YUGOSLAVIA
AND THE
SOVIET UNION
1939 – 1973

The Royal Institute of International Affairs is an unofficial body which promotes the scientific study of international questions and does not express opinions of its own. The opinions expressed in this publication are the responsibility of the author.

The Institute and its Research Committee gratefully acknowledge the comments and suggestions of the following who have read the manuscript: Malcolm Macintosh, Professor Hugh Seton-Watson, and Professor Marcus Wheeler.

YUGOSLAVIA
AND THE
SOVIET UNION
1939 – 1973

A DOCUMENTARY SURVEY

edited by

Stephen Clissold

Published for

THE ROYAL INSTITUTE OF
INTERNATIONAL AFFAIRS
by
OXFORD UNIVERSITY PRESS
LONDON   NEW YORK   TORONTO
1975

Oxford University Press, Ely House, London W.1
GLASGOW NEW YORK TORONTO MELBOURNE WELLINGTON
CAPE TOWN IBADAN NAIROBI DAR ES SALAAM LUSAKA ADDIS ABABA
DELHI BOMBAY CALCUTTA MADRAS KARACHI LAHORE DACCA
KUALA LUMPUR SINGAPORE HONG KONG TOKYO

ISBN 0 19 218315 x

Printed in Great Britain by
Ebenezer Baylis and Son, Limited
The Trinity Press, Worcester, and London

CONTENTS

PREFACE AND ACKNOWLEDGEMENTS

The relations between Yugoslavia and the Soviet Union during the three and a half decades covered by this study show vicissitudes which are reflected with considerable frankness in the documents available to us. For the first twenty years of her existence, Yugoslavia had no diplomatic links with the Soviet Union. Established in the face of the menace from the Axis powers, relations lapsed within a year following the invasion of Yugoslavia, but were resumed soon afterwards when Russia too fell victim to German aggression. King Peter's Government found itself in exile, whilst in the dismembered and occupied territories of Yugoslavia herself, two rival organizations struggled for postwar mastery. One, backed by the Government in Exile and strongest in the Serbian lands, was the Chetnik organization led by Draža Mihailović; the other, Partisans organized by the Communist Party, was led by Tito, its Secretary-General and the Comintern's nominee. From the start of guerrilla resistance in the summer of 1941 until the Red Army's approach to the Balkans three years later, the Russians kept their options open and maintained links with both sides—through normal diplomatic channels with the Government in Exile (but not with the Chetniks in the field, though this too was considered), and through courier and clandestine radio link with Tito's headquarters.

Enough documentation has survived from the wartime period to afford interesting insights into this two-tier relationship. The archives of the Government in Exile were brought to Yugoslavia following the formation early in 1945 of a Provisional Government which theoretically merged the de jure Royalist Government with Tito's de facto revolutionary regime. Dušan Plenča's *Medjunarodni odnosi Jugoslavije u toku drugog svjetskog rata* (1962) offers an account, based on these archives and reproducing a number of them, of the relations between the Soviet Government and the Government in Exile. The Foreign Office archives now available for the same period in the Public Record Office also provide valuable material. I am indebted to Miss Elisabeth Barker for her help in locating material from the latter quarry, and to Colonel Vojmir Kljaković for making available the text of some documents in the Military Historical Institute in Belgrade.

The archives of the Communist Party of Yugoslavia, including the signals exchanged between the Comintern and Tito's headquarters, were taken to Moscow for safe keeping towards the end of the war and were brought back to Yugoslavia under the agreement reached in 1955 when Khrushchev took the initiative in patching up the seven-year-old quarrel. They are now in the Institute for the Study of the Workers' Movement in Belgrade. Some have been published in the *Istoriski Arhiv Komunističke Partije Jugoslavije* (1949–58). Others, for the wartime period, will be found scattered through the remarkable 130-volume collection of documents, *Zbornik dokumenata i podataka o narodno-oslobodilačkom ratu jugoslavenskih naroda* (1950–60). A number of interesting wartime signals passed over Tito's secret radio link with the Comintern have also been published in Vlada Dedijer's *Josip Broz Tito—*

Prilozi za biografiju (1953), the fuller Serbo-Croat version of his well-known biography in English, *Tito speaks* (1953), and in his *The battle Stalin lost* (1971). Other interesting exchanges with the Russians, relating specially to the Partisans' desperate requests for supplies and showing incipient signs of the friction which was later to develop to such spectacular effect are to be found in the brochure by Tito's close associate Moša Pijade, *About the legend that the Yugoslav uprising owed its existence to Soviet assistance* (1950).

The documents relating to the postwar period also fall into two categories, but their interest is of a different nature. On the one hand we find the bland, cliché ridden surface material of official communiqués and formal exchanges; on the other, the intimate, often abrasive, correspondence passing between the Central Committees of the two CPs and subsequently released for publicity purposes once differences could no longer be concealed. The most remarkable exchanges of this nature are those between the Yugoslav and Soviet leaders in the spring of 1948, culminating in Yugoslavia's expulsion from the Cominform. The Russians were the first to publish their side of the story in an attempt to discredit and overawe the heretics and to drive a wedge between the leaders and the rank and file of the CPY. The Yugoslavs replied by publishing both their letters and those received from the CPSU. The result (published in an English version by the Royal Institute of International Affairs in 1948 under the title *The Soviet–Yugoslav dispute*) is a unique revelation of the sort of relationship which, during the Stalinist period, the Russian communist leaders assumed should exist between their Party and state and those of the client regimes emerging in Eastern Europe after World War II. It is no less revealing of the cast of mind and character of the Yugoslav leaders and the genesis of the brand of communism which has come to distinguish their Party and state over the last two and a half decades.

We thus find, in the postwar period, that the documents of greatest interest relate to those moments of crisis which have punctuated the course of Soviet–Yugoslav relations; the expulsion of Yugoslavia from the Cominform and its aftermath, down to the death of Stalin; the deterioration which ensued once it became clear that the reconciliation set in motion by Khrushchev would not result in the unconditional political and ideological return of Yugoslavia to the Soviet fold; and the Russian suppression of attempts, first by Hungary and then by Czechoslovakia, to introduce more liberal, independent regimes, which Moscow was quick to blame on the Yugoslav example. If less of the confidential exchanges during these later crises was released for publication than during the earlier Cominform dispute, the Yugoslavs' natural tendency to outspokenness found free vent and colours many of the speeches and public statements of Tito and his colleagues. As tension gives place to détente, the observer is offered little more than the bland surface of uninformative communiqués and official speeches. The account given in these pages of the calmer recent phases of Yugoslav–Soviet relations is thus perforce briefer and more provisional than for the better documented wartime and early postwar periods.

The propensity to outspokenness, to indiscretion even, coupled with the relaxation of censorship in Yugoslavia, lends a special interest to some of the memoirs published by prominent Yugoslavs. If Tito's own autobiography, long under preparation with the help of a team of specialists, still awaits completion and publication, much of Dedijer's invaluable biography is based on long conversations with his chief, whilst other interesting particulars, as indicated in the notes to the Introduction to this volume, have been confided by Tito to other biographers such as Sir Fitzroy Maclean and Miss Phyllis Auty. The memoirs (*Revolucija koja teče*, 1971) of Vukmanović-Tempo, for many years a close associate of Tito, contain glimpses of the friction building up between Yugoslavs and Russians during the apparent postwar honeymoon period, and a spirited account of the clash between the hot-blooded Yugoslav communist and the Soviet leader during the latter's visit of reconciliation. Tempo's account broadly confirms the description of the same visit given in the memoirs ascribed to Khrushchev (*Khrushchev remembers*, 1971–4), a source which has otherwise been used with reserve. The rarity of such frank memoirs by Soviet protagonists has meant that Yugoslav sources have been more freely drawn upon.

The case of Milovan Djilas is of unique interest for our study. One of Tito's closest and most trusted collaborators from the conspiratorial prewar days (described in his *Memoirs of a revolutionary*, 1973), throughout the Partisan war, and down to his estrangement and expulsion from the Party, he was one of the Yugoslav leaders in closest touch with Stalin and other Soviet leaders, and later most bitterly execrated by them. His personal evolution from the fanatical, unquestioning loyalty of the neophyte to doubt, disillusionment and final renunciation, present in microcosm, though in more extreme form, the path travelled by the leadership of the CPY as a whole away from orthodox dependence on Moscow to an independent if still theoretically Marxist stance. His *Conversations with Stalin* (1962) provides one of the most revealing and authentic pictures of the Soviet despot seeking to bend a foreign communist leader to his will for the furtherance of his Balkan policies.

The documents reproduced in this volume have, with very few exceptions, been taken from published sources. For most of the extracts from the Soviet press I have relied on the translations furnished (with permission) by the *Current Digest of the Soviet Press* issued by the American Association for the Advancement of Slavic Studies at the Ohio State University. Where I have found an official English version of a document I have used it in preference to translating direct from the original, though minor amendments have sometimes been found necessary in the interests of accuracy or consistency. I have kept explanatory notes to the documents to the minimum, but have permitted myself greater latitude in the notes attached to the Introduction in the hope that others may be assisted to pursue further research into the many fascinating byways waiting to be explored.

In order to provide an immediate link between the text of each document and the relevant section of the Introduction, a reference to that page is given in parentheses, in italic type after the title of each document, and at the end of each title in the list of documents and extracts. In the text of the Introduction, figures in parentheses in bold type provide cross references to the number of the relevant documents or extracts which make up the text.

I am greatly indebted to the friends and colleagues who have given generously of their time and expertise by reading through parts of the Introduction in draft and have helped me in other ways. Any errors of fact or assessment which remain are of course my responsibility alone. My thanks are specially due to Professor Phyllis Auty, Miss Elisabeth Barker, Mr E. H. Carr,

Mr K. F. Cviić, Sir William Deakin, Mr Michael Duncan, Sir Terence Garvey, Dr Richard Kindersley, Sir Fitzroy Maclean, Sir Thomas Rapp, Mr Peter Rennie, Miss Nada Saban, Professor Hugh Seton-Watson, and Sir Duncan Wilson. A special debt of gratitude is due to Miss Hermia Oliver and Mrs Judith Gurney for their invaluable collaboration in preparing the manuscript of this book for publication.

London, 9 July 1974   S.C.

ABBREVIATIONS

AVNOJ	Anti-Fascist Council for the National Liberation of Yugoslavia.
CC	Central Committee.
CMEA	Council for Mutual Economic Assistance.
CP	Communist Party.
CPB	Communist Party of Bulgaria.
CPSU	Communist Party of the Soviet Union.
CPY	Communist Party of Yugoslavia.
FPRY	Federal People's Republic of Yugoslavia.
IMRO	Internal Macedonian Revolutionary Organisation.
LCY	League of Communists of Yugoslavia.
PR	People's Republic
PRC	People's Republic of China.
SFRY	Socialist Federal Republic of Yugoslavia.
SNOF	Slav National Liberation Front.
UDBA	Yugoslav State Security Service.
UNRRA	United Nations Relief and Rehabilitation Administration

LIST OF DOCUMENTS AND EXTRACTS

Note: Italic figures in parentheses denote page references to the Introduction.

I THE WAR PERIOD

II THE POSTWAR PERIOD

III POST-STALIN RAPPROCHEMENT, RECOIL, AND NON-ALIGNMENT

RUSSIAN OVERTURES FOR RECONCILIATION

KHRUSHCHEV'S VISIT TO YUGOSLAVIA: THE BELGRADE DECLARATION

TOWARDS THE RE-ESTABLISHMENT OF PARTY LINKS: THE MOSCOW DECLARATION

Introduction

I THE WAR PERIOD

The outbreak of World War II left Yugoslavia clinging to a precarious neutrality. Her geographical position astride the plains and valleys which formed the gateway to South East Europe had been a standing invitation to acquisitive neighbours and ambitious great powers, and the history of her peoples one long struggle to preserve their individuality, and if possible their independence, in the face of these competing pressures. They had been left a legacy of national, social, and political tensions which two decades of coexistence in the kingdom of Yugoslavia had done little to relieve. Fascist Italy had long coveted the Adriatic coast and now lost no time in establishing herself in Albania. Nazi Germany, having swallowed up Austria, was displaying an ominous interest in Yugoslavia's Volksdeutsche and showed every sign of renewing the Drang nach Osten. Some of Yugoslavia's rulers believed that the only hope of safety for their country was to come to terms with the Axis powers. Others, specially in Serbia where memories of the alliance of World War I remained strong, looked to the Western democracies. And almost everywhere men cherished feelings of mingled hope, apprehension and curiosity for the great and enigmatic Slav power, Soviet Russia, who had yet to declare her role in the developing conflagration.

The reluctance of the Belgrade Government to maintain diplomatic relations with Moscow had deep roots.[1] The Soviet Government looked with little favour on the kingdom of the Serbs, Croats, and Slovenes set up by the Versailles settlement and ruled by the Karadjordjević dynasty which had been closely associated with the deposed Romanovs. The new state had given a warm welcome to thousands of Russian émigrés who became influential in Yugoslav professional and social life and educated their sons in a special military academy in Belgrade and their daughters in a replica of the Smolny Institute. A former counsellor of the imperial Russian embassy continued to represent the old regime in the Yugoslav capital down to the end of 1939. Prince Paul, the Prince Regent, like the late King Alexander, was strongly anti-communist, and feared Soviet influence as a catalyst both of social revolution and nationalist separatism.[2] But from the mid-30s, the expansionist appetite of fascist Italy and Nazi Germany began to loom as another and perhaps more immediate danger to Yugoslavia. The Soviet Union, faced with the same threat and anxious to strengthen anti-fascist forces, instructed the Yugoslav communists to drop their call for the dismemberment of Yugoslavia and campaign for the defence of the Yugoslav state and alliance with the Soviet Union. Nor were the communists alone in wanting to see links established between their country and Moscow. Pan-Slav sentiment was strong, if latent, amongst many sections of the Yugoslav people, particularly the Serbs and Montenegrins. The government, alarmed at the prospect of the eventual

3

'bolshevization' of the Balkans, remained extremely wary of allowing any opening for Soviet influence (3).

Some informal contacts between the two countries had nevertheless taken place at the League of Nations, and a protocol had been signed in Geneva providing for mutual abstention from hostile propaganda. In April 1940 it was announced that Šumenković, the Yugoslav minister in Ankara, had approached his Soviet counterpart to inquire whether the Soviet Government would be prepared to establish economic relations. He also conveyed his government's concern at Italy's expansionist ambitions and expressed his conviction that the Soviet Government ought not to condone them. Moscow replied that it wished to see the status quo maintained in the Balkans and was prepared to discuss economic links with Yugoslavia. At the same time Lavrentiev, the Soviet minister to Sofia, was instructed to sound out the Yugoslav Government on the diplomatic level.[3]

On 21 April a Yugoslav commercial delegation headed by Milorad Djordjević, a former Minister of Finance, left for Moscow. On 11 May a trade and shipping agreement was signed (5), together with a protocol on methods of payment and an agreement to open commercial missions in Belgrade and Moscow. The Yugoslavs hoped that the trade agreement would enable them to export minerals, tobacco, and cattle to the Soviet Union and to import such goods as machinery, cotton, and oil which wartime restrictions made it difficult to obtain. The importance of the trade agreement was however expected to lie less in promoting a flow of trade than in paving the way for the establishment of diplomatic relations. Although a démenti was issued disclaiming any such intentions on the part of the Soviet Government (4), the reception given to the Yugoslav delegates was cordial. The Russians confidentially assured them that they had no wish to see any Axis advance into the Balkans, and whilst not explicitly saying so, left them with the impression that they would oppose it.[4] At the end of May Šumenković received instructions to ascertain from Terentiev, the Soviet ambassador to Turkey, whether Moscow was prepared to establish political links. The Russians indicated their readiness for negotiations, and on 24 June Šumenković and Terentiev signed an agreement in Ankara establishing diplomatic relations between their respective countries (6).

POLICY AND TACTICS OF THE CPY

The CPY, though banned by and hostile to the Yugoslav Government, had been amongst the most vociferous advocates of formal political links between Belgrade and Moscow. Its attitude towards the Yugoslav state had varied with the successive phases of the national question inside Yugoslavia and the exigencies of Soviet foreign policy.[5] In the euphoria of the CPY's 2nd Congress (Vukovar, 1920) it had expressed the hope that the new state would become a Soviet republic and join a Balkan–Danubian federation of like nature. Until the mid-20s its course had been charted by its Serbian Secretary-General Sima Marković, who held that the Party should not allow itself to be diverted from its revolutionary class aims by the nationalities issue and opposed Comintern directives to exploit national resentments for tactical ends. In 1925 Marković even crossed swords with Stalin himself and was finally obliged to renounce his unitarist views. After unsuccessful attempts to follow Comintern guidance by collaborating with Stjepan Radić's Peasant Party and the Macedonian terrorists, the CPY, at its 4th Congress (Dresden, 1928) called openly for the self-determination, to the point of secession, of Yugoslavia's constituent peoples and minorities.[6] By the spring of 1934, the Comintern was still demanding the secession of Croatia, Slovenia, and Macedonia. The rise of Hitler, with his manifest threat to the Soviet Union, led to a sudden change of tune. The demand for secession was now denounced as playing into the hands of Nazi and fascist expansionists. The need for Yugoslav unity was stressed and the right to self-determination played down,[7] though it was assumed that national rights would be safeguarded in any multinational state once the socialist revolution had occurred.

This fateful shift in the communists' attitude towards the Yugoslav state, which they now professed to defend against the threats of internal and external fascism, whilst of course not ceasing to work for its eventual socialist transformation, was the outcome less of any rethinking on the part of the Yugoslav communist leaders themselves than of changed directives from the Comintern resulting from the new requirements of Soviet national security. An attempt by a group of Yugoslav communists to secure formal autonomy for each constituent member of the Third International had been frustrated as early as 1920 and its proponents expelled. Marković had then for a time defended his unitarist thesis against the call for secession and had been crushed. He was succeeded by a series of Secretaries-General, nominated by the Comintern and successively discarded for inefficiency rather than for any independence of mind. The fierce repression unleashed against the Party after the proclamation of King Alexander's dictatorship in 1929 seriously impaired its operations and threw its émigré leadership into a still more thoroughgoing dependence on Moscow. By 1938, when Stalin's purges of Moscow's foreign communist community were taking their toll, the CPY's stock had fallen so low that its dissolution was seriously considered.

It was at this stage that Tito began to make his mark in the Comintern.[8] Josip Broz, known by the conspiratorial names of Tito in Yugoslavia and Valter in Moscow, was a Croat metal worker who had been sent to fight with the Austrian army on the Russian front where he was captured and joined the Red Guards. Returning to his native Yugoslavia, he became active in the CP and attracted the favourable attention of the Comintern who summoned him to Moscow in 1936 to work in its Balkan secretariat. He was sent to Paris to organize the flow of volunteers to fight in Spain, and then returned to Yugoslavia to reorganize the Party there. At the beginning of 1939 the Comintern confirmed his appointment as Secretary-General and some months later registered its formal approval of his reorganization of the CPY (2). Valter-Tito seemed in every way a man in whom Moscow could have full confidence. Of impeccable working-class origin, he had married a Russian wife and fathered a son who was to serve as an officer in the Red Army. He spoke fluent Russian, and though he never attained the dangerous distinction of holding high office in the Comintern, he was well versed in its ways and well regarded by its leaders, particularly by its Secretary-General, the Bulgarian Georgi Dimitrov.

The inexorable approach of war in Europe led Stalin to fresh expedients to buy time. The signing of the German–Soviet Pact in August 1939—which the

CPY endeavoured to present as a move by which 'German fascism has been compelled to capitulate before the strength of victorious socialism' (1)—nevertheless caused consternation amongst some Yugoslav communists and brought popular odium upon the Party as allies of the Nazis (9). Some comrades reasoned that, if Russia was no longer at odds with Germany, there was no reason to defend Yugoslavia against Russia's ally. In some parts of Yugoslavia, particularly Montenegro, the communists accordingly refused to respond to their call-up papers.[9] The Party leaders maintained that the pact did not involve any reconsideration of the tactics of 'defending Yugoslavia' and informed subordinate party organizations accordingly. But 'harm had been done and the good name of the Party injured, as many communists failed to report to the army'.[10] Tito, who had been recalled to Moscow shortly before and evidently showed less than his usual sensitivity to popular reactions in Yugoslavia, commented blandly in the columns of the Comintern journal that the

> 'Pact for Mutual Aid between the Soviet Union and Germany, and the entry of Soviet troops into western White Russia, have aroused great enthusiasm amongst the broad masses of the Yugoslav population. The Yugoslav people have understood that these events facilitate the struggle for national independence.[11]

Early in 1940 Tito was authorized by the Comintern to return to Yugoslavia. Exactly what directives he brought back with him we do not know. Certainly he was to press on with the thorough reorganization of the Party and prepare for the Party Conference which was to be held in the greatest secrecy in Zagreb the following autumn. That event apart, it is probably true to say that, for the next year and more, the Party was content to wait upon events and see how best to turn them to its advantage. Though it was to claim credit for forcing the Belgrade government to enter into diplomatic relations with Moscow by mobilizing massive popular support, the initiative for that, as for the momentous coup of 27 March 1941, stemmed from other quarters. The communists limited their role to extracting the maximum propaganda advantage from these developments by organizing pro-Soviet demonstrations, sending their orators into the streets to put the communist gloss on the current situation, and turning out appropriate handbills and leaflets from their clandestine presses. Nor could the Party claim credit for the Friendship and Non-Aggression Pact (13) concluded on the eve of the German invasion between Yugoslavia and the Soviet Union. If this fell short of the Pact of Mutual Assistance for which they continued to agitate, they shared the sentiments of mingled disappointment and hope in the power of an invincible Mother Russia which animated many who were far from sympathetic to their revolutionary aims.

The CPY had several good and secure lines of communication with Moscow at this time, and it is reasonable to conclude that close contact with the Comintern was maintained. Correspondence was mainly with Georgi Dimitrov, who had a team of émigré Yugoslav communists headed by Veljko Vlahović to assist him, but all decisions of importance were taken by Stalin and carried into effect by Manuilsky.[12] After the Soviet legation was opened in Belgrade, the Party was able to maintain discreet contact with its staff.[13] More important however were the two radio links which the Party maintained direct with

Moscow. One clandestine transmitter operated from a medical institute in Belgrade, but it was put out of action and its operator killed in the air raids of April 1941.[14] The other transmitter was housed in a private villa in Zagreb and was operated by a Comintern agent who appears to have been vested by Moscow with some supervisory powers over the Party as well.[15] In addition, the Kremlin maintained its own network of intelligence agents which operated separately from the Party, though they too might be called upon in emergencies for direct action.[16]

The 5th Conference of the CPY was held in Zagreb in October 1940 in conditions of strict secrecy. According to the report which Tito sent to the Comintern (7), it was attended by just over a hundred delegates and 'complete unity was manifested'. By failing to report that some friction had occurred over the Macedonian question—[17] a foretaste of graver discord to come—Tito was perhaps, even at this early stage, already showing signs of a certain independence vis-à-vis the Comintern. But the report he delivered to the Conference, and the resolutions adopted by the latter, were impeccably faithful to the current Moscow line. The war, as the Party manifesto issued on its outbreak had been quick to point out (1), was being waged between the bourgeois imperialists of the pseudo-democracies and the German and Italian fascists; but the Yugoslav people looked for salvation to the Soviet Union and its great leader Stalin, whilst the CPY, the vanguard of its workers, was striving to follow the trail blazed by the Bolsheviks and to keep the country from being dragged into the war (8, 10).

Little information is available as to the Party's activities during the next five months. One important objective was to increase pressure on the government, by means of demonstrations and clandestine propaganda, for the conclusion of a military alliance with the Soviet Union. The announcement, on 5 April 1941, that a pact had at last been signed, though for Friendship and Non-Aggression rather than military assistance, was received with mixed feelings of disappointment and satisfaction, for some comrades believed that the government would at least now feel obliged to legalize the Party and even take its representatives into the cabinet.[18] The German attack on Belgrade the following morning found the local communist leaders busily preparing popular rallies to celebrate the conclusion of the new alliance.[19]

The speedy collapse of organized resistance in Yugoslavia was followed by dismemberment of the country by Germany, Italy, Hungary, and Bulgaria. Yugoslavia had ceased to exist. Hitler had accomplished in a matter of hours what all the Comintern directives of the 20s and early 30s had failed to achieve —the disruption and destruction of the bourgeois Yugoslav state. The policy of 'defending Yugoslavia' which the Yugoslav communists had subsequently been instructed to pursue for the last half a dozen years had failed; there was nothing left to defend. If Germany lost the war, Yugoslavia might one day be restored. But what sort of Yugoslavia—the old bourgeois monarchy, or an entirely new 'socialist' republic? Tito, both as a dedicated communist and a shrewd realist, had no doubt as to the answer. At a clandestine gathering of such members of the CC as still remained in Zagreb, he spoke of the need to prepare for armed resistance and, since the old Yugoslavia had been swept away, to lay the foundations for an entirely new social order and a revolutionary people's government.[20] He also informed the Comintern, in a lengthy report on the collapse of the Yugoslav state, the events leading up to it, and the tactics followed by the CPY, that 'all Party forums, from the Central Committee to the lowest ones, have remained for the most part intact and are discharging their functions' in the dramatically changed conditions' (18).

SOVIET REACTION TO THE INVASION AND DISMEMBERMENT OF YUGOSLAVIA

If the collapse of the old Yugoslav state opened up new prospects for the CPY, its immediate effect was a severe setback for Soviet policies. Less than a year had passed since Moscow decided to enter into diplomatic relations with the Yugoslav Government as a means of strengthening her position in the Balkans. Another and more ominous move to the same end had followed almost immediately; the Red Army had advanced into Romania and occupied Bessarabia and Northern Bukovina. Russia thereby dramatically demonstrated that she was not indifferent to events in South East Europe and entered the Balkans— but whether she came as friend or foe seemed uncertain in Belgrade. One disturbing indication of Soviet ambivalence was the failure to supply any of the arms and war material for which discussions had for some time been in progress. In November these discussions were discontinued, and although the Yugoslavs constantly reverted to the subject and furnished Plotnikov, the Soviet minister to Belgrade, with a full list of their military requirements before he left for consultations in Moscow in March 1941, no deliveries were ever made.[21]

The hope that the establishment of new links between Belgrade and Moscow would deter Hitler from pressing his designs in the Balkans proved illusory.[22] German pressure on Yugoslavia steadily increased, and after Prince Paul had complied with the summons to see Hitler in Berchtesgaden, Prime Minister Cvetković signed Yugoslavia's adhesion to the Tripartite Pact between Germany, Italy, and Japan on 25 March 1941. The outburst of national indignation which followed two days later, overthrowing the Cvetković Government and forcing Prince Paul into exile, drew a characteristically ambivalent response from the Soviet Government. Reports that the latter had sent congratulations to General Simović, the head of the new government, brought a démenti couched in terms which left Moscow's real sentiments in doubt[23] (11). The Kremlin, it seemed, welcomed the coup as reaffirming Yugoslavia's will to resist German pressure, but deplored it as likely to provoke Hitler to move openly into the Balkans.

Five days after the coup, Momčilo Ninčić, Foreign Minister in the new government, informed his envoy, Gavrilović, in Moscow that the Soviet chargé d'affaires had indicated his government's readiness to sign a military and political pact with Yugoslavia and that a military delegation was being dispatched with instructions and full authorization for Gavrilović to sign such a pact.[24] The delegates brought with them the draft for a Pact of Mutual Assistance, but on presenting it to Molotov on 4 April, the Yugoslav negotiators were informed that the pact was unacceptable, as it would undoubtedly put an end to the Soviet Union's friendly relations with Germany. The Russians then produced an alternative draft Friendship and Non-Aggression Pact. After referring the matter back to General Simović in Belgrade and holding out for at least a pledge of continuing Russian friendship in the event of a German attack on Yugoslavia, Gavrilović was instructed to sign. On 4 April, the day before the pact was signed, Molotov summoned the German ambassador to inform him of what was proposed and to assure him that the pact was in no way directed against Germany but was meant solely as a contribution towards preserving peace. Molotov 'added the repeated and urgent request that Germany also do all she could to preserve peace in the Balkans' (12).

The signing of the Yugoslav–Soviet Pact of Friendship and Non-Aggression (13) in effect did nothing to deter Hitler from the resolve which he had already formed of attacking and annihilating the Yugoslav state.[25] The German ambassador was instructed to demand an urgent interview with Molotov on the morning of 6 April to break the news that the Reich had felt impelled to undertake military action against Yugoslavia and Greece. He was told to say nothing of the Yugoslav pact signed only the day before unless Molotov himself raised the matter (15). The Soviet Foreign Minister listened to the ambassador's communication but made no reference to the pact, confining himself to declaring 'several times that it was extremely deplorable that an extension of the war had thus proved inevitable after all' (16).

Whilst Russian readers were learning from their morning papers that the new Soviet–Yugoslav pact would make a valuable contribution towards preventing the spread of war (14), Hitler's bombs were beginning to fall on Belgrade and his forces to smash through the Yugoslav defences. Had the Yugoslav armies succeeded in withdrawing to positions where they might have been able at least to slow up the enemy's advance, the supply of war material from abroad might have been considered feasible. 'Between the date of the signing of the Pact and the defeat of the Yugoslav armies', the United States ambassador to the Soviet Union informed his government in a report of a conversation with Gavrilović, 'the Soviet authorities had promised him armaments, munitions and planes, and . . . although there had been sufficient time at least to have discussed the quantities and means of shipment no steps had been taken by the Soviet authorities to implement their assurances. He expressed the opinion that the Soviet Government, at the time the assurances were given him, contemplated watching developments before commencing deliveries and that had Yugoslavia been able to offer effective resistance deliveries probably would have been made.'[26]

But Yugoslavia's collapse was speedy and complete. The government, taking the young king with them, managed to make their way to Montenegro and from there were flown out to allied territory. As they passed through Bosnia, General Simović and his Foreign Minister were approached by Soviet emissaries who appear to have held out promises of Russian support in return for far-reaching political concessions after the war.[27] But the German onslaught had put an end to official relations between the Soviet and the Yugoslav governments and these were not resumed until General Simović and his colleagues had established themselves in London as the Government in Exile.

THE GERMAN INVASION OF RUSSIA AND CPY PREPARATIONS
FOR ARMED RESISTANCE

The news that the German armies had started to cross the German–Soviet frontier on 22 June opened up fresh perspectives for the Yugoslav communists. Their naïve faith in the invincibility of the Red Army led them to believe that the war would soon be over and that the Russians would counterattack and liberate Yugoslavia within a couple of months; Djilas, who was in charge of its Agitprop, proposed that the Party should issue bulletins twice a day to record each stage in the Red Army's anticipated advance.[28] Tito alone appears to have taken the more realistic view that the fighting was likely to be grim and protracted and that it would call for many sacrifices by the Party and the Yugoslav people before final victory could be achieved. He held a meeting of the Politburo in Belgrade on the afternoon of the 22nd, and drafted an emotional manifesto calling upon the CP not to 'stand idly by whilst the precious blood of the heroic people of Soviet Russia is shed' but 'to prepare for this grim struggle' and 'organize the working masses' (**19**). The same evening a courier arrived from Zagreb with a signal received over the link with Moscow. This urged that 'the defence of the USSR is at the same time the defence of the countries which Germany has occupied' and the Party should therefore 'take all measures to support and facilitate the rightful struggle of the Soviet people'. The directive also cautioned that 'at this present stage what you are concerned with is liberation from fascist oppression, and not socialist revolution' (**20**).

Tito rightly reckoned that the call to armed resistance would find a readier response amongst the Serbs and Montenegrins, with their traditions of heroic revolt, than amongst the Croats, who had not yet had time to become disillusioned with their 'independent' state. Some Croat communists, moreover, had themselves nationalist sympathies which, until the Comintern's change of tactics in the mid-30s, had led them to regard the Ustashe less as enemies than as allies in the struggle against Serbian hegemony.[29] One of the leaders of this faction was Andrija Hebrang,[30] the Moscow-trained communist subsequently appointed Secretary of the Croat CP in succession to Rade Končar, a Serb from Croatia and a member of the CPY CC who remained in Zagreb to see that the local organizations kept in step with the strategy laid down by the Politburo in Belgrade. Other prominent Croat communists, including some who had been disciplined by the Party for nationalist deviation, had been arrested by the Yugoslav authorities before the German invasion and were still detained in Ustashe prisons.[31]

The communist organization in Croatia was thus hardly in a position to respond promptly and efficiently to the Comintern's instructions for immediate armed action. Though Tito's authority was absolute over the Politburo, and, (through Končar) strong over the CC of the Croat CP, the Zagreb Municipal Committee grew restive and soon showed signs of wishing to strike out on its own in the belief that conditions were already ripe and that Moscow's call for armed action should be immediately and literally carried out. In this, they were backed by Srebrnjak, a leading member of the Soviet intelligence service in Yugoslavia, who had already fallen out with the CPY leaders by making unauthorized attempts to recruit agents from amongst the party cadres.[32] The first attempt of the Zagreb activists was to attack and kill an Ustasha policeman; in reprisal, a group of arrested communist leaders, writers and intellectuals for the most part, were executed. Fearing that their remaining comrades would share a like fate, the Zagreb Municipal Committee next organized a mass break-out from the concentration camp at Kerestinec. But the Ustashe had wind of the affair and massacred some eighty escaping prisoners in an ambush. Bitter mutual recrimination followed, the Municipal Committee being accused by the Politburo of bungling, indiscipline, and precipitate action, whilst the dissidents countered with charges of betrayal.

For these setbacks in Croatia Moscow was itself largely to blame. At the end of July, dissatisfied with the delay in carrying out the instructions for immediate diversionary action sent scarcely a month before, the Comintern ordered Kopinič, the operator of the Zagreb radio link, to assume the leadership of the organization himself.[33] The Municipal Committee followed his lead and attempted to implement its disastrous activist policy whilst efforts were also made to win over the CC of the Croat CP. Kardelj and Vladimir Popović were hastily commissioned to settle the crisis and restore the authority of the Politburo. The Municipal Committee was replaced and Kopinič induced to return to his transmitter; the Party could take no disciplinary steps against him as he had only been carrying out the Comintern's orders and controlled what was then its only link with the Party. The dispute was patched up, but its effect may have had more than local significance. It suggests that Moscow had, at that time, some reservations regarding Tito's leadership and was at least anxious to keep other ties in Yugoslavia. It also raises the question of whether Tito's reports of the events which were soon to develop in Serbia were given due credence.[34]

RUPTURE AND RESUMPTION OF DIPLOMATIC RELATIONS

The sudden collapse and dismemberment of Yugoslavia faced the Russians with a wholly new and difficult situation in the Balkans. Should they resign themselves to the disappearance of the state with which they had just concluded a Pact of Friendship and Non-Aggression and accept all the consequences of Hitler's ruthless fait accompli? Should they, for instance, recognize the establishment and probable viability of the 'Independent Croat State' which he had erected on the ruins of the old kingdom of Yugoslavia? Should it be regarded as a mere puppet state, wholly subservient to German and Italian influence, or as the fulfilment of aspirations for national statehood widely held by the Croatian people? Until the mid-30s the Comintern line had been to encourage Croat separatism and the setting up of just such an independent republic. That the latter had now been formed under the aegis of the Axis powers was regrettable, but so long as the German–Soviet Pact remained in force, the possibility was not excluded that the Soviet Union might exert some influence in it, and perhaps encourage currents in favour of a real independence rather than the fictitious independence conferred upon it by grace of the dictators. Feelers in this direction seem to have been put out by Moscow with a view to recognizing the new state,[35] but neither the Ustashe leaders nor their Italian and German mentors saw any advantage in responding to them.

Moscow seems to have been in no hurry to surrender its valuable observation post by winding up the Soviet legation in Belgrade. Tito, who had moved to the former Yugoslav capital from Zagreb at the beginning of May, was still able to maintain discreet contact and to pass to the Soviet military attaché a report that German troop movements indicated an impending attack on the Soviet Union.[36] But on 4 May the Germans handed to the Soviet Government in Moscow a stiff note complaining that the Russians still retained diplomatic relations with Yugoslavia, as well as with Holland and Belgium, which had ceased to exist as states. Four days later, Vyshinsky sent for Gavrilović and informed him that his government considered diplomatic relations between their two countries to be at an end (17). Gavrilović was told that he might stay on in Moscow if he wished in a private capacity, but ten days later he left for Turkey where some contact continued to be maintained between the Soviet and Yugoslav Governments on an informal diplomatic level. The Yugoslav Government, for its part, was most unwilling to reconcile itself to this summary withdrawal of recognition, and on 12 May Foreign Minister Ninčić, during his stay in Cairo en route for London, asked the British ambassador there to request his government to intervene with Soviet authorities in Moscow and persuade them to reconsider their decision.

The following month, as Germany's hostile intentions towards Russia became increasingly clear, the Soviet Government gave signs of modifying its negative attitude towards the Yugoslav Government in Exile. Šumenković, Yugoslav ambassador in Ankara, received assurances from his Soviet colleague that the Soviet Union still entertained sentiments of friendship for Yugoslavia, and on 18 June Ambassador Maisky informed the Yugoslav ambassador in London that his government was ready to restore diplomatic relations.[37]

With the start of the German invasion four days later, Russia ceased to be an associate and found herself a fellow victim of German aggression. Britain lost no time in announcing full solidarity with the Russian people in the common war effort, and the Yugoslav Government in Exile hastened to issue a statement to the same effect (21). But the formalization of relations between the Yugoslav and Soviet Governments presented difficulties. The Russians first proposed, in line with similar offers made to the Czechs and Poles, to facilitate the setting up in the USSR of a Yugoslav National Committee which would raise a military force, armed and equipped by the Russians, to fight the Germans.[38] The Government in Exile saw this as a thinly disguised attempt to sponsor a body which might challenge its own authority, and pressed for the resumption of normal diplomatic relations. General Simović's Government was composed mainly of anti-communists and conservatives, deeply distrustful of the Russians; the latter saw in them the representatives of the same monarchical, anti-Soviet regime which had been hostile to their interests in Eastern Europe for the last two decades. However, Russia was now in desperate need of allies. The Yugoslav Government in Exile had already been taken under the wing of the British, and whether or not it proved able to give a lead to any resistance amongst the population now under German occupation or would eventually be restored to power, Moscow saw advantage in being able to exert some influence over it. The Yugoslav politicians, their thoughts already on a postwar settlement, pressed the Soviet representatives in London for undertakings that the Soviet Government would help to restore an independent Yugoslav state with its prewar frontiers and would leave its internal order to be determined by the Yugoslav people and government.[39] Verbal assurances to this effect were given by Ambassador Maisky and an agreement of 19 July to reopen the Yugoslav legation in Moscow signified the effective resumption of relations. But it was not until 28 August 1941 that a formal agreement to restore diplomatic relations was signed, and shortly afterwards a Soviet minister was accredited to the Yugoslav Government in Exile (**22**). As for the Friendship and Non-Aggression Pact concluded between the two governments on the eve of the German invasion of Yugoslavia, a statement by a Soviet spokesman indicated that his government considered this to be still in force.[40] This was a matter which was to be taken up later, when the issue had been complicated by the growth of the resistance movement and civil war in Yugoslavia. In the meantime the Soviet Government's sponsorship of a Pan–Slav Congress in Moscow (10 August), which asserted the right of the Montenegrin and Macedonian peoples to seek self-determination, provoked a protest from the Yugoslav Government and indicated that the course of relations between the two governments was unlikely to be smooth.[41] Graver issues, however, were soon to be raised by reports of the insurrection which was beginning to spread throughout Serbia.

THE RISING IN SERBIA
On 4 July 1941, and again six days later, the CC issued proclamations echoing the call to arms contained in a new Comintern directive: 'the hour has struck when communists must launch an open fight by the people against the invaders' (**23**). Isolated cases of sabotage and attacks on the occupying authorities and their collaborators were already occurring throughout Serbia; one of these, the shooting of two gendarmes in the village of Bela Crkva by an ex-volunteer in the Spanish Civil War, is commonly taken to mark the beginning of the general rising. Tito, with a small staff constituted as the military headquarters of the communist-led Partisan movement, worked hard throughout July and August to give the popular rising cohesion and direction. Emissaries were sent out to organize the revolt in Montenegro, Bosnia, Slovenia, and other parts of the country, and on 16 September Tito himself left Belgrade to take personal command in the field. The rising had now assumed major proportions, as Tito continued to report in a series of messages and progress reports destined for Moscow[42] (**24–8**).

How many of these messages reached their destination, and whether those that did gave the Russians a true appraisal of what was happening in Serbia is open to doubt. Russian efforts were now bent on staving off the German thrust against Moscow, and such space as their papers could spare for news items from Yugoslavia was filled mostly with reports from the allied and neutral press. That a major diversion had been created in the Balkans seemed clear enough. A report issued by the Russian High Command on 7 August declared that an open revolt had started against the forces of occupation in Serbia, with armed clashes between guerrilla fighters and acts of sabotage occurring in many places.[43] But the form this diversion was taking—a genuine national rising, blurred with elements of civil war, instead of the diversionary hit-and-run tactics which characterized the activity of the Soviet Partisans, acting always as ancillary to the Red Army—was disconcerting. Some officials in the Balkan Secretariat of the Comintern were inclined, at the time, to criticize the whole concept of a national rising as frankly 'adventurist', doomed to failure through the assumed passivity of the peasant masses.[44]

A further complication was the emergence of Colonel Draža Mihailović, an officer of the regular Yugoslav army who had evaded surrender and established himself on Ravna Gora, in western Serbia, where he claimed to be rallying all Serbian forces loyal to the king. By the middle of September Mihailović was in radio contact with the British and with the Government in Exile, who eagerly seized on this opportunity of building up the figure of one who claimed to be an uncompromising anti-German resistance leader and whose conservative, great-Serb, and anti-communist convictions were shared by many of the leading Yugoslav politicians in exile. The rising was thus flawed from its inception by a dangerous duality of leadership and purpose. Tito and his communist-led Partians stood for all-out and immediate resistance, regardless of cost, in response to Comintern directives and the need to relieve enemy pressure on the eastern front; Mihailović was more concerned to avoid enemy retaliation and reprisals on the civilian population and to husband his resources until they could be used to assist eventual intervention by the allies in the Balkans. In Tito's communist-led Partians they saw rivals for power and the most serious challenge to their aims, and they came to regard the destruction of the Partisans as of greater urgency than armed action against the Germans.[45]

The Serbs were proud of their tradition of guerrilla warfare against the Turks and possessed a paramilitary organization of irregulars or 'Chetniks' commanded by Kosta Pećanac, a hero of World War I. These Chetniks, Tito reported to the Comintern (29), declared themselves for the puppet administration which the Germans set up under General Nedić. Others who called themselves 'Chetniks' looked to Mihailović. During the fighting which raged in Serbia during the autumn and early winter of 1941, some Chetnik commanders went into action against the Germans, either on their own account or in alliance with the Partisans. But co-operation between the two groups proved short-lived and co-operation soon gave way to open hostility. Twice Tito conferred in person with Mihailović, who for some reason took him to be a Russian.[46] The Chetnik leader now had a British liaison officer at his headquarters and was confident not only of allied support but of receiving arms and supplies. The British and Yugoslav Governments were already urging Moscow to bring pressure on the Partisans to recognize Mihailović's authority as the supreme resistance leader and place themselves under his command.[47] In aims and outlook the two sides were already irreconcilable. The fragile alliance cracked under the pressure of the German offensive, and at the end of December Tito reported to Moscow that the Partisans had been driven out of Serbia into the Sandžak and Bosnia, whilst the Chetniks had given up all pretence of fighting the Germans and most of them had gone over to Nedić (31).

During the critical fighting in Serbia Tito had only tenuous links with Moscow,[48] and the Partisan leaders were largely dependent on what they could pick up from Radio Free Yugoslavia, the transmitter operated by the Comintern,[49] or from Radio Moscow. These gave a very muddled picture of what was happening in Yugoslavia. It was after listening to a broadcast from Moscow describing Mihailović as the leader of all Yugoslav resistance and attributing the Partisans' anti-German exploits to the Chetniks that Tito ordered his forces to break off an attack on Mihailović's headquarters 'so as not to make difficulties for Soviet foreign policy'.[50] The following day he sent an indignant signal to Moscow protesting against such distortion of the facts (30).

EFFORTS BY THE GOVERNMENT IN EXILE TO SECURE SOVIET
RECOGNITION FOR MIHAILOVIĆ

Tito's messages to the Comintern were not the only reports to reach the Russians of the events in Serbia. They had also received, through information passed to them by undercover representatives in Turkey of the Yugoslav Government, reports regarding the Chetnik organization headed by Mihailović and his claim to be the leader of the whole resistance movement in the country. Moscow appears at first to have been impressed by this claim. Whilst divulging nothing of what they knew of Tito and the Partisans, they proposed, through their agents in Istanbul, to fly in a joint Soviet–British–Yugoslav military mission to Mihailović—an offer which was at first welcomed by the British and subsequently, under pressure from the Yugoslav Government, which wished to exclude any Russian influence over the developing resistance movement, declined.[51] Had the proposed initiative for joint Anglo–Soviet co-operation born fruit, events in Yugoslavia might have taken a very different turn.

Despite the rebuff of this early offer to send in a joint mission to Mihailović, the Soviet Government believed that it was desirable and feasible to encourage the formation of a 'united anti-Fascist front' which might rally both Partisans and Chetniks in a maximum effort against the Germans. It also wished to avoid antagonizing its British and other allies, who held broadly the same view, but would probably jib at the prospect of backing a communist resistance leader with overtly revolutionary aims. When, on 22 October, Ambassador Maisky discussed the rising with Eden and 'expressed the opinion that it should be encouraged and helped in every way',[52] Mihailović and the Chetnik movement were the assumed beneficiaries. The Russians seem to have been slow to accept Tito's allegations that Mihailović was bent on fighting the Partisans rather than the Germans and they maintained an ambivalent attitude towards the Chetnik leader. This was to persist even after the British reluctantly reached the conclusion that he would contribute nothing effective to the war effort; the Russians continued to harbour the suspicion that they might be tricked into cold-shouldering a figure who, in Serbia at least, could be a powerful factor in the postwar settlement.

The Yugoslav politicians in London, fed with the reports sent to them by Mihailović which gave a totally different version from that received by the Comintern of the fighting going on in Yugoslavia, pressed three main aims on the Soviet Government. They wanted Moscow to order the Partisans to stop fighting the Chetniks, to recognize Mihailović as the supreme resistance leader in Yugoslavia, and to place their forces under his command. In reality, the Government in Exile had a good deal of sympathy with a policy of passivity as a means of avoiding bloody reprisals against the civilian population, and on 29 October General Simović told Eden that he had accordingly instructed the rebels to go slow. Two weeks later he broadcast an appeal to 'discontinue sabotage and individual attacks which serve the enemy only as an excuse for cruelties and murders'.[53] Allied propaganda, however, needed a resistance leader who was actually resisting and the Yugoslav Government in Exile saw the opportunity of bolstering its prestige by publicizing one who claimed to be playing this role. Whilst the Soviet Government, wedded to its tradition of secrecy and fearful of alarming its allies by disclosing that the man who was doing most of the fighting in Yugoslavia was a trained and trusted Comintern agent, kept silent about Tito and the scale of his operations, the Western allies had every inducement to inflate the reputation of their self-proclaimed resistance leader. So rapidly and powerfully did the Mihailović myth grow that the Russians themselves seem to have been impressed by it and to have modified their attitude to Tito accordingly.

On 28 October, and again on 4 and 18 November, General Simović called on Ambassador Maisky to press the views of the Yugoslav Government. The credit for the rising in Serbia was attributed solely to the Chetniks and their leader, whilst the Partisans were depicted as irresponsible bands bent only on fomenting social revolution and civil war. The Soviet Government was urged to use its influence with the Partisans to stop the fratricidal strife and to place themselves under the command of Mihailović. On 17 November, on instructions from the Government in Exile (32), the Yugoslav chargé d'affaires in the USSR made a parallel approach to the Deputy Foreign Minister; Vyshinsky gave a non-committal reply and said he would refer the matter to his government (33). On the following day, Sir Stafford Cripps, the British ambassador, supported the Yugoslav initiative with a similar démarche, and a week later, a memorandum setting out the same case on grounds of military expediency was presented to the Soviet authorities by the British military mission. Both the Soviet and the Yugoslav Governments were already concealing from each other vital information about the rising in Serbia. Ambassador Gavrilović, fearing that the Russians would openly support the Partisans, did not tell Vyshinsky that the two sides were known to be fighting each other. Vyshinsky professed ignorance of this fact when Cripps raised the subject of Yugoslavia with him, and asked why this should be. Cripps answered that the Yugoslav Government had initially tried to persuade Mihailović that resistance was premature, and that he had consequently sought some contact with Nedić, which might have turned the other resistance groups against him. Cripps added however that the Yugoslav Government had now changed its line and was anxious to support Mihailović in a policy of resistance.[54]

These démarches were not without their effect. On the evening of 24 November Radio Moscow began to refer to Colonel Mihailović. From then on, as Tito was later to complain, not only the British but the Russians

> spoke only of Draža Mihailović. With the exception of one speech by Voroshilov in November 1941, in which he mentioned the Partisans of Yugoslavia, the whole Yugoslav uprising, our entire efforts, were ascribed to Draža Mihailović. . . . Soviet propaganda never mentioned the Partisans, although Stalin received detailed daily reports on the situation in Yugoslavia, broadcast through the secret transmitter in Zagreb.[55]

During this initial phase of the Yugoslav resistance movement the policies of the Soviet and Yugoslav Governments remained broadly in line, though their sources for an appraisal of events inside the country and their ultimate aims, in so far as these had been consciously formulated at this stage, were very different. The overriding need for the moment was to make common cause against the enemy. Attempts to patch up a truce were made by both sides, and when, at the end of November, Mihailović reported success to his government, the latter briefly believed that its main objective had been achieved. But the outbreak of renewed hostilities between Chetniks and Partisans, and the re-establishment of German authority in Serbia, shattered the illusion. Though the Yugoslav Government was to continue pressing the Russians to order the Partisans to stop fighting Mihailović and recognize his leadership, the growing ambiguity of the Chetniks' relations with the occupying powers, the spread and increasing strength of the Partisan movement, and the manifest impossibility of reaching any compromise between them, were to impose sharp strains on the relations between the Soviet and Yugoslav Governments.

On 9 January 1942, General Simović was succeeded by Professor Slobodan Jovanović as head of the Yugoslav Government in Exile. The latter soon showed itself even more insistent than its predecessor in pressing the claims of Mihailović, whom it promoted to the rank of general and nominated Minister of Defence in the new cabinet, to be considered the only authorized leader of the resistance movement in Yugoslavia. Three days before the change of government, the Yugoslav chargé d'affaires in Kuibyshev raised this question with the Russians, but Vyshinsky replied somewhat curtly that 'the Soviet Government does not consider it opportune to intervene in the rising in Yugoslavia'.[56] This continued to be the official Soviet attitude. Since Gavrilović had been given a seat in the cabinet of Professor Jovanović, the latter appointed a new minister to the Soviet Union, Stanoje Simić, who was briefed to keep a sharp eye open for 'any eventual help which the USSR may propose giving to the Partisans' and report it at once to his government (34). On 29 April Simić was instructed to urge the Russians to order the Partisans to cease opposing the Chetniks and to recognize the authority of Mihailović, as the French communists had agreed to recognize that of General de Gaulle in France (35). Simić cabled back that the Russians, whilst disclaiming any locus standi in Yugoslavia's internal affairs, had put out feelers for establishing contact with Mihailović (36). The Government in Exile, repeating its instructions to go on pressing the Russians to intervene with the Partisans, informed him that local attempts to stop the fratricidal strife had failed, and that 'we are doing what we can to prevent premature action on a large scale ... Greater guerrilla resistance, unaided by the allies, would bring about the destruction of the Serbian people' (37). On 16 May the government sent a further cable to inform the minister that Prime Minister Jovanović had had an interview with the Soviet ambassador who had repeated his government's refusal to intervene with the Partisans (38).

Despite the wariness with which each government regarded the other, relations between the Yugoslav and Soviet authorities remained reasonably good during the first half of 1942 and some overtures were made with a view to improving them still further. Professor Jovanović's Government proposed that the Friendship and Non-Aggression Pact, concluded the previous April but never ratified, should be brought up to date and reactivated. The Soviet Government put forward a counterproposal for the conclusion of a new treaty which would provide not only for mutual assistance in the war but for co-operation in the postwar period. The British Government however cautioned the Yugoslavs that 'the conclusion of such a treaty between countries of disparate power might reduce the weaker partner to the position of a protectorate of the greater' and also pointed out that it was 'undesirable at this stage for the Yugoslav government to enter into any commitment which might subsequently run counter to the plans for a Balkan Confederation'.[57] Such an arrangement would moreover set an undesirable precedent and encourage other allied governments to approach the major powers for similar treaties, 'thereby beginning a treaty race between His Majesty's Government and the Soviet Government'.[58] The latter argument, which Eden put to Molotov on 9 June, was one which carried some weight with the Soviet Government. On the Yugoslav side, meanwhile, the Slovene and Croat representatives felt little enthusiasm for an initiative which they feared might be a manœuvre to secure Russian support for the Serbs. The Serbian politicians, who showed most eagerness to conclude some arrangement with the Soviet Government and had even proposed that King Peter should undertake a state visit to the Soviet Union,[59] began themselves to have second thoughts about the wisdom of tying the destinies of their country too closely to the Soviet Union. By the end of June 1942 the proposal for a treaty between the latter and the Yugoslav Government in Exile had lost support on all sides and was quietly dropped.

Within the next few weeks it became clear from the tenor of Russian press and broadcast comment that the Soviet attitude towards the Government in Exile and General Mihailović's movement which it backed in Yugoslavia was beginning to harden. On 19 July Tass publicized a Free Yugoslavia broadcast report alleging that the Chetniks were collaborating with the enemy in Yugoslavia. This was the first time that the official Soviet news agency had come out openly against the Chetniks, and the report was taken up and reproduced in the communist press. The Yugoslav minister to the Soviet Union reported to his government that he and his British colleague had enquired whether the Tass report represented the official Soviet view of the situation in Yugoslavia, and added that Vyshinsky had told his British colleague that, whilst the report did not have the force of an official policy statement, it did reflect the increasing divergence of view between the Soviet Government and the Yugoslav Government in Exile.[60] On 28 July Ninčić handed Ambassador Bogomolov a note protesting against the Tass report and asking that a démenti should be issued.[61] The Russian reply took the form of a statement, which Lozovsky handed to Simić on 3 August, listing a number of specific cases of Chetnik collaboration with the Italians and even with the Ustashe[62] (39). He added that the charges were based on information supplied by Partisan headquarters, thus confirming —as the Yugoslav Government in Exile had long suspected—that the Russians were in direct touch with General Mihailović's rivals.

On instructions from his government (40), the Yugoslav minister replied with a note verbale rejecting the charges of the Chetnik leader's collaboration with the enemy and reaffirming that his government's policy had always been to work for the unity of all resistance forces under the leadership of Mihailović. As a counterblast to the charges against the latter, the government asked Mihailović to send material for a dossier on the misdeeds and atrocities attributed to the Partisans.[63] This was handed by Simić to the Soviet Government on 18 November in the form of an aide-mémoire which set out to show that, under the cover of fighting the Germans and Italians, the Partisans were really aiming to destroy General Mihailović's resistance movement.[64] Simić and his military attaché were told to impress on the Russians that, before there could be any talk of co-operation, they must cease their campaign of calumny against Mihailović and tell the Partisans to stop fighting the Chetniks and to place themselves under his command (**44, 46**). Simić cabled back to his government in some bewilderment that 'here in Russia it is impossible to read or hear anything against Mihailović', and that although he was no longer being mentioned by name in the press and on the radio he was still being spoken of as a national hero (**47**).

Throughout 1942 the Russians appear to have remained in some doubt as to the real situation in Yugoslavia and how best to react to it. In August, despite their mutual distrust and recurrent outbreaks of friction, the Soviet and Yugoslav Governments agreed to raise their respective diplomatic missions to embassy level (**41**)—a move which provoked Tito to an irritated protest (**42**). Moscow, still cautious, again asked Tito to send definite proof of Chetnik collaboration (**43**). Despite the evidence he had been providing that the Chetniks were more interested in settling accounts with the Partisans than in going into action against the Germans, the Russians still seem to have believed —as did the British—that pressure could be brought to bear on Mihailović to make him an effective resistance leader. They even considered sending a military mission to him and broached the subject with the Yugoslav Government. On 16 September Lozovsky sounded out Simić, suggesting that if Soviet liaison officers sent to his headquarters reported that he was seriously fighting the Germans, the Red Army would be willing to train Yugoslav pilots who could fly supplies in to the Chetniks.[65] Simić reported this surprising offer to his government which brusquely turned it down. Mihailović was informed by Prime Minister Jovanović of the Soviet proposal and his reasons for refusing it; the Russians had been told that it could not be considered until they agreed to instruct the Partisans to cease all attacks on his forces and place themselves under his command, and until their radio and press campaign against him ceased (**45**).

During Secretary of State Eden's visit to Moscow at the end of 1942, Yugoslavia was amongst the subjects discussed. The British had been receiving more and more reports of Chetnik collaboration with the enemy and found force in the Russian argument that the Yugoslav Government in Exile should be told plainly that a radical change of attitude was required from its Minister of Defence. On his return to London, Eden pressed the Yugoslav Prime Minister to urge Mihailović to cease his action against the Partisans and turn his arms against the Germans, and promised that he could then expect continued backing from the British. To Jovanović's complaint that the Russians were supporting the Partisans, Eden replied that 'the Russian case, as I understand it, was that the Partisans killed Germans. General Mihailović was busy killing Partisans. Consequently the Russians did not like General Mihailović. There seemed to be some force in that'.[66] Jovanović was also urged to improve relations with the Soviet Government. But these relations came under increasing strain. On 26 January 1943 Ambassador Simić was summoned to receive the Soviet reply to the Yugoslav aide-mémoire of 18 November and was informed that the Yugoslav representations were based on 'one-sided data which do not correspond to reality' (**48**).

At the beginning of February Jovanović confided to Eden that the deterioration in Soviet–Yugoslav relations was causing his government grave anxiety. He had been informed by Bogomolov that the Soviet Government would not be satisfied with anything less than a complete change of attitude on the part of

Mihailović. The Yugoslav Government had no intention, the Prime Minister declared, of withdrawing its confidence from the minister. It was wiser to stop recriminations as to who was responsible for the Chetnik–Partisan clash and to seek some modus vivendi.[67] On 19 February Simić again approached the Soviet authorities to ask them to intervene with the Partisans to stop fighting the Chetniks and to place themselves under Draža Mihailović's command. In rejecting this request, the Soviet spokesman declared that the Partisan movement was not composed merely of communists, as alleged by the Government in Exile, but was a movement of national liberation, all parties being represented on the Anti-Fascist Council.[68] Bogomolov went still further, when replying to a similar démarche from the Yugoslav Prime Minister on the following day. If the Chetniks wanted to fight the Germans, he said, they should join the Partisans, where they would be guaranteed full rights. To attempt to bring Partisans and Chetniks together on any other basis was now useless, since Mihailović was collaborating with the Germans and Italians.[69]

However the Chetniks showed less and less disposition to fight the Germans, and their wait and see attitude seemed to have the full endorsement of King Peter's Government. 'It is important that you should not launch any activities on a large scale until the time is ripe', the king exhorted his people in a broadcast commemorating the 27 March coup. 'For the moment, confine yourselves to organization. Gather round your supreme command in the country, around General Mihailović.'[70] This appeal was not well received in Moscow. If taken to heart by the people of Yugoslavia it would have taken the pressure off the Germans and permitted them to move some of their divisions from the Balkans to the eastern front. On 2 April the Soviet Government sent a sharp note calling upon the Yugoslav Government to put an end to all Chetnik collaboration and dissolve the formations making common cause with the enemy in Montenegro and Hercegovina. The Yugoslav Government's reply was to recall their minister from Moscow and virtually to suspend diplomatic relations.[71]

British policy, in the meanwhile, was also becoming increasingly critical of Mihailović and of the Yugoslav Government apparently condoning Chetnik collaboration.[72] At the end of March, in a personal letter to Jovanović, Churchill declared that 'His Majesty's Government are becoming seriously disturbed at recent developments in Yugoslavia', and complained that in a speech of 20 February, Mihailović had attacked Britain and frankly admitted that his forces were collaborating with the Italians.[73] At the same time the British Government hoped that it would still be possible to secure Russian collaboration for putting an end to what increasingly appeared to be a state of civil war in Yugoslavia. When the British ambassador in Moscow raised this question with Molotov, the latter replied that the Chetniks had the backing of the Yugoslav Government in Exile, and that any attempt by the Soviet Union to intervene with their Partisan rivals would be meddling in Yugoslavia's internal affairs.[74] British endeavours to restore a little more cordiality to the relations between the Yugoslav and Soviet Governments met with more success. On 20 April Jovanović and the Yugoslav Government held an official reception in honour of Ambassador Bogomolov in token of the desire of both governments to put their relations on a friendlier footing.[75] Seven days later, the Yugoslav cabinet met to take stock of its international position and passed a resolution that 'the Government will take all measures to ensure that its relations with the Soviet Union develop in a spirit of good intentions and friendly ties'.[76]

By the summer of 1943 the tide of war seemed to be turning in favour of the allies. In the Mediterranean theatre the Germans had been driven from North Africa, while the Anglo–American armies were pushing up through Italy and the capitulation of that country seemed only a matter of time. In August the Yugoslav Government, which had moved to Cairo to be nearer the scene of operations, was reformed under Božidar Purić, former ambassador in Paris, supposedly with a view to relegating contentious political issues until after the war and confining itself to administrative tasks. Mihailović nevertheless continued in the cabinet as Minister of Defence. Even at this stage the Russians were not convinced that the Chetnik leader was a spent force or should be written off as an incorrigible collaborator. At the beginning of September Moscow sent a signal to Tito requesting further details of the documents allegedly proving Mihailović's collusion with the enemy and asking for their authenticity to be carefully checked, since they might have been planted by the Germans as a means of splitting the resistance movement (43). Shortly afterwards, the Soviet Government, presumably wishing to study matters at first hand, renewed its proposal to the Yugoslav ambassador in Moscow that a Soviet mission should be sent to Mihailović's headquarters.[77] The Purić Government declined this suggestion, as it did a further proposal (on the grounds that the soldiers had violated their oath of loyalty to the king) that the Soviet Government should form a Yugoslav air force unit out of captured members of Pavelić's Croat Legion.[78] It still appeared to consider itself strong enough to take an intransigent line in its dealings with the Russians.

MOSCOW AND THE PARTISANS
Expectations of Russian military aid
Whilst the Kremlin and the Yugoslav Government in Exile continued their uneasy dialogue, the Partisans were struggling to make good their claim to be the one true resistance movement in Yugoslavia and the future masters of their country. Their immediate problem, in the grim months which followed the Partisans' withdrawal from Serbia at the end of 1941, was that of physical survival. As the remnants of his army battered their way through Bosnia, Tito turned to Moscow for prompt and generous help, which he wanted for its psychological no less than for its material effects (31). During the fighting in Serbia, outside assistance had scarcely been feasible on account of the speed with which operations had developed and the logistical difficulties which the Russians would have to overcome. Early in February, however, he succeeded in setting up a transmitter at his headquarters and establishing direct contact with the Comintern.[79] This meant that the sending in of men and supplies could now be considered a practical possibility. At the end of December Tito had sent a message to say that the airfield at Sokolac in east Bosnia was still in Partisan hands, and Moscow had replied that they would soon fly in an aeroplane with supplies (49, 50). An attempt to do so may have been made,[80] but no aeroplane appeared. On 17 February Tito signalled over his radio set that although deep snow had put the Sokolac airfield out of action supplies could be dropped near Žablak, at the foot of Mt Durmitor, in Montenegro; he gave

the co-ordinates of this landing ground and a detailed list of the arms and supplies needed (**51**). Moša Pijade, one of his most trusted lieutenants, was sent to organize the reception of the expected material. Tito's signals became more detailed and demanding. He listed a whole range of weapons and explosives, even down to the binoculars required for his officers, and declared he could mobilize another 100,000 men provided they would send in arms. If some Russian parachutists could be dropped, that would have 'enormous moral and political effect' (**52**). For 38 nights Moša Pijade and his party waited on the bleak, snow-covered landing ground but no sign came of any Soviet aircraft.

A note of growing impatience could now be detected in Tito's signals. 'We need arms and ammunition. That is the best way of creating a national liberation front,' he riposted to Moscow's political counselling (**64**). By the middle of March he reported that the situation had become critical for lack of ammunition, and asked to be told frankly whether they could expect help (**53**). At the end of the month came the answer; the Russians were still trying to find ways of helping, but 'the technical difficulties are enormous' and probably could not be overcome in the near future; the Partisans were advised to concentrate on seizing arms from the enemy and making the best use of those they already had (**54**). Throughout the following weeks of stern fighting Tito repeated his appeals and received the same answer: 'unfortunately you cannot expect to get either munitions or automatic weapons from here in the near future. . . . Make the best . . . use . . . of equipping yourselves there on the spot' (**55**).

Despite bitter disappointment over the Russians' failure to send in arms, Tito still faithfully believed that the struggle of his Partisans should be seen as an integral part of the vaster duel between the German and the Soviet armies. It was now time to launch a spring offensive, he wrote to Djilas, then in Montenegro, 'for we owe it to the oppressed peoples of Yugoslavia, we owe it Stalin, who paid a great tribute to our struggle in his First of May Proclamation'.[81] At the end of June the Partisans set out on their 'long march'—the three-months' trek which was to take them from eastern Bosnia and Montenegro to western Bosnia and the borders of Croatia. Despite losses and lack of equipment, the Partisan detachments had grown into a seasoned army, and their commander was able to address his Russian comrades-in-arms with a new sense of dignity and equality: 'The Supreme Staff requests the General Staff of the Red Army to help us with military equipment. . . . Through lack of arms we are unable to accept thousands of volunteers for our liberation army' (**56**).

From the outset of the revolt in the summer of 1941 until the advent of the Red Army more than three years later, no effective military aid or supplies were sent in to the Partisans by the Russians. From about March 1942 they seem even to have dropped any proposals to do so. This failure, temporarily overlooked in the euphoria of the final phase of victorious joint military operations against the Germans and the establishment of a communist regime in Yugoslavia, was later held against the Russians as one of the Yugoslavs' bitterest grievances.[82] The technical difficulty of sending in supplies from the eastern front was indeed great; but was it sufficient to explain total Soviet passivity? By the spring of 1942 Tito had begun to suspect that it was not. The

Government in Exile, he had written to Pijade, who was waiting in vain near Žablak for the promised aircraft, was to blame.[83] The Soviet authorities had to take political, and not merely military, factors into account.

POLITICAL EXCHANGES WITH THE COMINTERN

These political factors had been implicit in the resistance movement ever since the Partisans fired the first shot, and soon became only too obtrusive. On the day that the Comintern had first signalled Tito to make common cause with the Red Army now bearing the full weight of the German attack, he had been cautioned to 'bear in mind that, at this present stage, what you are concerned with is liberation from fascist oppression, and not socialist revolution' (20). As the rising gathered momentum, Tito reported that he was setting up a National Liberation Committee to serve as a sort of central people's government (60). He followed this up at the end of September 1941 by describing the efforts he had been making to form an alliance with certain other political parties for common action against the Germans 'on the basis of brotherly understanding between all the peoples of Yugoslavia' (61). But few political leaders were willing to co-operate with a Communist Party which clearly intended to retain the leading role.[84] The rift, moreover, between Partisans and the Chetniks of Draža Mihailović had become unbridgeable and hopes of constructing a broadly based national resistance even at this stage were clearly illusory. The struggle against the occupying forces, despite attempts to patch up the deepening quarrel, soon acquired the characteristics of a civil war.

Soviet misgivings about this state of affairs found expression at the beginning of March 1942 in a lengthy signal repeating the need to 'unite all anti-Nazi movements' and avoid giving any grounds for the charge that the Partisans were aiming at the 'Sovietization of Yugoslavia'. Why, for instance, had it been thought necessary to form a special 'Proletarian Brigade'? (62). In a further signal, Tito was urged to bear in mind that 'the Soviet Union has treaty relations with the Yugoslav King and Government and that taking an open stand against these would create new difficulties'; he should look at things not 'only from your own, national standpoint, but also from the international standpoint of the British–American–Soviet coalition' (63). To these criticisms Tito reacted sharply, explaining—as he confided to Pijade in Montenegro— that the Comintern

> has drawn the wrong conclusions from our reports; that we have a broad national liberation front, not in common with fifth-columnists, but with the great majority of true patriots; that the supporters of London are not working with the label London, but that of the occupying forces, i.e., the Nedić label, in their struggle against us; that we have sufficient documentary proofs of this; that the setting up of proletarian brigades was an indispensable step, when the partisan movement was in danger of being broken up by fifth-columnists, and that the proletarian brigades are not fighting for sovietization, but by their heroism are an example to our people how to fight . . . for one's freedom and independence.[85]

A cable was sent to the Comintern (67), which replied in conciliatory terms: 'We made you no reproaches . . . you enjoy our complete, unbreakable confidence', but for the moment, 'it is not opportune . . . to emphasize that the struggle is mainly against the Chetniks' (65).

In response to Comintern requests, Tito continued to report fully on conditions in the territories liberated by the Partisans, on the political, military, and economic measures they were taking, and on the political programme and slogans they had adopted. He also sent detailed reports on the strength of their Chetnik rivals, the location of their forces, their political and social background, and backed up this information by captured documents which he sent out of the country by courier. His denunciations of the Chetniks—'who are knifing us in the back just as we are waging a fierce and bloody war against the invaders' (66)—and the Yugoslav Government which supported them grew more and more bitter. Moscow's explanations as to why his own men were not receiving due psychological and propaganda backing hardly seemed to convince him. 'The whole people curse the Yugoslav Government in London which, through Draža Mihailović, is aiding the invader', he declared. 'Is it really quite impossible to do something in London against the present treacherous policy of the Yugoslav Government?' (67). And again, as the fighting on the Montenegrin front grew ever more bitter,

> All the Chetniks in Yugoslavia, particularly those of Mihailović, fight on the side of the invaders, against our national liberation units. . . . We are deeply convinced that the Yugoslav Government in London is also involved in this and knows it all. Please do all you can to expose this terrible treachery. . . . In a few days, we propose to issue a proclamation against the Chetniks and the Yugoslav Government in London (68).

In March an incident occurred which seemed to offer Tito an unexpected opportunity for opening the eyes of the allies to the reality of Chetnik collaboration.[86] He reported to the Comintern that a British officer had reached his headquarters and appeared anxious to learn the facts about what was happening in Yugoslavia. Major Atherton had been shown evidence of Mihailović's treachery and had declared that the British were badly informed, but that the Partisans were themselves to blame for this state of affairs for failing to publicize what they were doing. In a further telegram Tito reported that the British mission had been told of the CC's view that a new Yugoslav Government, composed of sound elements from both inside and outside the country, should be set up to rally the people against the enemy. If Tito had hoped that these views would have been reported back to London and influenced the thinking of the British and the Yugoslav Government in Exile his expectations were to be disappointed. Major Atherton shortly afterwards slipped away from his headquarters, presumably to make contact with some Chetnik group, and was never seen again.[87] The episode deepened Tito's suspicion of the British and his conviction that, though solidarity with all the allies was outwardly to be maintained, the Russians alone were to be trusted.[88] The end of the year found him complaining that 'it is simply nauseating that the English go on praising Mihailović' when his Chetniks were collaborating with the enemy (69).

Even trust in the Russians could sometimes be brought under heavy strain, The decision of the Soviet and Yugoslav Governments to raise the status of their respective diplomatic missions to embassy level (41) suggested an apparent rapprochement which was the more surprising in that, after repeated representations by Tito, Radio Free Yugoslavia had at last begun to publicize the exploits of individual Partisan commanders and their units and to carry reports of Mihailović's collusion with the occupying forces.[89] But this publicity for the Partisans evidently did not yet represent any real change in the Soviet attitude towards events in Yugoslavia. The following month Tito was again complaining that Radio Moscow was still keeping inexplicably silent about Chetnik atrocities; why did it continue to deny the Partisans the publicity and moral support they deserved? (**70**). Though the Soviet Government had in fact begun to tax the Yugoslav Government in Exile with the collusion of its Minister of Defence, it was still only half convinced by the incriminating evidence supplied by the Partisans. The latter were again requested to send further details of the documents which they claimed gave proof of his treachery, and to make sure that these had not been forged and planted on them by the enemy as a means of splitting the resistance movement (**43**).

By mid-October Tito could note with satisfaction that the Russians seemed at last to be seeing the Chetniks in their true light and to be giving the Partisans their due. In presenting the colours to the Second Proletarian Brigade, he could claim that almost every broadcast from Russia now paid some tribute to the Partisans, and that 'we have won recognition from the greatest and most cultured of nations'; he blamed 'Fifth Columnists' in Britain and the United States for hampering the common war effort. Both the political and military situation of the Partisans had become more favourable. Their movement had assumed national dimensions and was gaining Moscow's open support. The main body of their troops had fought their way through to western Bosnia and controlled a large liberated area centring round the town of Bihać and maintained contact with detachments operating in many other parts of the country. These detachments, Tito reported to the Comintern, were

> no longer called partisan units, but shock divisions of the National Liberation Army of Yugoslavia. We shall now [he went on to say] set up something like a government which is to be called the National Liberation Committee of Yugoslavia (**71**).

Founding of the Anti-Fascist Council (AVNOJ)

On 26 November 1942 delegates from the main regions of Yugoslavia assembled in Bihać and proceeded to form an Anti-Fascist Council for the National Liberation of Yugoslavia (AVNOJ), which in turn elected its own executive, the National Liberation Committee. The Comintern commented that 'the creation of a National Liberation Committee of Yugoslavia is very necessary and of exceptional importance', but warned Tito not to look to it as a sort of government in opposition to the Government in Exile; the question of abolishing the monarchy and setting up a republic in its place should not be raised at that stage but should be deferred until after the occupying forces had been driven from the country (**72**). To this Tito replied that 'we agree to the advice you gave in your telegram and shall follow it', but added that the Government in Exile was execrated as traitorous by the people of Yugoslavia and that, since the old administrative structure of the state had been completely destroyed, the newly formed Committee would 'have to look after all state business and occupy itself with the war', even though it did not possess the formal status of a government (73).

The setting up of AVNOJ marked a new stage in the evolution of the Partisan movement. 'It served notice on the Russians that Tito now considered he had both an army and a state. It marked Tito's political coming of age.'[90] He was careful to keep the Russians fully informed and to secure their agreement for this important step. In the open sessions of AVNOJ he also made a point of stressing the Partisans' gratitude to the Russians and emphasized that faith in the strength of the Soviet Union had sustained them from the beginning of their struggle. Nevertheless it is clear that in his interpretation of the general instructions received from Moscow, Tito was now resolved to secure as much liberty of action as possible. The Russians had no representatives, either military or political, at his headquarters, and they appeared to assume that the directives transmitted over the Comintern's radio link would continue to be a sufficient means of exercising control over a movement whose steadily developing national character and independence they persistently underrated. Nor, in the military crisis which shortly confronted the Partisans, were they able to provide any urgently needed help.

The Partisans were not left long in undisturbed occupation of Bihać and the surrounding liberated territory. In the middle of January 1943 they were forced to begin a long withdrawal, taking a great train of wounded and refugees with them, through Hercegovina and into Montenegro as the enemy launched their fourth offensive against them. A new note of urgency now marked Tito's calls for help. 'Is it really impossible, after twenty months of fighting, to find some way of helping us?' he radioed (57). And why, he asked testily some days later, does Radio Free Yugoslavia make no mention of this new enemy offensive?[91] Moscow replied in flattering terms—but sent no help. The Soviet people were full of admiration for the Partisans, Dimitrov assured Tito. He and Stalin in person had frequently discussed how they could help them, although unfortunately the difficulties were still insurmountable. But Tito and his heroic comrades should rest assured that the Soviet people would never forget them (58).

Yet did Moscow really grasp the plight of the Partisans, and did it really trust them? An incident occurred at the height of this German offensive which taxed Tito's patience to the utmost. The Partisan withdrawal was severely handicapped by the great numbers of wounded they were obliged to take with them and who could expect short shrift if they fell into the hands of the enemy. Tito therefore decided that he had no alternative but to negotiate with the German High Command for a truce and exchange, as he had already negotiated the previous September with the Ustashe, who had exchanged two high-ranking officers for some thirty arrested communists. Tito reported his intentions to the Russians who disapproved and distrusted the secret negotiations. Perhaps their suspicions were to some extent justified, since, after the previous exchange, the Partisans had themselves executed three of the men handed over to them as agents and were later to denounce Hebrang, who was amongst those exchanged, as a spy. But Tito reacted sharply to Russian disapproval. 'If you cannot understand what a hard time we are having', he radioed back, 'and if you cannot help us, at least do not hinder us'.[92] 'Our first duty', he declared to his intimates, 'is to look after our own army and our own people'. This, Djilas was later to recall, 'was the first time anyone in the Central Committee openly stated that our interests might be different from Moscow's'.[93]

On 13 March Tito reported to the Comintern that his troops had crossed the Neretva, broken through the enemy ring, and were overrunning the Chetnik positions barring their way into Montenegro.[94] Instead of a sanctuary, this mountain fortress soon threatened to become itself a trap round which the enemy was concentrating large numbers of fresh troops. In mid-May, in the fiercest fighting of the war, Tito launched a desperate thrust to break out of the steel ring in the direction of the Sandžak. At this critical juncture an event occurred which, though it brought no help in the immediate military emergency, marked the beginning of a new phase in Tito's relations with the allies. On the night of 27 May a British military mission was dropped by parachute to his headquarters.[95] A fortnight later Tito signalled to Moscow: 'We are still in a difficult position. . . . Today the British Captain Stewart [Stuart] was killed by a bomb, while Captain Deakin and I were lightly wounded. . . . We request your support in this supreme trial' (59).

By the end of June, despite crippling losses, the core of Tito's army had broken out of Montenegro and started to reform in east Bosnia. The capitulation of Italy brought it a welcome accession of arms and equipment. Partisan morale was again high, the international political conjuncture favourable, and the time ripe for a fresh political initiative—the second session of the AVNOJ which was summoned to meet at Jajce, in Bosnia, at the end of November, at the same time as Stalin, Roosevelt, and Churchill were conferring at Teheran. Tito reported his intention to hold this meeting (75), as he reported all his moves, to Moscow, but on this occasion he did not disclose in advance the details of the politically significant resolutions to be put before the Council[96] though the broad lines on which he was thinking were sufficiently clear from the telegram he had previously sent (and which the Russians had ignored) (74) for the Foreign Ministers' Meeting in Moscow. The most important of the decisions taken at Jajce, which the Russians only learned after the event, were that the Council had resolved not to recognize King Peter and his government or to allow them to return to Yugoslavia after the war, and had constituted itself the supreme authority in the country (76).

The Russians were extremely displeased when they received the report of the Jajce decisions. Manuilsky sent for Vlahović and told him that 'the Boss [Stalin] is very angry. He says that this is a stab in the back for the Soviet Union and the Teheran decisions', and forbade him to broadcast details of the decisions.[97] Stalin expected that the British and American Governments would be displeased by the Partisans' precipitate action in breaking with the king and his government, whom the allies were still pledged to support, and would assume that Stalin had secretly put them up to it. Certainly they were far from imagining at this stage that Tito was capable of striking out on a line of his own without waiting for Moscow's prompting. Their reactions to the Jajce decisions were not particularly hostile, however, perhaps because they did not wish to make the issue a bone of contention with Stalin. When the Russians noted this mild response, and the coverage given to the Jajce meeting in the Western press, they were to some extent mollified and permitted Free Yugoslavia to broadcast the text of the decisions and commented favourably on them in the press (77). This sign of growing and potentially dangerous independence on the part of Tito and his fellow communists was probably not lost on Stalin.

Disbanding of the Comintern

Whilst Tito was in the thick of the savage fighting in Hercegovina in early May 1943 he received a signal from the Comintern saying that it was felt that 'the centralized form of international organization no longer corresponds to the further development of the Communist Parties of the different countries, and has even become an obstacle to this development', and proposing its own dissolution. The CC of the CPY was asked to notify Moscow of its views (92). Tito did not reply at once to this proposal, probably less on account of its seemingly startling nature than because the Partisans were still heavily engaged in critical military operations. On 6 June Moscow sent a reminder asking for a reply and for information as to what had been the reaction of the CPY to the proposed demise of the Comintern, whether there were any elements in the Party which had attempted to exploit the opportunity for 'fractional work', and what counter-precautionary measures might have been thought necessary to take against hostile propaganda dismissing Moscow's proposal as a mere manœuvre.[98]

In a message signed by himself and five members of the Politburo, Tito duly replied that 'the Central Committee of the CPY finds itself in full agreement'. He paid a tribute to the Comintern, through whose assistance the CPY had grown into a powerful mass party, and pledged that the Party would 'remain faithful to the principles of the International' (93). Despite the disappointments and differences of view which had sometimes marked the exchanges with Moscow, there seems to be no evidence that, at this stage, the disbanding of the Comintern was looked upon by the Yugoslav leaders as giving them the green light to strike out on a more independent line of their own;[99] the Russians certainly did not intend them to draw any such conclusions. The decision of the Comintern to put a formal end to its own existence was a tactical move designed primarily to allay allied fears that the Russians were intervening, through the control they exercised over local CPs, in their internal affairs and were bent on subverting the social order. The realities of the subordinate relationship of the foreign CPs to Moscow remained unaffected. Tito continued as before to report to the Russians through Dimitrov and his assistants and to receive guidance and directives. The administrative machinery which had served as Comintern headquarters was maintained as an integral part of the state and Party apparatus of the Soviet Union.

INTERNATIONAL ISSUES AND THE PARTISAN MOVEMENT
The abortive Proclamation to the Peoples of Occupied Europe

The development of a vigorous communist-led resistance movement in Yugoslavia offered the Comintern opportunities for extending Moscow's influence to countries too remote for direct contact or lacking indigenous CPs of their own. The Yugoslav communists were only too ready to play the part not only of intermediaries but of mentors, and though the Comintern saw advantage in using them in this way, the experience they thereby acquired encouraged in time the growing spirit of self-confidence and independence which was to set them at odds with Moscow. The signals exchanged early in 1942 over the proposed drafting of a Proclamation to the Peoples of Occupied Europe already reveal Russian hesitations as to how far the Yugoslavs could safely be assigned a leading role.

In mid-February the Comintern asked the Partisan Supreme Staff to draft a proclamation which would encourage the resistance movements elsewhere in Europe, particularly in France and Czechoslovakia, and promised to give it the widest publicity (**87**). Tito readily agreed (**88**); the proposal was a tacit recognition of the pre-eminent part which the Yugoslav CP was playing in the organization of resistance in occupied Europe. A text was quickly drafted and radioed to Moscow. The latter replied suggesting certain amendments; these consisted mainly in the omission of references to the leading role assumed by the communists in organizing resistance in Yugoslavia and of slogans expressing excessive adulation of Stalin and the Red Army (**89**). Tito wired back his concurrence and asked to be informed when the revised version of the proclamation might be published (**90**). Eleven days later he was told that it had been decided to defer publication 'until certain matters in the relations between the Soviet and Yugoslav Government have been cleared up' (**91**). The Russians were, in fact, considering entering into a treaty of mutual assistance with the Government in Exile and the proclamation, which might prove a stumbling block, was quietly shelved.

Italy

Mussolini's fascist regime had destroyed the communist organization in Italy, but Umberto Massola ('Quinto'), an Italian communist who had found asylum in Zagreb in 1940, had been making attempts to rebuild it in north Italy. In May of the following year he was joined in the task by a Comintern agent, Rigoleto Martini ('Quarto'). The latter was able to use the Zagreb radio link with Moscow, but his relations with the CPY were clouded by the Comintern's policy towards the Croat and Slovene minority in Venezia Giulia which ruled that its future was a matter to be decided after the war, whereas the Yugoslav communists claimed that it should be given the right of self-determination and encouraged to wage a 'struggle for national liberation'.[100]

Early in July 1941 the Comintern sent a directive urging Martini to step up subversive activities in Italy 'for the defence of the Soviet Union', in particular amongst the workers in the Italian war industry, to incite Italian soldiers to desert, and to stir up dissension between the fascists and their German allies (**78**). In an attempt to carry out these instructions, Martini made his way back to Italy but was caught and sentenced to a heavy term of imprisonment. The work was carried on by Massola, who showed himself more accommodating with regard to the Yugoslav communists' attitude over Italy's Slavs. Though he would not agree that work amongst them should be organized within the framework of the CPY, he recognized that, on practical grounds, the Slovene CP should develop links with them, and delegates were sent into Venezia Giulia to organize branches of the clandestine Slovene Freedom Front. Partisan detachments were also developed in that area and were regarded by the Yugoslav communists as an integral part of the military and political movement led by Tito and as a useful means of strengthening the claims which it was later to advance—in the teeth of opposition from the Italian CP—to Trieste.

Austria

A somewhat similar situation developed in Austria over the Slovene minority in Carinthia and Lower Styria. After the outbreak of World War II, Franz Honner, a prominent Austrian communist, sought asylum in Yugoslavia and made contact with the CPY before moving to Moscow the following May. Four years later he returned to Črnomelj in Slovenia with instructions to raise an Austrian Partisan detachment, officered mainly by former Austrian volunteers in the Spanish Civil War, for operations in Austria. Two units thus formed co-operated closely with Slovene Partisans and the Slovene CP. On 5 September 1944 Kardelj reported that Honner had agreed that the anti-Nazi activities of the Slovenes of Carinthia amounted to a practical plebiscite expressing their wish to be incorporated in Yugoslavia.[101] As in the case of Venezia Giulia however nationalist sentiment in Austria militated against any public expression of such views, and though Moscow for a time backed Yugoslavia's postwar territorial claims against Austria, this support was later withdrawn and the Slovene Carinthians were left in Austria (**149–52**). (See below, pp.75–6.)

Albania

The Albanian CP and Partisan movement were created and nurtured by the CPY in much the same way as the CPs of other countries had been developed under the wing of the Comintern.[102] The latter appears to have been content to entrust this role to the CPY and to let it have a fairly free hand so long as Moscow was kept fully informed and consulted on major issues. Yugoslavia possessed a considerable Albanian, or Skiptar, minority of its own in Kosovo and Metohija, where the CPY had local organizations. In mid-1939 Tito sent Miladin Popović, the Party Secretary for that region, and later another delegate, Dušan Mugoša, into Albania with instructions to weld together the various Marxist groups, some of which had been infected by Trotskyist and anarchist tendencies, into a disciplined CP on standard Moscow lines. Under the sponsorship of these Yugoslav delegates, the Albanian CP was formally founded in November 1941, and during the course of 1942 the Party organization was built up throughout the country and the first Partisan detachments were formed. In September of that year Tito was able to inform Popović that the Comintern had approved the organizers' preparatory work and prescribed guidelines for the election of a CC and the formulation of Party policy (**79**).

Bulgaria and the Macedonian problem

Macedonia, byword for racial complexity and the coveted object of rival ambitions, was to prove as much an apple of discord amongst the CPs of Eastern Europe as it had been amongst other parties and governments.[103] Its major part (Vardar Macedonia) had belonged to Yugoslavia (smaller slices,

Pirin and Aegean Macedonia, forming parts respectively of Bulgaria and Greece) but had been given to Bulgaria after the Axis dismemberment of the Yugoslav state. The Comintern line on Macedonia remained unusually opportunistic and ambivalent. So long as its policy had been to work for the break-up of the Yugoslav state it had looked with favour on Macedonian separatism and sponsored its own branch of the notorious terrorist organization IMRO, the *Obidinena* or united IMRO, whose leader, Dimitar Vlahov, was the delegate for Macedonia at Comintern headquarters. The issue was complicated by the fact that the Comintern's Secretary-General, Georgi Dimitrov, and other influential officials were Bulgarians, and tended to view the Balkans through Bulgarian spectacles. The Bulgarian CP was frankly in favour of Macedonia's incorporation in Bulgaria.

Following the Axis invasion of Yugoslavia in 1941, Moscow appears to have accepted Bulgaria's annexation of Vardar Macedonia as a fait accompli and to have regarded the local CP organization there, which had hitherto been a part of the CPY, as now coming within the framework of the Bulgarian CP. Instructions to this effect appear to have been sent to the secretary of the local organization, Metodij Šatorov-Šarlo.[104] The following August, as the Partisan movement began to gather momentum in Serbia and other parts of Yugoslavia, the Comintern exhorted the Yugoslav and Bulgarian CPs to work together and ruled that responsibility for Macedonia should remain with the Yugoslavs, since it was necessary to develop Partisan activity there and the Partisan movement was under Yugoslav leadership; but the directive also told both Parties to support self-determination for the Macedonian people **(80)**. At the end of the month, the CPB informed its Yugoslav counterpart that it unreservedly accepted this ruling and would send a representative to Macedonia to liaise with the Yugoslav comrades.[105] It also reminded the latter that the Comintern's decision had been taken 'on grounds of practicality and expediency' and seemed to have been reached without a full knowledge of the situation.[106] At the beginning of September Tito complained to Moscow that Metodij Šatorov-Šarlo had repudiated his authority and aligned the local Party organization with the Bulgarian communists, on whose support, as well as on Dimitrov's, he was confident he could rely **(81)**. Tito also sent an angry protest to the CPB **(82)**. By the end of September he was able to write to the Macedonian Party organization to confirm that the Comintern had ruled in favour of their remaining within the framework of the CPY whilst permitting them, on practical grounds, to retain special links with the Bulgarian Party **(83)**.

This ruling left the dispute virtually unsettled and satisfied neither side. The Yugoslavs redoubled their efforts to make good their grip on the local organization by sending delegates from the CC and circulating an Open Letter to its members. The Bulgarian communists had easier channels of communication with Sofia, and determined to exploit to the full the advantages which the occupation of Macedonia by the Bulgarian army gave them. They argued that the policy of all-out resistance to the forces of occupation approved for other areas of the former Yugoslav state was not valid for Macedonia, where the Party's organization was weak and the people in no mood to respond to the watchword of national liberation, since the Bulgarian army, though under fascist command, had in a sense already brought them national liberation. The task was rather to infiltrate that army and so hasten the collapse of the whole fascist regime in Bulgaria, instead of raising Partisan detachments to fight against it. The Party organization in Macedonia was split on these issues.

At the beginning of 1942 the Bulgarian CP presented a new proposal to the Comintern to the effect that the Macedonian communists should form their own Party independent of both the Yugoslav and Bulgarian Parties (84). Tito reacted sharply against this proposal and told the Comintern that he was sending a delegate to try to settle matters with the Bulgarian communists (85). The latter stuck to their line and nearly a year later Tito was still complaining to Dimitrov that their demand for an independent Macedonia was tantamount to German propaganda, and that they would do better to concentrate their efforts on getting the Bulgarian army to stop fighting his forces (86). With the advent of the Red Army, and Bulgaria's eleventh-hour switch to the allied side, the position was radically altered. Macedonia was re-established within the prewar Yugoslav frontiers as one of the constituent units of the new Federal Yugoslav Republic. But the friction between the Bulgarian and Yugoslav comrades over the status of Macedonia and the future of Pirin Macedonia was never far below the surface and could readily be revived when it suited Moscow to bring pressure upon a recalcitrant protégé. The status of Aegean Macedonia was similarly to become a complicating factor in the communist rising in Greece.[107]

EFFORTS TO INDUCE THE GOVERNMENT IN EXILE
TO COME TO TERMS WITH TITO

By the end of 1943 the pattern of relationships between the Yugoslav, British, and Soviet Governments had undergone a marked change. British and Yugoslav efforts to induce the Soviet Government to back Mihailović had given place to British and Soviet efforts to induce the Government in Exile to come to terms with Tito. The capitulation of Italy in September strengthened the Partisans' military situation and enhanced the strategic importance of Yugoslavia. One of the plans which the allies now began to consider was a commando operation across the Adriatic which would cut off the German armies in the Balkans and strike into central Europe. For the success of such an operation, co-operation with Tito's forces would be of the first importance. In July Tito reported to Moscow that he was starting to receive military equipment through his British liaison officers, but that 'we are cautious and are keeping a watch on them'.[108] Early in October he sent a further telegram to Moscow for consideration by the Foreign Ministers who were to meet there shortly to prepare the conference between the war leaders at the end of November. The Yugoslav people, he declared, would never permit the return to Yugoslavia of a king and government compromised by their association with Mihailović and the collaborationist Chetniks; the sole lawful authorities were the National Liberation Committees and the AVNOJ (74). Neither the Russian nor the Western Foreign Ministers took cognizance of this communication, but the trend of events in Yugoslavia was clearly in the direction indicated in Tito's claim.

When, shortly afterwards, the Teheran Conference took place between Stalin, Roosevelt, and Churchill, the latter had words of warm commendation for Tito 'who had done much more than Mihailović' against the Germans, and to whom the British intended to increase their military aid to the maximum.[109]

The Russians made few references to the situation in Yugoslavia. Stalin was recorded as saying that

> there was no difference of opinion as to the importance of helping the Partisans, but that he must say that, from the Russian point of view, the questions of Turkey, the Partisans, and even the occupation of Rome were not really important operations.[110]

He said that 'Overlord' (the opening of a Second Front) was the most important, and nothing should be done to distract attention from that operation. Later during the conference he repeated that 'we feel it desirable to help Yugoslavia and to give two or three divisions, if it would be necessary to do so. The Soviets however do not consider this an important matter.' Stalin personally was rather dismissive about the Partisans' war effort and insisted that they were holding down a mere eight German divisions against Churchill's affirmation that there were twenty-two German divisions in Yugoslavia, to say nothing of numerous Quisling troops.[111]

Eden repeated a suggestion which he had discussed with Molotov the previous month to the effect that the Russians might wish to send a military mission to the Partisans and offered to place a base at their disposal in North Africa for this purpose. Molotov expressed gratitude for this offer, but 'asked whether it would not be better to have a mission to Mihailović rather than Tito in order to get better information'.[112] The British, who were moving towards the decision to withdraw all support from Mihailović, showed little enthusiasm for this suggestion and it was not taken up. In a statement published after the conference, the Russians announced their intention to send a military mission to the Partisans and criticized, but in moderate language, the attitude of Mihailović which 'has not facilitated but has rather brought harm to the cause of the struggle of the Yugoslav peoples against the German invaders' **(100)**. The secret military conclusions reached at the conference included an agreement that 'the Partisans in Yugoslavia should be supported by supplies and equipment to the greatest possible extent, and also by commando operations.[113] The Government in Exile was informed through its ambassador in London that the allies were agreed that 'Yugoslavia, as a state entity, will be restored in full territorial integrity and independence, the question of her western frontier and her claims against Italy being settled after the war, bearing in mind the proposal put forward by President Wilson in 1919'.[114]

The allies' decisions at Teheran to increase their help to Tito, and their mild public reaction to the Jajce declarations denouncing the Government in Exile aroused the latter to a belated effort to improve its relations with Moscow. On 10 December Dr Purić reopened with Novikov, the Soviet representative in Cairo, the idea of a Soviet–Yugoslav pact for which the Soviet Government had shown some interest the previous year. But circumstances had now changed, and Moscow saw little advantage in committing itself to an exiled government whose prospects of returning to the country were clearly diminishing. The Soviet ambassador declared that, in view of the unsettled situation in Yugoslavia, his government did not think it opportune to start negotiations, and hinted that a prerequisite for any such treaty would be for the Government in Exile to come to some understanding with Tito. In a note handed to the British Foreign Secretary by the Soviet ambassador in London, the Soviet

Government stressed the need 'to find a basis for collaboration between the two sides' and, despite the great difficulties which would clearly attend it, affirmed its readiness to do everything possible to further this aim (94).

Dr Purić nevertheless remained optimistic, and at the end of December asked for a signal to be sent to Mihailović informing him that

> I have offered to negotiate with the Soviet Government to place relations between our two countries on a basis of closer collaboration and alliance during the present war as well as after it. While doing this I made it quite clear that our people are not for Communism and that in no case shall we sacrifice you personally or the Yugoslav Army in the Fatherland.[115]

To smooth the course of the negotiations, Purić asked him to moderate the attacks on the communists contained in his communiqués. The unpromising exchanges between the Soviet Government and the Government in Exile were continued until the beginning of February when Moscow Radio announced that the Soviet Union had declined the proposals made by Dr Purić's government for a pact in view of the unsettled situation in Yugoslavia. The defection of Simić, its ambassador in Moscow, to the Partisan cause was a pointer to the steadily weakening position of the Government in Exile[116] (95).

At the end of May, following British diplomatic pressure, King Peter dismissed Dr Purić and entrusted Dr Ivan Šubašić with a mandate to reach agreement with Tito for the formation of a united provisional government. Efforts to this end continued throughout the summer of 1944 and were endorsed when, in October, Stalin received Churchill in Moscow. The future of Eastern Europe was discussed[117] and broad agreement reached that, until a general settlement was concluded at the peace settlement, the Soviet Union's influence should be predominant in Romania and Bulgaria, that of Britain in Greece, whilst the allies should each have a say in Yugoslav and Hungarian affairs on a fifty-fifty basis.[118] Though this proposed sharing of influence carried no territorial connotations and was an almost casual arrangement (the figures were jotted down on a scrap of paper and passed across the table to Stalin, who ticked them with his pencil), its implications were clearly of capital importance to the Yugoslav leaders, who do not appear to have been given any hint of them when Tito conferred with Stalin a few days before. Nor were they subsequently informed by the Russians, but were left to discover the deal through other sources. Although it was never carried into effect, for Soviet influence was paramount from the outset in postwar Yugoslavia, the Yugoslav leaders felt keenly affronted by what seemed to them a proposal to carve up their country over their heads into spheres of influence.[119] The maintenance of a rough equilibrium of influence between East and West was indeed to prove the cornerstone of Tito's own policies in later years and the best guarantee of the country's independence, but it was a balance which Tito intended to adjust with his own hands, and not see imposed by the great powers according to a pre-arranged formula devised without him.

To induce a reluctant royalist government, in the person of Dr Šubašić, to come to some agreement with Tito was left to British diplomatic initiative and proved a difficult and protracted task. Moscow expressed official satisfaction at the progress achieved when Šubašić and Kardelj held talks there with the Soviet leaders in November (96), but was soon attacking King Peter for attempting to wreck the agreement (97). Opposition from this quarter was overcome by inducing the king, under strong British pressure, to vest his royal powers in a Council of Regency. A settlement of the Yugoslav question was rendered urgent by the increasing strategic importance of the country as the Red Army continued to drive the Germans from the Balkans. It figured on the agenda when Churchill, Stalin, and Roosevelt met at Yalta at the beginning of the following February. Churchill reverted to his proposal that the Anglo–American forces in Italy should strike through the Ljubljana gap in Yugoslav territory, towards Vienna.[120] Stalin gave no encouragement to this proposal, as he had no wish to see an Anglo–American force interposed between the advancing Red Army and Central Europe. In the political sphere, discussion turned on the Tito–Šubašić agreement which, though agreed in principle, was still hanging fire. Stalin said that 'he would like to know what is holding back the formation of a united Government'. Churchill replied that 'the King had been persuaded, or even forced, to agree to a Regency'. He went on to say that the British Government would like some slight amendments to the Agreement to be adopted and that he was sure that Tito would readily accept them if Stalin were to say the word.[121] Molotov opposed this proposal, but after further discussion it was agreed to include in the communiqué issued at the end of the conference two amendments recommending that AVNOJ be enlarged to include uncompromised members of the former Yugoslav legislature, and that legislation passed by the new body should subsequently be ratified by a Constituent Assembly[122] (98).

At the beginning of 1945 Churchill informed the House of Commons that the British and Soviet Governments were pursuing a joint policy of encouraging the representatives of the Yugoslav Government in Exile to reach agreement with the regime which Tito had now installed in Belgrade (99). On 7 March it was announced that a new Provisional Government had been formed under the nominal authority of the Regency, in which Tito figured as Prime Minister and Šubašić as his Minister of Foreign Affairs.[123] This was officially recognized by the Soviet Government on 29 March, and a fortnight later, exactly four years after the German armies had shattered the structure of the old Yugoslav state, a Treaty of Friendship, Mutual Aid, and Postwar Collaboration was signed between the Soviet and Provisional Yugoslav Governments (106). It was a clear indication of the path which the new Yugoslavia had chosen to take and the special relationship which its leaders were eager to cultivate with their great Soviet ally.

THE RED ARMY IN YUGOSLAVIA
Exchange of military missions
One factor which, quite apart from the ideological allegiance of the Yugoslav communist leaders, was potent in determining the direction which the political destinies of Yugoslavia would take after the war was the advent of the Red Army. The establishment of any physical presence in the resistance movement had been tardy, and it was not until the end of 1943 that the Russians announced their intention of sending a military mission to Tito's headquarters (100). That they had not done so earlier seems a surprising and unwise omission, due perhaps in part to their continuing suspicion that the Chetniks might,

after all, prove a more powerful force to back.[124] Tito's unquestioning co-operation, and the role of his Partisans as ancillary to the main operations of the Red Army, were no doubt taken for granted. But a Russian presence at an earlier stage would not only have given Moscow a clearer realization of Yugoslav realities, but could hardly have failed to ensure closer military and political control. By February 1944, when the military mission finally arrived, it was to find a movement which, though pledged to objectives broadly in line with its own, had acquired a strong national character, with its distinctive traditions and outlook, and with its own links to the Western allies from whom it was now obtaining valuable supplies.

The Soviet military mission was headed by Lt General Korneyev and his staff included General Gorshkov, an expert on Russian guerrilla warfare, and a number of political intelligence officers. Its arrival was greeted with great enthusiasm by the Partisans and received a fulsome tribute from Tito (**101**). It represented their first official contact with the Red Army and indicated the public recognition the Russians were beginning to accord them. But the Russian officers were soon made aware that the Yugoslav Partisans' way of life and fighting differed from their own and the mutual enthusiasm of the initial encounter soon began to pass off. 'When it became apparent to them', the head of the British military mission noted, 'that there was no question of their taking over command of the Partisan forces, as they had evidently expected to do, they became even less enthusiastic'.[125]

Shortly after the arrival of the Soviet military mission, Tito was invited to send a delegation to Moscow. The main purpose of the delegation, which was headed on the military side by General Velimir Terzić, Deputy Chief of Staff, and on the political side by Milovan Djilas, was to arrange Soviet military aid for the Partisans and to sound out the Soviet Government on whether they would recognize the National Committee as the provisional legal government, and would influence the Western allies to do so too.[126] It was also to ask for a loan of $200,000, arrange, through Soviet or other channels, for help from UNRRA, deposit the archives of the CC of the CPY and the Partisans' Supreme Staff with the Russians for safe keeping,[127] and settle the question of the Croats captured by the Red Army on the eastern front.[128] The Partisan delegation soon agreed that the Croats should constitute a Yugoslav brigade which was already under formation in the Soviet Union despite the objections voiced by the Government in Exile. The Partisan delegation also reached agreement with the Soviet authorities for the latter to fly in military supplies from Romania and to open a million-rouble credit for the purchase of war material.[129] Stalin raised the possibility of supplying larger quantities of war material by sea in ships purchased in Egypt, but nothing came of this proposal.[130]

Tito had also commissioned Djilas to find out from Dimitrov, or from Stalin if possible, 'whether there was any dissatisfaction with the work of our party'. 'This order of Tito', Djilas later commented, 'was purely formal—to call attention to our disciplined relations with Moscow—for he was utterly convinced that the CPY had brilliantly passed the test, and uniquely so'. When he spoke with Djilas, Stalin raised the question of the Partisans' relations with the Western allies and cautioned them 'not to "frighten" the English, by which he meant that we were to avoid anything that might alarm them into thinking that a revolution was going on in Yugoslavia or an attempt at Communist control'. Why, for instance, he asked Djilas, had the Partisans thought fit to wear the Red Star in their caps? He warned Djilas repeatedly against the duplicity of the British, and of Churchill in particular, and declared that the intelligence service might make an attempt on the life of Tito as—he alleged— it had successfully done against General Sikorski. With regard to the Government in Exile, Stalin advised the Partisans to come to an agreement with Šubašić. This advice, which Djilas duly passed on to Tito, no doubt helped to bring about the Tito–Šubašić agreement. Despite Stalin's wish that the Yugoslavs should make a temporary accommodation of this nature, Djilas gained the impression that 'Stalin was deliberately frightening the Yugoslav leaders in order to weaken their ties with the West, and at the same time he tried to subordinate their policy to his interests and to his relations with the Western states, especially Great Britain'. For all the cordial reception accorded him, Djilas did not secure the main objective of his mission—the recognition of Tito's National Committee as the legal government of Yugoslavia. Before taking his leave Djilas asked—as Tito had instructed him—whether Stalin had any comments to make concerning the work of the CPY. 'No, I have not', Stalin replied. 'You yourselves know best what is to be done'.[131] In the light of future events, these words had an ironic ring.

Joint military operations

Whilst his military mission was in Moscow, an event occurred in Yugoslavia which served as a harsh reminder that Tito's forces were still exposed to the hazards of Partisan warfare. Launching an airborne attack on his Bosnian headquarters at Drvar, the Germans nearly succeeded in capturing the whole of the Supreme Staff and political leadership. Tito was flown out to Italy, from where he returned to set up a new headquarters on the island of Vis, which a joint British and Yugoslav garrison rendered secure against enemy attack. The fact that he had been flown out to safety by a Soviet-piloted plane but was now relying heavily, at this phase of the war, on military co-operation with the British was a measure of the competing interest shown by the allies in strengthening their influence over what appeared more and more likely to be the dominant force in postwar Yugoslavia. By the end of May the British had withdrawn all assistance from Mihailović, and Dr Šubašić was working to bring into his cabinet ministers who were acceptable to Tito and prepared to work with him. In the broad lines of their policy towards Yugoslavia the allies still managed to keep in step (though the Americans remained loath to drop Mihailović). But the inexorable approach of the Red Army towards the Balkans left little doubt as to who would wield the dominant influence. At the beginning of July Tito sent a personal letter to Stalin in which he declared that 'in these decisive days, Soviet help is needed more than ever. . . . The strongest support you could possibly give would consist in the Red Army crossing across Romania and moving south'.[132]

In the meantime it was necessary to come to an understanding with the British on closer military co-operation. In August Tito and his advisers left to confer with Churchill and senior British commanders in Italy. Talks between Tito and Šubašić also made progress and held out hopes that the allies would soon be able to reconcile their de jure obligations to the king with the de facto control of much of Yugoslavia by the Partisans, whose power they hoped to see tempered by the influence of other political groupings. A new relationship of trust and co-operation with the West seemed, in short, to be in the making. This assumption was rudely shaken when, in the night of 18–19 September, Tito flew in all secrecy from Vis to Marshal Tolbukhin's headquarters in Romania and then on to Moscow.[133] A few days later it was officially announced that agreement had been reached between the Russians and the National Liberation Committee over the entry of the Red Army into Yugoslavia (102). The Russians agreed to recognize the authority of the civil administration set up by that Committee, and though they also undertook to withdraw their troops as soon as the Germans had been driven out, there could now be little doubt as to the shape which postwar Yugoslavia was likely to take or the direction to which the regime would primarily look.

Tito was given a hero's welcome in Moscow. But beneath the rough cordiality with which Stalin received him lay the barely concealed assumption that the man who was now the master of a victorious army and a vigorous national movement would continue, with the unquestioning obedience of a Comintern subordinate, to accept the guidelines prescribed for him. Tito, for his part, whilst continuing to treat the Russian leader with the deference due to the undisputed head of the communist world, had formed views of his own and had no hesitation in expressing them, even when they contradicted those of Stalin himself. When the latter counselled him to proceed with caution in Serbia as the bourgeoisie was still strong there and mentioned the name of other politicians with whom he might co-operate, Tito answered that, on the contrary, the Serbian bourgeoisie was quite weak and that the politicians mentioned were all compromised as collaborators. Nor did he show any disposition to drop his insistence that the king should never return to Yugoslavia, even after Stalin's cynical remark that 'you need not restore him for ever. Take him back temporarily; then you can slip a knife into his back at a suitable moment!' Only with regard to the British did Tito's attitude give the Russians full satisfaction. A report had just come in that some artillery units, which General Alexander had promised to send to assist in the Partisans' operations, had landed in Dalmatia. Stalin misrepresented this as the start of a general invasion, and drew from Tito the pledge that, if this were indeed the case, he would offer determined resistance. The Russian leaders were reassured by this indication that the national pride and assertiveness of the Partisans, no less than their ideological orientation, would rule out anything more than a purely opportunistic alliance with the West; they could hardly have begun to suspect that these same qualities would one day make the Partisans such a thorn in their own flesh.[134]

After conferring with Stalin, Tito returned to Soviet military headquarters at Craiova where—according to a Yugoslav version—

> he worked out a plan with Marshal Tolbukhin for joint operations between the Army of National Liberation and units of the Red Army for the liberation of Belgrade. . . . From Craiova he went on to Bela Crkva where he commanded operations for the liberation of Belgrade.[135]

But whatever agreement in principle may have been reached with Tolbukhin the Soviet operational commander, General Zhdanov, showed little concern for the Yugoslavs' insistence that they should be assigned an equal and visible role in liberating the capital of their country. 'I am advancing according to my own plan, and you may use yours and you may advance if you can. The enemy is weak and I shall simply walk over him', he is reported to have told the Partisan commanders. 'Come tomorrow and have tea with me in Belgrade!' This unco-operative attitude—according to Yugoslav accounts[136]— ruled out any effective joint operations and obliged the Partisans to launch a virtually independent attack on Belgrade, until Zhdanov, finding the reduction of the city more difficult than he had anticipated, turned to them for assistance. The Soviet account glosses over these differences and states somewhat patronizingly that

> the Soviet command courteously complied with the wishes expressed by Partisan leaders and by Tito personally that the Yugoslav troops be the first to enter the capital of Yugoslavia. The commander of the Soviet 4th Guard Moto-Mechanized corps, General Zhdanov, accordingly issued orders to his crews to have the Yugoslav partisans seated on their tanks. In this way, the Soviet and Yugoslav forces entered Belgrade simultaneously.[137]

No shadow of any misunderstanding between the Partisans and their great ally was certainly to be deduced from the official communiqué announcing the liberation of Belgrade[138] or from the fervent expressions of gratitude sent by Tito to Stalin (**104**).

A good deal of initial confusion seems nevertheless to have occurred when the Russians entered Yugoslav territory as to who were their allies and how they should be treated. Even after some Partisan detachments had assisted the Russian units to clear the Germans from Mladenovac and the heights of Topola, at the approaches to Belgrade, one Yugoslav commander felt obliged to report to Tito that 'they ignore the fact that . . . we have been assigned the main role in taking Belgrade (with the assistance of Soviet armour, transport, and artillery). They do not even know of the existence of our liberated territory' (**103**). Elsewhere things went more smoothly. A British liaison officer attached to the Partisans in the Banat observed that

> once military needs had been safeguarded, the Russians left the entire civil administrative machine in Partisan hands. In the first stages, Russians and Partisans worked together. Joint control was established in each town captured. Joint patrols searched for fugitive Germans lurking in cellars, patrolled the streets together and guarded strategic points, bridges and important buildings. Once law and order were assured, the Yugoslavs took over complete control, the only Russians remaining being those on duty organizing for the constant streams of troops moving to the front.[139]

The advent of the Red Army sounded the death-knell to Mihailović's hopes. He had always held that it was folly for his guerrilla forces to challenge the Germans until the latter were weakened by an allied onslaught; the allies were now in Serbia, but they were Russians, not Anglo–Americans. In those parts of Serbia which the Chetniks managed to control as the Germans withdrew and before the Partisans broke in, Mihailović's commanders offered their collaboration to the advancing Russians. Though the Soviet leadership had at last lost its lingering illusion that the Chetniks, rather than the Partisans, might be worth backing in Serbia, the Russian field commanders, unversed in the complexities of Balkan politics, saw little difference between Partisans and Chetniks. Short-lived tactical collaboration between Chetniks and Russians thus sometimes ensued. But

> as soon as the Red Army had established contact with the main partisan contingents in Serbia, its treatment of Mihailović's men radically changed. His officers and commanders, often on liaison duties at Soviet command posts, were arrested without warning, abducted from their units, delivered into partisan custody, deported to the USSR, or assassinated on the spot. His units fared no better. They were disarmed, disbanded, or dragooned into new Soviet-equipped partisan formations. Mihailović's position became hopeless. Under the circumstances, his plans of sustained action against the Germans could not materialize. Realizing that nothing could prevent the Soviet imposition of the partisan regime, and to avoid further collisions, let alone armed resistance to an Allied force, his forces staged a mass exodus from Serbia into Sandžak and Bosnia. Thus the partisans won control of Serbia without having defeated their rivals in a decisive military or political contest. The Soviet dispersal of the bulk of Mihailović's forces altered the internal balance of power in favour of the Partisans. The arms and supplies furnished by the Soviets consolidated their intervention in the internal conflict. Only after the Red Army had dispersed, disarmed, or forced the exodus of Mihailović's forces from Serbia, were the Partisans able to retain power without Soviet support.[140]

Mihailović himself reported to the allied Commander-in-Chief in Italy that he had ordered his men to offer co-operation with the Russians but that the latter had turned it down and seemed resolved to hand over Serbia to the communists (**105**).

With the capital and the government of the country in their hands, the Partisans were able, for the first time since the war began, to receive arms and supplies from their Soviet allies on a large scale.[141] These they needed both for the liquidation of their domestic enemies and in order to transform themselves into a regular army for operations against the withdrawing Germans. The latter were still strong enough to offer a stubborn resistance and even to launch a counteroffensive on the Srem front. The Yugoslav forces, used to the different tactics of guerrilla warfare and diluted by forcibly mobilized recruits, suffered heavy losses. The last Russian operational units withdrew into Hungary from Yugoslav soil on 12 November, and a communiqué was issued expressing gratitude for the unselfish help and friendly attitude shown to the Red Army by the Yugoslav people.[142] But when Tito visited Moscow again the following April, Stalin taunted him with the slow progress his forces were making and drew from him the angry retort that they would soon overcome their shortcomings.[143] It was not until the middle of May, when the Russians had taken Vienna, liberated parts of Slovenia, and threatened to cut off the remaining enemy forces holding out in the Balkans, that the German forces left in Yugoslavia finally surrendered to the Partisans.

The scope and significance of the Soviet military operations in Yugoslavia have been variously evaluated. 'Our peoples know very well that without the Soviet Union and without the Red Army, our liberation struggle could not have ended successfully', declared the commander of the Partisan army corps that welcomed the Soviet troops in Serbia. 'The brunt of the war was carried by the Soviet Union. The Soviet forces defeated Nazi Germany; all other anti-Fascist troops were of secondary and ancillary significance, and their successes possible only because of the victories of the Soviet army.'[144] Later, when the dispute between Moscow and Belgrade was at its height, the Russians declared that their intervention had been decisive at a much earlier stage and that they had saved Tito's whole movement from disintegration after the Germans nearly captured his headquarters in their parachute attack on Drvar. Yugoslav polemicists could not retrospectively deny the significance of Russia's role, but they claimed that

> the aid rendered by the Red Army, on its way to Budapest and Vienna, to the Partisan forces in the liberation of Belgrade, Banat, and Bačka was significant, but in no way decisive for victory. The National Liberation Movement had already won the definitive political victory, had an organized state, and the Partisan forces consisted of an army numbering three quarters of a million.[145]

These differing assessments of the value of the Soviet military intervention in Yugoslavia gained significance once the immediate postwar euphoria had given way to concern to establish Yugoslavia's rightful place in the 'socialist camp'. If Russia's military power had been virtually the only factor of consequence in the triumph of the allied cause, the whole Partisan epic which legitimized Tito's status as ruler of the new Yugoslavia was correspondingly devalued, and the achievements of the Yugoslav communists could be rated no higher than those of their East European comrades who had returned home in the wake of the Red Army, seized power, and carried through their revolutions by grace and favour of the Russians. But the Yugoslav CP believed that its successful leadership in the four years' struggle against the occupying forces and their Quisling allies had vested it with a more solid indigenous authority. Though it had looked for inspiration to the Soviet Union and welcomed Soviet co-operation in the last stages of the struggle, the Party prided itself on forging a movement with deep national roots and on having liberated its own country. This in no way invalidated its membership of the 'socialist camp'; rather, it had earned for the Party a specially privileged and honourable position within this camp, second only to that of the Soviet Union itself.

There was no question at this stage of the Yugoslav communists doubting the leadership of Moscow or looking elsewhere for the blueprint of the new social and political order they intended to construct in their country. But contact with Soviet political and military representatives had not been entirely without friction. Little of this was visible to outside observers. 'The Russians felt themselves amongst friends, had been treated with open hospitality, and did not repay kindness with looting', reported a correspondent of *The Times*.[146] Yugoslav accounts paint a rather different picture;

3

according to complaints filed by citizens, there were 121 cases of rape, of which 111 involved rape with murder, and 1,204 cases of looting with assault—figures that are hardly insignificant if it is borne in mind that the Red Army crossed only the northeastern corner of Yugoslavia.[147]

The indignation aroused by such incidents caused considerable resentment against the Russians and the new regime which was being established with their support. The consequences were felt to be sufficiently serious for the matter to be taken up between Tito and General Korneyev, the head of the Soviet military mission.[148] Korneyev sharply rejected the Yugoslav complaints and took particular exception to a remark by Djilas that people were making unfavourable comparisons between the correct behaviour of the British liaison officers attached to the Partisan forces and the excesses of the Red Army men (**109**). These and other incidents were reported to Moscow and noted as indicating a growing spirit of arrogance and insubordination which was in time to bring down Stalin's wrath upon the heads of the Yugoslav leaders.[149]

II THE POSTWAR PERIOD

FRIENDSHIP AND FRICTION

For the first three years after the end of World War II, Yugoslavia appeared to be the staunchest, the most thoroughgoing, and the most militant of Moscow's followers. The fiction of the Regency and the Provisional Government was quickly discarded. Though the façade of a Popular Front was maintained, the communists everywhere secured the levers of power, their Chetnik rivals having been eliminated and Mihailović himself captured, brought to trial, and executed. Industry was brought wholly under the state and a Five Year Plan was prepared for implementation once the immediate tasks of making good the ravages of war had been completed. A drastic agrarian reform abolished all large and medium-sized landholdings and set up peasant co-operatives as the first step towards the collectivization of agriculture. A new constitution converting Yugoslavia into a 'People's Republic' was introduced. In this, as in the concentration of power in the hands of a single party controlling the armed forces, the secret police, and the apparatus of propaganda, press, and education, the new Yugoslavia seemed to be reconstructing herself closely on the Soviet model, and Russian advisers were to be found promoting the process in key sectors of civilian and military life. The new Yugoslavia, Djilas declared, 'pursues, and will consistently pursue, the most friendly policy towards the Soviet Union. . . . No force on earth . . . could break the fraternal alliance' (**108**).

The alliance with the Soviet Union brought with it a corresponding weakening of Yugoslavia's ties with her wartime Western allies. Belgrade and Moscow both came out strongly against the Marshall Plan, 'the former largely out of revolutionary dogmatism, and the latter for fear that American economic aid might shake up the empire it had so recently acquired militarily'.[150] The Yugoslav communists were resolved to develop their country solely with the aid of the socialist bloc. At the end of May 1946 Tito, accompanied by his senior political, military, and economic colleagues, visited Moscow for talks with Stalin and other Soviet leaders. The outcome was an agreement on economic co-operation, supplemented in July of the following year by a further trade agreement for deliveries of Soviet industrial plant and equipment against a $135 million credit (**113**). The negotiation of these agreements revealed certain differences of view as to the goals of Yugoslavia's economic development and the forms which should be taken to achieve it. The Russians showed themselves unenthusiastic about Yugoslavia's ambitious plans for industrialization, arguing that they could supply her with all the products of heavy industry and that it would be preferable to concentrate on the development of her rich mineral resources of which they themselves stood in need. Moscow, in short, regarded her weaker partner—as the Yugoslavs were later to complain—as a source of colonial raw materials and showed no real wish to help her escape from her underdevelopment. The forms proposed as channels for their economic co-operation, the joint companies already operating in other People's Democracies, appeared designed to work to the unfair advantage of the Soviet Union (**147**). The Yugoslavs accordingly agreed to establish only two such bodies, one for commercial aviation and the other for Danubian shipping, and the operation even of these they subsequently denounced as highly exploitive.[151] In the face of obvious Yugoslav reluctance, Stalin finally dropped proposals for other joint companies and offered credits instead.

In the field of military co-operation, the Yugoslav communists quickly turned their backs on their wartime Western allies and looked for arms, equipment and guidance from the Soviet Union. The difficulty of converting Partisan units into a regular army had already become apparent in the final phases of the war, when the Russians had at last been able to offer valuable assistance in arms and supplies and had provided tactical co-operation with the Red Army. But how far was this process to go? Should the Yugoslavs develop their armed forces in every respect—not only in arms and equipment, but in organization, training, strategy, and tactics—as a carbon copy of the Red Army, or should they, whilst benefiting from Soviet arms and equipment and from the rich military experience of their Russian comrades, rely primarily on their own fighting experience and on the geographical and local factors which must affect any future operations in their own country? Some military leaders, including General Arso Jovanović, Tito's wartime Chief of Staff, and some of the many cadets and younger officers sent for training in Russian military academies, favoured total adherence to the Soviet model, and the large body of Russian military advisers in Yugoslavia exerted their influence in the same direction. But the majority of the Yugoslav leaders remained convinced that, however great their debt to the Russians, their own distinctive experience of the Partisan war should determine the main lines of future military development.[152]

The close relationship taken for granted between the Yugoslav and Soviet CPs had delicate implications in another field—that of intelligence and state security. Could a loyal member of another party have secrets from his more experienced Soviet comrades? Had he the right to conceal from them any aspect of his state or Party affairs, or any dubious attitude or action on the part of his colleagues? 'To give information to the Soviet Party was at that time not in itself considered a deadly sin, for no Yugoslav Communist set his own Central Committee against the Soviet', records Djilas, who describes the approach made to him by Russian intelligence officers during his first visit to Moscow and his embarrassed response to their questioning, for 'I knew that it was my duty as a Communist to give them the information they wanted'.[153] Two of his colleagues in the Yugoslav CC had fewer scruples. One was Sreten Žujović, a Moscow-trained communist, Partisan general, and cabinet member, who kept the Soviet ambassador in Belgrade informed of the CC's proceedings. Another was the Croat communist Andrija Hebrang who, as Minister for Heavy Industry, headed a large Yugoslav delegation to Moscow during the winter of 1944–5 and on his return to Belgrade continued to maintain close links with the Soviet authorities. In 1946 Hebrang, whose personal relations with Tito had become strained, was expelled from the CC on the grounds that doubts had arisen as to the circumstances in which he had been released by the Ustashe during the war. Djilas and Kardelj reported his expulsion to Molotov, who maintained an enigmatic silence. Hebrang continued to exercise some influence in his capacity of Chairman of the Federal Planning Commission and to enjoy the confidence of the Soviet leaders who kept him in mind for the new plans which they were beginning to consider for Yugoslavia.

The introduction of revolutionary changes at home was accompanied by the pursuit of energetic, and sometimes aggressive, policies abroad. Here, even more than in the domestic field, the Yugoslav communists ardently followed Moscow's lead, never questioning that their national interests could best be served by a wholehearted espousal of Soviet policies and adding their own quota to the international tensions which were transforming wartime co-operation with the West into the Cold War. Only gradually and painfully was experience to show that their country's interests and aims might not always be identical with those of the Soviet Union, and that the latter would have as little compunction as the capitalist powers in sacrificing them to her own. Yugoslavia's immediate foreign policy objectives were the expansion of her frontiers to include as much as possible of those areas of Italy and Austria where a Slav minority could be found; the consolidation of a sphere of influence tantamount to a protectorate over Albania; support for the communist-led rebels in Greece in order to remove the danger of an Anglo–American counter-revolutionary base and bring the whole of the Balkans within the socialist camp; close relations with the other People's Democracies and the conclusion of a federation with Bulgaria, whose Pirin province, like Greece's Aegean Macedonia, they hoped to see joined to Vardar Macedonia, which already formed one of the constituent republics of the Yugoslav state.

The occupation of Trieste and the entire territory of Venezia Giulia was an immediate objective, for Tito realized that possession would prove nine-tenths of the law. On 2 May 1945 his shock troops broke through the German defences, and for a time the city was held jointly, and with growing tension, by Yugoslav and New Zealand troops. General Alexander, the allied Commander-in-Chief, objected that the Yugoslavs had acted in violation of an understanding previously reached with Tito, and after some weeks of deadlock the Yugoslavs were forced to withdraw. Tito was not only bitterly aggrieved with the Western allies, but disappointed at the lukewarm support received from the Russians. He suspected that a deal had been concluded over the heads of the Yugoslavs in the spirit of the 50/50 division of influence agreed upon at Moscow between Stalin and Churchill. The new Yugoslavia, he declared in an outspoken speech at Ljubljana, would no longer put up with such treatment; 'this Yugoslavia is not an object for barter and bargaining' (**110**). Tito's outburst was directed against the Western powers, but it was also seen and resented by the Russians as an implied criticism. The Soviet ambassador in Belgrade was instructed to lodge a sharp protest with the Yugoslav Government, and the Kremlin did not show itself mollified by the explanations and assurances offered by Kardelj (**111, 112**).

The Western allies remained, of course, quite unaware of the friction which had begun to arise between Belgrade and Moscow over Yugoslavia's territorial claims against Italy which, to judge from the sharp tone of the message sent to Churchill by Stalin on 21 June, the Russians seemed resolved to support unreservedly. Molotov continued to press the Yugoslav case at the meeting of the Foreign Ministers in Paris but, encountering strong resistance from the Western allies, then proposed that Trieste and its surrounding countryside should constitute an autonomous state governed by a statute to be drafted by the four great powers but under Yugoslav sovereignty. Finally, dropping their demand for Yugoslav sovereignty, they agreed to a French compromise line by which the disputed territory should be divided provisionally into Zone A, comprising the city of Trieste and a strip of territory to the west, to be controlled by the Western allies, whilst the remainder, Zone B, stayed in Yugoslav hands until such time as the inhabitants of both zones were able to make their wishes known by means of a plebiscite. Yugoslav dissatisfaction over the decision was coupled with aggrieved surprise that Russian acquiescence should have been announced following an evening spent in talks between Kardelj and Molotov, during which the latter gave no hint of the steps his delegation had already decided to take on the following day.[154] However, the Russians subsequently made some amends to the Yugoslavs by attempting to cripple the arrangements envisaged for Trieste by circumscribing the Governor's powers and by pressing for a customs union and other concessions which would have given the Yugoslavs virtual control of the city after all. But the support given by the Russians to the Yugoslav case was inescapably ambivalent; they were held back not only by fear of a head-on clash with the Western allies but by reluctance to offend nationalist opinion in Italy and so prejudice the Italian CP's prospects in the forthcoming elections.

Yugoslavia's territorial claims against Austria were less soundly based and her total failure to achieve them gave other grounds for resentment against Moscow. By pursuing the Quisling forces across the prewar frontier and establishing themselves in Klagenfurt and Villach, the Partisans hoped to face the Western allies with a fait accompli, but the latter's peremptory demand forced them to withdraw. Nor did the Russians deal any more gently with the Partisan units which found themselves in the territory under Soviet occupation; the orders issued to them to withdraw behind the prewar frontiers were obeyed but bitterly resented.[155] Nevertheless, the Soviet Government agreed to support the Yugoslav claims at the Peace Conference but met with firm resistance from the

Western negotiators, who insisted that the prewar frontier should be restored. Stalin, in a personal letter to Chancellor Renner, himself gave what was generally regarded as a pledge to the same effect, though the Russians later argued that it did not bear this interpretation (152). What did emerge clearly was the Russians' prime interest in securing for themselves the substantial German assets in Austria, and their eventual realization that the Western allies would acquiesce if the Soviet Union ceased supporting the Yugoslav case and so made an early conclusion of a peace treaty with Austria possible. In March 1947 Molotov and Vyshinsky informed Kardelj that they were now convinced that the allies would never agree to substantial territorial concessions, and asked him to draft statements of the Yugoslav maximum and minimum demands 'so as to enable them to bargain better with the Western statesmen and try to get as much as possible'.[156] The Russians in fact got nothing for their clients and later adduced Kardelj's letter outlining his country's minimum demands (115) as evidence that it was the Yugoslav, and not the Soviet, Government which had abandoned the cause of the Carinthian Slovenes (150).

The close relationship established during the war, with Comintern blessing, between the Yugoslav and Albanian CPs continued into the postwar period, Belgrade assuming a tutelary role over Tirana even more pronounced than Moscow's over Belgrade. Though this proved deeply offensive to Albanian national pride, the Yugoslav communists succeeded in dominating their smaller neighbour's army and economy and placing reliably pro-Yugoslav communists in key positions in the Albanian Party. Despite their own complaints to the Russians that joint companies operated to the disadvantage of the weaker party, the Yugoslavs established a number of these bodies as their main channels for aid and trade with Albania,[157] and in November 1946 signed a commercial treaty envisaging the closest economic links with that country. At the end of the following year however Stalin asked the CC of the CPY to send Djilas to Moscow for discussions to bring Soviet and Yugoslav policies over Albania into line. Stalin confided to Djilas that 'we have no special interest in Albania—we agree to Yugoslavia swallowing Albania'.[158] This appears to have been a ruse to encourage the Yugoslavs to overreach themselves, whilst Soviet envoys in Tirana were secretly working to place their own men in the leadership of the Albanian CP and reverse its pro-Yugoslav policies.

Yugoslavia's relations with her Bulgarian neighbours, transformed in the last stages of the war from enemies into allies, were close if not always cordial. The possibility of a federation between the two countries had long figured in communist thinking and had been discussed between Tito and Dimitrov. In a conversation with Kardelj, Simić, and Šubašić on 22 November 1944, Stalin urged them to go ahead with the federation.[159] By the end of 1944 the Yugoslavs had prepared a draft plan which Kardelj took with him to Sofia for discussion with the Bulgarian comrades, and in the following January Moša Pijade headed a Yugoslav delegation to Moscow for further discussions with the Bulgarians and the Russians. But though there was general agreement that federation was desirable, there were differences as to the form it should take. The Bulgarians hoped that both countries would enter into the association on equal terms, whilst the Yugoslavs wanted Pirin Macedonia to be joined to the Macedonian Republic, which already constituted one of the six components of the Yugoslav state, and the rest of Bulgaria to join the latter simply as a seventh unit. If this seemed a loss of face for an independent country, the Yugoslavs could argue that Serbia and Montenegro too had once been fully independent; and after all, had not Yugoslavia proved her superior status by her heroic resistance during the war, whereas Bulgaria, until the eleventh hour, had chosen the losing side? The Russians at first favoured the Bulgarian thesis and then supported that of the Yugoslavs, whilst the Bulgarians were forced to acquiesce. Moscow's policy, nevertheless, remained obscure and contradictory. The Bulgarians had been traditionally amenable to Russian influence and had none of the truculent independence of mind which successful wartime resistance had bred in the Yugoslavs; to dilute the leadership of the Yugoslav Party and state with a Bulgarian element might well be to Moscow's advantage. But could not the proposed federation itself become undesirably strong and powerful? The Western allies too would be against it, and the issue could become another bone of contention with them. So plans for the federation hung fire, and it was not until August 1947 that Tito and Dimitrov, after meeting at Bled, concluded an agreement on co-operation between their two countries envisaging a customs union and gradual progress towards federation. Three months later, after the Russians had seen and approved the draft, and had amended the proposed duration from perpetuity to twenty years, a Yugoslav–Bulgarian Treaty of Friendship, Co-operation, and Assistance was signed.

The question of a Yugoslav-Bulgarian federation was linked to that of a wider grouping of the East European states on a federal or confederal basis. The Comintern had sponsored a projected Balkan communist federation on these lines during the 20s and early 30s. During the war, as the Yugoslav Partisan movement developed and extended its influence into Macedonia, Albania, and even northern Greece, the Russians had considered setting up a military-political centre under Tito's auspices for the whole Balkans.[160] Though this plan was not pursued, Soviet diplomats had dropped alarming hints of the lines on which Moscow was likely to favour the postwar reorganization of Eastern Europe.[161] The pattern seems to have envisaged a federation between Bulgaria and Yugoslavia (including Albania), another between Poland and Czechoslovakia, and a third between Romania and Hungary, possibly as a preliminary stage before bringing these groupings within the borders of the USSR itself.[162] By undertaking a series of state visits to the East European capitals in the course of 1946 and 1947, which were followed up by a corresponding series of bilateral treaties, Tito appeared to have been assigned a leading role in preparing the ground for such a plan.

Greece presented a special problem, for that country remained in the Western, not the Soviet, sphere of influence. Tito's emissary, Vukmanović-Tempo, had attempted without much success to strengthen communist influence in the leadership of the Greek resistance movement EAM, to wean it away from military co-operation with the British and induce it to adopt Yugoslav tactics of guerrilla fighting. The Greek communists made their bid to seize power in the autumn of 1944 and failed. At the end of the following year their leaders met with Yugoslav and Bulgarian representatives at Petrich (Bulgaria) and agreed to launch a new guerrilla rising. Yugoslavia offered the main support—at first, food, transport facilities, and the use of camps, ostensibly for the use of Greek refugees, and later, arms, ammunitions, artillery, and the services of a strong military mission headed by Peko Dapčević, one of Tito's most experienced generals. This assistance was steadily extended and forma-lized by an agreement concluded at Bled on 2 August 1947 between Yugoslav, Bulgarian, and Albanian representatives who undertook 'to organise the rear defences of the Greek Democratic Army with artillery, aviation, and in-fantry.'[163] Operations, which continued to increase in scope throughout 1946 and 1947, were under the command of 'General Markos', the former Greek trade union leader Vaphiadis, whose tactical thinking was much influenced by Yugoslav Partisan experience. The value of the assistance provided for his guerrilla forces by their Bulgarian, Albanian, and particularly their Yugoslav backers was amply confirmed by the Balkan Commission of Enquiry which the UN sent to investigate matters in Northern Greece.

The degree of direct Soviet responsibility for the rising in Greece is difficult to assess. Some observers believe that 'in their support of the Greek com-munist insurgents the Yugoslavs went further than Stalin considered advis-able'[164] or even that 'Yugoslavia's aid to the insurgents . . . was given on her own initiative, and not at Soviet request'.[165] Others take the view that Stalin wanted to see Tito committed more deeply in Greece, both for his nuisance value and as the best means to gain full control over him.[166] It is difficult to believe that Tito's support for the Greek rebels was *initially* given without the full knowledge and concurrence of Stalin, who had not at the time come to have serious doubts about his reliability. Soviet military representatives attended the meeting at Bled in August 1947 which set up the Joint Balkan Staff designed to organize support for the Greek guerrillas.[167] Whether or not, as prospects for the success of the rebellion faded, Stalin may have found Tito slower to discontinue support than seemed prudent, or whether, on the con-trary, Stalin continued to egg him on in secret we have no evidence. Strategy for Greece may well have been discussed during Tito's visit to Moscow in May–June 1946. According to a statement attributed to Markos, the Greek guerrillas had launched their rising on Stalin's instructions but had eventually been left by him to their fate.[168] Though Russian officers were attached to some guerrilla units as observers, the Soviet Government seems to have been anxious to confine its visible support for the Greek rebellion to the use of its veto in order to block effective action by the UN Security Council to halt it.

Moscow's policy in Greece thus seems to have been to fight the war by proxy, allowing a free hand to the Yugoslavs, who had formed a separate Slav National Liberation Front (SNOF), recruited from the Slavophone population of Greek Macedonia, within the Greek wartime resistance movement, and hoped eventually to be rewarded by the incorporation of Aegean Macedonia into their Macedonian Republic in return for the provision of arms and sup-plies to the Greek rebels and the use of secure bases on the Yugoslav side of the Greek frontier.[169] The formulation in March 1947 of the 'Truman Doctrine' pledging the United States 'to support free peoples who are resisting attempted subjugation by armed minorities or by outside pressure', named Greece as one such threatened area. The escalation of the fighting there prompted the United States to give corresponding help to the Greek Government forces. The Soviet Government, unwilling to become over-extended in the Cold War or to pro-voke a full-scale American intervention, grew still more cautious. When, at the end of the year, Markos proclaimed the establishment of a 'Provisional Demo-cratic Government of Greece', with himself as Prime Minister and Minister of

Defence, neither the Soviet Government, nor its three Balkan protégés, found it expedient to recognize it. By the beginning of 1948 the prospects of a military victory by Markos were receding, dissensions over the perennial Macedonian problem were weakening the alliance between the Greek, Bulgarian, Yugoslav, and Albanian communists, and storm clouds were blowing up between Moscow and Belgrade which threatened to change the whole Balkan scene.

After the dissolution of the Comintern in 1943, no formal machinery existed for the international co-ordination and control of the world's CPs, though each continued much as before to look to Moscow and to receive guidance from the Russian communist leaders. At the end of the war proposals were mooted to revive the Comintern, ostensibly on a more democratic and limited basis. Tito himself is credited with putting such a proposal to Stalin,[170] stressing that the new body would be a useful vehicle for consultation, and the exchange of experience—fields in which he believed its wartime achievements had given the Yugoslav Party much of value to contribute to the world communist movement. Stalin readily agreed, though his designs for the new organization proved to be rather different, and after further discussions in 1946, the Communist Information Bureau (Cominform) held its inaugural meeting in September 1947. It comprised representatives from the East European CPs—those of the Soviet Union, Yugoslavia, Bulgaria, Romania, Hungary, Czechoslovakia, and Poland—and from the two leading Parties of Western Europe, those of Italy and France. In the resolution announcing the formation of the new body its primarily consultative character was stressed, and it was also announced that it would sponsor the publication of a special journal (**114**). On Stalin's personal insistence, Belgrade was chosen as the seat for its Secretariat, the Yugoslav delegates—Djilas and Kardelj—were encouraged to play a prominent role, and the primacy of the CPY, after that of the CPSU, was tacitly acknowledged.

At the time of the Cominform's formation, the Yugoslav leaders were still in a state of revolutionary euphoria, confident that their vigorous policies towards Italy, Albania, Greece, and Bulgaria would soon yield rich rewards, and that their wartime exploits and the thoroughness with which they were 'building socialism' in their country had won them a unique and universally recognized position of authority within the socialist camp. But, in the suspicious eyes of the Kremlin, the very magnitude of the Yugoslav comrades' success was beginning to render them suspect. Moscow did not welcome communist regimes with strong indigenous roots; it wanted regimes which drew their sustenance and strength solely from Moscow. The gestures made apparently as compliments to the Yugoslavs—the choice of their capital as the Cominform's seat and the encouragement given to their delegates at the inaugural session to berate the Italian and French representatives for the shortcomings of their respective Parties—were in reality snares laid to encompass their fall. The Cominform headquarters revealed itself as a centre for keeping the Yugoslav leaders under observation and attempting to influence their activities, whilst the resentment aroused in the Italian and French Parties by the arrogant criticism of the Yugoslavs ensured that, when the time came, those Parties would not be backward in turning the tables on their comrades. The Yugoslavs were soon to discover that the alleged opportunities for consultation and 'exchange of experience' within the new organization were a fiction, and that it was as much under Soviet domination as ever the Comintern had been.

The Kremlin conference of 10 February 1948
By early 1948—the year which was to see an intensification of the Cold War and the consolidation of Soviet power over Eastern Europe through the communist coup in Czechoslovakia—Stalin had decided that it was time to call the Yugoslav leaders to order. Tito's growing prestige with the People's Democracies and the independence and sometimes misguided vigour with which he was pursuing his foreign policy aims, even though these were framed for the general promotion of communist power and influence, coupled with the numerous complaints received of his way of conducting his domestic affairs without the unquestioning deference towards his Russian mentors expected of him, all indicated that the Yugoslavs were overreaching themselves. The immediate causes of the ensuing rift might seem trivial, but the Kremlin saw in them the culmination of a process of insubordination and the expression of an arrogant and intractable frame of mind stretching back to the conduct of the wartime Partisan struggle and now constituting an obstacle to the Russians' designs for the complete domination, on their own terms, of Eastern Europe. Tito and his colleagues had the bit between their teeth and threatened Soviet plans through their heedless Leftism. They must be taught a lesson or, if necessary, be replaced.

Whilst Djilas, who had travelled to Moscow at the beginning of January in answer to the summons to discuss policy towards Albania, found Stalin apparently willing for Yugoslavia to 'swallow' Albania, the government in Belgrade received a peremptory demand from Molotov to halt their plans for that country. They were told to countermand the arrangements to send two Yugoslav divisions which, in answer to a request from the pro-Yugoslav leadership of the Albanian CP, were about to be dispatched as a safeguard against any Greek attempts to pursue Markos's retreating guerrillas across the Albanian–Greek frontier. A Yugoslav airforce regiment was already stationed in Albania. Belgrade had not thought it necessary to seek prior agreement from the Soviet Government before ordering its armed forces to move, since it had grown accustomed to acting on its own within the agreed policy of extending 'fraternal aid' to Albania and the Greek guerrilla movement. But Molotov's message, which threatened the publication of an open reprimand if the Yugoslavs failed to comply immediately, was a clear indication of Russian displeasure.

At the end of January another storm blew up. Dimitrov, on a visit to Romania, issued a statement on the prospects for forming a federation or confederation between the East European countries which was promptly repudiated in *Pravda*. Dimitrov obediently retracted his remarks, but telegrams were at once sent to Belgrade and Sofia instructing the Yugoslav and Bulgarian Governments to send delegations for talks in Moscow immediately. Tito, feigning indisposition, decided not to respond in person to the summons —though the Russians clearly expected him to do so—but instead sent Kardelj and Bakarić, Secretary of the Croat CP, to join Djilas and the members of the Yugoslav military and economic delegations already in Moscow.

The meeting took place in the Kremlin on 10 February.[171] Molotov opened the proceedings by stating that serious differences had arisen between Yugoslavia and Bulgaria on the one side, and the USSR on the other. The ensuing discussions turned mainly on the proposed Bulgarian–Yugoslav federation and the situations in Albania and Greece. They were marked by violent and hectoring outbursts on the part of Stalin, directed primarily against Dimitrov and his colleagues and indirectly against the Yugoslavs. The latter, like the Bulgarians, went to great pains to profess complete acceptance of the Russian line and to deny, or minimize, any serious divergences or failure to consult with Moscow. On Albania, Stalin repeated his charges that Belgrade was sending two divisions into that country without reference to him. He finished by asserting that it should be annexed to Yugoslavia, but only after Yugoslavia had federated with Bulgaria. On the latter project, he repeated—after again berating Dimitrov for his ill judged public utterances and his failure to consult —that he favoured such a federation (though not one between Bulgaria and Romania) and that it should take place as soon as possible. On Greece, he brushed aside Kardelj's optimistic forecast of success by declaring that, on the contrary, the guerrillas had no prospect whatsoever of winning and that the uprising must be stopped, and as quickly as possible.

The following day the Bulgarian and Yugoslav delegations met for further talks on the proposed federation and agreed to continue discussions after reporting to their respective governments. The Yugoslavs returned to Belgrade dispirited and confused. A military delegation which had been in Moscow hoping to arrange for substantial deliveries of arms and for the equipment needed for the country's war industry and shipyards was obliged to leave empty-handed. A Yugoslav economic delegation had also met with a firm refusal when it presented proposals for the increase in commercial exchanges envisaged under the Five Year Plan and was unable to secure Russian agreement for the protocol regulating bilateral trade for the current year. The only new engagement entered into by the Yugoslavs had been a Treaty of Consultation pledging their government to consult with Moscow on all foreign policy issues. The Yugoslav delegates had been given no say in the drafting of this treaty and Molotov had simply put the text in front of Kardelj and told him to sign it.[172] Even with this evidence of Soviet hostility the Yugoslavs were reluctant to believe the worst. Djilas, who presented the report on the Kremlin meeting to the CC of the CPY, concluded hopefully that 'there is no need to doubt for a moment the great love Comrade Stalin bears our entire Party, the Central Committee, and particularly Comrade Tito'.[173] But already, as a French newspaper correspondent reported from Bucharest two days after the Kremlin meeting, rumour was rife that 'Marshal Tito's position was not as secure as was commonly believed' and that the Romanian CP had ordered his portrait to be removed from all public buildings and offices.[174]

On 1 March Tito called a meeting of the CC to consider the reports of the delegations returning from Moscow and to review relations with the Soviet Union. He made no attempt to conceal the gravity of the situation. The restructuring of Yugoslavia's economic life was based on the assumption of large scale trade and aid from the Soviet Union, and the latter's evident unwillingness to provide it could have the most serious consequences for the country. The withholding of arms and supplies for the Yugoslav war industry was similarly aimed at weakening the country's capacity for defence. The proposed federation with Bulgaria, desirable as it was in principle, was now being urged by the Russians as an obvious Trojan Horse, a means of destroying the unity of the Party and state and disrupting the economic expansion envisaged under the Five Year Plan. All the members of the CC, with the exception of Žujović, agreed that it would be inopportune at present to press on with the proposed federation. The momentous decision was taken to ignore Stalin's directive.

Inter-party polemic
Eighteen days later General Barskov, head of the Soviet military mission, informed the chief of the Yugoslav General Staff that he had been instructed to withdraw all military advisers and instructors immediately from Yugoslavia since they were 'surrounded by hostility'. The following day, 19 March, the Soviet chargé d'affaires announced that he had received similar instructions with regard to all Russian civilian advisers. Tito immediately composed a letter to Molotov expressing pained surprise at the Soviet action,[175] protesting that the Soviet Union's representatives had, on the contrary, always been treated in the most friendly fashion. He denied Russian complaints that Yugoslav officials had ever shown them 'lack of hospitality and lack of confidence' or had refused them any economic information asked for through the proper channels. Such reports, he hinted, must have emanated from untrustworthy and ill-intentioned sources. He asked to be told frankly what was behind the Russian decision and what grounds they had for their evident dissatisfaction with the present state of Soviet–Yugoslav relations (117).

The Russian reply, a long and sharply worded letter dated 27 March—the anniversary of the famous coup of seven years ago—and signed on behalf of the CC of the CPSU by Molotov and Stalin, was handed to Tito by the Soviet ambassador. It repeated the charges that the Soviet advisers had found themselves working in an increasingly hostile atmosphere and recalled with indignation the derogatory remarks ascribed to Djilas about the conduct of Red Army officers. Not only were Soviet officials denied legitimate information, the letter charged, but they were placed under the surveillance of Yugoslav security officials, just as in a hostile bourgeois country. Turning to the broader reasons for dissatisfaction, the letter referred to the disparagement of Soviet achievements by 'such questionable Marxists as Djilas, Vukmanović, Kidrič, Ranković and others' behind a hypocritical façade of official friendship, and observed menacingly that, in this connection 'we think the political career of Trotsky quite instructive.'[176] The CPY was criticized for retaining its illegal, conspiratorial character, with a CC run on non-democratic lines, since most of its members had been co-opted rather than elected and there was virtually no criticism or self-criticism practised within it. Instead of the Party controlling the secret police, the latter controlled the party. It could not be considered truly Marxist-Leninist, since instead of being the 'controlling force in the country' it had merged its identity with that of the Popular Front. Nor did it show the proper spirit of class struggle, for it was doing nothing to check the growing influence of 'capitalist elements' in the villages. Turning to the state administration, the letter expressed indignant surprise that an 'English spy', in the person of Vlatko Velebit, who had incurred Russian displeasure by his defence of Yugoslavia's economic interests in the negotiations over the joint companies and by protesting against mis-statements in the Russian press (**147, 116**), should hold the key post of Assistant Foreign Minister (**118**).

After consultation with his Politburo—most of whose members had been branded as 'questionable Marxists' in Stalin's letter—Tito decided to summon the CC and seek its endorsement for the terms in which he proposed to frame his reply. The sneering, threatening tone of the letter, and the injustice of the charges contained in it, had struck him with the force of a thunderbolt.[177] That he and his closest colleagues could be accused of anti-Soviet, non-Marxist practices, when they had been politically nurtured by Moscow, had proved their loyalty by the heroic sacrifices of the Partisan movement, and were now zealously seeking to apply the Soviet model to the rebuilding of their own state and the extension of communist power throughout the Balkans seemed to him so monstrously unjust as to be almost unthinkable. Yet Stalin was clearly resolved on a confrontation and there was nothing for it but to accept the challenge. Weak though Yugoslavia's position might be compared with the might of the Soviet Union and her influence over the satellites, Tito could at least choose combat on his own ground. The best chance of survival, he saw, would be to make a stand on the issue of national sovereignty and independence and not on the ideological purity called in question in Stalin's letter. Official relations between the two countries must also be kept correct as far and as long as possible. 11 April, the day before the holding of the CC's plenum, was also the third anniversary of the signing of the Treaty of Friendship, Mutual Aid, and Postwar Collaboration between Yugoslavia and the Soviet Union. Tito took the occasion to send a message to Stalin and the Soviet people stressing the 'unbreakable bonds' which linked the two nations together and the Yugoslav people's warmest wishes for their comrades' continued progress and prosperity. Stalin's reply was somewhat less fulsome and confined to the expression of good wishes to 'the fraternal peoples of Yugoslavia'.[178]

Tito's decision to call a CC plenum was a bold step designed to test how far he could count on his Party's support in the growing confrontation with Stalin; it was, in fact, the first time since it had been set up nearly eight years earlier that the CC had ever met in plenary session.[179] The only open opposition was voiced by Žujović, who was in turn accused of passing confidential information on party affairs to Lavrentiev, the Soviet ambassador. Both he and Hebrang, previously expelled from the CC, were placed under investigation. The rest of the CC endorsed the draft which Tito and Kardelj laid before it in reply to Stalin's letter of 27 March. After again expressing indignant surprise at its harsh tone and rejecting the Russian allegations, which were assumed to be based on the false information supplied by Hebrang and Žujović, the reply formulated the Yugoslav party's profession of faith: 'No matter how much each of us loves the land of Socialism, the USSR, he can in no case love his country less'. It was explained that a previous Yugoslav request to reduce the number of Russian military advisers was not an expression of anti-Sovietism but a mere measure of economy, since these advisers were each paid a salary four times that of a Yugoslav army commander and three times that of a federal minister. The remarks attributed to Djilas about Soviet officers, it was repeated, had been maliciously distorted. The comparison with Trotsky was unmerited and insulting. The Yugoslav communists had never belittled Soviet achievements; on the contrary, they had worked long and hard to inculcate love and admiration for the Soviet Union and its Party. Nor was it true that the CPY was controlled by the secret police, run on undemocratic lines, indistinguishable from the Popular Front, and blind to the emergence of 'capitalist elements'. Far from it; the drastic revolutionary changes carried through in Yugoslavia by the CPY were well known. Though these were based on Soviet experience, 'we are developing socialism in our country in somewhat different forms'. As to Velebit, the Party was investigating his past, but had so far found nothing to justify the charges against him. Passing over to the offensive, the Yugoslav letter then accused the Russian intelligence services of recruiting Yugoslav agents and spying on the state and Party leaders. It concluded with an appeal for a restoration of correct relations and a fairer appraisal of the situation in Yugoslavia, and invited the CPSU CC to send one or two delegates to judge matters for themselves (**119**).

The Russians returned to the charge with a long letter rehearsing their former grievances and adding a number of new ones; not only Velebit, but the Yugoslav ambassador in London and three members of his staff were English spies; the Soviet ambassador in Belgrade was treated like the representative of any bourgeois state, whereas the American ambassador behaved 'as if he owned the place'; the Yugoslavs evidently put the foreign policies of the USSR on a par with those of the bourgeois imperialists—Tito's Ljubljana speech of May 1945 (**110**) was quoted as an instance of this—and yet expected Moscow to press their claims on Trieste even to the point of going to war; the social reforms which the CPY boasted about were 'almost negligible'; the land had not been collectivized and the peasants had been pandered to; the CPY, in short, was a Menshevik party, and the situation within it had become alarming, thanks to the 'unbounded arrogance' of its leaders whose heads had been turned by their wartime successes. But past services did not make them immune from present errors—Trotsky's example was here again invoked—and in any case the Yugoslavs exaggerated their military achievements, for their movement had been all but destroyed by the German parachute attack on its headquarters at Drvar, after which 'the Soviet Army came to the aid of the Yugoslav people, crushed the German invader, [and] liberated Belgrade'. No Soviet representative would be sent, as Tito had suggested, to look into current differences, 'since it is not a matter of verifying individual facts but of differences of principle'. The Yugoslavs were urged instead to submit the dispute to the Cominform (**120**).

The CC met in Belgrade to consider the new Soviet letter and agreed to send a reply that was short and firm, but not intransigent. The Yugoslavs expressed regret that their explanations had failed to carry conviction, but declared themselves unwilling to refer the dispute to the Cominform where they believed the issues to be already prejudged. They affirmed instead their intention to 'show by our deeds that the accusations against us are unjust. . . . We are resolutely building socialism and . . . remain loyal to the Soviet Union, loyal to the doctrine of Marx, Engels, Lenin, and Stalin' (**121**). At the same time the plenum approved the findings of the commission set up to look into the cases of Hebrang and Žujović and decreed the expulsion of both from the Party. A few days later it was announced that they had been placed under arrest. This elicited a fresh outburst from Moscow. A note was delivered by the Soviet ambassador threatening that the Yugoslav leaders would be denounced as 'criminal murderers' if any harm came to the two men, and demanding that their interrogation should be carried out in the presence of a representative of the CC of the CPSU.[180] These demands were indignantly rejected (122). On 22 May the Russians sent a further letter declaring that, by refusing to attend the Cominform meeting, the CPY was claiming a specially privileged position for itself and was thereby tacitly admitting the truth of the Soviet charges and 'laying the blame on innocent men, who were supposed to have misinformed the CPSU'. By following their anti-Soviet policies, Tito and his Politburo had destroyed all faith in their good intentions and were betraying 'the international solidarity of the workers'. Whether they attended or not, the Cominform would meet to consider the serious consequences of their actions (123).

THE FRONTAL ASSAULT
Yugoslavia's expulsion from the Cominform
Stalin had the Cominform meeting postponed for one month whilst he made further attempts to induce the Yugoslavs to attend. The satellite leaders, by obediently repeating the Soviet accusations, had already made their hostility clear. Only Dimitrov, who had sent a message of congratulations on Tito's birthday and managed to whisper 'Stand firm!' to Djilas whom he saw briefly as he passed through Belgrade on his way to Moscow, gave some signs of friendship;[181] but a communication later received from the Bulgarian CP contained the standard repetition of the Russian charges. When a formal invitation was received from the Cominform to attend a meeting in Bucharest (to which the organization's headquarters had already been transferred) the Yugoslav leaders therefore saw no reason to change their decision to reject it (124, 125). Their previous tactless criticism of the Italian and French CP leaders at the Cominform's first meeting ensured that no sympathy could be expected from that quarter now that it was their turn to be in the dock. The Bucharest meeting, which was attended by all the Cominform members except the Yugoslavs, accordingly pronounced the unanimous anathema expected of it. The CPY, through the errors and contumacy of its leaders, was declared to have 'placed itself . . . outside the united Communist front and consequently outside the ranks of the Information Bureau'. An appeal was made to the 'healthy elements' in the CPY to discipline its present leaders or replace them by a 'new internationalist leadership' (126). The CPY CC riposted with a statement rejecting the Soviet-inspired accusations and reaffirming its confidence in its leaders (127).

News of Yugoslavia's expulsion came as a sensational surprise, both inside the country and abroad. No hint of the growing tension between Moscow and Belgrade had been given, and there had been no sign of any relaxation in her intransigent anti-Western policies or the pace of her revolutionary domestic changes. Few expected that her leaders would be able to hold out for long against the combined pressures of the Soviet Union and her own communist neighbours, or realized the significance of the new trends which ostracism by the rest of the communist bloc had set in motion. The bloc had ceased to be a monolith, dedicated to the unquestioning implementation of whatever directives might emanate from Moscow. A crack had appeared which was to lead not—as the Russians claimed—to any defection to the 'imperialist camp', but to a phenomenon of ultimately greater significance; the emergence within the world communist movement of polycentrism, the 'separate roads to socialism' which parties other than the Yugoslavs were in time to choose or at least strive to take.

Attempts to subvert Party and state

By appealing to the 'healthy elements' within the CPY the Cominform hoped to apply the former Comintern tactics of going over the heads of a recalcitrant leadership and inviting the Party cadres to replace it. Tito was aware of this danger and had already decided on the bold step of convening a Party congress —the first to take place since the 4th Congress held in Dresden in 1928, when the Party was persecuted and illegal. In this way Tito counted on obtaining wider popular support without which resistance to Russian pressure would be impossible. He also thereby hoped—as he had claimed in his letters to the CPSU—that the Party would 'refute the accusations by its deeds' and demonstrate its democratic and representative character and the strength of the links between the leaders and the lower organizations. By bringing the dispute out into the open he knew that he was taking a calculated risk. For years the Party leaders had proclaimed the CPSU the vanguard of world revolution, the identity of state and Party interests between Yugoslavia and the Soviet Union, and the infallible genius and benevolence of Stalin. How then to explain the present rift and to convince bewildered comrades that it was not Yugoslavia, but the rest of the socialist camp, which had fallen out of step? When the 5th Congress opened on 21 July, Tito skilfully appealed to the Party's pride in its wartime role, its recent achievements in 'building socialism', and the general patriotism of the Yugoslav people. He concentrated his fire against the lesser Cominform members, particularly the unpopular Bulgars, whilst affirming his resolve to seek ways of restoring good relations with the Soviet Union (**128**). He won the firm support of the Congress, which ended with enthusiastic cries of 'Tito! Stalin!'. As he was later to explain, the immense prestige enjoyed by Stalin and the need to carry the Party rank and file with him meant that he must move very cautiously indeed; 'I had to give Stalin time to behave in such a way that people in Yugoslavia would say "Down with Stalin!" of their own accord, without any prompting on my part'.[182]

The 5th Congress showed Stalin that it was not enough, as he had boasted, for him to raise his little finger and Tito would disappear. But the Russians believed that they still had effective means of replacing him. They seem to have earmarked Žujović as the new Secretary-General of the Party and Hebrang as Prime Minister. This plan was frustrated by the timely arrest of the two men, but the Soviet intelligence service appears to have considered organizing their rescue, much as the Yugoslav communists had rescued Ranković from the Gestapo in Belgrade some seven years before.[183] A more feasible plan was to arrange the flight of General Arso Jovanović, who had returned from Moscow fully committed to the Soviet cause, and other senior officers, to Romania, where the Yugoslav ambassador had already declared himself for the Cominform and where the exiles might head a puppet government or an anti-Tito military force. Jovanović was reportedly shot by Yugoslav guards on 13 August whilst trying to cross the Romanian frontier, and two other officers, General Petričević, Deputy Head of the Political Administration of the Yugoslav Army, and Colonel Vlada Dapčević, brother of the well-known general, were also apprehended.

Attempts to subvert local Party organizations in Croatia, Bosnia, Montenegro, and Macedonia met with little more success. Ranković's police were omnipresent and efficient; if his figures are to be trusted, they arrested a total of some 8,400 Cominform sympathizers.[184] Several thousand young Yugoslavs however were beyond its reach and within that of the Russians. Though few of those studying or working in the Soviet Union succumbed to Russian pressure, the Yugoslav Government deemed it wise to demand their recall. A year later Belgrade was still complaining that the Soviet authorities were delaying their return and were also sponsoring the activities of a handful of 'traitors to their Socialist homeland' whom Moscow eulogized as 'patriot-exiles' and allowed ample press and radio facilities and the right to publish their own anti-Tito journal (**129–33**). These attempts to subvert the CPY and turn it against Tito and the Politburo were largely the work of Russian intelligence services, whose activities were the subject of frequent Yugoslav protests and of Soviet counter protests alleging unjustifiable ill treatment of Soviet citizens. Many of the latter were former White Russians who had lived as exiles in Yugoslavia and collaborated with the Germans before seeking to save themselves by taking out Soviet citizenship and agreeing to work for the intelligence services (**134–7**).

Other forms of political pressure

Tito's successful defiance brought with it the danger that other 'nationalist' communist leaders in Eastern Europe might be emboldened to stand up to Moscow. Stalin decided to take drastic steps to punish or deter any who might be tempted to take this course, and in the process to blacken Tito by implicating him in their alleged crimes. Yugoslav control over Albania had been immediately dismantled, and Koci Xoxe, the leader of the pro-Yugoslav faction, was executed in June 1949. Gomulka, Secretary of the Polish CP, had been stripped of office at the beginning of the year. Rajk, the Hungarian Foreign Minister, was disgraced, tried, and executed the following October, and Kostov, Secretary-General of the Bulgarian CP was executed in December. In the trials stagemanaged to discredit the fallen leaders—despite their signature of the Cominform resolution denouncing Tito—the most grotesque machinations were imputed to Tito, Ranković, and other Yugoslav communist leaders who were now discovered to have been traitors, renegades, and agents of the foreign imperialists before, during, and after the war.

So patently contrived and absurd were these charges that they served only to rally the Yugoslav CP and the nation as a whole behind their leaders. But they afforded a pretext for Moscow to denounce the Treaty of Friendship, Mutual Aid, and Postwar Collaboration which had already become a dead letter (**138, 139**), and to expel the Yugoslav ambassador to the Soviet Union (**140, 141**). Russian animosity also pursued Yugoslavia into the UN, where Soviet and satellite delegates attempted unsuccessfully to prevent Yugoslavia's election to the Security Council (**142**). The virulence of the Soviet onslaught was mirrored in a new denunciation by the Cominform, 'The Yugoslav Communist Party in the power of murderers and spies' (143).

Economic pressure

The political offensive against Yugoslavia was reinforced by an economic blockade which, coupled with the hardships caused by three disastrous harvests, the Russians believed would bring the country to its knees. The Five Year Plan for Yugoslavia's economic development had been drawn up on the assumption that the credits, loans, raw material, machinery, and technical aid needed for its implementation would be supplied by the Soviet Union. Well over half the country's foreign trade was already with the USSR and the other East European countries, and further substantial expansion was envisaged. The reluctance of the Soviet authorities at the beginning of 1948 to discuss this expansion had been one of the factors which brought friction between Belgrade and Moscow to a head. When the dispute came out into the open, the Soviet Union reduced her economic exchanges with Yugoslavia still more, and the satellite countries followed suit. Romania for a time even cut off all rail and postal communication in an effort to complete her neighbour's isolation. Only the two joint companies, by means of which the Russians strove to tighten their control over Yugoslavia's Danubian shipping and civil aviation, continued operations until the Russians at length agreed, on terms unfavourable to their weaker partners, to wind them up (147). A Yugoslav delegation sent to Moscow to negotiate trade arrangements for 1949 was unable to get the Russians to agree to a level higher than one eighth of the already inadequate 1948 levels (144). When, the following February, the socialist countries met in Moscow to form the Council for Mutual Economic Assistance (Comecon) Yugoslavia was not invited and protested at her exclusion (145). The Soviet Government replied with brutal frankness that membership would 'be possible only if the Yugoslav Government renounces its hostile policy' (146).

Threat of invasion

There remained the ultimate sanction—that of armed invasion. The Yugoslav leaders certainly took the threat very seriously indeed, and it has even been averred that in mid-1949 the decision to invade was taken but countermanded at the last minute.[185] Frontier incidents multiplied ominously, and Yugoslav intelligence reports spoke of at least seven Russian motorized divisions poised on the borders of Hungary and Romania. The Russian note of 18 August protesting against the arrest and maltreatment of Soviet citizens and concluding with the threat that the Soviet Government 'will not reconcile itself to such a state of affairs and . . . will be compelled to resort to other, more effective means' (136) was taken by the Yugoslavs as an ultimatum. In an address to army commanders in Skopje earlier that month Tito had declared that Yugoslavia would resist any attempt at invasion and had made it clear for the first time that this held good even if the aggressor should be the Red Army (148). Yugoslav security plans were revised to allow for a system of defence in depth based on zones of suitable terrain which could be made broadly self-sufficient in arms, munitions, food, and other supplies and in which the Partisan tactics their Soviet advisers had looked coolly upon could be effectively employed.[186]

During the second half of 1949 the danger of invasion remained serious, though Yugoslavia's determined preparations to resist and fear that the allies might come to her help and precipitate a wider conflict for which the Russians were not yet ready may have deterred Stalin from carrying out his threat. The start of the Korean war in June 1950 showed that he was prepared to strike, at least by proxy, where the prospects of success were judged good. But by then American arms as well as economic help had further increased Yugoslavia's defensive capacity and tension between Belgrade and Moscow had stiffened into mutual recrimination and uneasy vigilance.

CONSEQUENCES OF THE RIFT
Reshaping of economic policy
The Yugoslavs responded to the Soviet economic blockade in two ways. First, by a drastic tightening of the belt, reducing civilian consumption and attempting to wring more out of the economy by collectivization and enforced deliveries of agricultural products from the peasantry and by directing unemployed labour, including members of the dispossessed bourgeoisie, into the factories. Secondly, and more effectively, by turning to the West for loans and supplies to tide the country over the immediate crisis. These emergency measures were succeeded by long-term credits and trade agreements with the USA, France, and Britain, and by loans from the international monetary organizations. Thus through its boycott and blockade the Soviet Union forced the Belgrade Government to reorient its economic life towards the West. Stalin reckoned that if Tito could not at once be brought to his knees, he could at least be weakened and branded as a defector to the capitalist camp, his ultimate removal being thereby justified and facilitated. For Tito, the immediate problem was to survive without jeopardizing his national independence or the success of his socialist experiment. In the long run, he was to find Moscow's economic pressure a blessing in disguise. It forced him to scale down the over-ambitious targets of his Five Year Plan and substitute more realistic goals. It also offered a way out from subordination to the overall needs of Soviet economic planning and a chance of benefiting from the wider openings of Western trade, aid, and technology.

Reshaping of foreign policy
The dispute with Moscow also obliged Yugoslavia to reshape her foreign policies. This was not however immediately apparent to the Yugoslav leaders who, despite ostracism by the bloc, continued for a time to give undiminished support to Soviet positions in the UN and sided ostentatiously against the West at the Danubian Conference held in Belgrade in August 1948.[187] But it was not long before they began to see the necessity of moderating their aggressive stance if Yugoslavia was to survive through maintaining a delicate balancing act between East and West and work out the new relationship with third parties which became known as the policy of non-alignment.[188]

The loss of Soviet favour reduced Yugoslavia's chances of a favourable settlement of her territorial claims against Austria and Italy. In June 1948 the

Council of Foreign Ministers reached agreement on restoring the prewar frontier between Austria and Yugoslavia. This provoked accusations from Belgrade that Moscow had bartered away the rights of the Carinthian Slovenes to suit her selfish national interests, and counter-charges that it was Belgrade itself who had 'betrayed' Austria's Slav minority (**149–52**). Kardelj's letter to Vyshinsky of 20 April 1947 was cited in alleged proof of this (**115**).

A settlement of the Trieste problem proved more protracted and complex. The Russians temporized, reluctant even after their breach with Belgrade to withdraw all backing from the Yugoslav claims in the hope that Tito would be replaced by a more acceptable leadership. The Yugoslavs, even without the assurance of Russian support, remained quick to react sharply to Western moves, as in March 1948 when the Western allies issued a Tripartite Declaration in favour of Italy's claims to both zones A and B, and later, in 1952 and again in 1953, when the Allied Military Government of Zone A moved to make over the civil and then the military control of the zone to the Italians. The following year, despite these setbacks and no doubt as a reflection of the generally improved relations prevailing with the West, an arrangement was finally reached by which Yugoslavia was obliged to renounce the city of Trieste and its hinterland, but received all Zone B and some other frontier rectifications as well. Though less than her proclaimed right to Trieste and all the disputed area, these terms were by no means unfavourable to Yugoslavia and had moreover been secured with no thanks to Moscow.

Belgrade's Balkan policies were thrown into disarray by the dispute with Moscow. With the loss of her protectorate over Albania and of prospects for a federation with a friendly Bulgaria, Yugoslavia saw her own territorial integrity threatened by a revival of the old Comintern plan for an independent Great Macedonia. Markos, through whom the Yugoslavs had channelled their aid to the Greek rebels, vanished from the scene, whilst Zachariadis, the Secretary-General of the Greek CP, who had declared himself vociferously for the Cominform, took over the command in a last disastrous bid for victory. The time had come, the Yugoslavs ironically decided, to heed Stalin's earlier bidding which, in their revolutionary overconfidence, they had ignored. Kardelj announced[189] that Yugoslavia was closing the Greek frontier and withdrawing all help from the rebels (**153**)—a move which Moscow hastened to denounce as stabbing the Greek patriots in the back (**154**). The first step had been taken towards the normalization of relations with the non-communist states which was to result, five years later, in the conclusion of the Balkan Pact between Yugoslavia, Greece, and Turkey.

With the Trieste and Greek problems on the way to solution, and negotiation of loans and trade agreements with Britain, France, and the United States, whose support had secured her a seat on the UN Security Council, Yugoslavia's political relations with the West began to improve. The Russian-backed invasion of South Korea in mid-1950 served warning of the fate in store for any non-communist state which could not count on help from the West to deter Soviet aggression. Tito let it be known that he was accepting British and American aid in re-equipping his army, to match the build-up of arms in the neighbouring Cominform countries. Menacing manœuvres continued to be held along the latters' frontiers with Yugoslavia, but these were now less likely than ever to frighten Tito off the course which he had chosen to steer between East and West. In November 1951 Yugoslavia lodged a formal complaint with the UN against the hostile actions being carried out against her by the Soviet Union and satellite countries (**159**). Despite Soviet attempts to dismiss the charges as a 'tissue of lies and calumnies' designed to hide Yugoslavia's own provocative policies towards her neighbours (**160**), the UN General Assembly, by a majority of 47 votes against 5 (with two abstentions) voted a resolution taking note of the Yugoslav statement and her readiness to seek peaceful solutions and recommending a settlement of Soviet–Yugoslav differences 'in accordance with the spirit of the United Nations'.[190]

Emergence of the Yugoslav path to socialism

Tito and his Politburo comrades were far from imagining, when the thunderbolt of Soviet displeasure struck them in 1948, that they had begun to pioneer a new brand of socialism. They protested, on the contrary, that they were the purest of Marxist-Leninists, the staunchest of Stalinists, and that they would prove by their deeds that any suggestion to the contrary was false. Their immediate response was thus a radicalization, not a liberalization, of existing policies. Steps were hastily taken to strengthen the already great power of the CPY and to build up its grass roots organization and increase its membership; to nationalize all small traders, crafts and services; to direct class enemies and 'social idlers' into mines and factories; and, above all, to intensify the class struggle in the countryside by forcing the peasants into collectives—a policy continued, despite fierce resistance and falling agricultural production, into 1952.[191] The secret police, too, redoubled their activity, though this was now directed against pro-Cominformists more than anti-communists.

But gradually, beneath this conscious striving towards dogmatic communist orthodoxy, currents began to gather strength in the contrary direction. Whether they liked it or not, the logic of their independent stance impelled the Yugoslav leaders towards innovation. The broadening of the base of the Party started to release mounting forces of popular participation. Nor could the Party alone bear the weight of the Soviet assault; the whole people, non-communist as well as communist, had to be marshalled behind the leadership. The aid and trade emanating from outside the socialist bloc began to loosen the strait jacket into which the country's economy was being forced. Ostracized by the East, the leaders had to cast at least some glances towards the West. Once the immediate danger of Cominform subversion from within had been neutralized, harshly repressive measures began to appear counter-productive and anachronistic. New institutional forms were needed to suit new circumstances. In June 1950 a law was passed placing economic enterprises under the direct management of Workers' Councils—an innovation which was to develop into one of the most distinctive features of Yugoslavia's path to socialism. Other measures of decentralization and wider self-government followed. The drive for the collectivization of agriculture was dropped, and a mass exodus from the state farms followed. The government relaxed its anti-church measures, permitted a degree of public criticism, limited the abuses of Party officials' privileges, and took the first steps towards curbing the absolute powers of the secret police by introducing a new criminal code.

During 1952–3 these reforms were systematized and made more explicit.

A new Constitutional Law was introduced superseding the old Stalinist Constitution, and the Party itself—now rechristened the League of Communists (LCY)—was exhorted to operate by guidance and persuasion rather than by command and coercion. Official spokesmen began to vaunt Yugoslavia's distinctive contributions to the building of socialism, and to criticize, implicitly and then explicitly, the contrast between practice and principles in the Soviet Union, and the perversion of true Marxist-Leninist doctrines at the hands of Stalinist bureaucrats (155). Kardelj spoke of the Russians' 'hegemonistic policy' and 'unsocialistic methods' (156), and Tito answered Molotov's tirades (157) by recalling the crimes of genocide which disfigured the Soviet Government's record (158). By the end of 1952, when the Party held its defiant 6th Congress, the path which Yugoslavia had chosen for building its brand of socialism could be more clearly defined and just where this differed from the Soviet model more franky stated (162, 163).

Yugoslavia's path to socialism was pragmatic, determined as much by expediency and necessity, at least initially, as by deliberate choice. Her leaders moved along it gingerly, like the dancers in a Balkan *kolo*, taking many an intricate sidestep and here and there a pace back. Only later, as their self-confidence increased and the process of emancipation from Moscow's tutelage was seen to be irreversible, did they become fully aware of the need to formulate a historical and ideological justification for their stand. The Partisan movement was described as having raised, from its inception, the banner of social revolution, not merely that of national liberation;[192] the postwar socialist revolution thus drew its legitimacy not from any external prompting or prescription but from the efforts of the Yugoslav people and of their indigenous communist leaders. Marxism indeed provided them with the ideological framework, but it was a flexible, pragmatic Marxism—had not its author himself written that his teaching was 'not dogma, but a guide to action'? —and nearer to the humanitarian spirit of the 'young Marx' than to the hardened prescription of class warfare voiced by the older prophet. The Yugoslav people's desire for more personal and political freedom, more regional autonomy for the constituent Republics, and more scope for private ownership and economic enterprise had to be taken into account and harnessed for social and national ends. Adjusting his course between these popular pressures and the need to keep a firm grip of the tiller, Tito was to tack dexterously for more than two decades.

III POST-STALIN RAPPROCHEMENT, RECOIL, AND NON-ALIGNMENT

RUSSIAN OVERTURES FOR RECONCILIATION

So long as Stalin lived, there could be little prospect of bridging the rift which had opened between Belgrade and Moscow. On 17 June 1953, however, little more than three months after his death, the Soviet Government indicated its intention of working for a normalization of relations with Yugoslavia by reappointing an ambassador to Belgrade (**165**). Tito's response was cautious; he was prepared to agree to an exchange of ambassadors, but he had yet to be convinced that the Soviet offer was made in good faith as an earnest of a real change of attitude and was not merely a manœuvre to impede Yugoslavia's developing relations with her Balkan neighbours and the Western powers (**164, 166**). Though the Russians relaxed their economic pressure and started talks for a new trade agreement, which was signed at the beginning of 1955, the composition and true nature of the post-Stalin leadership was not immediately apparent. Malenkov, the new Chairman of the Council of Ministers, who only a few months before had described Yugoslavia as an American colony and its rulers as agents engaged in espionage and subversion against the Soviet Union (**161**), declared in the Supreme Soviet on 14 August 1953 that his government was resolved to normalize its relations with Yugoslavia. A statement a year and a half later by Molotov, co-signatory with Stalin of the letters anathematizing Tito, claiming that the first steps had been taken towards reconciliation, and implying that this was because the Yugoslavs had begun to see the error of their ways, drew a sharp retort from Tito (**167, 168**). Tito's speech was reported without comment in the Soviet press—a surprising departure from normal practice, and an indication that Molotov's own position could no longer be considered unassailable—and a few days later evoked only a mild Soviet reaction (**169**).

Both parties to the dispute stood to gain by burying the hatchet. Tito realized that some way must eventually be found to end Yugoslavia's ostracism from the socialist camp if the ultimate erosion of the communist basis for his regime was to be avoided, though he was resolved to accept an olive branch only on terms compatible with the independence and security of his Party and state. To be courted by the Russians might also strengthen his bargaining power with the West. The new masters of the Kremlin, manœuvring amongst themselves for position, saw, for their part, that there was much prestige to be gained by any leader who succeeded in restoring the unity of the socialist camp and projecting a more conciliatory image. The West would also be correspondingly weakened if Yugoslavia could be attracted back into the Soviet orbit. Molotov, Suslov, and other hardliners however objected that the Yugoslavs had sold out to the Western capitalists and that their country had ceased to be socialist.[193] An ad hoc committee comprising Shepilov and other CC members was set up to examine this question and found that there were no ideological grounds for considering that the Yugoslavs had placed themselves outside the socialist camp. Developments within the leadership of the CPY seemed favourable for reconciliation. Djilas, who had veered from an almost mystical faith in the Soviet Union to disillusionment and to an increasingly outspoken denunciation not only of Stalinism in the USSR but of the defects of the brand of communism his colleagues were trying to establish in Yugoslavia, had finally overstepped the mark and been expelled from the CC; though disgraced, he was to continue his criticisms of the 'new class' of Yugoslav communist bureaucrats, and ultimately Marxism itself, which were to earn him imprisonment and ostracism by his former comrades. His removal seemed to the Russians to offer the Yugoslav leaders a convenient face-saving formula for reconciliation. The letter from the CC of the CPSU, which bore the signature of Khrushchev and the stamp of his bold opportunism, argued that both CPs had now been purged of the anti-Party elements—Beria and Djilas respectively—who had been responsible for poisoning relations between them, so the way was now clear for normalization. The Yugoslavs replied that their stand had been determined by the Party leadership as a whole, not by Djilas, but that they were ready to settle the dispute on a basis of equality between socialist parties and states.[194]

The Russians had then to decide on their next move. The hardliners argued that the Yugoslavs should be asked to send a delegation to Moscow, but Khrushchev favoured making the unprecedented gesture of visiting Belgrade.[195] On 14 May a communiqué was issued simultaneously in Moscow and Belgrade announcing that delegations at the highest level would shortly hold discussions of mutual interest to both countries (**170**). The Soviet team was to consist of Khrushchev, Bulganin, Mikoyan, Shepilov, Gromyko, and Kumykin; Molotov, still Minister of Foreign Affairs, was a notable absentee.

The prospect that the bitter quarrel between Belgrade and Moscow was to be patched up aroused speculation that this would mark the end of Yugoslavia's independent stance and an unconditional return to the Soviet fold. In a speech delivered the day following the announcement Tito disclaimed any intention of a political volte face and affirmed his wish to maintain the best of relations with the West. But—in an apparent reference to some recent remarks of the Turkish Prime Minister that the existence of a 'brotherly link' between the Balkan alliance and the Atlantic Pact indicated that Yugoslavia was drawing closer to the West—he warned that it was not the fault of the Yugoslavs if certain people in the West who expected his country to be other than it was found themselves disappointed (**171**). The Russians, more crudely, berated 'reactionary circles' for threatening reprisals against Yugoslavia in order to keep her from normalizing her relations with Moscow, and disclaimed any wish to prejudice her links with the West (**172**).

KHRUSHCHEV'S VISIT TO YUGOSLAVIA:
THE BELGRADE DECLARATION

On 26 May the Soviet delegation flew into Belgrade. Khrushchev, addressing 'Comrade Tito' and the other Yugoslav leaders assembled to meet him at the airport, read a prepared statement affirming the Soviet desire to let bygones be bygones, alluding to the brotherhood in arms of the Russian and Yugoslav peoples during the war and the Marxist ideology which they held in common, and putting the blame for past troubles on Beria and his executed lieutenant Abakumov (**173**). He found, to his chagrin, that the speech was coolly received, the crowds being restrained in their welcome and the Yugoslav leaders frankly unimpressed by his crude attempt to use the former police chiefs as scapegoats.[196] Nor did the discussions between the two delegations run an easy course.[197] Khrushchev aimed at restoring relations on the old Party-to-Party basis which would have secured Yugoslavia's reincorporation into the Soviet bloc on honourable though unequal terms. Tito was determined that the talks should be conducted at governmental level, as between representatives of independent and sovereign states. The communiqué issued at the end of the Russians' visit indicated that his view had broadly prevailed; it was signed by himself, as President of the FPRY, and on the Soviet side, not by Khrushchev, the First Secretary of the CPSU, but by Bulganin, the titular head of government (**174**).

The Belgrade Declaration, as the communiqué came to be known, marked the formal ending of the seven-year rift between Belgrade and Moscow.[198] Though couched in general terms which left many outstanding issues to be settled, it denoted important concessions to the Yugoslav claim that each country had the right to build socialism in its own way, without interference or pressure from another, and to maintain the foreign links it saw fit. The existence of military blocs (though Moscow had just formalized her relations with the satellites of Eastern Europe in the Warsaw Pact) was pronounced harmful. Yugoslavia remained a communist state, and her attitude on most current world issues was declared to have much in common with the Soviet Union's. But the talks revealed important differences of emphasis. The Soviet concept of peaceful coexistence was that of two irreconcilable ideological blocs, which might do business together but would continue opposing each other by all means short of war since their mutual hostility was an expression of inevitable class struggle. The Yugoslavs preferred to see things in terms of what they came to describe as 'active coexistence', which implied a loosening up of the opposing blocs until differences of ideology and social system no longer proved determining factors in inter-state relations.

The Declaration was also significant for its omissions. It contained no references to Marxist–Leninist ideology or inter-Party relations. No mention was made of the Cominform, from which Tito had been solemnly expelled, though he may have been given assurances that it would shortly be dissolved. Nor was anything further said of Beria and Abakumov. The origins of the quarrel were tactfully passed over in silence. It was enough that the prodigal had returned. And there was rejoicing in Belgrade that it was not the erring son, but the father from the homeland of socialism itself, who had come, if not to confess his sins, at least to express regret that the estrangement had all been a most unfortunate mistake.

TITO'S VISIT TO THE USSR: THE MOSCOW DECLARATION
One year later, in response to pressing Russian invitations, Tito paid a state visit to the USSR. From the uncertain start with the Belgrade Declaration, events had rapidly evolved. On leaving Yugoslavia, Khrushchev visited the Bulgarian and Romanian capitals to ensure that the Balkan communist leaders followed the Soviet lead in making their peace with Belgrade, and also to allay their fears that Moscow might accord Yugoslavia a privileged position in some revived scheme for a Balkan federation. The Stalinists were weeded out from amongst the satellite leaders, the Titoists rehabilitated (not a few of them posthumously) and in April the Cominform was quietly dissolved. Molotov, censured the year before by the CC of the CPSU for resisting the normalization of relations with Yugoslavia, was removed from office as Minister for Foreign Affairs on the eve of Tito's arrival in Moscow. On the economic front, despite Soviet resentment at Yugoslavia's growing commercial links with the West,[199] agreements had been concluded for a substantial expansion of Soviet–Yugoslav trade and new offers of Soviet credit (**175**). On the

delicate issue of inter-Party affairs, the way had been cleared for the resumption of closer relations by a cordial message of greetings sent by Tito in February 1956 to the 20th CPSU Congress (**176**), and by Khrushchev's sensational disclosure of Stalin's personal responsibility for the abuses of his regime. In his famous 'secret speech' at a closed session of that Congress, the new master of the Soviet Union frankly admitted the 'shameful role' played by his predecessor in the quarrel with Belgrade. Stalin's attempts to overthrow Tito, he declared, had failed because of the unity which their wartime resistance had forged between the Yugoslav people and their leader; they were not without their shortcomings and mistakes, but these had been magnified by Stalin in a 'monstrous manner'. A solution had now happily been found, he concluded, acceptable alike to the Soviet Union, Yugoslavia, the People's Democracies and 'all progressive humanity' (**177**).

The 20th Congress endorsed several important shifts of ideology which indicated that the Soviet and Yugoslav CPs were drawing closer together; it recognized that there could be more than one road to socialism, that communists might use peaceful means to achieve power in democratic states, that war was no longer inevitable. Under its new leaders, the Kremlin seemed to be renouncing the claim to infallibility and unquestioned authority over other CPs and admitting the right of each to work out its own Marxist salvation. In this new and more liberal climate, the Yugoslavs felt able to sign the undertaking for closer inter-Party relations for which the Russians had been pressing. The Moscow Declaration, signed between Tito and Khrushchev on behalf of their respective Parties, reaffirmed the principles of independence and equality enshrined at the state level in the Belgrade Declaration, and pledged their Parties to closer co-operation through discussion, consultation, the exchange of views and experience, always within the context of the 'internationalist principles of Marxism–Leninism', equality and mutual respect, and mindful that 'the ways of socialist development vary in different countries and conditions' (**179**). A communiqué signed by Tito and Bulganin recorded progress made in the normalization of political relations and the resolve of the two governments to continue the process in the economic, cultural, and political fields (**178**). These two statements, particularly the Declaration on Inter-Party Relations, were the fruit of a visit where the official and popular acclaim accorded to Tito seemed to set the seal on a new era of Soviet–Yugoslav rapprochement.[200]

REPERCUSSIONS IN EASTERN EUROPE: THE HUNGARIAN RISING
The Soviet–Yugoslav rapprochement had an importance which transcended bilateral relations; it represented a facet of the de-Stalinization process within the Soviet Union which was hailed as a signal for the liberalization of the other East European communist regimes and a lessening of their dependence on Moscow.[201] The thaw in Eastern Europe was viewed in some Soviet quarters with alarm. A secret directive (**180**) was sent out to the satellite leaders warning them against following in the Yugoslavs' footsteps and reaffirming Moscow's claim to pre-eminence in the world communist movement.[202] Tito was indignant when he learned of the terms of the directive and protested to the Russians that they were backsliding from their recently concluded agreement. The

Soviet leaders were growing alarmed at the course events were taking, particularly in Hungary. The Soviet ambassador in Budapest reported that unless the hated Stalinist Party boss Rákosi was deposed there was danger of a nation-wide revolt. Tito, who hated Rákosi for the violent stand he had taken in the Cominform dispute, also pressed the Russians to have him removed. In July Mikoyan was dispatched to preside over a Hungarian CC meeting at which Rákosi was deposed and replaced by Gerö, another if less notorious Stalinist and an intimate associate of Rákosi, who proceded to do his utmost to stifle the mounting discontent with more repressive measures. On 19 September it was announced that Khrushchev had gone to Yugoslavia 'on holiday', and a week later, he and Tito left together for a 'hunting trip' in the Crimea.[203]

On 5 October Tito returned to Yugoslavia, which became the centre of intense diplomatic activity. Delegations came from Italy, Poland, Romania, Bulgaria, and Hungary—the latter sending a team headed by Gerö whom Tito liked little better than Rákosi and had rather unenthusiastically made his peace with, at Khrushchev's behest, in the Crimea. The Hungarian comrades were lectured on the dangers of a CP becoming separated from the masses, and sent off to study the operation of his Workers' Councils as one means of promoting wider popular participation.[204]

Although the Soviet leaders were prepared to make use of Tito as a trouble-shooter during this critical time, they were far from seeing eye to eye with him on the extent and modalities of liberalization. Khrushchev believed that, through their record in the war and their firmness in backing their own leaders against Stalin, the Yugoslav communists had reached a level of independence and maturity which it would be unwise to accord to less firmly established communist regimes. He did not himself share the suspicions of their enemies that the Yugoslavs were being drawn into the Western camp, nor did he doubt that they had smashed the power of their internal class enemies once and for all. The situation in the East European satellite countries however seemed to him quite different. There the communist regimes lacked strong indigenous roots, were often indeed bitterly hated, and had merely cowed, not crushed, the bourgeoisie. To allow their people the degree of freedom enjoyed by the Yugo-slavs would open the way for the collapse of the communist system and the defection of the countries from the Soviet camp. This was the fear which had inspired the Russians' secret directive that had so angered Tito. The latter saw that 'they are afraid that reactionary elements might then be victorious', and declared that 'they lack sufficient confidence in the internal revolutionary forces of these countries. In my opinion, this is wrong, and the root of all later mistakes lies in insufficient confidence in the socialist forces of those peoples' (181).

These differences of assessment explain the shifting Soviet and Yugoslav attitudes to the events in Hungary as they moved towards a climax at the end of October. If Tito appeared to have belatedly gone over to the Russians' view, and approved their action in suppressing the rising, he could argue that, had they followed his advice, things would never have come to such a pass. But 'in order not again to come into conflict with the Soviet comrades, we were not insistent enough with the Soviet leaders to have such a team as Rákosi and Gerö eliminated' (181). Whilst the Hungarian delegation was still in Yugo-slavia, news came that serious demonstrations had broken out in Budapest, following reports of the dramatic turn which events were taking in Poland. There, what had started as workers' riots in Poznan developed into an attack on the government and secret police and a demand for more freedom from Moscow. Pressure mounted for the replacement of Ochab, the Party's Secretary, by Gomulka, a communist leader imprisoned until recently for his 'Titoist' ideas on workers' councils and greater independence vis-à-vis the Russians. Ochab yielded to the clamour, and the Gomulka faction then succeeded in forcing the resignation of Marshal Rokossovsky, the Polish-born Red Army officer commanding the Polish forces, and securing his recall to the Soviet Union. Khrushchev and other Soviet leaders, after a stormy meeting with the new leadership in Warsaw and a spell of menacing indecision, acquiesced in this reassertion of national and ideological independence.

These dramatic developments in Poland aroused hopes that similar concessions could be wrung from the Russians in Hungary. The pro-Polish demonstrations of 23 October were accompanied by vigorous demands that Gerö should be replaced by Imre Nagy, a 'national communist' hitherto in disgrace. But Gerö, unlike Ochab, refused to bow to the storm. Instead, he called on the police and troops to restore order. When he saw his forces handing over their arms to the rebels, Gerö turned to the Russians, but in the face of the growing popular clamour, the Soviet troops were soon withdrawn from the capital. Suslov and Mikoyan, who had been hastily sent to retrieve the situation, saw themselves obliged to bow to Hungarian pressure and allowed Nagy to take office. The Russians temporized and agreed to discuss troop withdrawals from Hungary and a new basis for more equal inter-state relations.

A tense pause ensued, whilst the Soviet leaders weighed up the pros and cons of military action to restore their authority and tested out the likely reaction of the Chinese, Polish, Yugoslav, and other communist Parties. Khrushchev and Malenkov flew in to confer with Tito at his summer resort on the island of Brioni. Tito, who had welcomed the disappearance of Rákosi and Gerö and approved of Nagy, was now having second thoughts about the way things were going in Hungary. The Soviet leaders left Brioni satisfied that the impending action against that country might strain, but would not break, the painfully achieved rapprochement with Yugoslavia.[205] On their return to Moscow, the order was given to move against the Hungarian rebels. Meanwhile, the position of the Nagy Government had become increasingly precarious in face of the uncertain intentions of the Soviet military command. In a desperate attempt to secure help from the outside world, Nagy appealed to the UN to accept the neutralization of Hungary on Austrian lines. But the UN was too much absorbed by the Suez crisis to give adequate attention to the protection of a Hungary who was now appealing for an end to collectivization, one-party rule, and membership of the Warsaw Pact.

Tito instructed his delegates to abstain from the United States-sponsored resolution at the UN calling on the Soviet Union to order an immediate withdrawal of their forces from Hungary. As he later declared in a speech delivered one week after the Russian tanks had moved in for the liquidation of the movement,

> the justified revolt and uprising against a clique turned into an uprising of the whole nation against Socialism and against the Soviet Union. And

the Communists who were in the ranks of the rebels willy-nilly found themselves in a struggle not for socialism, but for a return to the past, as soon as the reactionaries took matters into their own hands. . . . The first intervention [of 24 October], coming at the invitation of Gerö, was absolutely wrong **(181)**.

The second intervention [of 4 November], though deeply regrettable, was justified by Tito. 'If it meant saving socialism in Hungary then . . . we can say, although we are against interference, Soviet intervention was necessary' **(181)**. Although, in his remarkably frank speech, Tito gave his reasons for approving the smashing of the 'counter-revolutionaries', the Soviet intervention in Budapest came as a traumatic shock. Nagy had made no secret of his pro-Yugoslav orientation. His friends and colleagues maintained the closest contact with the Yugoslav embassy in Budapest which kept its government closely informed of the crucial course of events. These were followed in Belgrade with sympathy tinged with deepening anxiety. The Workers' Councils which the Hungarians set up seemed to be based on the Yugoslav model, but they soon proved to be veritable 'soviets' ironically nurturing popular resistance to the Soviet Union. On 26 October the correspondent of the official Yugoslav journal *Borba* was still reporting of the upheaval that 'in any case it is not a counter-revolution'. Two days later, Tito himself sent a message to the Hungarian CP approving its just aims but warning that reactionaries might try 'to exploit present events for anti-social ends'. The note of alarm was increasingly sounded. On 31 October *Borba* detected the existence of 'basically anti-socialist ideas and reactionary claims' beneath the new, ostensibly democratic slogans, and on 1 November observed with concern that 'right wing elements are the most active . . . the workers' party does not seem to exist'. Nevertheless, it welcomed the sensational news of the same day that Hungary had withdrawn from the Warsaw Pact and proclaimed her neutrality.

The bloody destruction of the Nagy regime left in ruins not only the Hungarian capital but all dreams of de-Stalinized, Yugoslav-style communist regimes emerging throughout Eastern Europe. Nagy, so recently the symbol of these hopes in Hungary, was now a refugee in the Yugoslav embassy, whilst his erstwhile colleague János Kádár, who had become Secretary of the Party during the revolution, took over as the head of a new Soviet-sponsored Government. Despite the rapid tempo and disturbing nature of these events, Khrushchev and Tito nevertheless attempted to maintain their dialogue and minimize the danger likely to be caused to their relations,[206] though the Soviet leader raised a number of 'legitimate objections' to Tito's frank comments **(182)**. Kádár, for all the puppet role now assigned to him, had himself previously been under a cloud for his 'Titoist' ideas, and was in time to succeed in applying some of them to Hungary. The presence of Nagy as a refugee in their embassy was an embarrassment to the Yugoslavs, and on 22 November, after they had been given solemn assurances of safe conduct, he was released to Kádár's representatives. The latter, despite repeated protests and personal interventions by the Yugoslav diplomats in Budapest, handed him over to the Russians who, after holding him in custody for nearly two years,[207] had him shot **(183)**.

THE SECOND SOVIET–YUGOSLAV DISPUTE

Despite Khrushchev's efforts to minimize the damage to Soviet–Yugoslav relations, the Hungarian affair proved a grave setback. From being the trusted adviser in Khrushchev's cautious initiatives for de-Stalinization outside the Soviet Union, Tito found himself made the scapegoat for the loss of CP control which had led to the Hungarian 'mutiny'. The exchange of charge and counter-charge in the press of the two countries was accompanied, on the Soviet side, by hints of renewed economic pressure, the credits offered in 1956 for a number of important industrial projects being unilaterally 'postponed'. Criticism by the Yugoslav Foreign Minister of Stalinist attitudes which had done untold harm to the cause of socialism, and a statement that Yugoslavia intended to remain outside the organized Soviet bloc were denounced by *Pravda* as 'sacrilege' (**186, 187**). Mutual recrimination continued, despite the same paper's more conciliatory statement that the Yugoslavs had the right to build socialism in their own way though not to hold it up as a model for others (**187**), and a declaration by Foreign Minister Shepilov that relations had been normalized although some 'manifestations of ill will' persisted on the Yugo-slav side (**185**).

Both sides now spoke more in sorrow than in anger, eschewing the vitupera-tion of previous polemics, for neither wished for the total discomfiture of the other. Khrushchev had favoured conciliation and co-operation with Tito, and sought to use his prestige in Eastern Europe to further his own policies and consolidate his personal position. He still had enemies in the CC, the hard-liners like Molotov who could point to the events in Hungary as justifying their forebodings. Tito had equally strong, though quite different, reasons for criticizing Khrushchev's handling of the crisis, but did not wish to add to his difficulties or see him displaced by leaders less well disposed towards Yugo-slavia.

By mid-1957, when things had settled down somewhat in Eastern Europe, there were signs of renewed Yugoslav–Soviet détente. Tito had already hinted in one of his speeches that the chief stumbling block in the path of normaliza-tion with the Soviet Union was the attitude of 'individual leaders who are not able as yet to get rid of old concepts of relationships between socialist coun-tries' (**188**). By the beginning of July Khrushchev had established his ascend-ancy over the CPSU CC through the expulsion of the 'anti-Party group'. Molotov, arraigned for, amongst other things, his 'erroneous stand in the Yugoslav question' (**189**), the man who, with Stalin, had signed the letters precipitating Yugoslavia's expulsion from the Cominform and given many other signs of arrogant hostility towards the Yugoslav leaders, was at last removed from the scene. Khrushchev, now unchallenged in his domestic posi-tion, was free to press on with his policy of friendlier relations with Yugo-slavia. He hoped, in particular, to benefit from the prestige and influence Tito enjoyed in the non-aligned world with such figures as Nasser, whom the Soviet leader wished to cultivate as a means of furthering his ambitions in Egypt and throughout the Middle East.

By August 1957 Soviet–Yugoslav relations had recovered sufficiently for a high-level Yugoslav Party and government delegation led by Tito to visit Romania—a venue symbolically suggesting that each side was prepared to meet the other half-way—for talks with Khrushchev and other Soviet leaders.

The communiqué issued after the talks reaffirmed the principles embodied in the Belgrade and Moscow Declarations and the resolve 'to work for the further all-round extension of mutual relations and for the removal of the obstacles hampering this development' (190). One of these obstacles was a divergence of view regarding the German question. Tito had never recognized East Germany, which was ruled by the old Stalinist and Cominformist, Ulbricht. During the post-Hungary tightening of the economic screw, the Russians had gone back on an agreement which they had made jointly with the East Germans to finance aluminium production in Yugoslavia. The agreement was satisfactorily renegotiated, and before the end of the year Yugoslavia recognized the East German regime, at the cost of a breach in relations with West Germany. Another area in which Yugoslavia and the Soviet Union seemed to be drawing closer together was in military affairs. In June General Gošnjak, the Yugoslav Defence Minister, made a visit to the Soviet Union which was returned in October by Marshal Zhukov.[208]

But if relations between the two governments were patched up, strains began manifesting themselves again at the Party and ideological levels. In November 1957 the Yugoslavs accepted an invitation to send a delegation, headed by Kardelj, to attend the commemoration of the 40th anniversary of the October Revolution in Moscow, where a consultation between twelve ruling CPs also took place. Though the Yugoslavs endorsed the Peace Manifesto issued during the celebrations, they refused to sign the Declaration drawn up by the Parties on the grounds that it revived the concept of a bloc in which one country was assigned a leading role—'hegemonism'—and that it indirectly condemned the views and practices of the LCY whilst making no mention of the real deformation of Marxism–Leninism at the hands of Stalin. The Yugoslavs' refusal to sign the Declaration, which by Moscow's standards was a liberal document in so far as it conceded a certain latitude to the CPs for the definition of their ideological and national policies, angered Khrushchev, who is reported to have told Kardelj and Ranković that they could not go on 'sitting on two chairs' but would have to choose between allegiance to the East or the West.[209]

When Tito addressed the 7th LCY Congress five months later, he could still nevertheless claim that the improvement in relations with Moscow was continuing and 'that there is more trust between us, that we understand each other, that we can in a comradely and sincere fashion talk about our experiences in building socialism' (191). Other speakers however were less temperate, and the Congress itself represented a defiant formulation of the Yugoslav heresy and a scathing indictment of Soviet practice. Kardelj's speech contained a sharp criticism of the socialist countries, whilst Ranković's remarks were deemed so offensive that the diplomats who represented them in the capacity of observers—the invitation to send delegates had been declined—walked out in protest.[210] The Congress had before it a lengthy document known as the Draft Programme (192) which formulated the Party's ideological position in terms to which the theorists in Moscow took strong exception. The document had already been circulated amongst the other CPs and amended in a number of minor ways intended to make it less unpalatable to the CPSU. But the modifications were brushed aside as irrelevant or insufficient by the Russians, who evidently intended to make the document a casus belli.

The Draft Programme argued that, in the critical years following the October Revolution, when the Soviet Union was the only socialist country, revolutionaries the world over had the duty of defending her interests and acknowledging her leadership. But history had now moved on and socialism had triumphed in other countries where conditions and experience were different. The Soviet Union was thus no longer entitled to a 'monopoly position in the workers' movement, least of all in the sphere of ideology' (**192**). A new, more equal relationship between socialist states, each of whom had their distinctive contribution to make, was required. Stalin, moreover, had distorted Marxism–Leninism through his personal dictatorship, which concentrated the machinery of state and Party power in his own hands, instead of allowing it, as Marxism postulated, to 'wither away' as power became more broadly distributed throughout the democratic organs of the working class. It was Stalin's claim to ideological monopoly and political hegemony which caused the 1948 rift with Yugoslavia. But sound socialist forces were strongly enough rooted in the Soviet Union for them to be able to correct these abuses after his death. The 20th CPSU Congress thus approved the rapprochement with Yugoslavia, which was evolving its own forms of socialism, such as the concept of social property and workers' management, in accord with the true tenets of Marxism–Leninism.

CHINA AS A FACTOR IN THE DISPUTE
The Draft Programme contained other theses, such as the possibility of a peaceful evolution to socialism in capitalist states and the danger of military blocs (the Soviet amongst them) contrasted with the peaceful role of such 'uncommitted' countries as Yugoslavia, which the Soviet ideologists strongly attacked. These theses, though now more fully developed, were not new. But positions which the Russians seemed prepared to tolerate in the conciliatory mood of 1956 were now denounced as inadmissible. What had led to this hardening of attitude in Moscow? One important factor was the emergence of China as a new and still inscrutable member of the Soviet family. When the Chinese CP first began to show interest in Eastern Europe, there were signs that it might throw its weight behind more relaxed, egalitarian policies. The contrary, however, soon proved to be the case. The Chinese declared themselves in favour of strong, centralized control and strict ideological uniformity and at first seemed content to see such authority exercised from Moscow. This suited Khrushchev's new line; a firmer hand with the satellites, after the Hungarian rising incited by Yugoslav meddling, would both serve to stabilize the position in Eastern Europe and keep Moscow in step with Peking. The latter, after urging caution on the Russians with regard to the Poles, advised firmness in dealing with the Hungarians.

The Yugoslavs were growing increasingly critical of the Chinese comrades since the ending of their 'Hundred Flowers' phase and their demands for tougher action by Moscow in the international sphere. On 5 May 1958, after the customary exchange of May Day messages, the *People's Daily* in Peking launched an onslaught endorsing the old Cominform strictures against the Yugoslavs and dubbing the Draft Programme a systematic and comprehensive revisionist programme. The following day, *Pravda* reprinted the article and three days later published a similar, though more moderately worded, attack. The Yugoslav leaders were arraigned for having arrogantly rejected the justified criticism of their Draft Programme, for following the path of revisionism, and for attempting to tar the Soviet camp with the imperialist brush, since they seemingly preferred American bribes to the disinterested Soviet aid which they branded as exploitive; but—with an ominous hint of renewed economic sanctions—'Yugoslavia could be relieved of such "exploitation" ' (**193**). As a mark of Russian displeasure, the visit of Voroshilov, the Soviet Head of State, was cancelled at short notice, and at the end of the month a note was sent announcing the suspension of important credits (**194**)—a move which the East Germans, despite Yugoslavia's recognition of the GDR the previous autumn—were quick to emulate. The Yugoslav Government replied that this unilateral suspension was unacceptable and likely to cause serious harm to the country's economy and its relations with the Soviet Union, from whom the FPRY would reserve the right to demand compensation (**195**). The Soviet Government indignantly rejected these contentions and argued that such a revision of trade agreements was normal and well-intentioned (**196**). Similar delaying tactics were also employed over the delivery of 200,000 tons of wheat due to Yugoslavia under existing arrangements.

Whilst the Yugoslavs were protesting at the suspension of Soviet credits, Khrushchev, in a speech at the 7th Congress of the Bulgarian CP in Sofia, delivered one of the sharpest attacks on the Yugoslavs to be made by any Russian statesman since Stalin's days (**197**). He too, like the Chinese, declared that the Cominform resolution attacking their errors had been justified, and that the LCY had proved itself a Trojan Horse aiming at the destruction of the whole socialist camp. These charges were no less vigorously rebutted a few days later in a speech by Tito, who trounced the Chinese for their distortion of Marxism–Leninism and the Russians for their continued tolerance of Stalinism, both at home and in their attitude to the building of socialism in Yugoslavia (**198**).

During the next eighteen months Chinese and Soviet attacks continued against Yugoslavia's 'schismatic and revisionist line', though Khrushchev showed some concern that 'we should not devote greater attention to the Yugoslav revisionists than they actually deserve' (**199**) and even pointed to some positive signs of Soviet–Yugoslav co-operation and the need for a further interchange of delegations (**200**). The 21st CPSU Congress, held early in 1959, provided however a forum for renewed criticism (**201**).

The tone of this second Soviet–Yugoslav dispute was nevertheless markedly more restrained than that of the first. There was sabre-rattling, but no troop movements on Yugoslavia's borders, a threat of economic sanctions, but no lasting interruption to the flow of Yugoslav–Soviet trade. One reason for this relative restraint was the gathering tension within the socialist camp which was to erupt in the open quarrel between Moscow and Peking. The shafts launched by the Chinese against the Yugoslav 'revisionists', as Tito was quick to perceive,[211] were in reality increasingly aimed against the Russians. Khrushchev, whilst intermittently joining in the fray against the Yugoslavs, was growing more deeply concerned at the threat from the Left. In May 1959 he paid a visit to Albania, which had made itself the most vociferous mouthpiece of the Chinese communists, in an apparent attempt to persuade Enver Hoxha, the

4

First Secretary of the Party, to moderate his attacks on Tito. But these increased in vehemence, and when, early in 1961, Tirana reported the arrest of a group of conspirators allegedly linked to Yugoslavia and the West, it transpired that the ringleader, Admiral Seyko, was in effect (as Khrushchev later confirmed) a Soviet agent. Diplomatic relations between the two countries were thereupon suspended. The microcosm of Albanian politics reflected Peking's challenge to Moscow which was in time to promote a new Soviet–Yugoslav rapprochement.

Some signs could be discerned, during 1960, of the impending realignment of forces. At the Russians' invitation, Vukmanović-Tempo, whom Khrushchev had clashed with on his first encounter in Yugoslavia and then taken a liking to, paid a visit to the USSR where, in a frank exchange of views with the Soviet leader, he learned that the CC had recently expressed itself in favour of normalizing relations with Yugoslavia.[212] There proved, however, to be little justification for these hopes. The Yugoslavs were not invited in June to the Romanian Party Congress where communist leaders met to prepare a mammoth gathering of 81 CPs in Moscow the following November, and where Khrushchev again attacked the Yugoslavs, criticizing them for advocating a phoney neutrality whereas they were aligned in the Balkan Pact. Nor were they invited to the Moscow Conference itself, whose closing statement included a ritual denunciation of Yugoslav revisionism (202) which in turn elicited a firm rebuttal from Tito (203). The pacemakers in this anti-Yugoslav campaign continued to be the Chinese, who were later to complain that

> on 1 December Khrushchev signed the statement on behalf of the Central Committee of the CPSU, and twenty-four hours later, violating what the fraternal parties had agreed upon, brazenly described Yugoslavia as a socialist country at the banquet for the delegations of the fraternal parties.[213]

Behind the sporadic firing directed against Yugoslav revisionism, the battle lines were being steadily drawn for the Sino–Soviet conflict. Warning shots had already been fired by Khrushchev in the previous October at the Chinese Tenth Anniversary celebrations in Peking. The following June, at Budapest, he crossed swords with the Chinese delegate, P'eng Chen. In August, the Yugoslav press reported the recall of Soviet advisers from key Chinese projects and was quick to perceive, from Yugoslavia's own experience, what that portended. In the same month, Kardelj published a series of articles in *Borba* in reply to the campaign which the Chinese Party journal *Red Flag* had been waging ostensibly against Yugoslav revisionism, and in defending the LCY he also defended the CPSU. The latter's theoreticians, embarrassed to find themselves vindicated by a heretic, repudiated in their journal *Kommunist* the claims advanced on behalf of the LCY. Moscow and Peking still kept up their duet of abuse against the Yugoslavs, but the trend to which the dynamism of the Chinese ideological offensive was leading could scarcely be mistaken.

Tito and Khrushchev had resumed personal contact in September 1960 when they met in New York whilst attending a session of the UN General Assembly. On most international questions, apart from those concerning relations within the socialist camp and the Yugoslav concept of non-alignment, they held similar or identical views. The announcement, in the following April, that their Foreign Ministers would exchange visits came therefore as no particular surprise. Koča Popović, the Yugoslav Foreign Minister, was nevertheless kept waiting for two months for his invitation (204), whilst Gromyko did not make his return visit until the middle of the following year. But the pendulum was swinging steadily towards détente. In September 1961 Belgrade became the venue for the first world conference of twenty-five 'non-aligned' nations. The Russians had oscillated in their attitude towards Tito's initiative in the non-aligned world between envious distrust (when relations with him were bad, and his influence judged likely to be detrimental) and satisfaction (when relations were good, and they could count on his propagating generally acceptable theses). They had even come to the point of themselves sponsoring a sort of triple division of the world (capitalist, socialist, non-aligned) for application at the UN. The strongly anti-Western tone adopted at the Belgrade Conference, and the indulgent reaction to the Soviet Union's resumption of nuclear testing were noted in Moscow with gratification.[214] The following month the CPSU held its 22nd Congress. The old clichés against Yugoslav revisionism could still be heard (205), but interest centred on Khrushchev's outburst against the Albanians and his renewed attempts to lay the ghost of Stalinism which caused the Chinese to leave Moscow in dudgeon.

The rapprochment continued into 1962. After four years of disapproving silence, the Soviet press began again to publish news of LCY activities. Following Gromyko's visit in May, Khrushchev referred to Yugoslavia as a country that was 'building socialism' and described relations with her as 'normal, even good'. The Yugoslavs were debating a new constitution, to be adopted the following April, which changed the official designation of their state to that of the Socialist Federal Republic of Yugoslavia. Khrushchev's remarks, together with a more explicit assertion later in the year that 'it is impossible to deny that Yugoslavia is a Socialist country',[215] seemed tantamount to Soviet recognition that Yugoslavia belonged in spirit, if not through formal membership, to the socialist camp.

THE SECOND RECONCILIATION

Before 1962 had run its course, the renewed rapprochement between Yugoslavia and the Soviet Union appeared to be virtually complete. Not all differences had been ironed out, but both sides seemed firmly committed to a policy of live and let live. The visit of a Yugoslav commercial delegation to Moscow in July prepared the way for a substantial expansion in bilateral trade. Two months later, a visit to Yugoslavia by Leonid Brezhnev demonstrated the new cordiality (206), though it could be noted that the Chairman of the Supreme Soviet chose to expatiate more on the economic headway achieved by his hosts rather than on the progress in 'building socialism' along their distinctive lines, and that his speeches were marked by a virulently anti-Western tone which evoked no sympathetic response from them. It was a critical juncture in international affairs, when Khrushchev was secretly preparing his coup de main in Cuba by which he hoped to shift the balance of global power dramatically in favour of the Soviet Union. The outcome of the October Cuban missile crisis, when the super-powers drew back from the very brink of nuclear war, shook Khrushchev's prestige both at home and in the socialist camp. To the sound of shrill Chinese recriminations, Tito prepared, at significantly short notice, to return Brezhnev's visit. In December the still unrepentant but now acclaimed dissident found himself once more an honoured guest in the capital of world communism. On being accorded the rare distinction of addressing the Supreme Soviet, he spoke of the resolve of both governments to complete the process of rapprochement and paid a tribute to Khrushchev's 'peace-loving' policies and his statesmanship in handling the Cuban missile crisis (**207**).

For most of the next two years, until Khrushchev's fall in October 1964, Yugoslavia's relations with the USSR continued to be warm, and her influence in Eastern Europe (except Albania, and to some extent Bulgaria) reached a peak unknown since the 1956 explosion in Hungary. The Kremlin, whilst stopping short of countenancing a dangerous descent into 'revisionism', was now concentrating its fire against Chinese 'dogmatism' and seemed to be 'using Tito to hold Titoism in check'.[216] The East European CPs were encouraged once again to welcome Yugoslav 'fraternal delegates' to their congresses, on the tacit understanding that the Yugoslavs would give general endorsement to Soviet policies and not press their own line too zealously. On 23 January 1963 in a speech to the 7th Youth Congress, Tito delivered a slashing attack on the Chinese comrades whom he described as following in the footsteps of Genghis Khan.[217] He believed that his country's interest could best be served by leaning —but not too far—towards Moscow in her dispute with Peking, and the dispute persisting with neither too sharp an escalation nor too marked a degree of reconciliation. However, as he took pains to impress on the Party leadership, in a report in May to the LCY CC, closer relations with Moscow should not be allowed to impair Yugoslavia's standing with the West (**208**). Other CPs were also beginning to see that, if it raised problems of allegiance and ideology, the rift between the two great communist powers also allowed them similar scope for manœuvre. When, therefore, in the course of 1963, the Russians began to canvass support for a new rally of CPs in Moscow, with the object of pronouncing a general anathema on the Chinese, the Yugoslavs were not alone in hanging back.

In August Khrushchev arrived in Yugoslavia for a 'holiday'—his first visit since the Hungarian crisis of 1956. Little was to be gleaned from the uninformative communiqué issued at the conclusions of his talks with Tito (**209**), though it seems probable that, since Yuri Andropov, the official concerned with inter-Party relations in Eastern Europe, took part in them, they may have touched on Soviet proposals for a new Moscow Conference, and for the inclusion of Yugoslavia in the Kremlin's master plan for the socialist 'division of labour' through membership of Comecon. The Yugoslavs did not agree to these proposals, though they were later to accept observer status in Comecon on conditions which safeguarded their economic independence. The atmosphere during the Soviet visit was cordial, and Khrushchev pleased his hosts by showing interest in the Workers' Councils and even suggesting that something on the same lines might be introduced in the Soviet Union, where fresh ideas were under consideration for possible inclusion in the new constitution. He proposed that a special Soviet delegation might be sent to Yugoslavia to look into the matter further. This ideological open-mindedness was not, however, reflected in the Soviet press which did not report his praise for a system of self-management alien to the centralized control traditional in Soviet industry.[218]

During this period of renewed Yugoslav influence in Eastern Europe Tito, with Moscow's blessing, engaged in a series of talks with the leaders of the respective Parties—Gomulka of Poland, Gheorghiu-Dej of Romania, Zhivkov of Bulgaria, Kádar of Hungary (whose role in the overthrow of Nagy seemed to have been forgiven)—and he even received the homage of such hardliners as Novotny of Czechoslovakia and Ulbricht of East Germany. Reports (discounted in the West) of a growing neo-Stalinist opposition continued to circulate in Belgrade. It may have been concern for these rumours, and for Khrushchev's known wish to call the CPs of the world to an anti-Chinese rally in Moscow, which prompted Tito's hasty visit to Leningrad on 8 June 1964 for a four-hour talk with Khrushchev which recalled the circumstances of the Khrushchev–Tito consultations on the eve of the Soviet intervention in Hungary. The official communiqué merely referred blandly to the 'successful development of Soviet–Yugoslav relations' and, more enigmatically, to the 'necessity for every Communist and Workers' Party to make its contribution to overcoming the difficulties arisen in the world communist movement'. A reference to the need for 'unity and a monolithic structure of the fraternal Communist . . . parties' suggested greater Yugoslav readiness to accept the Soviet line (**210**).

RELATIONS FOLLOWING KHRUSHCHEV'S FALL

The fall of Khrushchev four months later came to the Yugoslavs as an unwelcome surprise. Tito hurried back from a trip abroad and watched anxiously for indications of the policies which the ousted leader's successors intended to follow. A Moscow statement pledging loyalty to the 'decrees of the 20th, 21st and 22nd Congresses of the CPSU' was hardly encouraging, since the Resolution of the 21st Congress had included a sharp condemnation of Yugoslav revisionism. Nor were the friendly overtures from Moscow towards Peking, which seemed to foreshadow a Sino–Soviet rapprochement likely to be made at the expense of Yugoslavia. But reassuring signs could soon be noted. A Yugoslav delegation invited to attend the October Revolution anniversary celebrations in Moscow was ranked with those from other 'socialist' countries, and the message of congratulation sent at the end of November on Yugoslavia's National Day accorded the country the same status. When, in the following month, the LCY held its 8th Congress, the CPSU, for the first time since Tito's advent to power, sent a fraternal delegation, though its spokesman caused some disappointment by the perfunctory nature of his address. In his report to the Congress, in which he strongly criticized the Chinese and pointed out that the attacks they had been directing against Yugoslavia and against Khrushchev were no less aimed against the whole CC of the CPSU, Tito paid a tribute to the fallen leader for his services for the normalization of Soviet–Yugoslav relations (**211**).

For the next three years, Yugoslavia's relations with the new team in the Kremlin continued on a more or less even keel. In June 1965 Tito made his first visit to the Soviet Union after Khrushchev's fall. He was warmly received, and the communiqué issued at the end of his visit recorded a growth in economic co-operation and 'noted with satisfaction that contacts between the CPSU and the LCY have become broader and stronger' (**212**). The political pendulum seemed indeed to have swung further than ever before towards full Soviet–Yugoslav co-operation. On Vietnam and other current international issues, Tito re-echoed Soviet criticism of the West, and in a speech at Sverdlovsk he declared that despite past misunderstandings there was not a Yugoslav communist who could doubt that 'if difficult times were to come', his country would stand firmly on the side of the Soviet people.[219]

Closer economic co-operation between the two countries figured largely in Tito's discussions with the Soviet leaders, for his country's economy, after a remarkable expansion once the initial difficulties caused by the Cominform blockade had been overcome, was now causing concern. Shortly after Khrushchev's fall, a Yugoslav delegation had visited Moscow and negotiated an agreement providing for an expansion of Soviet–Yugoslav trade and the delivery of more Yugoslav-built ships to the Soviet Union. On the eve of Tito's 1965 visit a further agreement on economic co-operation was reached and a joint inter-governmental committee set up for this purpose. The latter move somewhat paradoxically coincided with the decisions reached by the LCY's CC for far-reaching reforms, tantamount almost to embarking on a market economy, in an attempt to give freer scope to the principle of self-management in industries and enterprises. Thus, at a time when state and Party ties were being consolidated on orthodox lines in Moscow, Belgrade was committing itself to a re-structuring of the national economy in a more liberal spirit than had been seen in any communist-controlled country before. Though the full scope of their social consequences could not be foreseen—a consumption-led boom, the emigration of many workers to the Western countries with which Yugoslavia was becoming integrated, and a general process of *embourgeoisement*—the reforms were opposed by conservatives within the LCY, particularly by Serbs who feared that they would lead to a decline of their influence in favour of their Croat and Slovene comrades.

Opposition came to centre round Ranković, the most powerful of the Serbian communists, who also feared a dismantling of the UDBA police apparatus he had so long controlled. Ranković, rather than Tito's other close associate Kardelj, who favoured the policies of decentralization and economic reform, was regarded by many as next in the line of succession, and some of his supporters held that a change of both policies and leadership was already overdue.[220] On the discovery that his agents had been 'bugging' even the Marshal's own office and home, Tito struck against his old comrade and, at the Brioni plenum of July 1966, Ranković was forced to resign from the CC and to give up his offices. His fall, which the Russians appear to have tried to prevent, cleared the way for a continuance of the movement towards decentralization and democratization which they viewed with disquiet.[221]

In the field of foreign affairs, however, the non-aligned course which the Yugoslav Government claimed to be following appeared to offer some advantage to the Soviet bloc. In April 1965 Tito had played a prominent part in the initiative taken by seventeen associated countries to propose a solution of the Vietnam war on neutralist lines. The failure of this initiative was laid squarely to the charge of the West, and the communiqué issued after the visit of the Yugoslav Minister of Foreign Affairs to Moscow in May 1966 was able to record with some justification 'the closeness or identity of the two countries' views on the chief problems of the present international situation' **(213)**. The death of Nehru, Khrushchev's fall, and the meagre results of the second conference of non-aligned countries (Cairo, 1964) tended to reduce Tito's prestige amongst the non-aligned nations and to give his 'non-alignment' an increasingly pro-Soviet bias in opposition both to the pro-Chinese orientation represented by Sukarno, and to the West. In September Brezhnev visited Yugoslavia to continue his dialogue with Tito (**214**), and the following year, on the outbreak of the Arab–Israeli war, Tito flew to Moscow for a conference of communist leaders, broke off diplomatic relations with Israel, provided the Russians with transit rights, and did everything in his power to help them restore Nasser's military position.[222] This drastic bending of Yugoslavia's non-alignment in favour of the Soviet-sponsored Arab cause brought Tito dangerously at variance with Yugoslav public opinion and the judgment of some of his own officials and advisers. But despite this solidarity with the Soviet Union over the Middle East crisis, and another visit to Moscow in November when he again had the honour of addressing the Supreme Soviet, Tito did not accept the invitation to send delegates to a meeting of CPs which the Russians, after many delays, eventually held in Moscow in June 1969. A new crisis had arisen in Eastern Europe, and once again it was the Yugoslav example which was to take the credit, and later the blame, for the trend towards ideological and national emancipation.

INVASION OF CZECHOSLOVAKIA AND THE DOCTRINE OF LIMITED SOVEREIGNTY

Behind the Yugoslavs' opposition to a gathering of the world's CPs, where tacit endorsement at least would be given to Soviet claims to pre-eminence and ideological infallibility, lay a revival of inter-Party polemics over the nature and scope of the economic and political reforms needed in the communist world. Recent years had seen the introduction, to varying extents, of economic changes in Eastern Europe, and even in the Soviet Union itself, designed to modify the out-dated, centrally planned economies so as to take into account some degree of consumer choice. Yugoslavia, which had gone further than others in this direction, posed the question of how far such reforms could be pushed without a corresponding measure of political liberalization. The Soviet answer—expressed in articles published in *Pravda* in February 1967 —was a categorical assertion that the maintenance of a strong state and Party machine would be needed for a long time to come.

The East European parties were not at one in this question. The Romanians were moving towards a solution of their own which combined conformity to Soviet practice in domestic policies with a growing assertion of national independence. Starting from the opposition successfully offered in 1963 to Soviet schemes for supranational economic integration, which would have checked Romania's industrial growth, they had gone on to increase trade with the West, remain uncommitted in the Sino–Soviet dispute, and question Moscow's claim to dominance of the socialist camp and the subordination implied by Romania's membership of the Warsaw Pact—all this through a skilfully controlled process of emancipation which stopped short at outright provocation whilst constantly enlarging the area of their freedom of action. The Czechoslovaks were striking out in directions which seemed similar to those chosen by

Yugoslavia, though they stemmed from deep rooted indigenous aspirations for a more genuinely democratic and political system—the desire, hesitatingly but honestly proclaimed by Dubček, who succeeded the ousted dictator Novotny as Party Secretary early in 1968, to give communism a 'human face'. The Action Programme outlined by the new leadership, whilst reaffirming that the alliance with the Soviet Union and other socialist countries would remain the cornerstone of foreign policy, advocated a radical democratization of political life, a free press and guarantees for personal liberty, the rehabilitation of political victims, a guiding rather than a controlling role for the Party, the decentralization of industrial decision-making, the opening of the country to world markets, honest electoral processes, and equal national rights for all national groups. These were aspirations to which the Yugoslavs could heartily subscribe, for some they could claim to have successfully applied themselves. When the Action Programme was announced in April, *Borba* (11 April 1968)—unlike the Polish and East German press which ignored it altogether, or the Soviet, Bulgarian, and Romanian papers which omitted the clauses they found unpalatable—gave a full and approving account of it.

At the end of April 1968 a Yugoslav delegation headed by Tito arrived in Moscow. The Russians were deeply suspicious of the new trends in Czechoslovakia and uncertain how best to deal with them. They were particularly distrustful of the Czechoslovaks' wish to play down the 'leading role' of the Party, which they saw as the virtual surrender of power by the communists and the weakening or loss of the accepted channels of Soviet control over a country which occupied a strategic position in the Soviet line of defences in Europe, and one from which 'counter-revolutionary' contagion could readily spread to the other satellites. In the events leading to the Soviet invasion of Czechoslovakia and the destruction of the reforms, the Russians could count on a more or less willing co-operation from the other East European communist leaders (except the Romanians). Tito not only sympathized with the Czechs but attempted to use his influence in Moscow on their behalf. He

> told Brezhnev and the other Soviet leaders that any attempt to use force in the solution of the problems of Czechoslovakia would have infinitely serious consequences not only for Czechoslovakia, but for the Soviet Union itself, and the international workers movement in general.[223]

Two and a half months later the representatives of the USSR, Poland, Hungary, East Germany, and Bulgaria dispatched the 'Warsaw Letter' to Prague threatening dire consequences from the alleged betrayal of socialism in Czechoslovakia. *Politika* published the letter under the laconic headline 'Cominform—1968', whilst Tito issued a statement hopefully declaring that there could be no elements in the USSR so short-sighted as to resort to a policy of force against a fraternal country (**216**). The LCY had already expressed its conviction that 'any outside action representing interference or an effort to limit the independence of the CP of Czechoslovakia . . . would have grave consequences' (**215**). It is not clear why the Yugoslavs expected that the Russians would allow more latitude to Dubček and the Czechs than they had been willing to grant to Nagy and the Hungarians. The latter had wanted to leave the 'socialist camp'; the Czechs—more subversively—were working to transform it. Yet the danger of loosening party controls, whether in Czechoslovakia or Yugoslavia, was ominously apparent. Yugoslavia too was experiencing its own sort of 'Prague spring', with a serious outbreak of student trouble in Belgrade and renewed squabbling between Serbs and Croats on the language issue.

On 9 August Tito arrived in Prague where he was enthusiastically received. At about the same time, or shortly afterwards, the Russians reached the conclusion that the alarming trend of events could only be arrested by military intervention. On the night of 20–21 August, Soviet troops moved into Prague, took over all key military and political posts and, with support from East German, Bulgarian, Polish, and Hungarian units, reasserted total control over Czechoslovakia. The news, so reminiscent of Soviet action against Hungary in 1956 except that the victim now offered no resistance, aroused consternation in Belgrade and Bucharest. Ceauçescu, who had paid a visit to Prague shortly after Tito and received an equally warm welcome there, denounced the Russians' move as a flagrant violation of the national sovereignty of a fraternal, socialist, free and independent state. Tito, in firm but more measured terms, expressed 'deep concern' at the 'very negative consequences' which must follow (**217**). In a statement on the following day, the Yugoslav Government deplored the invasion as 'the grossest form of violation of the sovereignty and territorial integrity of an independent country' and called for the immediate withdrawal of the invading forces (**218**); it also raised the matter in the UN. The CC of the LCY similarly expressed 'deep indignation and protest' and affirmed, in forthright words, its resolve to oppose any similar threat from outside (**219**). The mobilization of the armed forces underlined Yugoslavia's intention to resist.

On 24 August Tito and Ceauçescu met secretly on the Yugoslav–Romanian frontier to confer on the situation created by the Soviet invasion of Czechoslovakia and its likely consequences for their respective countries. *Pravda* was quick to accuse the latter of giving 'active assistance to the Czechoslovak anti-socialist forces' and of taking the same stand as the 'imperialist circles' and the 'Mao Tse-tung group in Peking' (**220**), as well as offering asylum to Czechoslovak 'political adventurers'—prominent figures in the Dubček regime. Soviet economic or even military action seemed to threaten Yugoslavia again as it had after the rift with the Cominform. Economically, the country was no longer so vulnerable to pressure, for though her trade with the Soviet Union had increased in absolute terms, it now comprised less than one-third, as against a previous two-thirds, of her total foreign trade. Militarily, her dependence on the Soviet Union had also decreased, though her strategic position had assumed greater and more dangerous significance as a result of the build-up of Soviet power in the Mediterranean.[224] The Yugoslav army could not expect to repel Soviet armour attacking through Bulgaria and Hungary any more than it had been able to repel the German panzers in 1941. Moreover, the Czech experience had demonstrated the ease with which a sudden Soviet descent in overwhelming force could secure a country's capital and other key sectors. A new strategy was accordingly devised aiming at 'total national defence' and involving the creation of territorial armies of citizen-soldiers, organized by the constituent Republics for combined operations with the regular army in protracted regional resistance to an invader. The organization of these territorial defence groups was begun in the autumn of 1968 and formalized under a new Defence Law in the following February. The Yugo-slavs thereby hoped to serve notice that any hope of subjugating their country by a sudden Prague-style attack would not be feasible, and that an invasion would meet with prolonged and bitter resistance, allow Yugoslavia to call for outside help, and perhaps precipitate a superpower confrontation.

On 30 August the Soviet ambassador handed Tito a note complaining of Yugoslavia's unfriendly attitude towards the 'aid operation' undertaken by the five Warsaw Pact countries for the benefit of Czechoslovakia[225] (**221**); a further note protesting against the continuance of hostile Yugoslav press comment was presented to the Yugoslav ambassador in Moscow on 19 October. The text of the Yugoslav replies has not been disclosed, but in his public speeches, Tito continued to voice his criticism of the Soviet action and of all attempts by one state or Party to impose its will on another (**222, 223**). The Yugoslavs found themselves once again the target of undisguised Soviet hostility. But much had changed since the Cominform campaign unleashed against them twenty years before. Their concern then had been to rebut criticism by proving 'through their deeds' that their Party was true to Marxist–Leninist–Stalinist orthodoxy. Now they were bent on vindicating their distinctive brand of socialism, and asserting that each Party and nation had the right to its own path. Though a few conservatives in the LCY pointed to the Czechoslovak example as proving the danger of ill-advised or over hasty reforms, the general effect of the Soviet action against the Czechs was to strengthen the progressives in the Party, confirming the process of liberalization to which it had pinned its colours, accelerating its pace, and facilitating the emergence of younger men to positions of leadership.

Whilst the Yugoslavs were reaffirming their resolve to 'build socialism' in their own way, Soviet spokesmen were becoming aware of the need to present an ex post facto justification for their action against Czechoslovakia which would both serve as a deterrent to other would-be offenders and offer a plausible pretext for any further military intervention which might be deemed necessary. *Pravda*, in an article on 25 September, argued that the independence of socialist countries was subordinate to the interests of the world communist movement—a theme which Brezhnev, in a speech delivered on 12 November to the 5th Congress of the Polish United Workers' Party, developed into the Doctrine of Limited Sovereignty with which his name was to be linked.

> When internal and external forces that are hostile to socialism try to turn the development of some socialist country towards the restoration of a capitalist regime . . . it becomes not only a problem of the people of the country concerned, but a common problem and concern of all socialist countries.[226]

The dangerous implications of such a claim were not lost on the Yugoslavs, particularly as the Soviet press continued to attack them for being the moral instigators of Czech 'revisionism' and reacted angrily to the hostile tone of Yugoslav newspaper comment.[227] The doctrine seemed clearly incompatible with Yugoslavia's thesis of 'separate roads to socialism' and designed to give the green light for further Soviet intervention.

'NORMALIZATION' AND THE TACTICS OF
LIMITED RAPPROCHEMENT

By the end of November, signs appeared that the political pendulum might be swinging back towards a certain normalization of relations. The congratulations sent from Moscow for Yugoslavia's National Day were couched in cordial terms, whilst *Pravda* even found some words of praise for Yugoslavia's economic reforms which had hitherto been denounced as contrary to Marxism and leading to stagnation. Tito, in his National Day speech at Jajce, refrained from any direct allusions to the Soviet Union, Czechoslovakia, or the Brezhnev Doctrine, but in reply to press correspondents' questions, discounted the threat of Soviet invasion and described the situation as still serious though not to be over-dramatized—remarks which were approvingly taken up by the Soviet press (**224**). The Consultative Meeting of world CPs organized by the Russians in Budapest held out promise that the Czechoslovaks would soon capitulate and that Moscow's writ would run again unchallenged throughout Eastern Europe. But Prague continued to fight its stubborn rearguard action, the Russians increased their pressure, and the Yugoslav press continued to comment disapprovingly on their systematic obliteration of all features of 'Socialism with a human face'. The Yugoslavs saw no real grounds to allay their alarm over the Soviet action against Czechoslovakia or the danger to themselves implicit in the Brezhnev Doctrine which Tito described, in the following March, when the LCY held its 9th Congress which the Russians boycotted, as 'contrary to the basic right of all peoples to independence, and as contrary to the principles of international law'. It was 'at variance with the interests of the struggle for socialism' (**225**).

The Russians, meanwhile, had found new grounds for dissatisfaction with Belgrade. The Chinese, after initially branding the Czech reformers as dangerous revisionists, were now siding with them against Moscow. The upheaval of the Cultural Revolution had subsided. A rapprochement between Peking and Belgrade could thus logically be expected, and the conclusion of a trade agreement in March 1969 between the two countries pointed in the same direction. As Sino–Soviet polemics increased in vehemence, the Yugoslav press saw to it that the Chinese case did not go by default. All this increased Russian anger and led to sharp accusations of anti-Soviet bias. Tito, in a bid to arrest this new deterioration, reiterated in a speech at Kraljevica on 1 May that his government was ready for talks with the Soviet Union and urged that political or ideological differences or critical press comment should not be allowed to prejudice good economic relations between the two countries (**226**). A fortnight later a communication was received from Moscow repeating the charges against the Yugoslav press, and declaring that the latter would have to change its tune before any real progress could be made in normalizing relations. The Yugoslav reply is believed to have argued that the poor state of relations between Moscow and Belgrade was not due to any alleged anti-Soviet bias on the part of the Yugoslav press, but to disquiet over the action which the Soviet Government had taken in Czechoslovakia.[228] A statement by Tepavac, the Yugoslav foreign minister, similarly put on record his government's unwillingness to muzzle the press,[229] defined the principles which determined its foreign policy, and repeated Yugoslavia's desire to find ways of improving relations despite existing differences.[230]

At the beginning of September Foreign Minister Gromyko arrived in Belgrade for a short visit. For more than a year the Czechoslovak issue had proved an apple of discord between Moscow and Belgrade, and both sides now seemed ready for a fresh attempt at rapprochement. The Yugoslavs reconciled themselves to the establishment of the Husak regime in Prague, whilst the Russians, by accepting a reference in the Soviet–Yugoslav joint communiqué (228) to the principles embodied in the Belgrade and Moscow Declarations, appeared to concede that the doctrine of limited sovereignty had no application to Yugoslavia. Tito, in stressing the importance of Gromyko's visit, was able to declare that 'we are on the right path' and to point to the need to turn to the future rather than dwell on the past (229). But, on the Party level, rapprochement proved more difficult. The LCY was not represented at the Consultative Meeting of CPs held in Moscow in the summer of 1969, and though the resolution passed there referred to the LCY in conciliatory terms (227), the Party rejected the redefinition of internationalism which that conference approved stressing the 'priority of the common interests of socialism over the particular national interests'. In November a LCY delegation did finally pay a visit to the Soviet Union—the first since the invasion of Czechoslovakia—but fresh irritants were soon apparent. The Yugoslavs took particular exception to a new history of the CPSU issued under the sponsorship of Ponomarev, a Secretary of the Party's CC, which belittled the role of the Partisans during the war and laid much of the blame for the 1948 dispute on the Yugoslav communists. This was seized on as evidence that the Russians had not changed their attitude of fundamental hostility, and Tito warned that 'we must be aware that any attempt to degrade our national liberation struggle is an attack on our socialist society based on self-management, on the equality of our peoples, on the independence of Yugoslavia'.[231] The Russians showed their displeasure by expelling the Moscow correspondent of *Politika* for allegedly biased reporting, and by reproducing Soviet press attacks on him in the propaganda bulletin disseminated by the Soviet embassy in Belgrade.[232]

The next two years were a time of intense activity in the field of diplomacy and foreign policy and of mounting pressure within Yugoslavia. During 1970 the process of normalization was carried forward by a series of high level contacts in Moscow—a delegation to attend the Lenin celebrations in April, and visits by the Yugoslav Minister of Defence and the Prime Minister in the two following months—but behind the guarded official communiqués much of the old differences remained. In the ideological field, the Yugoslavs showed no disposition to abandon their distinctive standpoints; in the military field, the Russians proved reluctant to find further credits for the purchase of arms and the Yugoslav General Staff took fresh stock of the possibilities of diversifying its sources of supply in the West; whilst in the political field, though the Belgrade Declaration was again invoked in the official communiqué following the visit of Prime Minister Ribičič to Moscow (230), the persistence of 'some differences of opinion' was also admitted. These hesitant moves towards rapprochement were balanced by other steps designed to reinforce Yugoslavia's independent position. Tito's attendance at the 3rd Conference of the Non-aligned Countries at Lusaka, the exchange of ambassadors with China, and particularly the visit paid by President Nixon at the end of September, demonstrated that the pursuit of better relations with the Soviet Union was only one of the several pillars on which they were determined to rest their foreign policy.

But in the foundations of the Yugoslav state itself cracks were appearing which gave increasing cause for alarm. The extravagance and conflicting projects of local authorities and the reassertion of native capitalist tendencies, leading to a spate of private building and small businesses, threatened economic chaos. More serious still, the factor to which all other strains and stresses were linked, was Yugoslavia's perennial nationalities problem. The process of decentralization and the de-emphasis on authoritarian Party control, the effects of workers' management and popular participation reaching up from the factory floor to the organs of regional administration, the impact of closer commercial and social contacts with the West which accentuated the disparity between the wealthier and the backward regions of Yugoslavia, all posed problems of where to draw the line between legitimate local patriotism and unacceptable national pretensions which might ultimately disrupt the common state. In these troubled domestic waters, despite the reassuring protestations of 'normalization' emanating from the capitals, the Russians seemed to be fishing. In the spring of 1970 the Croat émigré press began to float the notion that the Soviet Union would like to see the dismemberment of Yugoslavia and the establishment of an independent Croatia as a sort of Balkan Finland which would look to her for support and give her bases on the Adriatic.[233] One faction of hitherto fanatically anti-communist Croat separatists was reported to be in touch with Soviet agents in Berlin, whilst the Croat Party and Republican leaders in Zagreb were themselves rumoured by their opponents to have put out feelers in the same direction. It was noted that the official Soviet Party delegations visiting Yugoslavia were showing an unwonted and disquieting interest in making contact with the LCY's lower echelons and regional leadership.

Distrust and mutual recrimination, particularly between the Croat and Serb communist leaders, came to a head early in 1971. In April the CC of the Croat CP openly charged 'certain federal bodies' with helping to disseminate rumours of collusion between the pro-Soviet separatists and the Party leadership in order to discredit the latter and frustrate the constitutional reforms then under consideration for increasing the autonomy of Yugoslavia's constituent Republics. Those Serbian communists who distrusted the Croats and favoured the old centralist, Stalinist methods were accused of scheming to put the clock back, or to provoke the intervention of the army on the pretext of protecting the unity of Yugoslavia. At the end of April Tito summoned the Party Presidium to a secret emergency meeting at his Brioni residence where, after a three-day session, he succeeded in restoring some unity amongst the Party leaders and exacting from them a pledge of good behaviour and abstention from further polemics. Two months later the Federal Assembly adopted a series of constitutional amendments designed to ease the evolution of the Yugoslav state into a loose federation under a collective leadership which would take over on Tito's retirement.

There were other grounds, besides suspected collusion with the Croat separatists, for Yugoslav reserve with regard to the Soviet Union's professed readiness for 'normalization'. Since Sofia was known to be subservient to Soviet wishes, Russian encouragement seemed likely to be behind Bulgarian intransigence over the Macedonian question which frustrated the attempts at Bulgarian–Yugoslav rapprochement in the autumn of 1970. Another cause for disquiet was the increased activity shown by the pro-Cominform exiles since the Soviet invasion of Czechoslovakia. Proposals to sponsor the formation of a 'Revolutionary Communist Party of Yugoslavia in Exile' were reported by the Yugoslav press in the spring of 1970,[234] and in the following year bitter polemics broke out over a dispatch by *Politika*'s Moscow correspondent drawing attention to the hostile lectures which the Soviet authorities were permitting anti-Tito émigrés to deliver.[235] An official Yugoslav diplomatic protest, like the representations made by Foreign Minister Tepavac when he visited Moscow the previous February, were met with bland Soviet disclaimers. The official line continued to be that 'relations and co-operation between the USSR and the SFRY . . . have been developing successfully' (231), and—as Brezhnev reported to the 24th CPSU Congress in March—'the Soviet people want Socialism to gain strength in Yugoslavia and its ties with the Socialist Commonwealth to become firmer[236] (232).

By the summer of 1971 relations between Moscow and Belgrade appeared to be once more under strain. One reason for this was Russian concern at China's growing influence in the Balkans. At first confined to her small client Albania, it had extended to Romania and now seemed to be gaining ground in Yugoslavia. In June 1971 Foreign Minister Tepavac left on an official visit to the PRC where he was received by Chairman Mao and conferred with Chou En-lai and heard his country praised for 'having withstood foreign pressure and waged resolute struggles against the interference, subversion, and threat of aggression by the superpowers'.[237] None had once been fiercer than the Chinese in denouncing the Yugoslavs for their betrayal of socialism. But now, in the alchemy of converging national interests, the base metal of ideological heresy was transmuted into the pure gold of friendship. Yugoslavia also improved her once strained relations with Albania, whose leaders had grown alarmed at the lesson of Czechoslovakia and the threat to themselves implicit in the doctrine of limited sovereignty. It was even rumoured in the Bulgarian and Hungarian press that a pro-Chinese Tirana–Belgrade–Bucharest axis was in the making. This was at once denied by a government spokesman in Belgrade, who averred that good relations with China in no way implied bad relations with the Soviet Union. Yugoslavia's policy of non-alignment was applicable wherever there were opposing international groupings—within the socialist camp as well as outside it.

In July it was announced that the forces of the Warsaw Pact would hold manœuvres in southern Hungary, near the frontier with Yugoslavia and Romania, and also in Bulgaria. This was seen primarily as a threat to Romania who, although a member of the Pact, confined her participation to sending staff officers and would not permit the passage of foreign troops through her territory to Bulgaria. The Yugoslav Government, whilst discounting the likelihood of military intervention against herself at a time when Moscow's general policy was one of détente in preparation for a European Security Conference, could not rule out the danger entirely, and let it be known that Yugoslavia's resolve to defend her national independence remained unshaken, and that manœuvres would shortly be held to test her readiness for 'total national defence'.

NEW INITIATIVES AND OLD PROBLEMS

With the announcement that Brezhnev would pay a four-day visit to Yugoslavia at the end of September, relations between the two countries seemed set to take a turn for the better. Moscow's initiative could be seen as designed to counter the spread of Chinese influence in the Balkans, to weaken Yugoslavia's entente with a recalcitrant Romania by reasserting her own bilateral links, and also to further the general diplomatic campaign in favour of the proposed European Security Conference. The latter project was one which could count on a cautious welcome in Belgrade, though not for the same reasons as Moscow's. Whereas the Russians wished it to set the seal on a status quo favourable to their interests, the Yugoslavs hoped that it might afford them more elbow-room by reducing Soviet hegemony in Eastern Europe and the strength of both opposing power blocs. Their objectives in agreeing to Brezhnev's visit also differed from those of the Kremlin. The latter's aim remained Yugoslavia's eventual return to the fold. The Yugoslavs, for their part, were prepared for closer relations, with emphasis on state-to-state rather than Party-to-Party aspects, provided they could be assured that Moscow would abstain from all forms of interference and pressure and would reaffirm respect for Yugoslavia's independence and her right to build socialism in her own way. In particular, Tito intended to voice his disquiet over Moscow's continuing support for the Yugoslav émigrés, several hundred of whom had latterly been paying visits to Yugoslavia with obviously propagandist ends, whilst others were serving in the Soviet armed forces, some of them in units stationed near the borders of Yugoslavia.[238]

These differences of aim were reflected in the public speeches of the two leaders no less than in the compromise formulations of their final joint communiqué. In his speech of welcome at Belgrade airport, Tito expressed his wish to see the development of Soviet–Yugoslav co-operation 'based on equal rights and mutual respect', and stressed, at the banquet later given in the Russians' honour, that 'international co-operation can make no progress if it is based on any monopoly or on a negation of the legitimate rights and interests of individual countries and peoples'. In his reply, Brezhnev referred briefly to the years 'when Soviet–Yugoslav relations were seriously clouded' and to the legacy of this period which still persisted 'in some areas', but stressed 'the identity of our fundamental interests and our responsibility in the common struggle for the cause of peace, socialism and Communism'.[239] He paid tribute to the principles embodied in the Belgrade and Moscow Declarations, but emphasized the need to see 'how we can more fully and broadly realise these principles'—a gloss which Yugoslav commentators noted with some concern. He also denied the rumours that Soviet armies were preparing to move into the Balkans and 'the fable about the so-called "doctrine of limited sovereignty" '.[240] A reflection of that doctrine might nevertheless be noted in a speech made the following day to Yugoslav factory workers when Brezhnev declared that his country's foreign policy was to 'firmly defend the interests of socialism against all its enemies'. He went on to say that 'it is no secret that not everything which determines the specific character of the present organization of Yugoslav social life is acceptable to Soviet communists' who had different traditions and outlooks. But this, he assured his listeners, was no cause for 'any kind of alienation or distrust' since the choice of the specific forms of their social system was the internal affair of each communist Party and people.[241]

How much reliance could be placed on such Soviet assurances time alone would tell, but in general the Yugoslavs saw cause for satisfaction over Brezhnev's visit. The joint communiqué (233), it is true, contained a reference to 'allegiance to the principles of socialist internationalism' which, in the context of recent events, might seem uncomfortably close to the purportedly non-existent doctrine of limited sovereignty. Both sides also undertook to increase contacts, consultation, and exchanges of delegations at all levels, which the Yugoslavs would have preferred to restrict to a formal basis. But the reaffirmation of the principles of non-interference and mutual respect contained in the Belgrade and other Declarations, the avoidance of any formulation of attitude towards Peking and of denunciations (except over Vietnam) of Washington, where Tito was shortly expected on an official visit, the commendation of the 'anti-imperialist trend in the policy of the non-aligned countries', the promise of closer economic contacts, and the proposal that the Balkans should become a nuclear-free zone—all these suited the Yugoslavs' book and held promise of a reduction of tension in Eastern Europe. After leaving Belgrade, Brezhnev paid brief visits to Bulgaria and Hungary which were now required to tone down their criticism of Yugoslavia.

The understanding reached with Brezhnev left Yugoslavia's international position stronger than at any time since the end of World War II. A few weeks later, Tito paid a visit to Washington which resulted in improved prospects for American economic help and capital investments and an enlarged market for Yugoslav exports. Yugoslavia was now on cordial or correct terms with all her Balkan neighbours, and with the chief West European powers, both individually and through the EEC. The policy of non-alignment, though its early promise had somewhat faded, ensured her good standing in the Third World. Her relations with China, de-emphasized for Brezhnev's visit, had not been seriously impaired. With the Soviet Union, the strains caused by the invasion of Czechoslovakia seemed at last to have been eased. When a group of admirers in the West began to put forward Tito's name as a candidate for the Nobel Peace Prize, the proposal also drew warm support from Moscow[242]

But, internally, the country was still racked by tensions which placed all these gains in jeopardy. The policy of decentralization, and particularly the difficulty of determining which shares of Yugoslavia's economic cake should go to the constituent Republics, seemed to revive rather than assuage the old nationalist passion that had made the country such an easy prey to foreign intervention thirty years before. The crisis was most acute in Croatia, where aspirations for greater national autonomy mingled with demands for more political liberalization. The moderate leadership of the Croat CP, which sympathized with these trends but sought to keep them within acceptable bounds, found itself increasingly unable to curb the clamour led by Zagreb's students and intellectuals. Tito, aware that equally disruptive forces were gathering strength too in the other Republics and that the backlash could be particularly serious in Serbia, decided that the moment had come to apply drastic remedies. With the sanction of military force in the background, the chief nationalist firebrands were arrested, the leadership of the Croat CP thoroughly purged, and the Prime Minister of Croatia and other high officials replaced. Croatia had been slipping into chaos, Tito declared, and far-reaching measures were needed to forestall a civil war in which 'someone else' might intervene to restore order. Jakov Blažević, President of the Croatian Parliament, made the allusion still clearer when he told the CC of his party that the 'counter-revolution' wanted to provide a pretext for those who are ready to help, that is to say, for 'fraternal intervention'.[243] The Brezhnev doctrine of limited sovereignty, whatever its author might say, still seemed to be looming menacingly over a divided Yugoslavia. There were even critics of Tito's firm action in Croatia who complained that he was in fact already applying it himself against his own internal opponents and with a ruthlessness of which the Russians could only approve.[244]

The crisis in Croatia was a harsh reminder that the maintenance of internal stability was the precondition for Yugoslavia's ability to withstand external pressures. Albeit—as seemed likely—she had played little significant part in provoking them—the Soviet Union could only stand to profit from the excesses of nationalism. If they led to separatism and eventually to secession, the resulting mini-states would not be viable on their own and must fall into her lap. Alternatively, if Belgrade enforced unity, centralism and authoritarian rule would put an end to those reforms and experiments which set Yugoslavia apart from the Soviet model and would facilitate eventual reversion to Moscow's control. Though the immediate crisis was surmounted and the new leadership consolidated in Croatia at the beginning of 1972, the Yugoslav Government remained uneasily aware of these factors and the corresponding weakening of its position as 'normalization' developed into an ever closer relationship with the Soviet Union. When, in April, Marshal Grechko paid a long delayed visit to Yugoslavia, a government spokesman found it necessary to deny that the question of the use of Yugoslav ports by Soviet warships and overflight rights for Russian military aircraft had figured in the discussions held with him. The Soviet Defence Minister's visit nevertheless represented a strengthening of Russia's ties with that institution likely to play a crucial role as the country's most effective cohesive force in the post-Tito era, and one in which orthodox and conservative sympathies were reputed to be strong—the Yugoslav army.

In June Tito paid an official visit to Moscow—his first since the Czech crisis —in return for Brezhnev's of the previous September. The warmth of his reception, the ceremonious bestowal on him of the Order of Lenin, and his host's cordial allusions to Yugoslavia as a 'fraternal country' and to the improvement in bilateral relations, at Party as well as state level, combined to give the impression that the Russians were making real headway in drawing the errant Slav state back into their orbit. The joint communiqué emphasized 'the significance of the fruitful personal meetings' and 'the deepening of contacts and co-operation' which were now taking place at all levels. The principles of equality and non-interference enshrined in the Belgrade and Moscow Declarations were still invoked and stress was also laid on the need for closer co-ordination between the CPSU and the LCY and the common inspiration they drew from the teachings of Marx, Engels, and Lenin, but also—in an apparent concession to the Yugoslav view—on the fact that each party was 'creatively applying them in accordance with the specific features of their respective countries' (**234**).

Tito's visit to Moscow was seen by some Western observers as a step in the 're-Sovietization' of Yugoslavia. The Party purge which, by the end of the year, had led to the dismissal of hundreds of Party officials and the arrest and trial of prominent politicians and intellectuals in Croatia, was extended to Serbia and Slovenia against leaders accused of 'anarcho-liberalism', pro-Western sympathies, chauvinism, and other crimes. The reins of Party discipline and ideological orthodoxy were drawn tighter. Nationalist animosities were sharpened by the economic crisis through which the country was passing. The relaxation of controls had given Yugoslavia a form of market economy which, though more dynamic and productive than those of the orthodox socialist countries, had also produced inflation, sharp rises in the cost of living, and dangerous disparities of wealth between groups and individuals. The latter trend was breeding resentments threatening consequences similar to the outbursts which, two years before, led to the ousting of Gomulka in Poland. More consumer goods had been produced, but basic sectors of the economy, such as mining and electricity generating power, had suffered neglect. It was here that the government decided to look for Soviet development aid. By the end of the year, after difficult negotiations, it was announced that the Yugoslavs had been granted a credit of $540 million, which, though less than half the amount hoped for, was the largest sum ever offered their country by the Russians.

Yugoslavia's economic difficulties, compounded by her still unresolved political uncertainties, continued throughout 1973. Though the volume of Soviet–Yugoslav trade showed a gratifying expansion after Brezhnev's visit, the benefits expected from the proffered credit were slow to materialize. Nine months after the announcement of that offer, only three projects, accounting for less than 10 per cent of the credit available, had been negotiated. Agreement was proving difficult between a rigidly centralized system and Yugoslavia's largely autonomous, though sometimes financially weak, enterprises, whose expectations had been heightened by familiarity with the more sophisticated technology of the West. It was mainly with a view to ironing out these difficulties, and to improve the Soviet image in general without making any concessions of substance, that Prime Minister Kosygin accepted an invitation to return his Yugoslav colleague's visit in September 1973. The concrete upshot of this visit was the offer of a further $45 million financial credit to assist Yugoslav enterprises short of liquid capital to conclude deals with Soviet industry. Although the joint communiqué (235) spoke optimistically of the prospects for 'further comprehensive development' of economic co-operation and paid ritual tribute to the 1955 Belgrade Declaration and other statements pledging respect for the principles of sovereignty, equality, and non-interference, other observations by the Soviet Prime Minister were sufficiently ambiguous to cause concern. Addressing the workers of a Sarajevo firm which had concluded important deals with the Soviet Union, he extolled the latter's system of centralized planning as immunizing a country against the sort of crises and depressions to which theirs was now prone, and, whilst paying lipservice to Yugoslavia's independent road to socialism, implied that her current troubles stemmed from the refusal to follow the Soviet pattern.[245] The significance of such allusions was not lost on the Yugoslav press which, throughout the visit, took pains to emphasize that though an improvement in relations with the

Soviet Union was welcome, Yugoslavia would not be cajoled or coerced into forsaking her chosen path.

Little more than one month after Kosygin's visit came the unexpected news that Tito was to confer with Brezhnev and other Soviet leaders in Kiev. His visit was described as taking place at the invitation of the CPSU, but the inclusion of the Yugoslav Minister of Foreign Affairs and other high officials in the delegation accompanying him suggested that, whereas economic questions had figured largely in the recent talks with Kosygin, foreign affairs would now be high on the agenda. The renewal of fighting between Israel and the Arabs, and the scale of Soviet military support for the latter (with sophisticated weapons denied to the Yugoslavs), followed by the Soviet–American démarches to bring about a settlement, called for a clarification of Yugoslavia's position. Non-alignment, as a factor in world politics, had declined in importance. Tito's support for the Arabs remained as wholehearted as ever, and he had once again given Soviet planes carrying military supplies to them the right to overfly or refuel on Yugoslav territory. His policy of non-alignment, as far as the Arab–Israeli issue was concerned, continued to be inoperative. Nor had Tito made any secret of his conviction that socialism was the goal to which the non-aligned countries must all ultimately tend. Though these policies were broadly in line with Soviet interests, they were not presented by Tito, when he attended the conference of non-aligned states at Algiers in September 1973, with the wholeheartedly pro-Soviet spirit shown there, for example, by the Cubans. The Yugoslavs had clearly been worried lest, in the great issues of war and peace, the voice of the countries claiming to be non-aligned would not be heard and matters would be settled over their heads by the superpowers. It was to assert their right to a hearing, and for their interests to be taken into account, that Tito, as a founding father of the non-aligned group, now wished to confer with the Russians. The latter, anxious to carry the non-aligned countries with them in their Middle Eastern policies, and conscious of Yugoslavia's strategic position in the crucial Mediterranean theatre, welcomed his coming.

The course which Soviet–Yugoslav relations seemed to be taking gave the Russians grounds for cautious optimism. The area of common ground in foreign policy was considerable, and in bilateral relations there were now closer links at Party, as well as state, level. This was an aspect on which Brezhnev laid particular stress when greeting his guest at a banquet given in Tito's honour when he saluted the favourable prospects for deepening inter-Party co-operation and cited the 'dominant tendency' stemming from the fact that the two countries had the same social system and recognized 'the common objective laws governing the development of socialism' (236). Tito, in his reply, acknowledged the 'common goal' of building socialism but stressed the 'different methods of and specific paths in the creative application of the teaching of Marx, Engels and Lenin' (237). These differences of emphasis found no reflection in the anodyne phrases of the joint communiqué issued (238), which was equally silent as to whether, in the sphere of foreign policy, Yugoslavia and her non-aligned partners had been assured of any greater say in settlements likely to affect their interests, or whether, in ideological and political matters, the two sides had moved closer together. A short statement released in Belgrade soon after Tito's return from the Soviet Union announced that a delegation headed by a senior KGB official had been having talks with his

Yugoslav counterparts, and that the leaders of the CPs from the principal Yugoslav Republics had left for the Soviet Union on a 'fact-finding' mission.[246]

THE OUTLOOK

At the beginning of 1974 Yugoslavia and the Soviet Union seemed to have come closer together than at any time since 1948. State and Party relations had been restored at all levels and economic ties strengthened. The old dogmatic fiction that the interests of a socialist Yugoslavia must necessarily coincide with those of the homeland of socialism, and that what was good for the latter was right for the former, had long since been discarded and a measure of wary mutual tolerance established. A quarter of a century had gone by since Stalin had surprised the world by anathematizing the men who, up to that moment, had seemed to be wholly dedicated to building communism on the most orthodox lines. Uncertainly, and at first unwillingly, the Yugoslavs had struck out on a path of their own, surviving in the teeth of Soviet threats and blandishments, without exchanging dependence on the West for subordination to Moscow, and in time evolving foreign and domestic policies which marked their country as a socialist state which yet remained aloof from the socialist bloc. There had been times, first in Hungary and then in Czechoslovakia, when Eastern Europe seemed on the point of following their example. The Soviet Union itself, after Khrushchev had dared to lift the veil on the realities of Stalin's regime, had even seemed astir with the same currents. But the harsh authoritarian form of Soviet rule had been reimposed and Yugoslavia remained the Marxist maverick of Eastern Europe, no longer so direly threatened or so isolated, yet nevertheless still basically alone and vulnerable.

The political stance which Yugoslavia has come to assume during the last quarter of a century reflects the realities of her geographical position and her historical evolution as a land at the crossroads between East and West. To the West she looks for the technology and the financial aid which will speed the building of her distinctive brand of socialism. The West also provides employment for her 'Seventh Republic'—nearly one million workers whose remittances, together with the earnings from her expanding tourist industry, form a high proportion of her foreign exchange. Yet powerful forces still draw her towards the East and to that superpower which controls the destinies of several of her neighbours and looms on her own frontiers. Yugoslavia remains a communist state, albeit her communism is sui generis. There are those who argue that the authoritarianism of a ruling Party and a place in the disciplined ranks of the Soviet camp will be needed if the fissiparous tendencies of a small multinational country are to be held in check.

Any fresh attempt by Moscow to push rapprochement to the point of reincorporating Yugoslavia formally into the Soviet bloc seems hardly likely so long as the present climate of détente between the two superpowers persists. A government in Belgrade still ostensibly non-aligned and attached to the distinctive features of its chosen socialist path, but increasingly responsive to Soviet prompting and unlikely to make further trouble in Eastern Europe, probably suits Kremlin policy well enough for the time being. Nor does such a policy at the official level exclude the continued undercover encouragement of subversion for eventual use as a means of pressure or as a lever of power once Tito finally relinquishes his grip. The arrest, in the spring of 1974, of a dissident group in Montenegro, which was in touch with exiled Cominformists living in Eastern Europe who had helped them to found a small clandestine pro-Soviet CP, indicates that the Yugoslavs are well aware of this danger.[247]

For nearly forty years Tito has been the dominant figure among the Yugoslav communists and their country's ruler for thirty. The post-Tito era may well see a fresh Russian initiative to draw Yugoslavia closer into Moscow's orbit. But is this orbit necessarily analogous to that of the planets which, in the fullness of time, must ineluctably be sucked back into the centre? Or does it rather resemble a particle revolving round an atomic nucleus, which moves unpredictably from one orbit to another, now further from the centre of attraction, now nearer to it, but never drawn in and absorbed? Such, certainly, has been the pattern of Yugoslav–Soviet relations for the last twenty-five years, rapprochement alternating with recoil, détente with crisis, as if responding to some self-regulating mechanism or the changing international conjuncture and the shift of internal stresses.

NOTES

1 For a study of this early period see Vuk Vinaver, Jugoslovensko-Sovjetski odnosi, 1919–1929; *Istorija XX veka* (Inst. društvenih nauka, Zbornik rada VII, 1965), 93–183.

2 According to J. B. Hoptner, *Yugoslavia in crisis, 1934–41* (New York, 1962), 174 ff., the fullest account of Yugoslav policy towards the Soviet Union at this period, Prince Paul had addressed a memorandum to his government urging it 'to procrastinate as long as possible. . . . Recognise the Soviet Union only if absolutely necessary and only when conditions in the country become completely quiet and orderly. Keep in mind that the future Soviet minister will become the nucleus for all the dissatisfied elements [including] even the opposition. He would probably attract even the broader masses of the people by his Orthodoxy and Slavism'.

3 Ibid., 175.

4 Ibid., 176.

5 For the official history of the CPY, see Čolaković et al. eds, *Pregled istorije saveza komunista Jugoslavije* (Belgrade, 1963) and the useful collection of documents edited by E. Hasanagić, *Komunistička Partija Jugoslavije, 1919–41* (Zagreb, 1959). J. Marjanović, *Potsetnik iz istorije Komunističke Partije Jugoslavije* (Belgrade, 1953) is a work by a leading authority on the subject, and I. Avakumović, *History of the Communist Party of Yugoslavia* (Aberdeen, 1964), a well-informed critical appraisal. For a full study of the aspects referred to in this paragraph see P. Shoup, *Communism and the Yugoslav national question* (New York, 1968).

6 'The Party has the duty to aid the liberation movements of the oppressed nationalities and national minorities, to lead their fight against imperialism, and to defend without any reserve their right of self-determination, even to secession' *Istoriski arhiv KPJ* (Belgrade, 1950), ii. 195, quoted in US Senate, Cttee on the Judiciary, *Yugoslav communism—a critical study* (1961), 43.

7 The Politburo of the CPY, implementing the 7th Comintern Congress line on the Popular Front, drew up a new programme; 'whilst remaining in principle in favour of national self-determination with the right of secession, the Communists take into consideration the present international situation and . . . do not declare themselves for the secession of peoples from the present state community, Yugoslavia'. Ibid., 44.

8   The fullest biography in Serbo-Croat is by V. Dedijer, *Josip Broz Tito—Prilozi za biografiju (Belgrade, 1953)*, of which *Tito speaks* (London, 1953) is a shortened version in English. The best accounts in English are Fitzroy Maclean, *Disputed barricade* (London, 1957) and Phyllis Auty, *Tito* (London, 1970).

9   Djilas frankly states that 'the Central Committee stood against the mobilisation and against participation in an imperialist war' (*Memoirs of a revolutionary*, New York, 1973, 332–3). The virulence of the Yugoslav communists' denunciation of the 'imperialist character' of the war became a subsequent embarrassment which was officially played down. 'Our position was recorded in the resolutions of the Fifth Conference of the CPY in 1940', Djilas writes. 'In 1946 I had this resolution reprinted in *Komunist*, along with Tito's report to the Fifth Conference, but Tito insisted on deleting the portions explaining our position on the "imperialist character of the war" because it was "embarrassing today" I objected to that.' After the fall of France, the CPY 'evolved with events'. The 1939 mobilization was regarded as conducted 'under pressure from London and Paris', but in 1940 differences between Germany and the Soviet Union became apparent and 'we not only modified our position but started criticising the government for not taking measures to provide for national defence'. Tito's line was that 'we Communists would have to fight the Germans without basically changing our position on the general character of the war' (ibid., 334–9).

10 The memoirs of Vukmanović-Tempo (*Revolucija koja teče* (Belgrade, 1971), i. 109–10, frankly describe the consternation caused by news of the pact amongst Party members. Tito himself later declared that 'we accepted the pact like disciplined communists, considering it necessary for the security of the Soviet Union, at that time the only socialist state in the world. We were ignorant at that time of its secret clauses, countenancing Soviet interference in the rights of other nations, specially small ones' (Dedijer, *Prilozi*, 278).

11 Article signed W. Tito in the Comintern journal (*Die Welt*, 30 Nov. 1939, quoted in B. Lazitch, *Tito et la révolution Yougoslave*, Paris, 1957).

12 V. Dedijer, *The battle Stalin lost* (New York, 1971), 48.

13 This seems to have been maintained exclusively through Tito. Djilas states that he and his comrades in the CC were careful to avoid personal contact with the Soviet mission, though their zeal was such that they kept its staff under surveillance and reported one of its members who had made 'statements damaging to the reputation of the Soviet Union' whilst in his cups, to Tito, who in turn reported him to Moscow and secured his recall (*Memoirs*, 375). Tito's links were with the Soviet military attaché, whom he saw several times after the German invasion of Yugoslavia and gave reports for the Comintern in Moscow. Tito also passed to him a report on the movement of German troops towards the Soviet frontier (*Borba*, 7 July 1953).

14 Dedijer, *Prilozi*, 292.

15 The operator of the Zagreb transmitter was Josip Kopinič, a former warrant officer in the Yugoslav navy who had been trained in Moscow and fought in the Spanish Civil War; he is referred to in Party correspondence under the conspiratorial names of Vazduh ('air'), Valdés, or NN. He is said to have been working for Russian intelligence in Zagreb before the war (M. Milatović, *Slučaj Andrije Hebranga*, Belgrade, 1952, 21). His subsequent activities suggest that the Russians also entrusted him with the task of keeping check on Tito and other party leaders.

16 According to Yugoslav sources, the head of the Russian intelligence network in the Balkans was Ivan Srebrnjak, also known as Antonov, Ivančić, Doctor, and by other aliases, a Yugoslav worker from Slavonski Brod who had been trained by the NKVD and assigned to work in Spain and France before being transferred in 1939 to Belgrade. After the German invasion of Yugoslavia, he moved to Zagreb, where one of his contacts was Andrija Hebrang whom he appears to have recruited for the Russian service; he was executed by the Ustashe in 1942 (*Zbornik dokumenata i podataka o narodno-oslobodilačkom ratu Jugoslavenskih naroda* (Belgrade, 1960), ii/2. p. 42n. Another important figure in the Russian intelligence network was Mustafa Golubić, who was arrested in Belgrade shortly after the German invasion and tortured to death because of his refusal to disclose information (Auty, 95). According to Djilas (*Memoirs*, 375), 'he was hostile to our Central Committee and said it was composed of Trotskyites'. Ranković and Djilas suspected that *he* was a Trotskyite and that 'he might rally some support against the new leadership and make trouble for us in Moscow'. They shadowed

him and were even prepared to assassinate him until Tito, on being shown photographs, recognized him as an important agent on 'special assignment' and ordered them to leave him alone.

17 Tempo, i. 149–50.
18 Ibid., 163–4.
19 Ibid., 165.
20 Neither the text of the resolution passed at this meeting, nor Tito's report of it to the Comintern, have been published. Djilas (*Memoirs*, 387–8) says that 'at this Consultation Tito established a new thesis: the possibility of a direct Communist take-over of power, a denial of the need for the revolution to go through two stages, bourgeois democratic and proletarian, which had been the party position until then, following Comintern decisions. Tito also postulated a Communist take-over after the defeat of Germany, to prevent any other party or organization from doing so. Clearly the old machinery of state would be either defunct or compromised by collaboration with the enemy. Tito said that we Communists had to organize ourselves militarily so as to be able to attack our enemies at the time of their defeat and thus be able to take power. . . . Tito spoke as a pragmatist, and not as a theoretician.' Moscow distrusted these signs of incipient radicalism and independence. In a directive sent by the Comintern at the beginning of July after the Germans had invaded Russia, the Yugoslavs were warned to bear in mind that 'at this present stage what you are concerned with is liberation from fascist oppression and not socialist revolution' (**20**; see also Dedijer, *Battle*, 48).
21 Hoptner, 207. According to Ilija Jukić, then an official of the Yugoslav Ministry of Foreign Affairs, relations with Plotnikov had been strained by the arrest of a Russian journalist attached to the Soviet legation, and by complaints that Soviet diplomats were being followed by secret police agents. But he attributes a more fundamental reason for Soviet coolness to 'the secret negotiations with Mussolini, in which the Russians were willing to recognize Yugoslavia as an Italian sphere of interest in return for Italy's recognition of Bulgaria and the Dardanelles as a Soviet sphere of influence' (*The fall of Yugoslavia*, London, 1974, 34).
22 The Soviet Government does not appear to have made any efforts to influence the Yugoslav Government not to give way to German pressure. On 22 March the British ambassador to Moscow, acting on instructions, urged the Soviet Government to intervene in this sense but was told that it could do nothing (E.L. Woodward, *British foreign policy in the second world war*, London, 1970, i. 538–9, 602).
23 Vyshinsky informed the Yugoslav Minister that the article fully expressed his government's views towards the latest events in Yugoslavia.
24 For a full account of the negotiations between the Yugoslav delegation and the Russians, based on Gavrilović's reports to his government and conversations with the author, see Hoptner, 276–81. According to this account, the Russians wished to substitute for the crucial Article 2 of the draft treaty a statement to the effect that if one of the parties were attacked, the other would preserve its policy of neutrality and friendship. Gavrilović strongly objected to the introduction of the word 'neutrality', which he argued would completely destroy the effect of the treaty, and refused to sign the proposed text, even after receiving telephoned instructions from General Simović to do so. The impasse was resolved on Stalin's personal intervention, when the reference to neutrality was removed. The Soviet authorities also renewed their promises to arrange the immediate delivery of arms, munitions, and planes, though this was not specified in the treaty. No steps were taken, however, to implement these promises.
25 Eden, puzzled that the Soviet Government should have taken 'so defiant, if ineffective a step' as to conclude a treaty with a government brought to power by the anti-German coup of 27 March 1941, subsequently asked Stalin for his reasons. Stalin gave the unconvincing explanation that 'there was not really any new risk in it, because the Russians were fairly sure by then that they were going to be attacked', and secondly, that 'he wished to make a gesture of solidarity at that time to a fellow Slav nation'. Eden comments that 'it looks as if this were a rare occasion when Stalin allowed his head to be influenced by his heart' (*The reckoning*, London, 1965, 237–8).
26 FRUS, 1941, i. 311.
27 According to Stojan Gavrilović, an official accompanying the Yugoslav Government, the Russian emissaries were eight in number (FO 371/30226–R 6394/297/92). Djilas

states that the Yugoslav Foreign Minister was also approached with an offer of co-operation from the CPY by the Bosnian communist Avdo Humo who had married his daughter Olga, Tito's secretary-interpreter during the war (*Memoirs*, 384).

28 Tempo, i. 181.

29 For some interesting details, see Djilas (*Memoirs*, 131–4), who writes that in the 30s 'the Central Committee and the Comintern emphasized the importance of cooperation with "national revolutionaries" in certain areas. . . . We had a common enemy—the government and the regime. . . . Both groups believed that Yugoslavia should be broken up into its component parts. . . . We instinctively felt that the Ustashe's action could only help further our own aim—the destruction of Yugoslavia. . . . Our Communist friendship was conditional and temporary', but even after relations had deteriorated some personal friendships formed between Ustasha and Communist leaders during periods of common struggle or imprisonment sometimes persisted.

30 Djilas (*Memoirs*, 192–3) makes an interesting assessment of Hebrang, whom the Russians were later to back against Tito. 'A strong man, he stood up staunchly in all struggles . . . tough, dignified, courageous, above average intelligence . . . serious-minded, quick to blow up but never out of control, stubborn and patient, a skilful conversationalist, with a clean past and considerable experience.'

31 Ante Ciliga, *La crisi di stato della Jugoslavia di Tito* (Rome, 1972), 225.

32 Directive to Kardelj and Vladimir Popović from the CPY CC, 4 Sept. 1941 (*Zbornik dokumenata*, ii/2, p. 56–7).

33 In early June Kopinič, on his own initiative, reported to Moscow that the Croat communist leaders were proving passive and opportunistic (Jovan Marjanović, Jugoslavija, KPJ i Kominterna in *Zbornik filosofskog fakulteta*, Belgrade, 1970, xi/i). See also Milatović, 52, Ciliga, 222–7. I. Sible, *Zagreb, tisuću devetsto četrdeset prve* (Zagreb, 1967), 306–7, contains an account by the then Secretary of the Municipal Committee, Antun Rob, who states that the instructions radioed from the Comintern to Kopinič and shown by him to the Committee instructed the telegraphist 'to make contact with the Municipal Committee for Zagreb, take over the lead in organizing actions, and isolate the Central Committee of the Croat Communist Party'. Kardelj, in a letter to Tito of 2 August 1941, gives his version of the affair and explains that Kopinič had undertaken his disastrous actions 'out of panic, omitting the most necessary preparations, without realising what the real conditions were. And besides—I am convinced —out of a subconscious desire to attack you and the whole leadership. I say "subconscious", but I do not rule out some deliberate intent. He lied to Grandpa [the Comintern] at the most critical time and destroyed the Party. His role has been that of a real provocateur. Besides, he has been politically useless. He has had no idea of what advice to give. He simply said just what they have been saying—we must act. But how to set about it he has no idea. No wonder that the two actions he carried out ended in disaster. That is irreponsible behaviour which cannot be forgiven' (*Zbornik documenata* ii. 2, pp. 28–9).

34 See Tito's letter to the Secretary of the Croat CP, 12 September 1941, instructing him to inquire whether Tito's reports were being properly transmitted to Moscow over the secret radio link (*Zbornik dokumenata*, ii/2, p. 63).

35 Luka Fertilio, press attaché at the Croat legation in Berlin, describes an approach made to him at an official German press conference by a Soviet press correspondent who allegedly gave him the following message from his ambassador: 'The Government of the Soviet Union has always followed with great interest the struggle of the Croat people for state independence and has greeted with satisfaction the news of the proclamation of the Independent Croat State.' Fertilio wrote down this message and passed it to the head of his mission. The Soviet correspondent added that his government had withdrawn recognition from the Yugoslav minister in Moscow and implied that the way was now open for the accrediting of a Croat diplomat (*Hrvatska Revija*, Buenos Aires, Dec. 1960, 625).

36 Dedijer (*Prilozi*, 294; *Tito speaks*, 143), gives a slightly different version of this incident and states that Tito sent the report to Dimitrov in Moscow by radiogram.

37 Dušan Plenča, *Medjunarodni odnosi Jugoslavije u toku drugog svjetskog rata* (Belgrade, 1962), 30, which contains the fullest study of the relations between the Soviet Government and the Yugoslav Government in Exile, based on correspondence between the two governments now in archives in Belgrade. Some material is also to be found in C. Fotich,

Notes to pages 12–14   97

38 *The war we lost: Yugoslavia's tragedy and the failure of the West* (New York, 1948). FO371/33490.
39 Plenča, 30–2. The Yugoslav Government, Ninčić declared to a Foreign Office official, 'must at all costs avoid any attempt by the Soviet Union to try to send a force to Yugoslavia at the end of the war before the Yugoslav forces to be established in N. America and the Middle East could themselves return to Yugoslavia and bring back the rightful Government' (Minute of 11.7. 41, FO 371/30228).
40 Statement by Lozovsky, Deputy Chief of the Soviet Information Bureau (*The Times*, 6 Aug. 1941).
41 Plenča, 32.
42 'The messages were addressed to Dimitrov and signed by Tito with his Comintern name of Valter. They were written in Russian, usually in his own hand—mostly in pencil with his own corrections and careful punctuation, on sheets from an ordinary notebook which he kept in his satchel' (Auty, 203). Signals from the Comintern were signed 'Grandpa'. Since it was not until February of the following year that he managed to establish regular radio communications with Moscow from his headquarters at Foča, they had to be sent by courier to Zagreb for transmission over the secret transmitter. Some may also have been sent by courier to Sofia, where the Soviet legation served the Russians as a useful observation post in the Balkans.
43 *The Times*, 9 Aug. 1941.
44 Article by Veljko Vlahović, Yugoslav representative in the Comintern at that time, in *Socijalizam* (1959), 53.
45 Each side had been quick to recognize in the other its mortal enemy. Djilas writes that, at an early stage, 'a decision was made to denounce the [Chetnik] officers, to begin an armed struggle against them, as well as against the Ustashi and their crimes. The most important thing was to collect arms and set up committees. . . . Tito informed Moscow of the Central Committee's new position. Moscow responded with some fairly sharp criticism. Dimitrov pointed out that we Yugoslavs were now faced with a national liberation struggle, and not a proletarian revolution. Tito retreated from his position. At least in words. But words later had an important effect on deeds. Some of the Comintern's terminology of national struggle entered our own "people's liberation" jargon' (*Memoirs*, 389). The very term *narodno oslobodjenje* has an ambivalent connotation and can be variously rendered as 'national liberation' or 'people's liberation' (the former is preferred in the context of the war, when it was in common use, whereas in the postwar period, when the regime was frankly committed to a socialist revolution, *narodni* is generally translated as 'people's' or 'popular', e.g., People's Republic, People's Democracy, etc.).
46 Dedijer, *Prilozi*, 330. The belief that Tito was a Russian probably deepened Mihailović's suspicions of his movement and reduced the chances of any agreement being reached between them. It may also have prompted the early reports put about by Mihailović supporters in the West identifying the then unknown 'Tito' with V. Z. Lebedev, a Soviet official who had been sent to prepare the ground for the formal opening of the Soviet legation in Belgrade (F. W. D. Deakin, *The embattled mountain*, London, 1971, 203–6). After the Axis invasion of Yugoslavia, Lebedev reappeared in the Soviet legation in Sofia, through which the Partisans appear to have maintained contact by courier with Moscow. Lebedev later served as Soviet ambassador in Poland and Finland, being replaced by Stalin in the former post, according to Khrushchev, (*Khrushchev remembers*, London, 1974, ii. 168), 'because his activities exceeded the proper functions of an ambassador—he apparently tried to force his views on the Polish comrades and subjugate them'. No evidence, however, has come to light of his having made similar attempts to influence the Yugoslav communist leaders.
47 Though this is not explicitly stated in Partisan accounts, it seems probable that Tito did make an offer of subordination but hedged it round with conditions, e.g., all-out attacks on the Germans, to which he knew Mihailović would not agree. Tito himself is reported as saying, 'I offered him the supreme command; it was clear, however, that he would not accept it' (Auty, 191).
48 Dragičević, the Yugoslav wireless operator sent in with the first British military mission, stayed on with the Partisans when Captain Hudson left them for Mihailović's headquarters, and his set may have been used for a time for communications with Moscow (Deakin, 136–7, 146).

49 Radio Free Yugoslavia, which purported to be somewhere in Yugoslavia, operated from Ufa in the Urals and began broadcasting early in November 1941. It made no mention of the conflict between Partisans and Chetniks, or the latter's accommodations with the Germans, until April 1942.
50 Dedijer (*Prilozi*, 322) describes the consternation and indignation of Tito and his companions on listening to this broadcast.
51 According to Julian Amery (*Approach march*, London, 1973, 259–60), who was a member of the Special Operations Executive in touch with Djonović, the Yugoslav Government's undercover representative in Turkey, a message had been received there from Mihailović before the end of July 1941 and its contents communicated to the Russians. The latter, after consultations with Moscow, 'offered to provide an aircraft to fly in a mixed Yugoslav-British-Soviet military mission to Mihailović's head-quarters'. The aircraft was to fly in from a base at Leninaken in Soviet Armenia and was ready to leave in the middle of September. Preparations were set in train by SOE to recruit a British element for this joint venture at about the same time as the first British liaison officer (Captain Hudson) and two Yugoslav officers were on their way by submarine to land on the Montenegrin coast. However, the Yugoslav Government, through General Ilić, their War Minister in Cairo, induced SOE to countermand the instructions given. The Russians surmised from this that the British and the Yugoslav Government in Exile were determined to exclude their influence from the Balkans, and their representative in Istanbul was instructed 'not to do business with us'.
52 When Maisky saw Eden on 22 October he proposed that their two governments should 'concert plans' and encourage the rising in every way. He also presented a list, apparently obtained from the Yugoslav Government, of items urgently needed by the rebels. These included W/T sets, batteries of mountain artillery, 5 tons of dynamite, and large quantities of grenades and Bren guns. At a further meeting five days later, Eden told Maisky that the British were in radio contact with Mihailović and were preparing to send in supplies to him in aircraft operating from Malta and Cairo. Maisky urged that supplies should also be sent by sea to the rebels in Montenegro (FO 371/30220). To relieve the pressure of the German onslaught, the Russians would at this stage even have welcomed a British landing in the Balkans (or in France) and appeals for the speedy opening of such a front were made to Churchill by Stalin (Eden, *The reckoning*, 275). Moscow's attitude to a possible British landing in Yugoslavia changed as it became clear that the Red Army would itself be able to advance into the Balkans.
53 FO 371/30220. On 31 October Eden told the War Cabinet that he was 'disturbed' by the instructions broadcast by the Yugoslav Prime Minister to the insurgents to pursue a cautious policy. The need for sabotage against the Germans in Yugoslavia was also urged by some War Office departments (FO 371/30221).
54 FO 371/30221.
55 Dedijer, *Tito speaks*, 170–1.
56 V. Kljaković, Velika Britanija, Sovjetski Savez i Ustanak u Jugoslaviji 1941 godine, *Vojnoistorijski glasnik*, May–Aug. 1970, 101. A similar communication was made to the British Embassy in Kuibyshev by Vyshinsky, who declined to be more explicit even when it was pointed out to him that 'it was impossible to achieve that co-operation to which Molotov had agreed in principle unless HMG could be informed why joint action in this important matter was considered inexpedient'. The Foreign Office minute commenting on the cable reporting this conversation (13.1.42) concluded that the Russians 'don't want to send instructions which would hamper the Communist partisans; they hope the Communist faction will be the one with the greatest influence in Yugoslavia when the German armies finally retreat' (FO 371/33465).
57 FO 371/33490.
58 Ibid.
59 Fotich, 173–4.
60 Plenča, 149.
61 Ibid., 149–50.
62 A copy of the Soviet memorandum (39) was handed by Maisky to Eden who 'expressed great surprise at the information contained in the memorandum and said it did not at all bear out our own information which was to the effect that General Mihailović . . . and the partisans were both resisting the Axis separately'. The following day (8 August) the memorandum was discussed at a meeting held by Sir Orme Sargent and seems to

have proved an important factor in starting up the process of reconsidering British policy towards developments in Yugoslavia (FO 371/33490).

63 Plenča, 151.
64 Ibid., 154.
65 Ibid., 151.
66 Eden to Rendel FO 371/37578.
67 FO 371/37606.
68 Plenča, 161.
69 Ibid.
70 FO 371/37663.
71 Plenča, 176.
72 The fullest account so far available of British policy towards Yugoslavia during the war, and its interaction with Soviet policy, will be found in Woodward, iii. 278–382, and P. Auty & R. Clogg, eds, *British policy towards wartime resistance in Yugoslavia and Greece* (London, 1975).
73 Churchill to Jovanović FO 371/37582.
74 Plenča, 176–7. The British were by now seriously thinking of establishing contact with the Partisans and 'decided in the first instance to ask for Soviet assistance . . . [but] as a result of this rebuff we are now considering whether it is practically possible to establish contact with the Partisans without Soviet help' (FO 371/37583). This was done, and the Soviet Government was informed that liaison missions had been established with the Partisans with a view 'to effect co-operation and unity between all resistance groups in Yugoslavia' (FO 371/37588). This communication was acknowledged by Molotov in terms which—in view of his previously negative attitude—the Foreign Office considered 'most helpful and forthcoming' (ibid.).
75 Plenča, 177.
76 Ibid., 183.
77 *Hronologija oslobodilačke borbe naroda Jugoslavije 1941–5* (Belgrade, 1964), entry for 16 Sept. 1943.
78 Plenča, 207–8.
79 *Zbornik dokumenata*, ii/2, pp. 729–30.
80 There is some evidence from Yugoslav sources that the Russians did make an early and unsuccessful attempt to send in men to the Partisans, but there is no confirmation of this from Soviet sources. According to Djilas (*Conversations with Stalin*, 1962, 34), 'as early as 1941–2 Soviet pilots tried to get through to Yugoslav Partisan bases, and some homeward-bound Yugoslav émigrés who had flown with them had been frozen'.
81 *Zbornik dokumenata*, ii/4, p. 27.
82 See Pijade, *About the legend that the Yugoslav uprising owed its existence to Soviet assistance* (London, 1950). For the Serbo-Croat version of this tract, see Pijade's *Izabrani spisi* (Belgrade, 1966) i/5 pp. 771–96.
83 Auty, 205.
84 An exception was the small group headed by Dr Ivan Ribar, former President of the first National Assembly, whose son Ivo (Lola) was a leader of the Communist Youth.
85 *Zbornik dokumenata*, ii/3, p. 107. Pijade was inclined to think that the Comintern's criticisms were to some extent justified and called for some revision of the CPY's line. But Tito remained quite firm, and wrote to his friend on 26 March: 'You made me very angry with you when you began to philosophize as to whether we had indeed made a mistake and gone too far to the Left. You must know that long before I had received the Comintern telegram I had made our position quite clear about not attacking the pro-English elements simply because they were pro-English, but as lackeys of the invaders, and that we must not let Fifth Columnists entice us away from the line of the struggle of national liberation to that of the class struggle. The Comintern dropped the subject after my explanations', (ibid., 210).
86 Tito's signal reporting the arrival of Major Atherton is dated 5 March 1942. This appears to be an error, since his mission did not reach Partisan headquarters at Foča until 20 March. For an account of the Atherton affair, see Deakin, 155–77.
87 Atherton had instructions to obtain a broader and more accurate picture of resistance groups in Yugoslavia and to locate Captain Hudson, with whom radio contact had been lost after the suppression of the rising in Serbia. Atherton's W/T set also failed to work, but Tito suspected that it was being used to transmit secret reports about the

Partisans to the British. After slipping away from Tito's headquarter's, Atherton appears to have been robbed and killed by a Bosnian Chetnik, but Mihailović was quick to throw the blame on the Partisans.

88 On 8 April 1942 a confidential letter was sent by Tito to the Croatia CP CC warning that 'we have now certain proof that the British, through their agents in Yugoslavia, are working not to remove, but rather to intensify, the differences between ourselves and other groups such as the Chetniks. . . . In public, the alliance between the Soviet Union, Britain, and the United States must continue to be stressed, and the latter two Powers are to be depicted as our allies. But their agents and pawns inside our country must be opposed' (Deakin, 177–1; S. Clissold, *Whirlwind*, London, 1949, 86–7.

89 P. Morača, 'Odnosi izmedju Komunističke partije Jugoslavije i Kominterne od 1941 do 1943 godine' (*Jugoslovenski Istoriski Časopis*, 1961, No. 1. At the beginning of July Radio Free Yugoslavia broadcast a resolution of the 'Patriots of Montenegro, Sandžak and Bosnia', which Tito forwarded to the Comintern, branding the Chetniks of Draža Mihailović as collaborators and also denouncing the attitude of the Government in Exile. The initiative for broadcasting these criticisms seems to have been taken by Vlahović, who was reprimanded by Molotov for acting without orders and made to tighten up censorship procedures (*Socijalizam*, 1959, 53).

90 Auty, 209.

91 *Hronologija*, entry for 23 Jan. 1943.

92 The text of this signal has not been published, but its content was later communicated by Tito to Brigadier Maclean (Maclean, 206 & 468 n.). It is also referred to in Auty, 214 & 315. Yugoslav historians, still apparently fearful that the approaches made in February 1943 to the Germans would be misrepresented as collaboration, remain very reticent about the incident. But see Djilas (*Conversations*, 13–14) and W. R. Roberts, *Tito, Mihailović and the allies* (Rutgers, 1973), 106–12. For the earlier exchange of prisoners, the execution of the three agents, and Hebrang's alleged espionage, see Milatović, 203 ff.

93 Djilas, *Conversations*, 13–14.

94 Cable to the Comintern reporting that the Partisans were breaking through the Chetnik lines (*Hronologija*, entry for 13 Mar. 1943).

95 For this mission, and of the events leading to its dispatch, see the account written by its surviving officer, F. W. D. Deakin.

96 Djilas makes the reasons for this quite clear. 'During the preparations for the Resolutions in meetings of the Central Committee of the CPY, we were determined that Moscow should not be informed until after it was all over. We knew from previous experience of Moscow and its line of propaganda that it would not be capable of understanding' (*Conversations,* 14). Shortly before the Jajce meeting, the Russians had dropped an intelligence mission, the main purpose of which appears to have been infiltration into Bulgaria. Its Bulgarian-born leader, Sterija Atanasov-Viktor, was told about the proposed meeting and allowed to communicate over the link with Moscow; but the details of the proposed resolutions were not divulged to him (Dedijer, *Battle,* 51–2).

97 Dedijer, *Prilozi*, 358; Djilas, *Conversations*, 14; article by Vlahović, *Borba*, 29 Nov. 1953.

98 Morača, 128.

99 Following the 1948 break with the Cominform, Yugoslav apologists have claimed that the decision to disband the Comintern was 'accepted with great relief', that the Comintern's guiding hand, both before and during the war, had in fact hindered the growth of individual indigenous CPs, and that the disbanding of the Comintern amounted to the recognition that 'developments inside Yugoslavia were a matter for its own working class and not the concern of the Comintern and the USSR' (ibid., 128–30). It is hard to substantiate from contemporary evidence that this was the view of the Yugoslav communist leaders at the time.

100 Plenča, 70–1.

101 Ibid., 360–1; *Weg und Ziel* (Vienna), No. 9, 1973, pp. 334–8.

102 For the role of the Yugoslav communists in Albania, see V. Dedijer, *Jugoslovensko-albanski odnosi, 1939–48* (Belgrade, 1949), and N. L. Pano, *The People's Republic of Albania* (Baltimore, 1968).

103 For the Macedonia problem and the Soviet attitude to it, see Tempo, i. 307–61; Shoup,

82–3; Plenča, 64–9; S. E. Palmer & R. R. King, *Yugoslav communism and the Macedonian question* (Hamden, Conn., 1971); E. Barker, *Macedonia—its place in Balkan power politics* (London, 1950); E. Kofos, *Nationalism and communism in Macedonia* (Salonika, 1964), and *Macedonian nationalism and the communist Party of Yugoslavia* (Washington, 1954).

104 Šatorov-Šarlo (or 'Charlot', the name by which Charlie Chaplin was known, and a pseudonym popular at the time in left-wing circles) had attended the 5th Conference of the CPY in Zagreb where he had clashed with Djilas. As a disciplined communist, who had himself worked in the Comintern's headquarters and knew its thinking, it seems likely that his subsequent repudiation of CPY authority would have stemmed from Comintern instructions rather than personal initiative, especially as, although a former member of the Bulgarian CP, he is not thought to have had pro-Bulgarian sympathies (see Marjanović Jugoslavija, KPJ: Kominterna).

105 The Bulgarian representative was Bojan Bulgaranov, who had previously worked in Moscow for the Comintern. From conversations with him, Vukmanović-Tempo, the Yugoslav delegate, gained the impression that 'there were differences between us and Moscow, and that Moscow in reality did not approve the line we had taken'. Tempo exchanged heated words with Bulgaranov who threatened that he would be made to answer to the Comintern (Tempo, i. 317, 320).

106 *Zbornik dokumenata*, vii/1, pp. 16–17.

107 The Greek CP, after some initial reluctance, supported Comintern plans for an independent Macedonian state (which would have included Aegean Macedonia) until 1935, when the switch to Popular Front tactics necessitated a change of line. In 1949 the Party resumed agitation for an independent Macedonia as a means of making trouble for Yugoslavia, after the latter's expulsion from the Cominform (see G. Kousoulas, *Revolution and defeat*, London, 1965, 55–72 & 263).

108 Pijade, *Legend*, 23.

109 FRUS, *The conferences at Cairo and Teheran*, 537.

110 Ibid.

111 Churchill, *Closing the ring* (London, 1952), 370.

112 FRUS, *The conferences at Cairo and Teheran*, 575; FO 371/37591. The Soviet and British Governments seem to have shifted their ground on the question of a Soviet mission being sent to Mihailović. An early proposal for a joint British-Soviet mission had been put forward by the Russians and turned down by the British and Yugoslav Governments. By the spring of 1942, the British Government seems to have thought that the Russians may have established independent links with Mihailović, for on 27 March Eden approached Maisky for help in locating the whereabouts of the Chetnik leader, with whom the British had temporarily lost contact, since 'it occurs to Mr Eden that the Soviet Government may have means of communicating with General Mihailović' (FO 371/33466). Moscow replied that 'unfortunately they had no communication now with Yugoslavia at all' (FO 371/33467). The Foreign Office doubted the truth of this claim and thought it possible that they were in touch through their legation in Sofia with the Partisans and possibly with Mihailović as well (FO 371/33466; 371/33467). Though at Teheran the initiative for a proposed mission to Mihailović is described as coming from the Russians, Eden, in reporting his talks in Moscow only a few weeks before, says that he had himself proposed that the Russians should consider sending missions to both sides, 'or at least one or two officers to Mihailović. . . . Molotov did not much favour this idea and hinted that he might prefer to have no mission at all rather than one to each side' (Telegram from Moscow to the FO of 31.10.1943, FO 371/37614). Yet, when Stevenson, the British ambassador to the Government in Exile, reported that the senior British liaison officer at Mihailović's headquarters had been sounded out and believed that Mihailović would accept a Soviet mission if offered one (Cairo telegram to the FO of 20.11.1943, FO 371/37616), Sir Orme Sargent, the Permanent Under-Secretary at the FO, minuted (9.12.1943): 'Has anyone ever suggested that the Soviet Government should send a mission to Mihailović?'.

113 *Military conclusions of the Teheran Conference* (London, 1947).

114 Report dated 23.1.1944, quoted by Plenča, 220–1. President Wilson had proposed that the Italo-Yugoslav frontier in Istria should be drawn in accordance with the principle of national self-determination, but the Italian Government, with whom the allies had concluded the 1915 secret Treaty of London which envisaged the cession to Italy of

areas of Istria and Dalmatia predominantly inhabited by Slavs, rejected the proposed 'Wilson line'.

115 FO 371/37606.

116 Simić had decided to break with the Purić Government some months before. He had sent his letter to *Pravda* in November 1943, but publication was withheld until the following March.

117 Among the aspects of Yugoslav affairs discussed, according to a report of 12 October 1944 from Averell Harriman to Roosevelt, were the following: 'The Prime Minister took Stalin to task for receiving Tito without informing him. The only explanation that Stalin gave was that Tito had asked him to keep his visit secret. Stalin explained that he had never seen Tito before, although he had lived in Russia during 1917 and 1918. At Tito's request he had promised to give him arms, principally captured German but also some Russian. It was agreed between Stalin and the Prime Minister that they should work together in attempting to bring the Yugoslav peoples together for the establishment of a strong federation but that if it was found that such a federation was impracticable without continued internal strife Serbia should be established as an independent country. Both agreed that the former was far more desirable and the latter was only the last resort. This led to an interesting statement by Stalin on the subject of Pan-Slavism which he said he considered as an unrealistic conception. What the different Slavic people wanted was their independence. Pan-Slavism if pursued meant domination of the Slavic countries by Russia. This was against Russia's interest and would never satisfy the smaller Slavic countries. He said he felt he would have to make a public statement before long to make this clear. In connection with Yugoslavia, Churchill explained that England had no "sordid interests" but wished to see her moral obligations to the Yugoslavs fulfilled. Stalin brushed this side saying that he did not consider British [interests] in Yugoslavia as sordid. They were very real interests, both in mining concessions but principally because Yugoslavia had a long stretch of Mediterranean coast. Protection of the Mediterranean was vital to Great Britain's world communications. Stalin recognised and approved these interests' (FRUS, 1944, 1013–14).

118 Churchill, *Triumph and tragedy* (London, 1954), 198–204. Molotov subsequently tried to modify the 50–50 arrangement to 75–25 in favour of the Soviet Union, but desisted in face of strong opposition from Eden (Woodward, iii. 350). In a memo. of 12 October addressed 'to my colleagues' Churchill commented on the arrangement as follows: 'The symbol 50–50 is intended to be the foundation of joint action and an agreed policy between the two powers now closely involved, so as to favour the creation of a united Yugoslavia after all the elements there have been joined together to the utmost in driving out the Nazi invaders. It is intended to prevent, for instance, armed strife between the Croats and Slovenes on the one side and powerful and numerous elements in Serbia on the other, and also to produce a just and friendly policy towards Marshal Tito, while ensuring that weapons furnished to him are used against the common Nazi foe rather than for internal purposes. Such a policy, pursued in common by Britain and Soviet Russia, without any thought of special advantage to themselves, would be of real benefit.' That Churchill did not intend to conceal the arrangement from Tito, but assumed rather that the Russians would inform him of it, is clear from the following message he sent, via Brigadier Maclean, to Tito on 3 December 1944 complaining about lack of co-operation from subordinate Partisan commanders; 'As you know, we have made an arrangement with the Marshal and the Soviet Government to pursue as far as possible a joint policy towards Yugoslavia, and that our influence there should be held in equal balance. But you seem to be treating us in an increasingly invidious fashion' (FO 371/44293).

119 Speaking of the Yalta agreements in an interview (*Paris Match,* 16 Nov. 1968) Tito declared that 'the agreement stipulated a division on the basis of fifty-fifty, which meant putting in an estimate without consulting those who were to foot the bill. We have energetically rejected such an agreement, which was concluded to the disadvantage of our country. That was our first bone of contention with the Soviet Union. It certainly made Stalin lose his temper.' The issue of principle involved was defined in *Borba* (27 Aug. 1968) as follows: 'The League of Communists and the Socialist Alliance of Yugoslavia do not recognize any agreement—either explicit or implied—on spheres of interest which, by virtue of superior power, transform small nations into mere

political pawns.' Yet Yugoslavia nevertheless claimed just such a sphere of influence over her small neighbour Albania.

120 Churchill, *Triumph and tragedy*, 304–5.
121 Churchill declared that 'if Marshal Stalin said two words to Tito, this matter would be settled. Marshal Stalin replied that Tito is a proud man and he now was a popular head of a regime and might resist advice. The Prime Minister replied that Marshal Stalin could risk this. Marshal Stalin replied that he was not afraid' (FRUS, *The Conferences at Malta and Yalta*, 781–2). Churchill also referred to the situation after the war and expressed the hope 'that peace will come on the basis of amnesty, but they hate each other so much that they cannot keep their hands off each other in Yugoslavia. Stalin (smiling): "They are not yet accustomed to discussions. Instead, they cut each other's throats." ' (Ibid., 791).
122 The third amendment proposed by the British was to the effect that 'the Government is only temporary pending the free expression of the will of the people'. This the Russians refused to accept on the grounds that it would be offensive to Yugoslav susceptibilities. (Ibid., 909.)
123 Šubašić had been to Moscow the previous November to see Stalin who told him—perhaps to reassure his Western sponsors—that 'the Yugoslavs must not try any revolutionary experiments or attempt an imitation of the Soviet regime. The elections must be free and on democratic lines' (Woodward, iii. 353).
124 The Soviet mission flew into Yugoslavia via Egypt and Italy. Deakin, the British liaison officer who had the task of briefing them in Cairo, records that 'I sensed that my interpretation of Yugoslav affairs had made little impression upon the Russians, and that they had the conviction, possibly as the result of their own instructions, that the British were playing a highly subtle game; that we had little confidence in the military value of the Partisans of Tito, that our support of his movement had some subtle and devious political design; and that the only resistance group of any military significance was in effect that of Mihailović whom we now affected to ignore as a decisive factor. I had no confirmation at the time of this intuition, but recently I had occasion to meet a member of this delegation, who admitted to me that I had not made the wrong general assumption' (Deakin, 265). Shortly before the arrival of the mission, Stevenson, the British ambassador to the Yugoslav Government in Exile, reported to the FO that his Soviet colleague had confided to him his government's intention to send the mission first to Tito then to Mihailović. Stevenson pointed out the physical difficulty of such an operation, to which the Soviet representative replied that the mission could be divided and a part of it sent to each side. Stevenson then reminded him that policy towards Mihailović was under review by the British government, and that it was essential to preserve a common policy between the allies with regard to Yugoslavia (FO 371/37663).
125 Maclean, 253. Maclean adds that 'Tito had soon grasped that these were not the men to comprehend his point of view, still less to convey it successfully to Stalin. As to interpreting the Party line, Tito did not, or thought he did not, require their help. Still less did he want their advice on military matters. There was one thing he could hope for from them—that they would provide him with an additional channel of supply. When he realised that there was at present no question of this . . . he began to lose interest'. According to Djilas (*Conversations*, 103) Stalin himself had only a poor opinion of the man he had chosen to head the mission to Tito. 'The poor man is not stupid', Stalin is said to have remarked, 'but he is a drunkard, an incurable drunkard!'—an opinion which was to be borne out by the quantities of liquor the Russians had flown in.
126 Djilas, *Conversations*, 18.
127 Ibid.; Dedijer, *Dnevnik* (Belgrade, 1970) iii. 156. The completed section of Dedijer's diary, the fullest first-hand documentary source for the history of the Partisan war, was also sent to Russia for safe-keeping.
128 Pavelić had raised a Croat Legion, commanded by Colonel Marko Mesić, and sent it to fight on the eastern front as a gesture of solidarity with the Germans. It surrendered to the Russians in the fighting round Stalingrad.
129 Plenča, 244.
130 Djilas, *Conversations*, 62–3.
131 Ibid., 66–80. Djilas describes this revealing interview in detail.
132 Short excerpts only of this letter have been published in Russian sources (*Istoriya velikoi otechestvennoi voiny*, Moscow, 1962, iv. 417, 419, 420 quoted by Sava D. Bosnitch

in *Review*, London Study Centre for Yugoslav Affairs, 1969, No. 8, p. 697). Yugoslav historians make no mention of this letter.

133 The secrecy with which Tito left Vis, without notifying the British military mission or the authorities in operational control of the airfield, appears to have been on specific Russian advice and was in line with the warnings which Stalin had sent him through Djilas to be on his guard against the treachery of the British if he wished to avoid the fate of General Sikorski. 'It seems possible that the object of the Russians in insisting on secrecy was to make trouble between Tito and the British. If so, they were entirely successful. Mr Churchill was particularly annoyed by this clandestine departure and in an indignant telegram spoke of Tito as having "levanted" from Vis' (Maclean, 280 n.) Eden relates that when he complained of this incident in Moscow in October, 'Molotov hurriedly put all the blame on Tito. He said he was a peasant and did not understand anything about politics; that he had the secretiveness of his type and had not dared to impart his plans to anyone' (Eden, *The reckoning*, 482).

134 For Tito's visit to Moscow see Dedijer, *Prilozi*, 411–15, Maclean, 280–4, and Auty, 242–4.

135 Plenča, 343.

136 *Borba*, 25 Dec. 1951, and *Politika*, 20 Oct. 1951.

137 *Istoriya Iugoslavii* (Moscow, 1963), ii. 241; V. Volkov, Nekotorie voprosi osvoboditelnoi borbi iugoslavskikh narodov v godi vtoroi mirovoi voiny v osveshchenii iugoslavsko-istoricheskoi literaturi, *Novaya i noveishaya istoriya*, 1960, 126–38.

138 The message sent to King Peter II by King George VI congratulating him on 'the liberation of Belgrade by the forces of our gallant ally, helped by the stout resistance of its citizens' indicates the view taken by the British of the operations round the Yugoslav capital. A telegram from the FO to Cairo (1413 of 21.10.43) commenting on this message observes that 'we do not propose that any message should be sent to Tito whose troops in any case have played little or no part in Belgrade's liberation' (FO 371/44306).

139 *The Times*, 9 Mar. 1945.

140 Sava D. Bosnitch (705–6), who probably overestimates the Chetniks' capacity or will for 'sustained action against the Germans'. Though they were sometimes able to take over momentarily as the Germans began to pull out of Serbia, their strength had been eroded by the defection of several important commanders to the Partisans, and their morale sapped by habits of passivity vis-à-vis the Germans and of accommodation with the Nedić authorities. Their withdrawal with the latter from Serbia was more the outcome of their own policies and of the realization of their military inferiority to the Partisans than of action against them by the Red Army, which was heavily engaged in the operations against the Germans and attached little importance either to the Chetniks or to the Partisans.

141 According to Soviet sources, *Sovetskie vooruzhonnye sily v borbe za osvobozhdeniye Iugoslavii* (Moscow, 1960) 50–3 the total quantity of arms and equipment, not counting unspecified armounts of ammunition, uniforms, rations, medical and other supplies, amounted to 96,515 rifles and carbines, 20,528 revolvers, 68,819 machine-guns, sub-machine guns and automatic rifles, 3,797 anti-tank rifles, 3,364 mortars, 170 anti-tank guns, 895 guns of different calibre, 491 aeroplanes, 65 tanks, 1,329 wireless sets, and 11 field hospitals.

142 Plenča, 345.

143 Djilas, *Conversations*, 104.

144 *Borba*, 11 Nov. 1947, quoted by Bosnitch, who gives a useful survey of this polemic. He concludes that Yugoslav historians now tend 'to accept tacitly the Soviet interpretations that assigned the partisans a valiant, but somewhat minute auxiliary role in these historical events, and that the Soviet-Yugoslav symposium entitled *The Belgrade operation*, published to mark the 20th anniversary of the liberation of Serbia, represents a direct and explicit reversal of Yugoslav attitudes . . . a veritable historiographic Canossa'. Bosnitch himself believes that 'it was the Soviet army that liberated the major part of Serbia and Eastern Yugoslavia' and that 'it was the Red Army that made the Communist seizure of power an historical "inevitability" '.

145 F. Tudjman, *Stvaranje socijalističke Jugoslavije* (Zagreb, 1960) 95.

146 *The Times*, 9 Mar. 1945.

147 Djilas, *Conversations*, 82.

148 Though Tito put the matter mildly to General Korneyev, formality was given to the protest by the presence of two Partisan generals, Koča Popović and Peko Dapčević, as well as the political leaders, Kardelj, Ranković, and Djilas. The exact words used by the latter, according to his own account, were: 'our enemies are using this against us and are comparing the attacks by Red Army soldiers with the behaviour of the English officers who do not indulge in such excesses'. To this General Korneyev angrily replied: 'In the name of the Soviet Government, I protest against such insinuations of the Red Army. . . . I protest most sharply against the insult to the Red Army in comparing it with the armies of capitalist countries'. Djilas adds that 'the interview with Korneyev ended without results, though we did notice later that the Soviet commands treated their soldiers' misdemeanours more strictly'. Djilas' outspokenness was not forgiven by the Russians and his gradual change of attitude towards the latter even began to alarm his own comrades. 'These words of mine, and a few other matters, were the cause of the first friction between the Yugoslav and Soviet leaders. . . . Because of my declaration, I soon found myself almost isolated, not particularly because my closest friends condemned me—though there were indeed some severe reproaches—or because the Soviet leaders had exaggerated the incident, but . . . because of my own inner experiences' (*Conversations*, 82–4).
149 For other examples of friction between the Yugoslavs and the Soviet military see Tempo, Vol. ii, Chap. 2.
150 Djilas, *Conversations*, 115.
151 The operation of the joint companies and Yugoslav objections to them, are described in Dedijer, *Prilozi*, 454–67 and *Battle* 73–96, based on material supplied by Kardelj, the chief architect of Yugoslavia's economic plans, and Vlatko Velebit, the official in charge of negotiating them. Velebit had been a stalwart Party member, in whose Zagreb villa the Comintern's secret transmitter had operated during the war, but his refusal to accept the onerous conditions implicit in the joint companies led the Russians to brand him an 'English spy' (Dedijer, *Battle*, 84).
152 See Tempo (ii. 31), then in charge of the CPY's work in the Yugoslav army. On 22 December 1947 the Yugoslav leaders formally recognized the distinctive character of the Partisans' military tradition by introducing the celebration of 'Yugoslav Army Day', and thus 'for the first time, proclaimed that an important aspect of Soviet experience was not fully applicable to Yugoslavia' (A. Ross Johnson, *The transformation of communist ideology: the Yugoslav case, 1945–53*, Cambridge, Mass., 35).
153 Djilas, *Conversations*, 87, 43.
154 Dedijer, *Prilozi*, 443.
155 H. F. Armstrong, *Tito and Goliath* (London, 1951), 76.
156 Dedijer, *Battle*, 211.
157 Ibid., 193–6. Dedijer contends that the mixed Yugoslav-Albanian companies differed from the Soviet model in that they fully safeguarded Albania's interests and genuinely aimed at expanding her productive forces.
158 Djilas, *Conversations*, 120 ff.
159 Pijade, *Izabrani spisi*, i/5, 745.
160 On 9 October 1943 Tito wrote to Tempo: 'In our opinion, and also in that of Grandpa [the Comintern], we should be in the centre for the Balkan countries, both in the military and the political sense' (*Zbornik dokumenata*, xi/10, 360–1).
161 In confidential talks with the Yugoslav Government in Exile, Maisky had outlined proposals for a postwar system of interlocking federations in Eastern Europe which would 'lean economically and militarily on Russia' (FRUS, 1941, i. 337–8.)
162 Both Dedijer (*Battle*, 33, 101) and Djilas (*Conversations*, 160) affirm this, though corroborative evidence is lacking.
163 For the text of this agreement see F. A. Voigt, *The Greek sedition* (London, 1949), 251–3.
164 Maclean, 340 n.
165 Auty, in Vucinich, ed., *Contemporary Yugoslavia* (Berkeley, 1969), 165.
166 I. Jukić, *Tito between East and West* (London, 1961), 13.
167 E. O'Ballance, *The Greek civil war, 1944–9* (London, 1966), 150; Voigt, 251.
168 Voigt, 254–8. In a letter written, apparently in January 1948, to the Secretary of the Greek CP Zachariadis, who was then in Moscow, Markos recalls the successive phases of the guerrilla struggle: 'Comrade Stalin's historic message of December 1944 which

5

induced us to launch the popular uprising' that failed; the plans laid for its resumption a year later at Petrich, after which 'on orders from Comrade Stalin to our northern neighbours, supplies of arms and ammunition began to arrive'; the later agreements 'by which we received fresh aid', and the price exacted for it—promise of 'the readjustment of our frontier in favour of our neighbours'. In 1947, Markos continued, volunteers abroad began to be formed into 'Foreign Legions', but 'Molotov, always for the sake of diplomacy, postponed their entry into the struggle until at last we came to December 1947, when he told us: Establish an official government . . . and we shall immediately recognise you.' Konitsa was chosen as the seat for the new government, and the Greek guerrillas attempted to take it, expecting that the Foreign Legions would help by launching an attack. But 'the attack was postponed by Moscow until fresh orders, and so was the announcement that the government would be recognised, until Moscow could see what the reaction on the British and the Americans would be'. The letter concludes with the complaint that authority had now passed to the Yugoslav-dominated Balkan Joint Staff and that 'we have reached the stage of carrying out orders without being allowed any initiative', and the threat that unless Moscow and the other communist capitals did more to carry out their promises, he would repudiate agreements which were bringing the Greek rebels no benefit.

169   K. Younger, *The Greek passion* (London, 1969), 263, and E. O'Ballance, 122.

170   Dedijer, *Prilozi*, 470.

171   According to Yugoslav accounts (ibid., 495–505; Djilas, *Conversations*, 154–68) the meeting was attended on the Bulgarian side by Dimitrov, Kolarov, and Kostov, and on the Yugoslav, by Kardelj, Djilas, and Bakarić, whilst the Soviet Union was represented by Stalin, Molotov, Malenkov, Zhdanov, Suslov, and Zorin.

172   Kardelj was so dispirited and agitated by this humiliating treatment that he affixed his signature in the wrong place and fresh copies of the treaty had to be prepared and signed. The text of the Treaty of Consultation has never been made public. It was abrogated by the Russians on the following 24 April (Dedijer, *Prilozi*, 504–5).

173   Dedijer, *Battle*, 149.

174   *Figaro*, 12 Feb. 1948.

175   The acrimonious exchange of correspondence began some time earlier. The Soviet letter of 27 March (**18**) refers to a Yugoslav letter of 18 March apparently complaining about unfriendly remarks attributed to the Soviet official Gargarinov, and to the Russians' alleged refusal to enter into trade negotiations. The text of this letter has not been made public.

176   The charge of 'Trotskyism' had first been levelled against the Partisans—ironically enough—by Mihailović and the Government in Exile, in an apparent effort to discredit them in Moscow (**40**). Even after their break with Stalin in 1948, the Yugoslav communists stopped short of any move towards a rehabilitation of Trotsky, though several approaches were made to them by the Fourth International (the 'orthodox' Trotskyites). But 'Tito's claim of merit in unifying the CPY after 1937 was in part based on his claim of successful struggle against Yugoslav Trotskyism. If Trotsky himself were to be rehabilitated, that claim would be negated, the infallibility of the CPY's policies under Tito's leadership would be brought in question' (A. Ross Johnson, 115). There were also fundamental differences of outlook in international affairs between Trotskyites and Titoists. The former, for instance, regarded the offensive in North Korea as just, whereas the Yugoslavs looked upon it as one more expression of Stalin's 'hegemonistic' foreign policy. The divergencies between Trotskyites and Titoists grew more pronounced when relations between Belgrade and Moscow later improved. The jail sentences passed on a group of young Trotskyites in July 1972 led to anti-Yugoslav protests by militants abroad (letter from Robin Blackburn and Tariq Ali in the *Observer*, 24 June 1973).

177   In Tito's own phrase, reported by Dedijer (*Prilozi*, 511).

178   Text given ibid., 516.

179   *Tempo*, ii. 65. The normal practice had been to hold meetings of the Politburo, often enlarged (as at the meeting on 1 March) to include other CC members such as Tempo, Žujović, Kidrič, etc.

180   Ibid., 92–3.

181   Dedijer, *Prilozi*, 529, 536.

182   Ibid., 542; Maclean, 393.

183   Dedijer, *Battle*, 124, 141. Žujović recanted and was later released; Hebrang, it was announced in 1952, committed suicide in prison.

184   Woodford D. McClellan, in *Contemporary Yugoslavia*, 130, 380. G. W. Hoffman and F. W. Neal, *Tito's Yugoslavia* (Berkeley, 1960), 142, give the higher figure of 14,000 over a four-year period.

185   Tempo, ii. 108. In *Khrushchev remembers* (ii. 181), Khrushchev is reported to have observed: 'I'm absolutely sure that if the Soviet Union had a common border with Yugoslavia, Stalin would have intervened militarily. As it was, though, he would have had to go through Bulgaria, and Stalin knew we weren't strong enough to get away with that. He was afraid the American imperialists would have actively supported the Yugoslavs'.

186   Tempo, who was put in charge of these preparations for Partisan warfare, has described them (105–8).

187   E. Halperin, *The Triumphant heretic* (London, 1958), 79–80.

188   For a study of Yugoslavia's policy of non-alignment see Alvin Z. Rubinstein, *Yugoslavia and the non-aligned world* (Princeton, 1970) and Leo Mates, *Nonalignment— theory and current policy* (Belgrade, 1972). Mates claims that even in the immediate postwar period when Yugoslavia was fully 'aligned' with the USSR, certain differences over foreign policy could be discerned and cites as examples her advocacy of an Arab–Israeli confederation in place of the creation of an Israeli state then favoured by Moscow, and important amendments to the draft convention on the Danube, providing for the maintenance of national sovereignty over that part of the river within Yugoslavia's borders, which the Soviet Union first opposed and finally accepted (*Nonalignment* 197–8). 'Non-alignment' (first known as *neangažovanost* and later as *nesvrstanost*) did not however begin to take serious shape as a theory until after the reconciliation with Moscow, when the balancing act between East and West began to be underpinned by the doctrine that non-participation in military alliances afforded a degree of collective security to the Third World.

189   Kardelj made the official announcement on 23 July 1949, but Yugoslav help had ceased several months before.

190   *General Assembly Official Records*, 6th sess., suppl. 20, res. 509 (vi), 10.

191   The decision to adopt a course of radical collectivization was taken in January 1949; it was not until March 1953, when most other features of the Stalinist system had long been under fire, that the Party gave permission to dissolve most work co-operatives. The abandonment of collectivization was the fruit of pragmatic considerations; as Bakarić was to admit, 'the criticism of practice was faster than our theoretical criticism' (*O poljoprivredi*, Belgrade, 1960, 10).

192   During the war itself, the contrary tendency had prevailed. In accordance with Moscow's 'national front' line of emphasizing popular resistance to the Germans and dispelling the misgivings of the Western allies, the revolutionary implications of the Partisan movement had been played down and its predominantly patriotic, non-sectarian character stressed. For a discussion of this question and of the gradual genesis of the 'Yugoslav path to Socialism' see the illuminating study by A. Ross Johnson.

193   *Khrushchev remembers* (London, 1971), i. 374–91. According to this account, which diverges from the line taken in Khrushchev's 'secret speech' (where responsibility is placed firmly on Stalin's shoulders) and apparently reflects Khrushchev's thinking towards the end of his career after fresh differences had arisen to mar the Yugoslav–Soviet reconciliation, the Yugoslav leaders were also to blame for 'trying to pick a quarrel' and for persecuting those who refused to follow their 'anti-Soviet' line.

194   Tempo, ii. 210.

195   *Khrushchev remembers*, i. 379. According to Maclean (438), an invitation was first sent by the Russians early in 1955 to visit Moscow, but this was declined, though Tito made a counterproposal, which the Russians accepted, that they should visit him in Belgrade.

196   Khrushchev subsequently maintained that he and his colleagues had not at that time come to realize the full extent of Stalin's responsibility for the abuses and blunders of his regime. According to the confessions attributed to him in *Khrushchev remembers* (i. 343): 'When we touched on the whole subject of the terror and mentioned Beria as the culprit behind the Stalin period, the Yugoslav comrades smiled scornfully and made sarcastic remarks. We were irritated, and we launched into a long argument in defence of Stalin. Later I spoke out publicly in defence of Stalin when the Yugoslavs

criticized him. It's now clear to me that my position was wrong. I didn't fully realize the necessity not only of exposing the crimes but of putting the blame where it belonged so that Stalinist methods would never again be used in our Party. . . . The Yugoslavs quite correctly blamed Stalin for the split between our Parties. They didn't hold it against us personally, but against Stalin. We, too, were proceeding from the assumption that Stalin had started the conflict, but we tried to avoid bringing up the subject of who was to blame when we actually set about normalizing our relations with Yugoslavia. We were only beginning to realize the extent of Stalin's abuses of power and the carnage he had caused when he cut down the flower of our Party. . . . Psychologically, we were not prepared for our meeting with the Yugoslavs. We still hadn't freed ourselves from our slavish dependence on Stalin. However, the Yugoslavs agreed that we could come to some sort of understanding. They seemed receptive to our intentions'.

197   An interesting source for the course of the discussions are the memoirs of Vukmanović-Tempo (ii. 231–9), the most emotional and outspoken member of the Yugoslav delegation. After listening to Khrushchev's statement putting all the blame on Abakumov and Beria, Tempo burst out: 'Comrade Khrushchev, I can't understand how the dispute between our two parties can be explained away by saying that it was Beria who allegedly slandered our country. Let us assume that Beria spoke the truth, and that we had, for instance, adopted Bukharin's ideas about the development of relations in the villages. In that case, would the blockade and the pressure against our country have been justified? I ask you this as I am interested to know how you would react in similar situations in the future. If, for instance, we were to decide to build Bukharin-style socialism in the villages—what would you do about it? Would you again apply a blockade and pressure, or would you start discussions on these questions, leaving it for practice to show which solution gave the best results?' Khrushchev was taken aback by these questions and Tempo continued: 'I don't see, Comrade Khrushchev, how any person, whatever position he holds, could lead an entire Party to obviously unjust and unsocialist positions. Now you are blaming Beria, and I ask myself—who will guarantee that another Beria does not appear? As far as I know, you have always in the past put the blame on Ministers of the Interior. They have come to grief on account of policies previously carried into effect by the whole leadership—Yagoda, Yezhov, Beria. Who is going to guarantee that some fourth Beria does not arise?' Tempo concludes the scene: 'Khrushchev was very agitated and all red in the face. He quickly interrupted me and shouted angrily—"You—you petty bourgeois element!". I wanted to answer him back sharply, but Tito quickly got up. He looked very annoyed. And with that the morning's session was closed.'

Tempo's outburst was probably not altogether unwelcome to Tito, who wanted the Russians to realize how strongly his Party felt about the injustices suffered at Stalin's hands, and how determined it was to be treated as equals by them. He refused to accept Tempo's offer to withdraw from the Yugoslav delegation, but cautioned him to think more of future relations than of the past. Khrushchev, once he had got over his initial anger, took a liking to Tempo for his outspokenness: 'he impressed me very much with his sincerity, his genuineness, his human naturalness. I liked him, even though he spoke out very strongly against us. I don't think he should have let himself get so carried away. . . . I said at one meeting: "If ever again you want to aggravate tensions in your relations with some country, the man for the job is Comrade Tempo!" Tito glanced at me, then burst out laughing. Later, Vukmanović-Tempo and I got along fine.'

198   'The so-called Belgrade Declaration is no "declaration", but a fully fledged State treaty with a great number of concrete clauses and commitments' (Halperin, 272). It was no doubt preceded by much hard bargaining between the two sides before Khrushchev's visit to Belgrade. But it is harder to accept the same author's contention that Khrushchev's clumsy attempt to shrug off responsibility for the rift, and Tito's cool response to his guest's speech at the airport, were merely so much play-acting designed to conceal from Western observers that Yugoslavia had in fact returned to the Soviet fold.

199   'The rumour had been spread that Yugoslavia was forbidden by treaty to trade with the Soviet Union. In fact, this was a fabrication circulated by Yugoslavia's many ill-wishers in the USSR. Yugoslavia had no such treaty with the West. . . . [but] the West

was always making special deals with Yugoslavia. There was naturally a lot of resentment in the Soviet Union against Yugoslavia because of the amount of trade it did in the West. The resentment was based more on jealousy than ideology' (*Khrushchev remembers*, i. 382–3).

200   An assertion by Marshal Zhukov, on receiving a high Yugoslav decoration, that 'we shall fight again shoulder to shoulder' in the event of another war as the two countries had fought in the last caused some alarm amongst Western observers but elicited Yugoslav assurances that the Marshal's statement was no more than rhetorical hyperbole and not a reference to any secret military alliance (*Scotsman*, 22 June 1956).

201   One CP which refused to endorse Khrushchev's policy of rapprochement with Tito was that of Trieste, which had been granted a status of independence from the Italian CP and had reasons of its own for bearing a grudge against the Yugoslav communists. Vidali, the formidable boss of the Trieste communists and one of Stalin's trusted lieutenants, dissociated himself in his party journal, *Il Lavoratore*, from Khrushchev's initiative and declared that it was wrong to attribute Tito's misdeeds to the calumnies of Beria, since his Party had ample experience and documentation of its own to prove that Titoism was 'nothing but exaggerated nationalism, camouflaged under socialism, adventurism, sectarianism, and political and physical terrorism'. After considerable pressure, the Trieste communists were obliged to retract these accusations and toe the new Moscow line.

202   This directive was probably drafted by the hardline faction in the CPSU CC as an indirect attack upon Khrushchev and his policies (*New York Times*, 24 Sept. 1956).

203   According to *Khrushchev remembers* (i. 384) 'the hunt has been used for centuries as an opportunity for leaders of two or three different countries to get together and discuss issues of mutual interest and importance. The atmosphere of my discussions with Tito during our hunt together was warm and friendly'. Tito seems to have raised the question of the secret directive and to have received assurances that it represented no official departure from the policy of détente and of separate paths to socialism (*Borba*, 12 Oct. 1956).

204   *Tempo*, ii. 274.

205   'We reported to Tito on why we had come and confronted him with our decision to send troops into Budapest. We asked for his reaction. I expected even more strenuous objections from Tito than the ones we had encountered during our discussions with the Polish comrades. But we were pleasantly surprised. Tito said we were absolutely right and that we should send our soldiers into action as quickly as possible. He said we had an obligation to help Hungary crush the counter-revolution. He assured us that he completely understood the necessity of taking these measures. We had been ready for resistance, but instead we received his wholehearted support. I would even say he went further than we did in urging a speedy and decisive resolution of the problem' (*Khrushchev remembers*, i. 421).

206   Tito apparently managed to persuade Khrushchev that 'no particular importance should be given now to the question of whether or not the Yugoslav embassy in Budapest acted correctly in giving asylum to Imre Nagy and his companions', and Khrushchev wrote to him that 'we note with satisfaction that, since the Brioni talks, you have been in full agreement with our attitude towards Comrade Janoš Kádar as a distinguished personality with revolutionary authority in Hungary, capable of heading a new revolutionary government in these difficult times and conditions. (Extract from a letter sent to Tito by Khrushchev, as communicated by Ambassador Krylov to the Albanian CP CC; from a speech by Enver Hodja reported in *Zeri i Popullit*, 8 Nov. 1961 (W. E. Griffith, *Albania and the Sino-Soviet Rift*, Cambridge, Mass., 1963, 259).

207   There are grounds for believing that 'the Russians were at one time prepared to spare the life of Imre Nagy in exchange for the joining of the camp by Yugoslavia', and that upon the Yugoslav refusal to assent to this and the subsequent execution of Nagy, the publication of the documents relating to these secret negotiations was seriously considered in Belgrade (*Manchester Guardian*, 27 June 1958).

208   Zhukov, the most outstanding Soviet commander of World War II, had been disgraced by Stalin and subsequently re-emerged as an important ally of Khrushchev in the de-Stalinization process. After the purge of the 'anti-Party' group in June, his co-operation was no longer so necessary, and he was dismissed from his offices on a

charge of 'Bonapartism'. The timing of Zhukov's fall, which occurred immediately after his official visit to Yugoslavia where he had been cordially received by Tito, appeared as a calculated snub to the latter.

209 *New York Times*, 15 1958.
210 Except for the Polish delegate 'whose demonstration of solidarity with the Yugoslavs was tempered by the general impression that he was asleep' (John C. Campbell, *Tito's separate road*, New York, 1967, 42).
211 Speech of 23 November 1958, in which Tito declared that the Soviet bloc was not unanimous in its campaign against Yugoslavia and that China was, in fact, aiming its criticism against 'somebody else' whom it did not dare openly attack.
212 Tempo, ii. 359. Khrushchev also complained to Tempo that the Yugoslavs were organizing espionage and subversion in the socialist countries and warned them not to gamble on profiting from any deterioration in relations between Moscow and Peking which he maintained were very good. Tempo in turn complained to Mikoyan about the Soviet suspension of credits. The visit nevertheless passed in a friendly atmosphere, and Tempo returned home full of optimism which Tito, however, did not share. Tempo later learned that the Soviet leaders were letting it be known that he had been sent to the Soviet Union to seek a settlement of the quarrel and had been told that this would be possible only when the Yugoslavs had stopped engaging in espionage and subversion in socialist countries (ibid., 360).
213 *Origins and development of the differences between the leadership of the CPSU and ourselves* (Peking, 1963), 40–1. In a cordially worded New Year Message sent by Khrushchev to the LCY at the beginning of 1961 Yugoslavia was also classed amongst the socialist countries.
214 According to some press reports, however, Tito protested privately to the Russians against the tests (*New York Herald Tribune*, 18 Jan. 1962).
215 *Borba*, 12 Dec. 1962.
216 *Neue Zuercher Zeitung*, 10 June 1964.
217 *Borba*, 24 June 1963.
218 His unambiguous assertion to the workers of the Split shipyards that 'I like the form of the workers' council' (*New York Times*, 22 Aug. 1963) was watered down by *Pravda* (25 Aug. 1963) to 'I like the organization of labour at your yard'.
219 *Soviet News*, 25 June 1965.
220 According to P. Lendvai (*Eagles in cobwebs*, London, 1970, 161), 'in the winter of 1964, three leaders of the UDBA, headed by the then Minister of the Interior, paid a visit to Moscow and at a party, where they were slightly drunk, flatly remarked that "Tito is getting old, and it is time Ranković took over the helm" '.
221 Brezhnev is believed to have intervened on behalf of Ranković through Gomulka, and later in person when he paid a private visit to Yugoslavia between 22–5 September 1966. There is no reason to suppose that Ranković was particularly pro-Soviet—he had been attacked along with Tito, Kardelj, and the others at the time of the dispute with the Cominform—still less that he had attempted to enlist Soviet help to further his ambitions. But the Russians saw that the proposed reforms were likely to alienate Yugoslavia still further from the orthodox Soviet model and that Ranković, as the man who could be counted upon to reverse them, deserved their support. According to Ilija Jukić (Tito's legacy, *Survey*, Autumn 1970) some of his followers, and even a number of non-communist Serbs, contemplated turning to the Russians for backing against the Croats and Slovenes after they had lost their champion Ranković, but that wiser counsels prevailed and 'the conservatives' rejection of Soviet support became total after the Soviet invasion of Czechoslovakia'.
222 According to the memoirs of Mohammed Heikal, Nasser's confidant and adviser (*Sunday Telegraph*, 31 Oct. 1971), 'Tito set out to do what he could to rebuild Egypt's shattered forces. He called for and attended a meeting of the Communist party leaders of eight East European nations in Moscow and urged the rearmament of Egypt. When the Russians were preparing to fly in their huge Antonov transport planes filled with MIG fighters and other arms, they delayed, saying they had no landing rights in Yugoslavia where it was essential for them to refuel. Egypt's Ambassador in Belgrade explained this problem to Tito and he picked up the telephone and gave the order: open everything to the Antonovs, "no restrictions; as far as Egypt is concerned, I am no longer non-aligned". And the giant aircraft poured through Yugoslavia to Egypt,

three of them arriving every hour in a massive airlift of a new Army and new Air Force'.
223 Interview granted to *Paris Match*, 16 Nov. 1968.
224 In response to the manœuvres held by Cominform forces on her borders in 1948, Yugoslavia had undertaken a massive mobilization on conventional lines, supplemented by improvised plans for guerrilla resistance. From the mid-50s, as Soviet-Yugoslav relations improved, emphasis on defence was reduced so that by 1968 only 6 per cent of the national budget, as compared with 22 per cent in 1952, went on military expenditure.
225 The Tass announcement referring to the ambassador's démarche was interrupted and cancelled in the course of transmission, either as a result of divided counsels in the Kremlin or as part of Moscow's war of nerves against the Yugoslavs.
226 *Pravda*, 13 Nov. 1968.
227 A particularly serious indictment appeared in the Soviet theoretical journal *Kommunist* (17 Dec. 1968) under the heading 'Yugoslavia—a new variant of Socialism?' attacking the Yugoslavs for distorting Leninism in theory and practice, especially with regard to the role of their Party and the national economy.
228 *The Times,* 18 July 1969.
229 The freedom of the press was however understood to apply only in a limited and pragmatic way. Djilas, Mihajlov and others had received sentences for expressing their views too freely, and in the autumn of 1970, when the Yugoslav Government was moving again towards détente with Moscow, the editor of the *Književne novine* was imprisoned for publishing an article deemed hostile to the Soviet Union.
230 *Yugoslav Survey*, Aug. 1970, 143–4.
231 Speech at Ljubljana, 11 December 1969.
232 *Guardian*, 5 Feb. 1970.
233 The Croat émigrés were split into rival groups, a number of which, after the Soviet invasion of Czechoslovakia, addressed memoranda to the UN and to all diplomatic missions in Argentina (where there was a large émigré community) urging support for any action aimed at destroying the Yugoslav state and re-establishing an independent Croatia. One group, active in Spain and led by the former Ustasha police chief Max Luburić, claimed to have established its own secret links with Moscow (*Obrana*, Sept. 1970). Another, headed by Nahid Kulenović, son of the leader of the pro-Pavelić Moslems, operated from Monaco. Both Kulenović and Luburić were assassinated, reportedly by Titoist agents, in 1969. A third and more important group was led by Dr Branko Jelić, President of the self-styled Croat National Committee, who had been interned in Britain during World War II and thus escaped being personally compromised by the crimes of the Ustashe, campaigned in his journal *Hrvatska Država* for the creation of an 'independent, neutral Croatia', which would allow the Russians the use of naval and air facilities, whilst retaining an independent status similar to that of Finland. Jelić, who had become a naturalized West German citizen, was rumoured to have established contact with, and to have received encouragement from, Soviet authorities in Bonn and Berlin (Ciliga, 190–4, quoting reports in the *Neue Zuercher Zeitung* and in *Il Borghese* of 22 Feb. 1970, which drew a démenti from *Pravda* on 5 Mar. 1970). Whether the émigrés were exaggerating the degree of support they claimed to be receiving from the Russians in order to inflate their own importance, or whether Moscow was seriously encouraging them, either as a potential alternative to friendly relations with Belgrade, or simply as a means to bring pressure to bear on the latter, remains uncertain.
234 *Nedeljne informativne nivine* (NIN), 12 Apr. 1970. The formation of a separate League of Communists of Croatia, based on West Germany, was also reported, and was denounced on 10 August 1971 by the Croat communist leaders V. Bakarić and Savka Dabčević-Kučar as an act of 'usual provocation by hostile émigré circles'.
235 *Politika*, 9 June 1971; *Izvestiya*, 18 June 1971; *Politika*, 20 June 1971; *NIN*, 13 June 1971.
236 A different and more disquieting picture, which the Yugoslavs feared might be a truer reflection of Soviet thinking, was published, in the summer of 1971, in a book by Sergei Trapeznikov, head of the CPSU's Department of Science and Higher Education. This described Yugoslavia as a 'right-revisionist bridgehead established by world imperialism within the socialist camp'.

237 *The Times*, 16 June 1971.
238 One of the Yugoslav officers serving in the Red Army, Colonel Blažo Raspopović, was reportedly in charge of the training of both Yugoslav Cominformists and Croat extremists for espionage work in Yugoslavia (*Observer*, 16 June 1971).
239 *Pravda*, 23 Sept. 1971.
240 Ibid.
241 *Pravda*, 24 Sept. 1971.
242 Ibid., 15 Mar. 1973. The candidature was not, however, successful.
243 *Financial Times*, 17 Dec. 1971. According to the Czech general Jan Šejna, who defected to the West in February 1974, a plan code-named Operation Polarka had been worked out for the Warsaw Pact forces to move both against Austria, on the grounds that her neutrality had been compromised by allowing Ustashe bands to operate from her territory against Yugoslavia, and the latter, on the plea that order needed to be restored. He alleged that the incursion of a group of nineteen well-armed Ustashe in January 1972, which was routed by Yugoslav forces, had been undertaken with the knowledge and encouragement of Moscow (statement to Austrian news magazine *Profil*, quoted by the *Guardian*, 15 Feb. 1974).
244 *Izvestiya*, 2 June 1972, commended Tito for the 'destruction of putrid liberalism in Croatia'.
245 *The Times*, 2 Oct. 1973.
246 *Observer*, 25 Nov. 1973.
247 Thirty-two dissidents were brought to trial in Montenegro and given sentences of up to 14 years (*Borba*, 21 Sept. 1974). Tito described their attempt to form an alternative CP for which they held a clandestine congress, as 'fantasy, rather than anything serious', but called for their 'exemplary punishment' (ibid., 14 Sept. 1974). The dissidents were said to have taken orders from Mileta Perović, a Cominformist exile living in Kiev. Though the Soviet Union was not named during the trial, strong protests were reported to have been lodged with the Soviet and other East European governments over their role in the affair (*International Herald Tribune*, 14 Sept. 1974), and the recall of a Counsellor at the Soviet embassy was said to have followed as a result (*The Times*, 25 Sept. 1974). Tito is reported to have explained Moscow's double-faced policy at a special session of the Executive Committee of the LCY Presidium by postulating the existence of two schools of thought in the Kremlin: the moderates, led by Brezhnev and Kosygin, who favoured détente with Yugoslavia, and the hardliners, represented by the KGB chief Andropov and Defence Minister Grechko, who wanted Yugoslavia to be brought into the Warsaw Pact and the Soviet Union given the use of Yugoslav naval bases in the Adriatic (*Observer*, 22 Sept. 1974).

Documents and Extracts

I THE WAR PERIOD

1 CPY manifesto on the outbreak of the 'imperialist' war, September 1939: excerpt (*pp. 6, 7*)

The Soviet Union and the Communist International have for years made every effort to prevent the outbreak of the new world war prepared by the imperialist aggressors. The USSR and the Comintern have alone resolutely opposed the enslavement of the small nations . . . whereas the British and French reactionaries, in the persons of Daladier and Chamberlain, the representatives of great capital, did not want the fall of the fascist aggressors. Fearing the strengthening of the prestige of the USSR and the spread of the national struggles for democracy, they fought against the peace policy of the USSR and the Comintern, sabotaging their efforts to establish a firm defensive front against the aggressors and constantly striving by their double-faced policy to drag the Soviet Union into the war so as to pull their own chestnuts out of the fire for them.

But the Soviet Union, led by the Bolshevik Party and Comrade Stalin, the leader of genius of all progressive humanity, have unmasked the imperialist warmongers' foul trap. German fascism has been compelled to capitulate before the strength of victorious socialism, the USSR, and to conclude a non-aggression pact with it. The Soviet Union, the only real champion of peace, always ready to lead the struggle for peace, democracy, and national independence, conscious of its historic importance and duty towards the liberation struggle of the proletariat of the whole world, will never go to war for any imperialist interest, nor force the working masses of any other country to fight for such interests. Through the Non-Aggression Pact with Germany, the Soviet Union has won a great victory and limited the range of the present war.

2 Comintern Secretariat approves Tito's reorganization of the CPY, end of November, 1939: excerpt (*p. 5*)

. . . We have taken note of the report of friend Valter [the pseudonym used by Tito in the Comintern] on the work of the Party and the situation in the Party and record that the leadership has succeeded in gaining the full confidence of their working class through its work, and that the Party has made a serious start with carrying out our decisions of 5 January 1939 (a) to liquidate the state of chaos and disorganization in which the Party found itself as a result of the harmful work of previous leaders, to strengthen the Party ranks in a political and organizational sense, and to increase vigilance, and (b) to improve mass political work, to extend its influence over the working masses and strengthen the position of the Party in the trade unions and other mass organizations, and in the youth movement.

The most important task now is to take a stand in regard to the new situation created in the country as a result of the European war, and to analyse the present tasks which this calls for from the Party, and to take energetic steps to carry them into effect.

3 Foreign Minister Cincar-Marković discounts talk of 'bolshevization' of the Balkans to Yugoslav minister in Stockholm, 13 December 1939 (*p. 4*)

There has recently been some speculation in the international press regarding the danger of the alleged bolshevization said to be threatening the Balkan countries. A few insignificant incidents in Yugoslavia have been exaggeratedly cited in support of these allegations.

Please follow this campaign carefully and try to nip the rumours in the bud as thoroughly tendentious.

As far as Yugoslavia is concerned, there is not the slightest danger of bolshevization nor is any influence, either in domestic or foreign affairs, possible on the part of the Soviet Union. Our people are basically anti-bolshevik, and the state authorities are resolved, now as heretofore, to crush any bolshevik action.

4 Soviet Government announces arrival of a Yugoslav economic delegation, but denies rumours of any political negotiations, 20 April 1940 (*p. 4*)

At the end of March 1940 the Yugoslav Government, through the Soviet ambassador in Turkey, approached the Government of the USSR with a proposal for the establishment of economic relations between the two countries and suggested that with this object in view negotiations be begun on the following questions:

(1) The conclusion of a trade agreement
(2) A payments agreement
(3) The establishment of commercial agencies in the capitals of both states.

The Soviet Government has agreed to negotiations on these questions and has entrusted the matter to the People's Commissariat of Foreign Trade.

In this connection a Yugoslav Economic Mission is expected to arrive shortly in Moscow to conduct negotiations with the People's Commissariat of Foreign Trade headed by the Director of one of the Belgrade banks, Milan Djordjević, and Vice-Minister of Trade and Industry, Sava Obradović. . . .

The foreign press is spreading rumours about forthcoming political negotiations between the Soviet Government and the Yugoslav delegation which is to visit Moscow, alleging as their purpose the strengthening of Yugoslavia's position in relation to its neighbours. Tass is authorized to state that this report is a complete fabrication. A Yugoslav economic delegation is to come to Moscow for negotiations with the appropriate Soviet economic bodies concerning the establishment of trade relations between the two countries.

5 Signature of trade and shipping agreement, 11 May 1940 (*p. 4*)

On 11 May 1940 a trade and shipping agreement, a protocol to it regarding the trade representation of the USSR in Yugoslavia and the temporary trade delegation of Yugoslavia in the USSR, and a turnover and payments agreement for 1940–1941, were signed in Moscow by the Soviet Union and Yugoslavia.

The total turnover between the USSR and Yugoslavia for 1940–41 will, on the basis of the turnover and payments agreement, amount to 176 million dinars.

The Soviet Union proposes to import from Yugoslavia copper, concentrated lead and zinc ores, pig's fat, and other goods, and to deliver to Yugoslavia agricultural and other machinery, kerosene, cotton, and other goods.

The above agreements were signed on behalf of the Soviet Union by the People's Commissar of Foreign Trade of the USSR Comrade A. I. Mikoyan, and on behalf of Yugoslavia by the former Minister of Finance, M. Djordjević and the Vice-Minister of Trade and Industry, M. S. Obradović.

6 Establishment of diplomatic relations, 24 June 1940 (*p. 4*)

Following on the highly successful conclusion of economic negotiations between the USSR and Yugoslavia and the exchange of the instruments of ratification, the Soviet and Yugoslav Governments have decided to establish normal diplomatic relations and with that end in view have appointed diplomatic representatives.

The Soviet Government have nominated comrade Victor Andreyevich Plotnikov their plenipotentiary, whilst the Yugoslav Government have nominated Milan Gavrilović. The necessary agréments have been given by their respective governments.

7 Tito reports to the Comintern on the results of the 5th Conference of the CPY, October 1940 (*p. 7*)

The 5th Conference of the CPY was held from 19–23 October. One hundred and one delegates from all over the country participated. A Central Committee of twenty-two members was elected, among them two women, and sixteen candidates. Complete unity was manifested.

8 Tito (at 5th CPY Conference) assesses Yugoslavia's situation after one year's neutrality, October 1940: excerpts (*p. 7*)

The Conference is of historical importance because it is taking place at a time when the second World War is in full spate, when the danger of fascism is increasing in every country, and terror against the working class is growing in all capitalist countries including Yugoslavia, and class contradictions are acquiring ever sharper character. . . .

The Cvetković–Maček Government, whose policy is directed against the people, is sparing no effort in order to harness the peoples of Yugoslavia to the imperialist war chariot of the Axis powers, to make them assume part of the burden of the imperialist war these powers are waging, to make them into the slaves, not merely of their own capitalists, but also of the ruling financial oligarchy in Berlin and Rome.

The peoples of Yugoslavia, however, are opposed to the treacherous foreign and domestic policy of the Cvetković–Maček Government. The Yugoslav working peoples are opposed to the hypocritical, even hostile, policy their government is conducting towards the Soviet Union, just as they are opposed to the nauseatingly subservient attitude of this government towards the Axis powers, an attitude which is finding expression every day in the press, in the behaviour of the regime, etc. The numerous demonstrations and clashes which have occurred within the last few months are evidence of this. The peoples of Yugoslavia do not want fascism, they do not want a totalitarian regime, they refuse to become the slaves of the German and Italian financial oligarchies just as they were never reconciled to the condition of semi-colonial dependence which the so-called Western democracies had forced upon them after the first imperialist war. The peoples of Yugoslavia are persistently seeking to rely on the USSR, on the land of progress and welfare, the protector of the independence of small nations. All the working peoples of Yugoslavia are looking towards the great and powerful land of socialism with confidence and hope, and they are prepared to fight for their demands. . . .

Our Party held its 4th Congress in the autumn of 1928, on the eve of the introduction of the military dictatorship. That Congress was held with a view to the internal consolidation of the Party, and the struggle against the fractions, both of the Right and of the Left, which was being waged by an activist loyal to the Party at the head of the Zagreb party organization and with the assistance of the Comintern. With the help of an open letter sent by the Comintern to members of the CPY, all those cadres which had escaped fractional infection and remained loyal to the Party began to mobilize. . . .

Those fractions and groups in the higher party echelons who were fighting each other for the leadership and stopped at nothing, were nevertheless united in one thing; they systematically lied to the Communist International, sent false reports, and deceitfully misrepresented the real situation. . . . How, it may be asked, did they manage to maintain themselves at the top for so long? It was possible, in the first place, because for a long time there was no sound working class nucleus to lead the struggle against those alien elements in our Party. . . .

The war confronted our Party, because of the changed situation, with a number of important tasks. We had to give a new orientation to the entire struggle and work of the Party. All attempts at agreement with the leaders of the bourgeois, so-called democratic parties, which were assuming an increasingly reactionary character and had become agencies of English and French reactionary circles, were abandoned. The following tasks now faced our Party, as for all the sections of the Communist International—the struggle for the working masses by means of establishing a Popular Front from below, by organizing and waging a struggle against fascism and reaction, the struggle for the everyday needs of the masses, the struggle against high prices, against war, for freedom and the democratic national rights of the toiling and nationally oppressed masses of Yugoslavia.

The Central Committee of our Party tirelessly demanded that the part played by the imperialist warmongers be unmasked. It was necessary to explain to the masses the causes of the war, and the pseudo-democracy of the British and French imperialists. It was necessary to unmask and to wage a relentless struggle against the different foreign agents who were doing everything to push

Yugoslavia into the war. It was necessary to prevent the peoples of Yugoslavia being driven into such a catastrophe. Our Party has achieved significant results in this respect. . . .

Our Party, like all the other sections of the Communist International, received a year and a half ago a powerful theoretical weapon, the *History of the Communist Party of the Soviet Union* (b). This magnificent book, which was written with the co-operation of our great teacher and leader, Comrade Stalin himself, contains, in the condensed form of a history, the most popular form, the tremendous experience of the most revolutionary party, the Bolshevik Party. This book gives an outline of the heroic path followed by the Bolshevik Party which overthrew capitalism and built socialism. From this history, the proletariat throughout the world is learning today, and it is from this history that our Party members and the proletariat of Yugoslavia should learn. . . . If we follow and learn correctly from the experience of the most revolutionary and heroic CPSU, our Party will be able to accomplish its historic mission of vanguard of the working class of Yugoslavia.

9 A communist report at 5th CPY Conference on the impact of the German–Soviet Pact and on the work of the Party in the Army, October 1940: excerpts (*p. 6*)

The Non-Aggression Pact between the USSR and Germany had a deep political impact on the army. By disseminating the reactionary bourgeois press and by means of lectures, an attempt was made to stir up hatred against the USSR and its peace-loving policy through frightful slander and lies. The government and General Staff, and all the agents of British and French imperialism, carried out a planned and systematic propaganda in the army on behalf of London and Paris. To drive a wedge between the communists and the people, they spread shameless lies and slanders and dubbed us German spies. But despite all this rabble-rousing against the USSR on the part of the reaction and the Social Democrat leaders, our Party succeeded, by dint of vigorous agitation and propaganda, in clarifying the historical importance of the Non-Aggression Pact. The strength of the USSR has made an impression in the army, illusions about the strength of German fascism have begun to fade, and the popularity of the USSR to grow. . . .

When the imperialist war broke out in the heart of Europe, and when the government declared partial mobilization, the Central Committee's manifesto making clear the nature of the war and the mobilization was greeted with enthusiasm in the army. The rapid course of events and the work of our Party in the army have been influential in arousing the political consciousness of the soldiers. Political events have been publicly discussed in camps and barracks. Party members and sympathizers come forward and explain the Central Committee's manifesto to the soldiers, popularize the USSR as the only protector of small nations and the champion of peace, unmask the warmongering policy of the government and stress the need for links with the USSR. This has won enormous results for our Party. . . .

The young officers show an indescribable longing to fight in the ranks of the Red Army. In all public meetings it is openly said that the Red Army will liberate us. This indescribable enthusiasm reached its height on the breaking of the Mannerheim Line [Finnish defensive positions] . . . which nailed once and for all the foul lie about the weakness of the Red Army. . . . The peace concluded between Finland and the Soviet Union put an end to the basest of lies spread with one accord by the bourgeoisie of the world and their filthy Social Democrat vanguard about Red and Russian Imperialism. All the bourgeois dogs must now acknowledge the power and might of the Red Army and the Soviet Union and its peace-loving policy.

10 5th CPY Conference denounces Axis powers and Western democracies as equally responsible for the 'imperialist war', and affirms its loyalty to the Comintern, October 1940: excerpts (*p. 7*)

In the course of the past year, in which the imperialist war has been raging, the mask behind which the aggressors from both camps have been attempting to conceal themselves has been completely dropped. It has become clear as day that the English and French imperialists have not unleashed the conflagration of war in defence of the freedom, democracy, and independence of the small nations, but in order to defend their own colonial dominions and hegemony acquired through their victory in the last imperialist war; it has become as clear as day that the German and Italian imperialists are not waging war in order to right the wrongs of the Versailles settlement allegedly imposed upon their nations and on other smaller nations after the last war, but rather to win colonies and markets from their rivals and enslave independent nations, particularly those which are defenceless, and to win hegemony in Europe and the rest of the world.

The capitalist world, led by the English financial oligarchy and with the help of the treacherous Social Democrat leaders, has been furiously attempting, up to the second imperialist war, to find a way out of the contradictions and conflicting interests which cannot be solved so long as capitalism lasts, and which have been rendered more dangerous to them on account of the existence of the Soviet Union. The imperialist bloc which won the first imperialist war places all its hopes on setting its chief rival, Germany, at odds with the Soviet Union, so that both of them should be bled and weakened by fighting each other, and with the help of German imperialism thwart the triumphant construction of socialism in the USSR, which they regard as the greatest enemy and danger to the imperialist world, and afterwards render a weakened imperialist Germany harmless. . . .

The English and French imperialists have been doing everything through their different machinations to draw the Soviet Union into the war so as to pull their chestnuts out of the fire for them. But thanks to Stalin's wise peace policy, thanks to its gigantic strength, the Soviet Union has averted the danger of war from its frontiers, has kept the conflagration of war within bounds and, in the course of this year, has liberated 23 millions of the working masses from the national and capitalist yoke [following the annexation of territory from the Baltic, Finnish, and Polish states]. . . .

The 5th Conference approves the assessment contained in the reports on the errors in political organization and the harmful work of the former leaders of the CPY already denounced by the Communist International.

The 5th Conference unanimously welcomes the measures taken, and the help given, by the Communist International in the matter of purging our CC of various harmful fractionist and anti-Party elements. . . .

Concious of these hard and fateful times, the 5th Conference considers that it is necessary for the Party to redouble its efforts in working to carry out the tasks before it; in the struggle for discipline and against all deviations in the Party, in the struggle to preserve Party unity, to purge the Party mercilessly of all harmful elements, to forge and consolidate the Party through struggle, as we have been taught by the great Lenin, and by the great Stalin, the creator of the most revolutionary party in history—the CPSU. In the struggle for the oppressed and down-trodden masses, always with the masses in their every struggle, at the head of those masses, under the banner of the Communist International, the CPY will win the trust of the workers and oppressed masses, will carry out its role as vanguard of the Yugoslav working class, and will take a worthy place amongst the sections of the Communist International.

11 Ambivalent Soviet attitude towards the coup of 27 March: démenti that the government sent congratulations, 1 April 1941: excerpts (*p. 8*)

The Belgrade correspondent of the British United Press . . . filed a report that the Soviet Union had sent a message of congratulations to Yugoslavia. He even claims to know the text of the message, which allegedly states that 'the Yugoslav people has proved itself worthy of its glorious past'. . . .

But there is no such phrase in the telegram. Moreover, there is not even any such telegram. The Soviet Union sent no message of congratulations. It is all a fabrication, from first to last. . . .

The Yugoslav people undoubtedly has a glorious past. A people worthy of its glorious past does deserve congratulations, and if a message of congratulations were to be sent, there would be nothing surprising about it. All the same, congratulations were not sent, perhaps because of an oversight on the part of the Soviet Government, or because the idea did not occur to anyone.

12 German Ambassador in Moscow reports to his government on the proposed Soviet–Yugoslav Pact, 4 April 1941 (*p. 9*)

Molotov just summoned me to the Kremlin to inform me of the following, in accordance with the agreement to consult existing between Germany and the Soviet Union:

The Yugoslav Government had proposed to the Soviet Government the negotiation of a Treaty of Friendship and Non-aggression, and the Soviet Government had accepted the proposal. This agreement would be signed today or tomorrow. In its decision to accede to the proposal of the Yugoslav Government, the Soviet Government had been actuated solely by the desire to preserve peace. It knew that in this desire it was in harmony with the Reich Government, which was likewise opposed to an extension of the war. The Soviet Government therefore hoped that the German Government, too, in its present relations to Yugoslavia, would do everything to maintain peace. The agreement between the Soviet Union and Yugoslavia was analogous to the Turko–Soviet Agreement of 1925, and relations of the Soviet Union to other countries were not affected by the agreement with Yugoslavia. The Soviet–

Yugoslav agreement was directed against no one and was not aimed at any other state.

I replied to Molotov that in my estimation the moment chosen by the Soviet Union for the negotiation of such a treaty had been very unfortunate, and the very signing would create an undesirable impression in the world. The policy of the Yugoslav Government was entirely unclear, and its attitude, as well as the behaviour of the Yugoslav public toward Germany, was challenging.

Molotov replied that Yugoslavia had concluded a treaty with Germany regarding accession to the Tripartite Pact, and the Yugoslav Minister here, who was at the same time a member of the new Cabinet, had assured the Soviet Government that the new Yugoslav Government was observing this treaty. In these circumstances, the Soviet Government had thought that it could, for its part, conclude an agreement with Yugoslavia that was not even so far-reaching as the German–Yugoslav Treaty.

To my objection that, to my knowledge, we had thus far received no statement from the Yugoslav Government regarding the observance of its accession to the Tripartite Pact and had been given every reason to doubt its good will, Molotov countered with the assertion that he was convinced of the peaceful intention of the Yugoslav Government. The latter had restored peace and order to its country and strove to create good relations with all its neighbours.

At my objection that the behaviour of the new Yugoslav Government actually revealed no striving toward good relations with Germany—and despite all my efforts to obtain from Molotov the promise that the Soviet Government might reconsider the matter—Molotov repeatedly stated that the Soviet Government had reached its decision after mature deliberation. It was convinced that the step it had taken was a positive contribution to peace, which was also desired by Germany. To this Molotov added the repeated and urgent request that Germany also do all she could to preserve peace in the Balkans.

13 Friendship and Non-Aggression Pact between Yugoslavia and the USSR, 5 April 1941 (*pp. 6, 9*)

The Presidium of the Supreme Council of the USSR and His Majesty the King of Yugoslavia, inspired by the friendship existing between two countries which are convinced that it is in their common interest to preserve peace, have decided to conclude a Pact of Friendship and Non-Aggression, and for this purpose have appointed as their plenipotentiaries . . . who, having exchanged their full powers, which were found in good and due order, have agreed upon the following:

1

Both contracting parties undertake to refrain from any attack upon each other and undertake to respect the independence, sovereignty, and territorial integrity of the USSR and of Yugoslavia.

2

In the event of one of the contracting parties being the object of attack by a third State, the other party undertakes to preserve a policy of friendly relations towards it.

3

The present pact is concluded for five years. Unless one of the contracting parties considers it necessary to denounce the present pact one year before the expiration of the period stipulated, the pact shall be automatically prolonged for a subsequent period of five years.

4

The present pact comes into operation from the moment of its signature. The pact shall be ratified within the shortest possible time, and the instruments of ratification shall be exchanged at Belgrade.

5

The pact is drawn up in two copies, each in the Russian and Serbo–Croat languages, both texts having equal force.

**14 Pravda hails the pact as likely to prevent the spread of war,
6 April 1941: excerpts** (*p. 9*)

As will be seen from paragraphs 1 and 2 of the Pact, the two contracting parties undertake to refrain from attacking each other and to respect the independence, sovereign rights and territorial integrity of the USSR and Yugoslavia.

The day the Pact of Friendship and Non-Aggression between the USSR and Yugoslavia was signed is not only a landmark in the development of friendly relations between the two states, but denotes the common efforts of the USSR and Yugoslavia for the strengthening of peace and preventing the spread of war. . . .

Recent events in Yugoslavia have clearly shown that the people of Yugoslavia do not wish their country to be drawn into the vortex of war. In numerous demonstrations and meetings, the broad masses of the Yugoslav people have made their protest against the government of Dragiša Cvetković which threatened to drag Yugoslavia into the war. . . .

The course of events has clearly shown that the Government of General Simović has assumed the duty of setting the internal conditions in his country to rights. In this endeavour, as in the domain of foreign policy, it has the support of the majority of the people.

THE INVASION AND DISMEMBERMENT OF YUGOSLAVIA;
THE SOVIET REACTION

**15 German ambassador in Moscow instructed by his government to inform
Molotov that Germany has invaded Yugoslavia, 6 April 1941** (*p. 9*)

Please call on M Molotov early Sunday morning, 6 April, and tell him that the Government of the Reich had felt itself impelled to proceed to a military action in Greece and Yugoslavia. The Government of the Reich had been forced to take this step because of the arrival of British military forces on the Greek mainland in ever-increasing numbers, and because of the fact that the Yugoslav Government which had come to power illegally by the coup d'état of 27 March had made common cause with England and Greece. The Reich government had accurate information for several days to the effect that the Yugoslav General Staff, in conjunction with the Greek General Staff and the High Command of the English Expeditionary Army that had landed in Greece, had prepared for joint operations against Germany and Italy, which were on the verge of being carried out. Moreover, the constantly increasing number of reports on excesses against Germans in Yugoslavia had made it impossible for the Government of the Reich to remain inactive further in the face of such development. The new Yugoslav Government had taken this course contrary to all law and reason, after Germany had for years pursued a policy of friendship with that country, which was to have its culmination in the recent accession to the Tripartite Pact. Moreover, I would ask you in this connection to refer to the communications made to M Molotov on various occasions, which you had already made to the Soviet Government, regarding the aims and intentions of the German Government in the Balkan Peninsula: that is, that Germany has absolutely no political or territorial interests in this area; and that German troops would be withdrawn when their tasks in the Balkans are finished. Please make these statements without any special emphasis, in an objective and dispassionate manner.

Please do not on this occasion mention the communication made to you by Molotov regarding the conclusion of a Soviet–Yugoslav Friendship Pact. Should Molotov, on his part, speak of it, then please confine yourself to the comment that you have transmitted his communication to Berlin, but have not yet received any reply.

16 German ambassador reports Molotov's reaction to the news, 6 April 1941 (*p. 9*)

Since Molotov always spends Sunday out of town, I was able to speak with him only this afternoon at 4 o'clock. Molotov came to Moscow expressly for this purpose.

After I had made to Molotov the communications prescribed, he repeated several times that it was extremely deplorable that an extension of the war had thus proved inevitable after all.

Molotov did not on this occasion mention the negotiation of the Soviet–Yugoslav Pact. Therefore I, too, as instructed, did not revert to this subject.

17 Soviet Government informs Yugoslav minister in Moscow that it considers diplomatic relations to be at an end, 8 May 1941 (*p. 12*)

I am instructed by my government to inform you that, on grounds of foreign policy, I see no legal justification at the present time for the Yugoslav legation to continue its work in the Soviet Union.

The Government of the USSR has recently ceased to have a diplomatic representative in Yugoslavia. After the Yugoslav Government's move from the territory of Yugoslavia to Palestine, the Soviet Union has had no contact with the Yugoslav Government. It must be admitted that in such circumstances there is no legal basis for the Yugoslav legation to continue to operate in the Soviet Union.

The Soviet Government accordingly considers that there is no longer a Yugoslav minister in the Soviet Union, and that, as from today, his officials should be regarded as private persons.

18 Tito reports to Comintern on the tactics of the CPY before, during, and following the invasion, end of May 1941: excerpts (*pp. 8, 24*)

During the entire period of the imperialist war, the CPY has had a clearly defined line on the question of war and the neutrality of Yugoslavia: (1) to struggle against Yugoslavia's being drawn into the imperialist war on the side of Britain and France, for such a danger did exist, as the followers and agents of Britain had strong positions among the ruling bourgeoisie, especially the Serbian, and worked vigorously along these lines; (2) to struggle against capitulation to the Axis powers and against Yugoslavia's joining the Tripartite Pact; (3) to launch the struggle to establish diplomatic relations with the Soviet Union, and later to work for close friendly relations and a mutual assistance pact; (4) to struggle against the numerous fifth columns of the Axis powers which worked persistently and systematically to weaken Yugoslavia and disrupt it from within; to rally the broad masses of the people around the struggle against that danger; (5) to struggle against the reactionary governments which refused to grant the people democratic rights and freedoms, and to establish a people's government which would give the peoples of Yugoslavia their democratic rights and freedoms, and the nationally-oppressed their equality, for the Party considered all these factors as pre-conditions for Yugoslavia's avoiding war and preserving her independence. The Party was successful in popularizing this line through its underground and semi-legal press, by way of Party proclamations and leaflets which were disseminated in hundreds of thousands of copies in virtually all the languages of the various nationalities living in Yugoslavia.

The success of these propaganda activities by the Party was reflected in large-scale demonstrations and manifestations: (1) mass demonstrations directed by the Party at the beginning of the imperialist war in Europe in 1939–40, in various localities in Yugoslavia, during which not a few were killed and injured; (2) numerous manifestations in favour of the Soviet Union, particularly at the time of the arrival of Soviet diplomatic representatives; (3) various actions and demonstrations in Belgrade and other towns against the Tripartite Pact and the Cvetković–Maček Government, on March 26 and 27 and before, which were largely responsible for the downfall of that Government and its replacement by the Simović Government. The Party characterized the taking of power by the Simović Government as a step forward in the struggle for attainment of the demands supported by the Party and put forward by the people. The Party based its stand on the fact that the Simović Government opposed the capitulation of Yugoslavia, that it concluded a Pact of Friendship and Neutrality with the Soviet Union. But it was still not a people's government, first of all, because most of the people in it had been seriously compromised during past regimes, some of them even having been leading figures in such regimes, like [former Prime Minister] Jevtić and others; secondly, because internally that government temporized in meeting the demands of the people, and thirdly, because there were several explicit Anglophiles in it.

The Party demanded that the Simović Government immediately release all Communists from prisons and concentration camps, that it amnesty without delay all those interned for political or military reasons, that it grant the people their political rights and freedoms, that it purge the government apparatus and undertake measures for the defence of the country. Of all these measures, the government only dissolved concentration camps on Serbian territory and released Communists in prison in Serbia, while leaving the Croatian and Slovene reactionaries a free hand in persecuting and arresting Communists, in imprisoning them and interning them in concentration camps, where all of them were later turned over to the Ustashe and Germans who have made hostages of them and keep them under constant threat of execution if the Party does not cease its activities.

In keeping with its line of defending the country, on the eve of the attack on Yugoslavia the Party issued directives to all Party members who were subject to the draft to join the Army and go to the front where they were to work among the soldiers in the spirit of Party policy. Party members acclaimed this decision; they made a strong and favourable impression on the army men when the latter saw the Communists were the first to volunteer for combat to defend the independence of Yugoslavia. Many commanders and the General Staff sabotaged the Communists at every step, often refusing to allow them to oin their units, endeavouring to put them under arrest, and so on. In all such cases, the Communists were saved by the soldiers themselves. Along fronts where the Communists were sufficiently strong in numbers, entire regiments took orders from them, as was the case in Montenegro, where an offensive was started against the Italians in Albania.

During the attack on Yugoslavia, while mobilization was being carried out, certain Party organizations, for example in Slovenia, Serbia, etc., made the mistake of asking military commands to allow the formation of special volunteer detachments made up of Communists. A battalion of Communist volunteers was formed in Slovenia where, instead of these men joining regular army units and winning the soldiers over, they were isolated and exposed to the danger of being shot by fifth column officers. Many Communists in the Army erred in not knowing how to implement organizationally the Party line in the army, in frequently acting too slowly in comparison with the fifth columnists who spread defeatism and chaos during combat. For instance, some regiments which deserted the front on the very first day without a fight contained more Communists than Ustashe ('Frankovtsi') but still the Communists did not know how to counter the defeatist activities of the Ustashe. There have been other cases of a want of resourcefulness in certain Party organizations; now all these weaknesses and errors are being discussed throughout the Party and lessons are being drawn from them.

During the entire period of the short but chaotic war, the Party preserved continuity in its work and maintained contact amongst the organizations. All Party forums, from the Central Committee to the lowest ones have remained, for the most part intact and are discharging their functions. . . . Before the occupation, the Party had on its rolls 8,000 Party members and 30,000 members of the Communist Youth. This number has now increased.

THE GERMAN INVASION OF RUSSIA; RELATIONS WITH THE
GOVERNMENT IN EXILE RESTORED AND CPY PREPARATIONS
FOR ARMED RESISTANCE

19 CPY CC manifesto on the German invasion of the USSR, June 1941: excerpt (*p. 10*)

Early in the morning of 22 June the frenzied German fascist bandits attacked
the great and peace-loving state of the workers and peasants—the Soviet
Union. . . .

A fateful hour has struck. The decisive battle against the greatest foe of the
working class has begun—the battle which the fascist criminals brought upon
themselves by their treacherous attack on the Soviet Union, the hope of all the
workers of the world. The precious blood of the heroic Soviet peoples is being
shed not only in defence of the land of socialism, but for the final social and
national liberation of the whole of labouring mankind. This is therefore our
struggle, which we are obliged to support with all our strength, and even with
our own lives.

Proletarians from all parts of Yugoslavia, to your posts—to the forefront of
the struggle! Rally round your vanguard, the CPY! Each to his place! Fulfil
your proletarian duty without fear or faltering! Make ready for the final fateful
struggle! Do not stand idly by while the precious blood of the heroic people of
Soviet Russia is shed! Your watchword must be: not a single working man and
woman to go to fascist Germany to strengthen the power of the fascist bandits
with their labour! Not a single gun, not a single rifle, not a single bullet, not a
single ear of corn must reach the hand of the fascist criminals through your
help! Mobilize all your strength to prevent our country from being turned into
a supply base for the fascist hordes who have unleashed their fury on the Soviet
Union, our dear socialist Fatherland, our hope, the beacon to which the eyes
of working folk throughout the world are turned in longing.

Communists of Yugoslavia! Do not waver for a moment, but make haste to
prepare for this grim struggle. Hurry to prepare your organizations and their
work for this decisive struggle. Do everything possible to safeguard our precious
cadres which are now needed more than ever for this struggle. Organize the
working masses and make available to them the experience you have painfully
acquired. Place yourselves at the head of the working and nationally oppressed
masses and lead them into the struggle against the fascist oppressors of our
peoples. Show courage, discipline, and steady nerves, for you must set others
an example. Fulfil your duty as the vanguard of the working class of Yugoslavia. Forward to the final decisive struggle for the freedom and happiness of
mankind!

Long live the great and invincible land of socialism—the Soviet Union!

Long live the heroic party of Bosheviks, the CPSU!

Long live the leader and organizer of past and future victories of the great
and mighty Soviet Union—Comrade Stalin!

Long live the Communist International!

Long live the CPY!

Long live the international solidarity of all oppressed and exploited
peoples!

Long live the unity and struggle of the working masses!

Down with the imperialist fascist criminals headed by the bloodstained Hitler, Mussolini and the other satraps!

20 Directive from Comintern urging CPY to organize resistance to the occupation, 22 June 1941 (*pp. 10, 23*)

Germany's treacherous attack on the USSR is not only a blow against the land of socialism, but also against the freedom and independence of all peoples. The defence of the USSR is at the same time the defence of the countries which Germany has occupied. The peoples of Yugoslavia are now offered the possibility of developing a liberation struggle on all sides against the German oppressors.

It is essential to take all measures to support and facilitate the rightful struggle of the Soviet people. It is essential to develop a movement with the slogan of forging a united national front and the united international front already formed, in the struggle against the German and Italian fascist bandits and to protect the oppressed peoples against fascism—a task inseparable from the victory of the USSR. Bear in mind that, at this present stage, what you are concerned with is liberation from fascist oppression, and not socialist revolution. Acknowledge receipt of this signal.

21 Prime Minister Simović pledges solidarity with the British Government in support of the USSR against Germany, 11 July 1941 (*p. 12*)

By reason of the aggression committed by the German army against the USSR, in spite of the promises given and the solemn engagements undertaken more than once by the Nazi Government towards the USSR, the British Prime Minister and the British Secretary of State for Foreign Affairs have defined the attitude of His Britannic Majesty's Government in the United Kingdom. They have declared that the British Government will give all possible aid to the USSR, which is engaged in the war against our common foe.

In the name of the Yugoslav Government I declare that they entirely agree with the position taken up by His Britannic Majesty's Government on the USSR and will observe the same attitude.

22 Soviet Government accredits a minister to King Peter II, 3 September 1941 (*p. 13*)

Desiring to ensure the friendly relations existing between the USSR and Yugoslavia, the Presidium of the Supreme Soviet of the USSR has decided to appoint citizen Aleksander Efremovitch Bogomolov to your government in the capacity of Minister Extraordinary and Plenipotentiary. In hereby accrediting citizen Aleksander Bogomolov the Presidium of the Supreme Soviet requests Your Majesty to receive him kindly and to have full confidence in what he may have the honour to communicate to you in the name of the government of the USSR.

THE RISING IN SERBIA

23 Comintern orders the start of Partisan actions in Yugoslavia, early July 1941 (*p. 13*)

The patriotic war being waged by the Soviet people against Hitler's bandit attack is a desperate life and death struggle, on the outcome of which hangs not only the fate of the Soviet Union but the freedom of your people. The hour has struck when communists must launch an open fight by the people against the invaders. Without wasting a moment, organize Partisan detachments and start a Partisan war behind the enemy's lines. Set fire to war factories, stores, fuel stocks (oil, petrol, etc), aerodromes; smash and destroy railways, the telephone and telegraph system; do not permit the transport of troops and munitions (or any war material). Organize the peasants to hide their grain and drive their cattle into the woods. It is absolutely essential to use all possible means to terrorize the enemy and make him feel he is under siege.

Acknowledge receipt of these instructions, and notify facts to show fulfilment.

24 Tito reports Partisan operations in Serbia, 17 August 1941 (*pp. 13, 24*)

Partisan actions and sabotage in Serbia are on the increase, despite the arrival of fresh German troops.

At Niš, the Partisans set fire to the German officers' home and killed seven German officers and wounded fifteen.

By Kragujevac, the Partisans destroyed a train, killing about fifty German officers and men.

In the night of 12 August, at Zemun, the Partisans bombed and destroyed the Zmaj aeroplane plant and at the same time damaged the Icarus aeroplane plant. Machine-gun and rifle engagements took place.

In Belgrade, the Beometal arms factory was destroyed.

In the Pomoravlje, the Partisans flooded the Senj mines and took the German commissioner prisoner.

By Valjevo, an engagement was fought between Partisans and German motorized units. We got the better of it. Afterwards German reinforcements arrived and burned down the village of Skela and hanged fifty peasants.

On 17 August, the Germans hanged five Partisans in Belgrade, in the middle of Terazija, and left them hanging there a whole day to the great indignation of the people.

In Čačak, the Partisans blew up a dump of munitions, arms and petrol, and all the windows in the town were blown in.

Our Partisans have taken over a number of places and disarmed Germans and gendarmes. Šabac, Bogotić, Lazarevac, etc. were in our hands for several hours. Successful engagements are being fought in a number of places.

In Grobljanska Street, Belgrade, a garage was burned down with eighty petrol trucks.

Our troops are still holding all Montenegro except for Četinje, which they have surrounded.

The savagery of the enemy is only helping to spread the revolt.

25 Moscow informed by Tito that the rising is spreading throughout Serbia and other parts of Yugoslavia, 23 August 1941 (*p. 13*)

Partisan operations in Serbia are taking on more and more the character of a popular rising. The Germans hold only the larger towns, whilst the villages and smaller places are under Partisan control. The Partisans are replacing the local administration, burning tax records, call-up registers and other papers, and people's committees are being set up to run things. Supporters of the Agrarian and other Parties are joining the Partisan detachments under the leadership of the Communist Party.

In many places fierce battles are being fought against the Germans and domestic fascists. By Umka a battle has lasted for about two days. The Germans have also been using aeroplanes.

The Germans have been exercising frightful terror. In their rage they have been hanging folk at the railway stations and leaving them hanging there to strike terror into the people. But the effect is just the opposite. The Partisans are attacking and destroying the railway track and other objectives. The railway workers are abandoning the trains and making off out of fear.

Three more German regiments have arrived in Belgrade as reinforcements. There are now about six German divisions in Serbia.

Arming our people by disarming gendarmes and Germans is making only slow headway. Lack of arms is the chief obstacle in the way of a mass rising.

In Bosnia the popular rising is spreading and fighting is going on in many places against Pavelić's Ustashe, the Germans, and the Italians.

The mass rising of Serbs in Bosnia and Hercegovina, Lika and Kordun, on account of the terrible atrocities perpetrated by Pavelić's Ustashe, is alarming the Germans and Italians, who have been taking over command and in many places disarming Pavelić's Ustashe and calling on the people to come back from the woods. By Sanski Most alone the Ustashe have killed around a thousand women, children, and old men. The villages of Amerska and Piskovce have been completely wiped out. They have been throwing the bodies of dead or wounded peasants into graves by the hundred and burying them there.

The Italians have reoccupied Dubrovnik and are sending their army on into Croatia to occupy the main towns, for Pavelić and his horde have shown themselves incapable of dealing with the Partisans. Stronger units of the German army have also been sent to Bosnia.

Montenegro is still in the hands of our army, but the Italians have been throwing strong forces into the struggle. Peasant insurgents taking to the woods are being accepted at once by our Partisans and organized into military formations.

All the staffs and commands of the Partisan detachments throughout Yugoslavia are in constant touch with the Supreme Staff of the Partisan detachments of Yugoslavia commanded by Valter. The Supreme Staff issues a weekly printed bulletin for the Partisans.

The question of arms is the most important thing for us. Please reply whether it is possible to receive arms from you. We will report where they must be dropped and when.

26 Tito describes the fighting round Kraljevo, early September 1941 (*p. 13*)

On 1 September, 150 Partisans captured the railway station at Kraljevo, seized three wagons of rifles and rifle ammunition (80 cases), several cases of bombs, 1 heavy machine-gun and 1 light machine-gun, with 1 case of ammunition for the latter, and much other material. Telegraph communications were cut, the large stone bridge over the river taken and destroyed, and the guards disarmed. The bridge over the Ibar was attacked and burned after breast to breast fighting, and the guards disarmed.

27 Report of railways and bridges destroyed, end of August or early September 1941 (*p. 13*)

The Partisans clashed with the Germans by Lončanik. The Germans threw in armoured cars. On 23 August fierce fighting broke out against 200 enemy troops around Grabovac and Orašac. The battle lasted a whole day. The Partisans repulsed the Germans and destroyed the bridges causing the loss of six trucks carrying soldiers. Sixteen Germans killed.

By Duboko near Umka the Partisans destroyed 2 trucks and 1 motor-car, killing several Germans. They blew up the railway line at four points. In this battle the Germans used 7 aircraft, but without success. These are only some of the actions in Serbia. All Serbia is ablaze under the German heel.

28 Tito reports that the Germans have been driven from the Mačva, 4 September 1941 (*p. 13*)

The people's rising in Serbia continues to spread. The people are coming over to the Partisans as one man and are helping their struggle. The Germans and their agents have been completely driven out of the Mačva.

The Germans attempted to burn down the villages of Slepčević, Duvanište, and Prnjavor, but the Partisans and peasants drove them back. Barricades have been set up in the villages and the peasants, armed with scythes and sickles, have been fighting alongside the Partisans, driving out the Germans, and destroying the railway track and telegraphs.

29 Tito reports that the Pećanac Chetniks are collaborating with the Germans, 4 September 1941 (*p. 14*)

With the help of the Germans, the Nedić puppet government in Serbia is organizing an army of 50,000 to fight the Partisans.

The Germans have reached an agreement with the Chetnik *vojvoda* Kosta Pećanac who has issued a proclamation against the Partisans and ordered the mobilization of the Chetniks. The people are full of rage against these traitors. The Chetniks have been coming over to us and agreement has been made with some junior Chetnik commanders for common action, although this is against the will of their leaders.

30 Tito protests against Russian propaganda in favour of Mihailović and accuses Chetniks of attacking the Partisans and collaborating with the Germans, 25 November 1941 (*p. 14*)

[To the operator of the clandestine wireless transmitter in Zagreb.] Send on this telegram urgently, as Radio Moscow is broadcasting frightful nonsense about Draža Mihailović against whom we have now been waging a bloody struggle for a month. He is in command of Chetniks, gendarmes and other riff-raff. He attacked us on 2 November and attempted to disarm us, but we routed him so thoroughly that he was left with only about 500 men—gendarmes.

He succeeded through trickery at Gornji Milanovac in disarming about 360 of our people and then turned them over to the Germans, after stripping them to their shirts and then handing them over without their clothes in Valjevo where most of them were executed and the rest put to work half-naked on the aerodrome.

At Mionica, by Valjevo, Draža had seventeen of our nurses and twenty others killed as they were making their way to our staff at Užice.

At Kosjerić his people horribly mutilated about fifteen of our Partisans and two schoolteachers. We found them and brought them mortally mangled to Užice where all could see them. They [the Chetniks] are wild beasts in human guise.

It was only on account of London that we refrained from completely liquidating Draža Mihailović, but we shall be hard put to it to hold the Partisans back from doing this.

Send on the message that they should stop broadcasting the nonsense spread abroad by Radio London.

We have full proof that Draža is co-operating openly with the Germans and fighting against us. Draža's people are not firing a single shot against the Germans. All the fighting is being done by the Partisans.

Four days ago these criminals caused a terrible catastrophe. They put an infernal machine in the tunnel [the vaults of the National Bank at Užice] where we had installed our munitions factory. This set off a frightful explosion which killed more than a hundred workers and citizens who had taken refuge in the next tunnel. On this occasion my own staff was all but blown up too, for our building stood some 5 metres in front of the tunnel. We somehow managed to escape, but some fifteen of our couriers and guards were horribly burned and are now in hospital.

Report this about Draža Mihailović. . . .

31 Tito reports that the Partisans, after being driven out of Serbia, are fighting on in Bosnia, and appeals for help, 29 December 1941 (*p. 14*)

On 22 November, three German motorized divisions, supported by tanks and aircraft and Nedić formations, launched a general offensive against the Partisans in Serbia over a 150 kilometre-wide front.

After eight days' fighting, we lost almost all the towns in West Serbia, including Užice. The Partisan Supreme Staff fell back with part of the army to the Sandžak, whilst the remaining Partisan units remained on Serbian soil and carry on a renewed struggle, in Partisan fashion, against the forces of occupation. The offensive resulted only in our losing the towns; the invaders did not succeed in breaking or destroying us.

The Partisan Supreme Staff fell back with one part of the Partisan units into the Sandžak, where we immediately began hostilities against the Italians. We captured Nova Varoš and some other places. Three thousand Montenegrin partisans are also, on our instructions, in the Sandžak.

In the fight against the invaders and the Nedić forces, the Partisans alone took part, whilst the greater part of Draža Mihailović's men went over to Nedić. Another, smaller part—two to three hundred strong—stayed with Draža Mihailović and stood passively by watching us fight, and then fled with him into Bosnia.

The Party's CC and the Partisan Supreme Staff have formed the First Proletarian Brigade in the Sandžak consisting of Serbs and Montenegrin Partisans. This is a shock brigade which will always have to face the most difficult tasks. On the way into Bosnia, the brigade dispersed three columns of the Italian army which, together with the Chetniks, attempted to attack us near the village of Rudo. One column two hundred strong was completely destroyed. One hundred and sixteen Italian soldiers were captured, including four officers. We captured 5 mine-throwers, 9 machine-guns, 2 heavy machine-guns, 600 bombs, 300 grenades, 15 horses, a quantity of ammunition, and supplies for one hundred and fifty Italian soldiers.

The Supreme Staff moved the Proletarian Brigade into Bosnia because of the straits in which the Bosnian Partisans found themselves, since the Germans and Italians are hurriedly arming the Chetniks and rallying all Serbian reactionaries, both in Bosnia and Serbia, who are making much propaganda against us and are now preparing to strike us a new blow in Bosnia. They are trying to split the Bosnian Partisans, and have in part succeeded, as a number of Partisan detachments have gone over to the Chetniks.

The arrival of help from you would put an end to that, for it would be of immense moral importance for the future of our liberation struggle.

MOSCOW AND THE GOVERNMENT IN EXILE: EFFORTS TO SECURE SOVIET RECOGNITION FOR MIHAILOVIĆ

32 Yugoslav minister instructed by Government in Exile to press the Russians to order the Partisans to co-operate with Mihailović, 13 November 1941 (*p. 16*)

Please approach the Russian Government and ask them to send urgent instructions directing the Communists to collaborate with Colonel Mihailović and to work under him in a united effort against the aggressor. According to his last report, the Communists are attacking Mihailović troops and thus preventing any success in their fight against the Germans.

Inform us immediately of the result.

33 Yugoslav minister reports Vyshinsky's reaction to request for recognition of Mihailović to Government in Exile, 17 November 1941 (*p. 16*)

I visited Vyshinsky today. I asked that the question of collaboration with the

Partisans should be taken very seriously, and that their intervention should be prompt, energetic and convincing. I explained the necessity of uniting all the rebel forces under one command, if it was desired that the movement should continue to lead to any sort of success. I said that the Yugoslav Government desired that the whole movement should be under the command of Colonel Mihailović, who was the soldier best able to organize and lead the fight against the enemy. As a staff officer, he would know how to make the best use of the terrain. If it was desired to give the movement a character of an extensive operation, it was necessary that an expert should lead it. I gave Mr Vyshinsky a whole series of examples from the Belgrade radio, and I pointed out to him that Colonel Mihailović's movement had taken a wider form.

Vyshinsky replied as follows: 'Your request is clear to me. Personally, I can give you no answer, for it is for the Government to decide the matter. I shall send an account of this conversation to Moscow. It is necessary also to discuss all this with military experts. I shall do what I can to get an answer in the course of the week.' From the whole of this conversation with Vyshinsky I could see that he knew nothing of your talk with Maisky, which is mentioned in the telegram about the same subject sent to the British Ambassador. So also as regards events in Yugoslavia. I immediately informed the British Ambassador of this conversation, as he is to see Vyshinsky tomorrow to speak to him in the same sense.

34 Prime Minister Jovanović instructs minister to report any signs of Soviet support for the Partisans, 5 February 1942: excerpt (*p. 17*)

Your main task is to follow carefully Moscow's communist propaganda with respect to our country. You should give early warning of any eventual help which the USSR may propose giving to the Partisans with a view to changing by force the social and state system in Yugoslavia. . . .

35 Government in Exile's report of the situation and démarche to get the Soviet Government to intervene with the Partisans, 29 April 1942 (*p. 17*)

The Partisans in Yugoslavia are attacking Draža's units. In Croatia, Slovenia and Dalmatia, the Trotskyists are attacking both Draža and the Partisans. The Germans, Italians, and Ustashe are helping them. Nedić's troops are attacking Draža and the Partisans. The Serbian Partisan forces have refused to work with Draža. Nedić is destroying them, for they have no experienced leaders. One unit of Nedić's consisting of 40 men can break up 300 Partisans.

Our principal and common enemies are the Germans, Italians and Hungarians. Everyone must attack them and refrain from mutual annihilation. Try to persuade the Soviet Government to invite the Partisans to put an end to the fratricidal struggle and to place themselves under Mihailović's command against the common enemy. The French Communists have been ordered to obey whatever leader the nation produces to lead the rebellion.

36 Yugoslav minister queries his instructions to approach the Soviet Government, 5 May 1942 (*p. 17*)

The Minister requests urgent instructions as to whether or not it is opportune for him to proceed with this question. He considers that the following points should be borne in mind:

1. Last year, when an approach was made, we received a negative answer.
2. The Soviet Government takes the line that all Communist activity abroad is outside their competence and that it is a purely internal question of the countries concerned.
3. The initiative for a change of attitude in France did not come from the French authorities in London, nor from their Minister in Russia.
4. The Minister says further that without a doubt the order came from Russia and that the agreement was reached on the spot.
5. The Minister is under the impression that something is desired in this sense. As the Russians are insisting on contact with Yugoslavia, he believes that they have this contact. They made inquiries about the sending of aeroplanes to one of the aerodromes in the hands of Mihailović. The Minister directed them to our connections via London. They did not wish to be officially involved in this. The Minister thinks that this question should not be dealt with officially but that until an understanding is reached all military activity on our part should cease, at least until such a time as greater Allied participation can be arranged for and we are in the position to get help from abroad for our struggle.

37 Government in Exile repeats its instructions and deprecates large scale guerrilla action, 7 May 1942 (*p. 17*)

Make another attempt in the sense of telegram SPVK 381 (**35**).

All attempts at an understanding on the spot have failed. Secretly and through the wireless we are doing what we can to prevent premature action on a large scale, which would be fruitless and lead to excessive sacrifice and terrible reprisals. Greater guerrilla resistance, unaided by the Allies, would bring about the destruction of the Serbian people. Let them at least tell the Partisans that the Germans are now the common enemy and that they should put an end to the fratricidal war.

38 Yugoslav Prime Minister complains of the Partisans to Soviet minister, who replies that if Mihailović is fighting the Germans, he too must be considered a Partisan, 16 May 1942 (*p. 17*)

Mr Bogomolov [Soviet Minister to the Yugoslav Government in Exile] came at the request of Mr Jovanović.

They discussed the harmful activities of the Partisans in Yugoslavia who, together with the Germans and Ustashe, were attacking Mihailović's forces in Bosnia and who even now, in spite of the war against Germany, were promoting a social revolution. The difficulties which the Communists were causing Mihailović were gone into. Mr Bogomolov's attention was drawn to the fact that the Communist leaders, by putting forward the social question in the middle of the war, were weakening Mihailović's power to resist the enemy. Mr Jovanović suggested it would be a good thing to persuade the Communist forces that they should place themselves under General Mihailović, who had been advised by us to work with all who were fighting the Germans and Italians, even if they were communists.

Mr Bogomolov interpreted this as a request on our part that the Soviet Government should intervene with the Communists and he immediately answered that the Government accepted no responsibility for the Comintern's activities, and that in any case the relations between Mihailović and individual Partisan units were our internal affair in which the Soviet Government did not wish to be mixed up. He reminded Mr Jovanović that at the recent Pan-Slav Congress, Stalin had invited all Slavs to fight the Germans and had thanked all Partisans without distinction. The Soviet Government did not wish to go further than this. Mr Bogomolov said that the Soviet Government considered every one a Partisan who was fighting the Germans—and consequently also General Mihailović.

39 Soviet note to Yugoslav minister at Kuibyshev on Chetnik collaboration with the enemy reported to Government in Exile, 3 August 1942 (*pp. 18, 98*)

Today, in the presence of Novikov, Lozovsky handed me the following aide-mémoire:

'The Foreign Commissariat deems it necessary to inform the Yugoslav Minister of confidential information in its possession concerning the activities of General Draža Mihailović and the Chetniks under his command. The information is as follows:

1. On 2 March at Višegrad the Partisans defeated an Italian detachment and captured the operational staff of Nedić. They took prisoner 120 Chetniks of General Mihailović and found correspondence which testifies to the collaboration between General Mihailović and the German–Italian forces of occupation [see **66**].

2. On 27 March of this year, when the Partisans defeated the 56th Italian Regiment by Bileće, it was established that the Chetniks under their leader Perišić were assisting the Italians.

3. On 5 April of this year, the national Partisan detachments in the Novi Pazar area fought against the Italian troops with which the Chetniks were collaborating.

4. In the middle of April, the Partisans defeated the Italians in the district of Nikšić. On this occasion the Chetniks, under their leader Stanišić, operated with the Italians against the Partisans.

5. In the operations carried out against the Partisans by the Germans and Italians in the district of Gornji Milanovac and Ravna Gora, the Chetniks acted jointly with the Nedić units.

6. On 13 May of this year, an Italian motorized column was defeated by the Partisans between Mostar and Nevesinje. In this action against the Partisans the Chetniks of General Mihailović and the Ustashe co-operated with the Italians.

7. At the end of May of this year, in the mountainous south western region of Yugoslavia near the Albanian frontier, the Chetniks of General Mihailović, under the leadership of Stanišić, took an active part in the Italian troops' operations against the national Partisan detachments.

8. It is reported that General Mihailović has with the Italian Occupation Authorities in Hercegovina as his permanent representative a certain Dobrosav Jevdjević, who, on instructions from General Mihailović,

travelled to Dalmatia to effect the mobilization of the Chetniks against the national Partisan movement in Bosnia and Hercegovina. Jevdjević issued a proclamation, widely circulated by the Italians, in which he appealed to the Serbs of Bosnia to join the Chetniks in order to fight the Partisans on the side of the Italians.'

He added that this was the reason why Vyshinsky asked me some months ago whether Mihailović really wanted to fight against Nedić and the Germans, and why the Soviet press did not mention his name. He emphasized that Mihailović was not the only one to have radio contact with abroad.

I told him that I would forward this grave and incredible indictment, which is not in keeping with the reports received from our country, to my government.

Recently the press has been publishing reports of the 'Partisans' struggle in Yugoslavia. I will send you cuttings by post. They should be checked to see whether they emanate from the sources ascribed to them or from sources of their own.

40 Yugoslav minister instructed to put the case for Mihailović to the Soviet Government, 12 August 1942 (*p. 18*)

Please communicate to Lozovsky the following:

As heretofore, the Royal Government is determined in its point of view that the unity of resistance in the country is a dire necessity and that any split-up of fighting forces benefits only the common enemy.

I. The Royal Government has been making every effort since October of last year to bring about co-operation between the Partisan groups and the forces of General Mihailović who himself has asked for the intervention of London and Moscow in this matter on several occasions since the end of October, last year.

The efforts of the Royal Government have been exerted constantly in two directions: Official interventions in London and Moscow and military radio broadcasts from London—which began on March 1 of this year, and in which all fighters constantly have been asked to unite in their action against the forces of occupation. The last official intervention was made on May 16, this year, when the Prime Minister, Mr. Jovanović, invited the Soviet Envoy, Mr. Bogomolov, and explained to him the situation in the country and expressed the wish for a cessation of mutual conflict.

II. From the telegrams of General Mihailović it is clear that no co-operation was attained, through the fault of the Partisan leaders especially, who not only refused to come to an agreement in the country, but had opened a fight against the forces of General Mihailović and that, just at the moment when the latter had asked London for intervention in order to bring about unity of action (in the beginning of November, last year). In a telegram of March 22, General Mihailović reported that he had 'positive proof that the forces of occupation supported the Partisans because they wished both sides to be busy fighting each other in the Spring'. In the same telegram it is reported that the Partisan groups in Bosnia had joined the Ustashe. The Partisans had condemned to death even General Mihailović. In a telegram, the General complains that the Partisans had killed off his best officers.

III. Aside from the irreconcilable attitude which they have shown in the

6

country toward the forces of General Mihailović, many Partisan groups, because of loose organization and lack of discipline, have carried out a thoroughly ill-advised policy of strong attacks against the strongest and most numerous element of our people—against the peasants. There were not a few murders of nationally prominent men by the Partisans as, for example, the murder of the well-known national worker and Sokol leader, Čeda Milić of Mostar.

All this provoked a turnabout in the disposition of the peasant masses toward the leaders of the Partisans. These masses had at first joined the Partisans because it was all the same to them under whose flag they fought against the Germans. When they saw that the Partisans fought not only against the Germans, but they also fought a civil war against the non-Communists, and were killing not only representatives of the bourgeoisie but also the peasants in large numbers, the peasants left the Partisan ranks individually and of their own accord, without any order of General Mihailović. That was one of the chief reasons for the collapse of the Partisan movement in individual parts of Yugoslavia.

IV. According to reports from the country, in some regions outside of Serbia there are splits among the Partisans themselves, such as the split into Trotskyists and Stalinists (in Slovenia, Croatia, Dalmatia, Bosnia and Herzegovina) which led to mutual betrayals and even local co-operation with the Ustashe and forces of occupation. There also is data to the effect that agents of the Gestapo had infiltrated into the ranks of certain Partisans, probably Trotskyists, and it is not improbable that the Germans, in whose interest it is, support the conflict between the two opposed fighting movements and forces to bring confusion into their ranks.

V. Any collaboration between General Mihailović and the Ustashe in any way whatsoever is out of the question. This can be seen from his fight in the country, from his dispatches and from the work of the Royal Government in London. Such a collaboration also is out of the question because of the horrible massacres carried out by the Ustashe among the Serbian population, in which over one-half million Serbs were victims.

VI. For the same purpose of creating dissension, rumors were spread about a collaboration of General Mihailović with Nedić. These false rumors are spread by the Germans, Nedić's and Ljotić's agents. However, it is clearly seen from General Mihailović's dispatches that such a collaboration does not exist, and also from his determined demands to have officers who are collaborators with Nedić and Ljotić degraded as well as condemned to death. The Royal Government, upon the request of General Mihailović, announced on June 2, 8 and 26, a strict denial in which Mihailović denied even the thought of any collaboration with the national traitors, Nedić and Ljotić; on July 30, again upon request of General Mihailović, the London radio broadcast a lengthy statement in which 'the traitor Nedić and the criminal Ljotić' were bitterly attacked. It is a well known fact that the Nedić Government promised a great reward in money to anyone killing General Mihailović.

In a dispatch, No. 352 of August 5, General Mihailović reported that Nedić had proclaimed all his units Communists in order to justify before the people their persecution. General Mihailović requested that the above be condemned over the radio.

VII. The Royal Government knows nothing of alleged collaboration of some units with the Italian forces in Western Bosnia. If it exists at all it could be only because General Mihailović has not sufficient control to prevent initiative on the part of individual units with which he has no direct contact.

It is out of the question that General Mihailović himself and his organization in any way collaborated with the Italians.

All these statements have documented proofs contained in a memoir of the Royal Government which will be handed, in the near future, to the Soviet Envoy.

The Royal Government furthermore insists on its readiness to make the greatest effort together with the Soviet Government and that of Great Britain for the sake of the realization of a united resistance in Yugoslavia.

The present relations are of benefit only to the enemy. Everything must be done to put an end to such a state of affairs and to establish a united common action against the common enemy instead of mutual extermination. In this regard, the Royal Government is convinced that effective action is possible through directives over the London and Moscow radios, which are listened to by everybody in Yugoslavia, and through other channels. Everything in this direction must be done together and as soon as possible. The Royal Government is prepared to carry out such an understanding immediately.

A copy of the memoir will be sent to you also. Strictly Confidential V.K. No. 711. Jovanović.

41 Soviet and Yugoslav Governments raise their respective legations to embassy status, August 1942 (*p. 19*)

The Yugoslav Government last night issued the following statement:

The Yugoslav Government and the Government of the Soviet Union have reached agreement following which their respective legations will be raised to the rank of embassies.

42 Tito urges the Soviet Government to recognize the treacherous role of the Chetniks and the Government in Exile, and deplores the decision to upgrade diplomatic missions, 11 August 1942 (*p. 19*)

The raising of the representation of the Yugoslav Government in Moscow to the rank of embassy has made an unfavourable impression on all patriots of Yugoslavia, particularly those in the ranks of our army, all the more so since this has come at a moment when the treacherous government of Yugoslavia is openly collaborating with the invaders, decorating every executioner with hands stained with the blood of the people, against whom we are waging a life and death struggle, just as we are against the invaders. Yesterday the Yugoslav Government demonstratively and openly decorated Pop Perišić, Djujić, and many other Chetnik executioners.

By this, our national liberation struggle has been made much more difficult. All wavering persons and open enemies of our fight quote this not as recognition by the Soviet Government of our national struggle, but as recognition of the policy of the Yugoslav Government in London. Can nothing be done to ensure that the Soviet Government is better informed concerning the treacherous role of the Yugoslav Government, and also of the superhuman sufferings and difficulties of our folk who are fighting the invaders, the Chetniks, the Ustashe and the rest of them? Do you really not believe our daily reports? We are asked on all sides what it all means, and however are we to explain it? There is already a lack of spirit showing in our ranks. This may have terrible consequences for our struggle.

We underline: the Yugoslav Government is openly collaborating with the Italians and under cover with the Germans. It is betraying our people and the Soviet Union. We are quite sure too that the intelligence service is in support of this policy.

43 Comintern asks Tito for evidence that Milhailović is collaborating with the enemy, early September 1942 (*pp. 19, 23, 25*)

Urgently communicate in brief contents of documents which you possess concerning the role of Draža Mihailović. Take care to check their authenticity well. It is possible that the invaders are particularly interested in stirring up an internecine struggle between the Partisans and Chetniks. It is not out of the question that some of these documents have been deliberately faked by the invaders themselves.

44 Government in Exile lays down its conditions for a Soviet approach to Mihailović, 18 November 1942 (*p. 19*)

Before there can be any agreement, the campaign against Mihailović must be stopped. Only then can there be talk of co-operation. To start with, it would be enough to tell the Partisans to stop fighting Mihailović. It would be of inestimable importance to order the Partisans to place themselves in our country under the command of Mihailović, who alone should co-ordinate all efforts.

The following three stages should be successively reached: the press and radio campaign against Mihailović should cease, the Partisans should be required to stop fighting him, and they should then be required to place themselves under the High Command [of Mihailović].

Only after this could there be any talk of sending Russian officers to the staff of the High Command.

45 Government in Exile inform Mihailović that the Russians wish to send a military mission but that they have rejected the proposal, 30 November 1942 (*p. 19*)

The Russians have suggested they send high-level officers to your HQ to set up direct contact with you, and form a squadron of yours in Russia to get assistance to you and organize joint broadcasting. Have rejected proposal. We are insisting, (1) immediate cessation of radio and press campaign against Yugoslav army under your command; (2) the Partisans being told not to attack our armed forces; (3) Partisans to be placed under your command. Only when this is done can there be talk of further cooperation. We shall inform you of further developments.

46 Yugoslav Foreign Minister repeats his conditions to the Soviet Government, 1 December 1942 (*p. 19*)

There can in no circumstances be any talk of cooperation until the campaign against Mihailović has been stopped.

As a preliminary to further work, the situation inside the country demands the cessation of the campaign. The ambassador and military attaché should direct all their endeavours to achieving the aims specified in my telegram No 958 [**44**].

47 Yugoslav ambassador reports that he knows of no Russian propaganda against Mihailović, 3 December 1942 (*p. 19*)

Please keep me informed how campaign against General Mihailović is developing. Here in Russia it is impossible to read or hear anything against Mihailović. If there is a campaign in the foreign press, then it is not reported here. What is more, uninformed persons in the Ministry of Foreign Affairs here speak of Mihailović as a national hero. The only thing one does notice is that his name is not mentioned in press or radio.

48 Soviet rejection of the Government in Exile's appraisal of the situation reported by ambassador, 26 January 1943: excerpt (*p. 19*)

Today Lozovsky handed me a short written answer in the form of an aide-mémoire declaring that 'the Russian Government considers it necessary to state the tendentious and frequently incredible nature of the allegations contained in the aide-mémoire regarding the Partisans and their relations with General Mihailović [**40**]. The character of such assertions is probably to be explained by their being based on one-sided data which do not correspond to reality. The information at the disposal of the Russian Government is completely different'.

He added orally to me that all their information points to Mihailović having an agreement with the Italians for joint action against [group omitted] and that he is acting according to this agreement.

MOSCOW AND THE PARTISANS

Expectations of Russian military aid

49 Tito reports an airfield in Bosnia ready to receive Russian supplies, 29 December 1941: excerpt (*p. 21*)

Since we have lost all airfields in Serbia, there is at present only one remaining in our hands in Bosnia—at Sokolac. It is suitable for heavy bombers to land. The airfield is being guarded by a battalion of the Proletarian Brigade. The identification signals and coordinates are as follows. . . .

We are waiting day and night for the planes. Send automatic arms, munitions, mortars, mountain guns and other arms. Send in some of your military experts too.

50 Comintern informs Tito that it may be able to fly men in to him, early February 1942: excerpt (*p. 21*)

There is a possibility of our sending men to you in the immediate future. . . . Give us details as to where our aircraft can come down. What reception signals can you make to ensure accurate and easy landing? Have you any aviation spirit?

51 Request to the Comintern for medical supplies, clothes, and arms, 17 February 1942 (*p. 22*)

We urgently require medicaments, particularly anti-typhoid serum. During offensive, there were 160 serious cases of frostbite.

Send us ammunition, automatic weapons, boots, and material for uniforms for the men. Send this by air and parachute to us at Žabljak at the foot of Mt. Durmitor in Montenegro. Here snow has fallen again and airfields are unfit for landing, unless aircraft are fitted with runners.

The Supreme Staff is in the town of Foča, on liberated Bosnian territory. Anything you can send would be of great moral and material significance.

. . . [Excerpt from another signal despatched later in the same day] . . . With regard to my telegram conveying directions for parachuting arms and men at Žablak in Montenegro, I wish to add: the site is fully safeguarded, on completely liberated territory. Both men and material can be dropped immediately, while we shall at once commence organization of reception ground.

To enable large aircraft at future date to land, we urgently need a supply of various automatic weapons, machine-guns, munitions, signals material, rockets, light infantry guns and munitions. Coordinates for aircraft; 43·8 degrees North Lat., 16 degrees 48 minutes east of Paris.

To your 3 red rockets we shall reply with 3 beacons at 50 metres distance from one another, commencing February 23.

52 Further requests for men and materials, 22 February 1942 (*p. 22*)

When we hear your planes approaching Žablak, we shall light a large fire and your pilots should reply with 3 red rockets. When we light 3 more fires, your pilots should release the parachutes.

We urgently need ammunition for our 7·8 mm guns and our Zbroyovka 7·9 sub-machine guns, as well as a range of explosives, together with instructions, for destroying railway tracks and bridges. As far as possible send bombs with instructions, signal rockets together with pistols, sub-machine guns and a number of anti-aircraft machine-guns, binoculars for officers, and canisters of camouflage-smoke material. If you send us sufficient military equipment, we can mobilize 100,000 more men.

The arrival here of a few dozen parachutists would have an enormous moral and political effect. They would be completely protected.

53 Request for help urgently repeated, 19 March 1942 (*p. 22*)

We are in a critical position owing to lack of ammunition. Please do everything possible to send us ammunition and military supplies. Tell us if we can expect anything, and when.

54 Comintern's reply to Tito's request, 29 March 1942 (*p. 22*)

All possible efforts are being made to help you with armament. But the technical difficulties are enormous. You should, alas, not count on our mastering them in the near future. Please bear that in mind. Do all you can to try to get arms from the enemy and to make the most economical use of what armament you have.

55 Comintern repeats that it cannot send arms and advises the Partisans to make a political approach to the Government in Exile, late April 1942: excerpts (*p. 22*)

As we informed you earlier, for reasons which you understand, you unfortunately cannot expect to get either munitions or automatic weapons from here in the near future. The principal reason is the impossibility of getting them to you.

It is therefore necessary for you to make the best and most economical use possible of all possibilities which do exist, amongst these the slenderest and most difficult possibility of equipping yourselves there on the spot. You will have to carry on like that, without regard to the devilish hard conditions, developing a war of liberation, holding out and beating off the enemy, until it becomes possible. . . .

It is certainly necessary to unmask the Chetniks to the people, concretely, with documentary proof, convincingly, but for the present it would be politically opportune for you to do so through a general approach to the Yugoslav Government, emphasizing that the Yugoslav patriots who are fighting have a right to expect support, and that those who claim to be acting in their name should not stick a knife in the back of the national liberation Partisan army when it is fighting against the vile invaders. That means, unmask them, but do not for the time being go over to a direct attack on the government itself.

It would be useful to set up the organization of a National Committee for helping the Army of Liberation of the Yugoslav People composed of persons well known to the Serb, Croat, Montenegrin, and Slovene fighters, to support, both at home and abroad, the fight of the national liberation Partisan army by a national political platform.

Please consider our advice and let us have your observations, and also tell us what concrete steps you take in that direction.

56 Tito requests arms to equip large numbers of volunteers, 26 August 1942: excerpt (*p. 22*)

The Supreme Staff requests the General Staff of the Red Army to help us with military equipment, particularly arms. We have huge possibilities of mobilizing men for a partisan and volunteer army. Through lack of arms we are unable to accept thousands of volunteers for our liberation army. . . .

57 Tito again appeals to Comintern for help, 31 January 1943 (*p. 26*)

I am obliged to ask you once again if it is really quite impossible to send us some sort of assistance? Hundreds of thousands of refugees are in danger of dying of starvation. Is it really impossible, after twenty months of heroic, almost superhuman fighting, to find some way of helping us? Twenty months we have been fighting without the least material assistance from any quarter. I do assure you that this wonderful, heroic people of Bosnia, the Lika, the Kordun, and Dalmatia have deserved to the full the maximum of aid. Typhus has now begun to rage here, yet we are without drugs; peoples are dying of starvation, yet they do not complain. These starving folk give our men their last crust, whilst themselves dying of hunger. They give their last sock, shirt, or boot, and themselves, in mid-winter, go barefoot. Do your utmost to help us.

58 Comintern expresses appreciation of the Partisans' struggle but repeats that it remains unable to send help, 11 February 1943: excerpts (*p. 26*)

You must not for an instant doubt that, were there the least possibility of giving your wonderful, heroic struggle any material aid, we should long ago have done so. The Soviet people, together with its leaders, is in its entirety on your side, full of enthusiasm and profound fraternal sympathy for the National Liberation Army. Josif Visarionovich [Stalin] and myself have many times discussed ways and means of helping you. Unfortunately, hitherto we have not been able to find a satisfactory solution to the problem on account of insurmountable difficulties [groups indecipherable] . . . possibility of affording you assistance. The moment it becomes possible, we shall do everything you most need. Is it possible to doubt this? Please grasp the present situation correctly and explain it all to your fighting comrades. Do not lose heart, but gather all your forces to bear the present exceptionally hard trials. You are doing a great thing, which our Soviet land and all freedom-loving peoples will never forget. With fraternal greetings to yourself and best wishes to all the comrades in their heroic fight against the accursed enemy.

59 Tito reports to Moscow on the Partisans' plight and the death of a British liaison officer, 12 June 1943 (*p. 27*)

We are still in a difficult position. The enemy is again trying to surround us. The enemy has occupied and fortified all the heights along the route of our advance into Central and Eastern Bosnia, placing artillery there, machine-gun posts and small garrisons, while with his main forces he is trying to surround us and is incessantly attacking from all sides. The enemy is suffering very heavy losses, but so are we, especially from aircraft. Today the British Captain Stewart [Stuart] was killed by a bomb, while Captain Deakin and I were lightly wounded. Captain Stewart [Stuart] was at the head of the Mission to our Headquarters. The British say they could have no conception what a hard fight we are waging. They can see that our units are on the march day and night, without sleep or food. We are at present feeding on horse-flesh, with no bread. Our position is hard, but we shall get out of it, even with heavy losses. The enemy is making extreme efforts to annihilate us, but he will not succeed. We request your support in this supreme trial.

Policy on United Front tactics, the Chetniks, and the Government in Exile

60 Tito informs Comintern of his preparations for a National Liberation Committee, 23 August 1941 (*p. 23*)

We are preparing to set up a National Liberation Committee to include well known representatives of the different democratic trends together with our own people. This will be a sort of central national government. It will issue a proclamation to the people calling for all-out struggle. We shall issue names later. The Committee will be clandestine.

61 Tito informs Comintern that he has reached agreement with the Serbian Agrarian Party, September 1941 (*p. 23*)

In all parts of the country the broad masses of the people have lost faith in all the former ruling bourgeois parties who are to blame for the speedy collapse of Yugoslavia and the present sufferings of the people, but towards the Soviet Union they look with vastly increased sympathy and pin all their hopes of salvation to it.

At the wish of the leadership of the Serbian Agrarian Party, the CC of the Yugoslav CP authorized Valter [the pseudonym used by Tito in the Comintern] and another member to negotiate with a view to co-operation during the current phase of events. Agreement was reached on the following: (1) Joint struggle against the invaders; (2) joint struggle for Soviet power and alliance with the USSR; (3) joint struggle against English agents and attempts to restore the old order; (4) joint struggle against incitement to national hatreds; (5) joint committees for alliance between workers and peasants. Dr Jovanović [leader of the left wing Agrarian Party] himself recognizes the need for our hegemony in the struggle and in defence of the powers already won. A similar agreement has been reached in Slovenia with the Christian Socialists, the Sokol, and other groups; (6) the struggle against the invaders is an integral part of our struggle for national freedom and equality for the peoples of Yugoslavia. National freedom and the equality of its peoples can only be achieved on the basis of brotherly understanding between all the peoples of Yugoslavia. In connection with this, the Party is mobilizing all its strength in the struggle against incitement to national hatreds, which the invaders and their agents, and likewise the agents of England, are doing everything they can to promote.

62 Comintern urges Tito to broaden the basis of the united national front and avoid signs of a communist character which might alarm Western allies, 5 March 1942: excerpt (*p. 23*)

Study of all the information you give leaves the impression that the adherents of Great Britain and the Yugoslav Government have some [? justification] in suspecting the Partisan movement of acquiring a communist character, and aiming at the sovietization of Yugoslavia. Why, for example, did you need to form a special Proletarian Brigade? The basic, immediate task is for the present to unite all anti-Nazi movements, smash the invaders, and achieve national liberation.

How is one to explain the fact that supporters of Great Britain are succeeding in forming armed units against the Partisan detachments? Are there really no other Yugoslav patriots—apart from communists and communist sympathizers—with whom you could join in a common struggle against the invaders?

It is difficult to agree that London and the Yugoslav Government are siding with the invaders. There must be some great misunderstanding here. We earnestly request you to give serious thought to your tactics in general and to your actions, and to make sure that you on your side have really done all you can to achieve a true united national front of all enemies of Hitler and Mussolini in Yugoslavia, in order to attain the common aim—the expulsion of the invader and would-be conquerors. If you have not already done so, you should urgently take the necessary measures and inform us.

63 Comintern congratulates Tito but urges him to avoid making difficulties in the USSR's relations with Western allies and Government in Exile, early March 1942 (*p. 23*)

Defeat of the Fascist bandits and liberation from the invader today constitute the main task, the task which stands above all others. Take into account that the Soviet Union has treaty relations with the Yugoslav King and Government and that taking an open stand against these would create new difficulties in the joint war efforts and the relations between the Soviet Union on the one hand and Great Britain and America on the other. Do not view the issues of your fight only from your own, national standpoint, but also from the international standpoint of the British–American–Soviet coalition. While doing all you can to consolidate positions won in the national liberation struggle, at the same time try to show political elasticity and some ability to manœuvre. We are all full of enthusiasm at your heroic fight and wholeheartedly delighted by your successes. We are trying to make your cause widely popular in all countries, and it justifiably excites the enthusiasm of the peoples fighting against Fascism, and among public workers, and serves as a fine example for popular resistance in other occupied countries. It is our wish to see you courageously come through all the trials ahead of you, and win further great successes. We firmly grip your plucky hands.

64 Tito replies to Comintern criticism and states his case, 9 March 1942 (*p. 22*)

You have drawn mistaken conclusions from our reports. The supporters of the London Government do not collaborate with the invaders openly in their fight against the Partisans and the Yugoslav volunteer army, not all of them at least. They fight against us in the name of Nedić, whom they call Serbia's best son. Draža Mihailović's detachments no longer exist; they are now all in the ranks of the Nedić army. They are gendarmes, officers and NCOs and the small Chetnik bandit groups of Kosta Pećanac.

From the start of the Partisan movement in Yugoslavia, the followers of the

London Government have forcefully declared themselves against an armed struggle against the invader on the plea that this brings down reprisals on the population. Draža Mihailović has also held these views. That is precisely why they have turned their arms against us. That is also why the invaders furnish them with war material for fighting against us. But they only constitute small groups just in Serbia and Bosnia. The Supreme Staff of the Partisans and the volunteer army has up to 200,000 fighters. These are not only communists and their sympathisers, but also followers of different parties—real patriots. And there are officers, even generals, with us too, and they are honourable patriots.

We did not form Proletarian Brigades right at the start, but in the winter, in December, when the need for it became apparent. They are mobile units of workers and peasants ready to go into action wherever they are ordered. They serve as an example of how one ought to fight for the independence of one's nation. This has made an enormous impact on the other Partisan and volunteer detachments.

Our peasants want to join the Proletarian Brigades en masse but this is not our practice. So we have also formed volunteer detachments which all patriots can join together in the fight against the invaders.

We are not setting up any sort of soviets, but we are forming committees of national liberation.

Send observers from the CPSU. We have all the documents on the treacherous work of the various followers of London. We are in possession of a report from General Novaković [an officer who had left the Chetniks for the Partisans] for the London Government which is sharply critical of Draža Mihailović and the fifth column. He would like to send this report through you to London. We need arms and ammunition. That is the best way to form a national liberation front. We have a huge number of men who want to fight the invader but there are no arms.

65 Comintern reaffirms its confidence in the Partisans but urges them not to emphasize their struggle against the Chetniks, March 1942 (*p. 24*)

Unfortunately, you misunderstood our telegram. We made you no reproaches. There was no thought of that. You enjoy our complete, unbreakable confidence. Our question had only one purpose—to obtain a necessary explanation of your latest report. Seeing that Soviet foreign broadcasting (for reasons of policy) for the present makes no mention of the Chetniks, it is not opportune . . . to emphasize that the struggle is mainly against the Chetniks. World public opinion must first and foremost be mobilized against the invaders; mentioning or unmasking the Chetniks is secondary. That of course at the present juncture. As for your heroic fight and its triumphs, we are doing all we can to give them publicity, which indeed, in the field of propaganda, is the most essential thing.

66 Tito reports clashes with the Chetniks and claims proof of their collaboration with the invaders, March 1942 (*p. 24*)

On 2 March we routed the Italians and Chetniks by Višegrad as they were trying to break through to our liberated territory. On 8 March we surrounded and captured by Višegrad the entire operational Nedić staff for that sector. We took five officers, one hundred and twenty Chetniks, the staff archives and a quantity of war material.

These records fully confirm our charges against the followers of Draža Mihailović and the Yugoslav Government in London that they have been collaborating, directly or indirectly, with the invaders.

Why have they been collaborating? Because the invaders have promised Bosnia both to the Croats and to the Serbs, provided they fight the Partisans. The invaders have been arousing the hegemonistic appetites of both Croats and Serbs in order to incite them to a fratricidal war and to divert the attention of the mass of the people in Serbia and in Croatia away from the war of national liberation against the invaders.

But this is being prevented by the Partisans and the CP which are fighting for the brotherhood and unity of all the peoples of Yugoslavia who are in favour of a resolute struggle against the invaders. That is why they hate us and with the help of the invaders organize different Chetnik detachments against us. That is why all the reactionary elements and riff-raff have rallied to fight against the movement for national liberation.

Please ask the Yugoslav Government in London for an explanation of this collaboration with the invaders. In the name of the whole Yugoslav people and of the national liberation Partisan and volunteer army we are resolutely combatting the treacherous work of Draža Mihailović's officers, Dangić [a Chetnik leader in Bosnia] and others, who are knifing us in the back just as we are waging a fierce and bloody war against the invaders and our many enemies for the cause of our country's freedom and independence.

67 Tito repeats his pleas for help and his protests against the Chetniks and the Government in Exile, 24 May 1942: excerpts (*pp. 23, 24*)

Since May 20th I have been . . . on the Montenegrin sector of the front. The situation here is critical. . . . Incessant fighting has left our Partisans exhausted; apart from that, there is no more ammunition. We shall have to get the larger part of our battalions out of Montenegro, if they are not to be annihilated.

The whole people curse the Yugoslav Government in London, which through Draža Mihailović, is aiding the invader. On all sides people and fighting men are asking why the Soviet Union does not send us aid, were it only automatic weapons and ammunition. Our Partisans are fighting with unprecedented heroism. . . . The question of assistance is a very serious one to us. In the name of the Supreme Staff, please pass on to the Supreme Staff of the Red Army our request for assistance. The enemy is making every possible effort to wipe us out; the lives of hundreds of thousands are in danger. We know it is out of the question, and are continuing the fight without regard to losses.

Is it really quite impossible to do something in London against the present treacherous policy of the Yugoslav Government?

68 Tito sends further reports of Chetnik collaboration and appeals to Comintern to make it known, 30 May 1942: excerpts (*p. 24*)

The Italian Command is doing all it can here, just as in Montenegro, to transfer authority to the Chetniks, to which end it is carrying through a conscription of the peasantry for the Chetnik ranks. The Chetniks now always attack in front of the Italians, and are much more dangerous, since they know every track and attack us from all sides. . . .

In Montenegro, fierce battles are being fought against the Chetniks of Mihailović and Stanišic and against the Italians. . . . We have suffered heavy losses in Montenegro. We have evacuated 600 wounded to Piva. Thanks to the treachery of the Chetniks, the Italians in Montenegro are now losing few men, since their camps are protected by Chetniks.

Radio London frequently broadcasts in Serbo–Croat about the common fight being waged by Partisans and Chetniks against the invaders. That is a horrible lie. All the Chetniks in Yugoslavia, particularly those of Mihailović, fight on the side of the invaders, against our national liberation units. In bestial murder and terrorization they exceed the invaders. The Chetnik detachments are set up by the invaders, who arm them and hand over authority to them. They are the faithful watchdogs of the invaders. We are deeply convinced that the Yugoslav Government in London is also involved in this, and knows it all. Please do all you can to expose this terrible treachery and acquaint the whole world with it. In a few days we propose to issue a proclamation against the Chetniks and the Yugoslav Government in London. We have kept silence so far, but it is now necessary to unmask this vile and treacherous game publicly. Please communicate your opinion. . . .

Hercegovina is now aflame with a veritable rising of the people against the invaders. Here our Partisan army is inflicting vast losses on the Italians, but the Italian invaders are making every exertion to suppress this rising with the help of the Chetniks. Draža Mihailović's Chetniks, together with Italian troops, are striving to break through from Montenegro into Hercegovina in order to drown the rising in blood. We are fighting in the teeth of great difficulties. We have little ammunition and no medicines and we have to defend the territory in which our hospitals are.

London's propaganda is deceiving people with its false communiqués. The enemies of the national liberation struggle in Yugoslavia are being aided from London. But despite all that, the morale of our units and of the people is high. The people are confident of the victory of the Soviet Union and of our own victory.

69 Tito repeats his request for an all-allied commission and protests against allied propaganda in support of Mihailović, 13 December 1942 (*p. 24*)

I have several times requested you to do everything you can to send an all-allied Commission to Yugoslavia to form a true opinion of the situation and of Mihailović's treachery. It is simply nauseating that the English go on praising Mihailović who has placed all his Chetnik formations at the service of the Italians and Germans against whom the English and Americans are fighting. Regardless of every sacrifice, we are destroying the railway lines to prevent the enemy from sending troops and material to Africa, but the Chetniks of Mihailović are guarding these lines.

70 Tito complains to the Comintern that the Partisans are not receiving enough moral support, 9 September 1942 (*p. 25*)

Why does Radio Moscow in its Serbo–Croat programme not speak of the Chetnik atrocities? Why does it not give publicity to our struggle? That is what many people are asking, and justifiably they demand at least moral support. Many are dissatisfied with the programmes of Radio Moscow in Serbo–Croat.

71 Tito reports the conversion of Partisan units into an army and proposes the creation of the National Liberation Committee as a 'government', 12 November 1942 (*p. 25*)

So far we have formed eight divisions of three brigades each, on the territory of Bosnia, Croatia and Dalmatia. In the other parts of Yugoslavia we have begun the formation of brigades from the stronger partisan detachments. Numerous partisan detachments and battalions, with their staffs, remain for partisan action. All these divisions are well armed, inclusive of artillery. This represents arms captured in engagements with the enemy.

These divisions are no longer called partisan units, but shock divisions of the National Liberation Army of Yugoslavia.

We shall now set up something like a government which is to be called the National Liberation Committee of Yugoslavia. This committee will include representatives of all the nationalities of Yugoslavia, drawn from various previous parties.

72 Comintern's instructions on the scope of the National Liberation Committee, November 1942 (*p. 25*)

The creation of a National Liberation Committee of Yugoslavia is very necessary and of exceptional importance. You must not fail to give the Committee an all-national Yugoslav and all-Party anti-fascist character, both in its composition and in its programme of work. Do not look upon the Committee as a sort of government, but as the political arm of the national liberation struggle.

Do not put it in opposition to the Yugoslav Government in London. At the present stage, do not raise the question of the abolition of the monarchy. Do not put forward any slogan of a republic. The question of the regime in Yugoslavia, as you understand it, will come up for settlement after the German–Italian coalition has been smashed and the country freed from the invaders.

73 Tito accepts Comintern's advice but reaffirms Partisans' view of the Government in Exile, 29 November 1942 (*p. 26*)

We agree to the advice you gave in your telegram and shall follow it. But I must inform you that it is precisely the civilian activists who have condemned the Yugoslav Government in London as traitorous. Although we do not look on this Executive Committee as a sort of government, it will nonetheless have to look after all state business and occupy itself with the war, in which it will have the support of the People's Liberation Committees which have been set up in nearly all districts on both liberated and unliberated territory. There are no other public authorities in Yugoslavia outside these committees and the military authority conducting the struggle. The session was summoned by the Supreme Staff of the National Army and Partisan Detachments of Yugoslavia, who enjoy immense authority throughout the whole country.

74 Tito sends a statement to the allied Foreign Ministers Meeting in Moscow, but it is ignored, early October 1943 (*pp. 27, 32*)

With reference to the preparations for a conference of representatives of the USSR, Great Britain, and America, it is probable that the question of Yugoslavia will come up. Will you please inform the Government of the USSR of the following:

The Anti-Fascist Council of Yugoslavia, of Croatia, and of Slovenia, and the Supreme Staff of the National Liberation Army and Partisan Detachments of Yugoslavia have authorized me to make the following declaration:

(1) We recognize neither the Yugoslav Government, nor the king who is abroad, because for two and a half years they have been supporting that collaborator with the invaders and traitor, Draža Mihailović, and hence bear full responsibility before the peoples of Yugoslavia for that treachery;

(2) We shall not permit them to come back to Yugoslavia, for that would mean civil war;

(3) Speaking in the name of the vast majority of the people, we declare that they desire a democratic republic based on the national liberation committees;

(4) The sole lawful authority of the people at the present time is in the people's liberation committees, headed by the Anti-Fascist Council.

We shall hand a similar declaration to the British Mission attached to our Staff. The British general [Brigadier Maclean, head of the British military mission] has already informed us that the British Government will not insist very much on supporting the king and the émigré government.

75 Tito informs Moscow of his proposal to set up a provisional government, 26 November 1943 (*p. 27*)

On 28 November the plenum of the Anti-Fascist Council of Yugoslavia will begin. Agenda: (1) Reorganization of the Council into the provisional legislative body for the peoples of Yugoslavia; (2) the creation of the National Committee as the provisional executive authority responsible to the Council.

Sessions of the peoples' councils have already been held in Slovenia, Croatia, Bosnia and Hercegovina, Montenegro, and the Sandžak, at which delegates to the plenum were elected. In Macedonia, too, delegates have been elected, including Dimitar Vlahov and Vlado Pop Tomov. Serbia has likewise sent delegates.

Some 200 delegates from different parts of the country have already arrived. It would be good to send them greetings from the Pan-Slav Committee. That would be a great contribution to the further development of the national liberation struggle in Yugoslavia and the Balkans.

76 Tito's report on the second session of the Anti-Fascist Council, early December 1943: excerpt (*p. 27*)

The Anti-Fascist Council for the National Liberation of Yugoslavia (AVNOJ) held its second session at Jajce at the end of November following the meeting of regional councils in Slovenia, Croatia, Bosnia and Hercegovina, Sandžak, and Montenegro.

Of the 208 delegates elected from all the constituent peoples, 142 attended and brought with them plenary and voting powers for the remaining 66. The constitution of the peoples' delegations shows that the national liberation movement brings together on the broadest basis persons from every democratic group, and the work of the meeting was an extraordinary manifestation of the fullest unity and brotherhood of all the peoples of Yugoslavia.

The main report on the development of the struggle for national liberation of the people of Yugoslavia in the context of international events was given by J. Broz Tito and was received with the greatest acclaim and enthusiasm.

The Bosnian delegate Dr Vojislav Kecmanović, a leader of the Serbian Democratic Party, moved the Council's Declaration and three important resolutions: (1) AVNOJ shall be constituted as the supreme legislative and executive-representative body, the presidency of which shall appoint the National Committee for the Liberation of Yugoslavia in the character of a Provisional Government; (2) the establishment of the federal principle for the structure of Yugoslavia; (3) the abrogation of all the rights of the Government in Exile and a ban on the return of King Peter until the liberation of the whole country, when the people will settle the question of the king and the monarchy. . . .

77 Communiqué of the Soviet Commissariat for Foreign Affairs endorsing the resolutions adopted by the Anti-Fascist Council, 14 December 1943: excerpt (*p. 27*)

These developments in Yugoslavia, which have already met with understanding in Britain and the USSR, are considered by the government of the USSR as a positive factor which should contribute to the further successful struggle of the peoples of Yugoslavia against Hitlerite Germany. These developments also bear witness to the solid success achieved by the new leaders of Yugoslavia in the matter of uniting all the peoples of Yugoslavia. . . .

INTERNATIONAL ISSUES AND THE PARTISANS

Italy

78 CPY asked to transmit Comintern instructions to the Italian communists, early July 1941: excerpt (*p. 29*)

Tell the Italian comrades that their task is immediately to send a group of comrades into the country [Italy] to organize a movement for the defence of the Soviet Union, mainly amongst the workers in the war industry. Aim—to slow down production and organize sabotage in the war industry; to organize the peasants to resist requisitioning and [group corrupt]. . . .

In Slovenia and Croatia all means must be used to bring about the demoralization of the Italian army, the desertion of Italian troops, and to get the soldiers to resist being sent to the front against the USSR and to cause armed clashes between soldiers and militiamen. Stir up hostility specially between Italian and German fascists and provoke armed clashes between them.

Albania

79 Tito transmits Comintern's instructions to the Albanian CP, 22 September 1942: excerpt (*p. 30*)

. . . We asked the Comintern in your name for permission to hold the Albanian CP conference and to elect a permanent CC. Yesterday we at last got an answer authorizing the conference and stating amongst other things: '(1) The conference must be thoroughly safeguarded on all sides against any penetration and on no account must suspect persons or provocateurs be allowed to attend. (2) The basic task of the conference should be the formation of a reliable party leadership and the adoption of concrete decisions. (3) The organizing and strengthening of the national front of all Albanian patriots, avoiding for the time being launching slogans which go beyond the scope of the national liberation of Albania. (4) Inclusion in the leadership of the Partisan struggle as many honest Albanian nationalists and patriots as possible as well as communists.'

Bulgaria and the Macedonian problem

80 Comintern rules that responsibility for Macedonia should remain with the CPY, but speaks of self-determination for the Macedonian people, August 1941 (*p. 31*)

Macedonia should remain with Yugoslavia on the grounds practicality and expediency.

The main struggle is now being waged against the German and Italian forces of occupation and their agents. The chief means of struggle is now the Partisan movement. This movement is now developing on Yugoslav territory and under Yugoslav leadership. Serbian Macedonia should become a base for this movement, harassing the German and Italian rear in the Balkans.

Bearing in mind the position of Macedonia, it is essential to forge the closest co-operation between Yugoslavia and Bulgaria, particularly on the terrain.

Bulgaria should tell . . . Bulgarian CP members who find themselves on Yugoslav territory to co-operate and give all possible help to Yugoslavia, and both parties should adopt an attitude in favour of self-determination for the Macedonian people.

An effort must be made to ensure co-operation between the Yugoslav and Bulgarian people against the common enemy.

81 Tito complains to Moscow about the attitude of the Macedonian and Bulgarian communists and requests clarification of Comintern policy, 4 September, 1941 (*p. 31*)

The Macedonian Regional Committee refused to remain in contact with us and linked up with Bulgarian CP as soon as the occupation of Macedonia started. Šarlo [Metodij Šatorov, Secretary of the Macedonian Regional Committee] refused to answer the CC's thrice repeated summons to come to Belgrade for a meeting in which the Macedonian question could be thrashed out. He refused to distribute the proclamation of the CPY CC calling for military actions, issued a directive that all arms should be surrendered to the authorities and adopted a stance in favour of a Soviet Macedonia and of awaiting the coming of the Red Army. He adopted a hostile attitude towards the Serbian comrades in Macedonia. Šarlo has been making speeches to the members against the leadership of the CPY and its Secretary, dubbing him pro-British because it was stated in the proclamation that Yugoslavia has been enslaved [i.e. that Macedonia was not 'liberated', as the Bulgars claimed].

We sent a delegate to Macedonia and Sofia. The CPB supports Šarlo and says that Macedonia has been attached to the CPB on instructions from the Comintern. We consider the CPB's conduct to be incorrect. We have expelled Šarlo from the Party for sabotage, grave infraction of discipline, making speeches against the leadership, and for national chauvinism, etc.

Up to now there have been no operations of any sort and no Partisan detachments because of this criminal attitude.

We are sending our delegate to organize Partisan detachments, operations, and other activity, and we shall bring the wrong-doers before our Partisan military court. Please inform us whether it is true that the Regional Committee for Macedonia has really been attached to Bulgaria on your instructions. We consider that this is not a good thing, for the Bulgarian Party is in a bad position with regard to operations and communications, since its communications have been cut.

82 Tito rebukes the Bulgarian CP for disregarding Comintern directives and failing in its duty to the USSR, 6 September 1941: excerpts (*p. 31*)

The situation in the Macedonian organization has obliged us to address this letter to you, as we consider you in some degree responsible for what has been happening in the Macedonian organization. The leaders of the Regional Committee in Macedonia have justified their conduct on the grounds that it has allegedly been arranged that it should be attached to you, that it has been receiving directives from you, and that the Comintern has confirmed this attachment. We consider such conduct quite incorrect, as this is a question which should be discussed and arranged with us. . . .

A fierce struggle, with mass actions and sabotage, is now being waged in every part of Yugoslavia by our Partisans, led and organized by our Party against the invaders and their domestic agents. Only in Macedonia is there no action, no Partisan detachments, despite the extremely favourable conditions, both subjective and objective, and our offers of material help. No excuses can justify this sabotage. . . .

We are in constant touch with Georgi [Georgi Dimitrov, Secretary-General of the Comintern], who has been urging upon us the most vigorous action and promotion of the rising. We consider it our duty to draw your attention to this, since this is a directive from the Comintern, and your duty towards the heroic Soviet people as well as to the Bulgarian people.

83 Tito informs the Macedonian communists the Comintern has decided they should remain within the framework of the CPY, 22 September 1942: excerpt (*p. 31*)

We have received a reply direct from the Comintern to the observations we made concerning the mistakes committed in your organization by those comrades whom we expelled from the Party. The Comintern has agreed with us in regard to our standpoint that the Regional Committee for Macedonia should remain until further notice under our leadership and within the framework of the CPY. They only commented on the weak links and the difficulties which arise in keeping in touch with you. Through the Comintern we have also received and agreed to proposals from the CPB CC to the effect that the Regional Committee for Macedonia should be allowed a certain autonomy, whilst remaining within the CPY and under our leadership, and in so far as it continues to be difficult to keep in touch with it, that it should get all the help it can from the CPB CC. We are naturally in full agreement with this, and we have never been against a solution on these lines.

84 Comintern adopts an ambiguous stance on the Macedonian question, 27 February 1942: excerpts (*p. 32*)

The CPB CC sends us the following reports:

(1) Your advice about handing over the Macedonian organization to the leadership of the CPY has been carried out. The situation in Macedonia continues to be difficult. For the last three months the Macedonian comrades have no links with the CPY CC. The leaders in Macedonia often turn to the CPB for advice. The CPB has been sending both advice and material help. . . . The CPB CC has not yet managed to make direct contact with the CPY CC. . . . (4) The CPB CC considers that, in present circumstances, the Macedonian party organizations ought to be formed into a separate Macedonian Party.

The subordination of everything to the CPY CC and the control by it of the Macedonian party organizations should bring about a corresponding improvement of the situation in Macedonia, and calls for the disavowal of the Great Serb policy previously followed with regard to Macedonia and the Macedonian people. That, in the view of the CPB CC, should help to facilitate work amongst the masses and attract the co-operation of the Macedonian comrades.

Please let us know what you think about this.

85 Tito repeats his request to the Comintern for clarification, 27 February 1942: excerpt (*p. 32*)

We have received the information from the CPB CC.

We cannot understand the last part of the telegram about reorganizing the CC for Macedonia as a separate party.

We are shortly sending a representative to Macedonia to make contact with the CPB CC and to help the comrades in Macedonia.

86 Tito protests to Comintern about Bulgarian propaganda for a separate Macedonian state, 24 January 1944 (*p. 32*)

The Bulgarian Fatherland Front has issued a leaflet on the Macedonian question. The line taken is in contradiction to the resolution of AVNOJ regarding federation and is a demand for a united Macedonia which should be attached to nobody but should be entirely separate.

That, in today's circumstances, is German propaganda and hostile to the struggle for national liberation.

In our view, the Fatherland Front would do better to appeal to the Bulgarian soldiers in Macedonia to stop fighting us.

THE ABORTIVE PROCLAMATION TO THE PEOPLES OF OCCUPIED EUROPE

87 Moscow requests the Partisans to prepare a proclamation to the Peoples of Occupied Europe, 13 February 1942: excerpt (*p. 29*)

It would be desirable for the Supreme Staff of the Partisans, on behalf of the Yugoslav people, to make a short proclamation to the peoples of the occupied countries, especially Czechoslovakia and France. In that proclamation, after pointing out that your people are fighting for liberty and independence, the Supreme Staff should call on those people to cease making war materials or supplying blood-stained Hitler with raw materials or foodstuffs, and in every way to do all they can to disrupt his war machine, and develop a Partisan movement against the invader, making every effort to achieve a total defeat of the mortal enemy of all the peoples of Europe—German-fascist imperialism. We could give such a proclamation the widest publicity in the press and by radio. Inform us of your opinion. . . .

88 Tito agrees to the request, 23 February 1942 (*p. 29*)

We have received your telegram of 13 February 1942. We welcome your suggestion about issuing a proclamation in the name of the Supreme Staff of the Partisan and Volunteer Army of Yugoslavia. Also give the proclamation by radio-telegraph in the Yugoslav or English language, for publication in our language in the press.

89 Comintern requires certain changes in the proclamation, 10 March 1942 (*p. 29*)

For your proclamation to have the desired result, there are passages in it which should be amended, since as they stand they lend it a Party character. I suggest:

(1) At the beginning of paragraph 2, delete: 'which were organized by the Communist Party'.

(2) At the end of paragraph 4, add: 'Hitler will not be able to withstand the powerful coalition of America, Great Britain, and the USSR, about which all freedom-loving peoples are rallying.'

(3) Amend the end of the final paragraph as follows: 'The victory of the heroic Red Army is the victory of all the peoples of Europe, though we, too, should fight, and in every possible way assist the just cause of the USSR, Great Britain, and America, and thereby hasten our own liberation.'

(4) Add two slogans only [i.e. omitting those proposed in the Yugoslav draft—'Long live the uprising of all enslaved peoples of Europe against the invader!', 'Long live the heroic Red Army!', 'Long live Comrade Stalin!', 'Long live the Soviet Union!']; 'Long live the united struggle of all downtrodden peoples against the invader!' and 'Long live our victory over the common enemy!'

(5) Could you not give the signatures of some members of the Supreme Staff?

(6) Why do you sign 'Tito'? Would it not be better to sign with your real name?

90 Tito accepts the proposed amendments, 11 March 1942 (*p. 29*)

We entirely agree with your observations concerning the need to correct the proclamation. Please make the corrections yourself and tell us when we may publish them.

Tito cannot yet sign with his real name as this would give away a great number of people in Croatia and put their lives in danger. The name of Tito is now very well known throughout our whole country, particularly in our liberated territory.

91 Comintern decides to withhold publication of the proclamation, 22 March 1942 (*p. 29*)

For Tito (personal). After discussion about the proposed publication of the Proclamation of the Supreme Staff, we have come to the conclusion that in the interests of the cause, publication should be withheld for a time, until certain matters in the relations between the Soviet Government and the Yugoslav Government have been cleared up. (We shall give you good notice when the Proclamation is to be published.)

Disbanding of the Comintern

92 CPY informed of the proposed disbanding of the Comintern, May 1943 (*p. 28*)

On 2 May a proposal was sent to the Sections for the disbanding of the Comintern as the leading centre of the international workers movement. The proposal is explained by the fact that this centralized form of international organization no longer corresponds to the needs of the further development of the Communist Parties of the different countries or of the national workers parties, and has even become an obstacle to this development. Please examine this proposal in detail in your Central Committee and inform us of your decision.

93 CPY informs Moscow that it approves the disbanding of the Comintern, June 1943: excerpt (*p. 28*)

After having considered the proposal of the Executive Committee of the Communist International concerning the disbanding of the Comintern, the Central Committee of the CPY finds itself in full agreement with this proposal as well as with the reasons given. The Central Committee of the CPY is profoundly convinced that this historical decision will not fail to yield tremendous results in the very near future in the struggle for victory over the enemies of mankind, the Fascist invaders. . . .

Thanks to the assistance of the Comintern, the CPY has grown into a powerful mass party which in these fateful days is conducting the struggle for national liberation and has won the goodwill of the people, of the majority of the masses of the Yugoslav people.

Under the banner of Marx, Engels, Lenin, Stalin, our Party will continue to do its duty to its people, regardless of sacrifices, in the struggle against Fascism and for the liberation of the oppressed people of Yugoslavia.

The CPY will remain faithful to the principles of the International.

EFFORTS TO INDUCE THE GOVERNMENT IN EXILE TO COME TO TERMS WITH TITO

94 Soviet Government informs British Foreign Secretary that it wishes to promote collaboration between Government in Exile and National Committee of Liberation, 21 December 1943 (*p. 34*)

The Soviet Government is aware that at the present time very strained relations exist between Marshal Tito and the National Committee of Liberation of Yugoslavia on the one hand and King Peter and his Government on the other. Mutual attacks and hard accusations on both sides, especially those which have recently taken place, have led to open hostilities, which hamper the cause of the struggle for the liberation of Yugoslavia. The Soviet Government shares the view of the British Government that in the interests of the fight of the Yugoslavian people against the German invaders it is necessary to make efforts to find a basis for collaboration between the two sides. The Soviet Government sees the great difficulties standing in the way of the realization of this task, but it is ready to do everything possible to find a compromise between the two sides, with the purpose of uniting all the forces of the Yugoslavian people in the interests of the common struggle of the Allies.

95 Stanoje Simić, ambassador in Moscow, disavows the Government in Exile and declares himself for Tito, March 1944: excerpts (*p. 34*)

With this letter I wish to state that I regard the Anti-Fascist Council as the only representative of the Yugoslav people and the only real organized national authority inside the country and abroad. . . .

The treachery of Draža Mihailović, Minister for War in the Government in Exile in Cairo, the rejection by the so-called government of all my proposals for the organization of Yugoslav military units to fight on the German–Russian front against our common enemy, the unjust measures taken against the

Yugoslav soldiers and officers in the Middle East who expressed a wish to fight in the ranks of the National Liberation Army in their country, all go to show that the Purić government does not represent its people at this most critical juncture of their heroic struggle.

As the representative of Yugoslavia in the Soviet Union I have always acted only in the interests of the struggle for national liberation. I have striven to convince each successive Government in Exile to provide unrestricted help to the people of Yugoslavia in their struggle, but all this has been in vain. Throughout my work I have never been ideologically linked to the anti-national Government in Exile and to the reactionary circles of Yugoslavia and now I believe the time has come to break completely with them, and I ask you to believe me that I place myself fully at your disposition and take my place in the ranks under your orders to play my part in your struggle of superhuman heroism for victory over our common enemy and the creation of a new, free, federal, and democratic Yugoslavia.

96 Soviet Government supports moves for a united Yugoslav Government, 25 November 1944 (*p. 34*)

In conversations held in Moscow from 20–23 November between Dr I. Šubašić, E. Kardelj, and S. Simić on the one side, and J. V. Stalin and V. M. Molotov on the other, a friendly discussion took place on fundamental Yugoslav problems arising out of the position of Yugoslavia among the United Nations.

In the course of this there was recognized the necessity for the formation of a united Yugoslav Government on the basis of the agreement concluded between Marshal Tito and Dr I. Šubašić.

The Soviet Government welcomes the efforts of Marshal Tito and Premier Šubašić to unify all the truly democratic forces of the people in the struggle against the common enemy and in the creation of a democratic federative Yugoslavia as a positive and constructive factor in the achievement of victory and the organization of peace in Europe.

97 Moscow criticizes King Peter for hampering the formation of a united government, January 1945: excerpt (*p. 35*)

The Tito–Šubašić Agreement has been welcomed by democratic opinion in Yugoslavia and by the allies. King Peter does not know the true situation in Yugoslavia. This is not a government crisis, but the personal crisis of King Peter.

He has no wish for a democratic Yugoslavia, but has been opposing it with the help of reactionary groups, including the Mihailović band.

Peter is in danger—in danger of cutting himself off completely from the people whose unanimous opinion is well known. Whatever the king's attitude may be, that cannot seriously influence internal political conditions.

98 Yalta Conference communiqué indicates Stalin in agreement with Churchill and Roosevelt on policy towards Yugoslavia, February 1945: excerpt (*p. 35*)

. . . We have agreed to recommend to Marshal Tito and Dr Šubašić that the

Agreement between them should be put into effect immediately and that a new Government should be formed on the basis of that Agreement.

We also recommend that, as soon as the new Government has been formed, it should declare that

(i) The Anti-fascist Assembly of National Liberation (AVNOJ) should be extended to include members of the last Yugoslav Parliament (Skupština) who have not compromised themselves by collaboration with the enemy, thus forming a body to be known as a temporary Parliament; and

(ii) Legislative acts passed by The Anti-fascist Assembly of National Liberation (AVNOJ) will be subject to subsequent ratification by a Constituent Assembly.

There was also a general review of other Balkan questions.

99 Churchill informs the House of Commons of the steps taken with USSR for a joint policy towards Yugoslavia, 18 January 1945: excerpt (*p. 35*)

. . . As we feared that there might be misunderstandings and contrary policies between us and the Soviet Government about Yugoslavia, which can easily arise when armies enter a country which is in great disorder, the Foreign Secretary and I reached at Moscow an understanding with Marshal Stalin by which our countries pursue a joint policy in these regions, after constant discussions. This agreement raised no question of divisions of territory or spheres of interest after the war. It arrived only at the avoidance, during these critical days, of frictions between the great allies. In practice, I exchange telegrams on behalf of His Majesty's Government personally with Marshal Stalin about the difficulties which arise, and about what is the best thing to do. We keep President Roosevelt informed constantly.

In pursuance of our joint policy, we encouraged the making of an agreement between the Tito government which, with Russian assistance, has now installed itself in Belgrade, and the Royal Government of Yugoslavia which is seated in London and recognized by us as, I believe, by all the Powers of the United Nations. Marshal Stalin and His Majesty's Government consider the arrangement on the whole to be wise.

THE RED ARMY IN YUGOSLAVIA

Exchange of military missions

100 Soviet decision to send a military mission to the Partisans, 13 December 1943: excerpt (*pp. 33, 35*)

The activity of the Chetniks of General Mihailović . . . has not facilitated but has rather brought harm to the cause of the struggle of the Yugoslav people against the German invaders, and therefore could not fail to be received unfavourably in the USSR.

The Soviet Government, considering it essential to receive more detailed information in regard to all Yugoslav events and concerning the Partisan organization, has decided to send to Yugoslavia a Soviet Military Mission, as the British Government has done previously.

101 Tito's tribute to the Soviet people and the Red Army, 24 February 1944
   (*p. 36*)

Our fighters—fighters for the freedom and brotherhood of the Yugoslav
peoples—have always been conscious that the Soviet Union's patriotic war is
at the same time a struggle for the liberation of all enslaved peoples. They have
been conscious that their sacred duty towards their native country requires
them to fight shoulder to shoulder with the Red Army. They have felt it a great
honour and responsibility to be fighting with the army led by the great Stalin.
Their fiercest attacks have been launched against the German bandits setting
off for the eastern front or returning from it. The tributes paid by the Soviet
peoples and its army to our struggle against the German fascists have been to
us the dearest of all tributes.

Joint military operations

102 Tass communiqué on the entry of Soviet forces into Yugoslavia,
   28 September 1944 (*p. 38*)

Several days ago the Soviet command—bearing in mind the interests of the
development of operations against the German and Hungarian troops in
Hungary—asked the National Committee of Liberation of Yugoslavia and
the Supreme Headquarters of the National Liberation Army and Partisan
Detachments of Yugoslavia to consent to the temporary entry of Soviet troops
into Yugoslav territory which borders on Hungary. The Soviet command on
this occasion declared that Soviet troops, having completed their operational
task, would be withdrawn from Yugoslavia.

The National Committee and Supreme Headquarters of Yugoslavia agreed
to meet the request of the Soviet command. The Soviet command accepted the
condition advanced by the Yugoslav side that the civil administration of the
National Committee of Liberation of Yugoslavia should be operative in
the territory of Yugoslavia in the area where the units of the Red Army
are located.

103 Report sent to Tito by the commander of a Partisan unit on lack of
   effective collaboration with the Soviet troops in the field, October 1944:
   excerpts (*p. 39*)

Today the Russians captured (with our co-operation) Mladenovac and
Topola. Their motorized corps proceeds further. It is necessary to co-ordinate
their advance with ours. From a talk with their divisional commander, we
gather that they ignore the fact that we have here our major forces and that
we have been assigned the main role in taking Belgrade (with the assistance of
Soviet armour, transport, and artillery). They do not even know of the existence
of our liberated territory. Help establish liaison between us and them.

104 Tito's message to Stalin on the liberation of Belgrade, 20 October 1944:
   excerpt (*p. 39*)

In connection with the liberation of Belgrade, the capital of Yugoslavia, allow me on behalf of the National Army of Liberation and the peoples of Yugo-slavia, to express gratitude to you, as the Supreme Commander of the great army of liberation which, in co-operation with the National Army of Libera-tion and the peoples of Yugoslavia, with exceptional heroism has liberated Belgrade. The liberation of Belgrade has an historic significance for our peoples, especially as the country of these tortured peoples is a place where the sons of the great Soviet Union and the gallant sons of Yugoslavia have died. Once more the brotherhood of the peoples of Yugoslavia and the peoples of the Soviet Union is sealed. Long live the heroic Red Army! Long live the great Soviet Union! Long live great Stalin, the Supreme Commander-in-Chief of the Red Army! Death to fascism, freedom to the people!

105 Mihailović informs General Wilson of his attempts to co-operate with the Russians in Serbia, 8 November 1944: excerpt (*p. 40*)

Russian troops which crossed the Danube in Yugoslavia enabled the Com-munists to break into Serbia . . . I ordered our commanders in Serbia who were in the direction of contacting the Russian troops to participate with the Russian troops in the fight against the occupier. The Communists rendered this cooperation impossible everywhere by compromising our commanders with the Russians who first of all accepted cooperation and later on turned it down and undertook the disarming of our units and taking them to concen-tration camps. Characteristic is the case of Colonel Keserović who took Kruševac from the Germans and who awaited the Russians as Allies in the freed town. Colonel Keserović was prepared together with all his units to con-tinue the fight against the occupier. In the meantime the Communists attacked out units in Kruševac after which the Russians disarmed a part of these units and wanted to disarm Colonel Keserović who succeeded in getting away.

Even after such cases I ordered our commanders to try and work further in military cooperation with the Russians as allies in the fight against the occu-piers and thereby to show our readiness to fight against them. On the basis of this order of mine Commander of the First and Second Ravna Gora Corps, Captain Raković gave battle in the fight against the Germans near Čačak and Kraljevo. When the Russian troops were contacted, Capt. Raković continued fighting in cooperation with them. Even now he is carrying on this fight to-gether with the Russian troops. . . .

II THE POSTWAR PERIOD

FRIENDSHIP AND FRICTION

106 Treaty of Friendship, Mutual Aid, and Postwar Collaboration between the USSR and Yugoslavia, 11 April 1945 (*pp. 35, 37*)

The Presidium of the Supreme Soviet of the USSR and the Regency Council of Yugoslavia,

Resolved to bring the war against the German aggressors to its final conclusion;

Desirous still further to consolidate the friendship existing between the peoples of the Soviet Union and Yugoslavia, which together are fighting against the common enemy—Hitlerite Germany; desirous to ensure close cooperation between the peoples of the two countries and all United Nations during the war and in peace time, and to make their contribution to the post-war organization of security and peace;

Convinced that the consolidation of friendship between the Soviet Union and Yugoslavia corresponds to the vital interests of the two peoples, and best serves the further economic development of the two countries,

Have decided, with this object in view, to conclude the present treaty, and have appointed as their authorized representatives:—

V. M. Molotov, People's Commissar for Foreign Affairs of the USSR;

Marshal Tito, President of the Council of Ministers of Yugoslavia;

Who, after exchanging their credentials, found in good and due order, agreed on the following:—

Article 1
Each of the contracting parties will continue the struggle in cooperation with one another and with all the United Nations against Germany until final victory. The two contracting parties pledge themselves to render each other military and other assistance and support of every kind.

Article 2
If one of the contracting parties should in the postwar period be drawn into military operations against Germany, which would have resumed her aggressive policy, or against any other State which had joined Germany either directly or in any other form in a war of this nature, the other contracting party shall immediately render military or any other support with all the means available.

Article 3
The two contracting parties state that they will participate, in the spirit of closest cooperation, in all international activities designed to ensure peace and security of peoples, and will make their contribution for attaining these lofty purposes.

The contracting parties state that the application of the present treaty will be in accordance with international principles in the acceptance of which they have participated.

Article 4
Each of the contracting parties undertakes not to conclude any alliance and not to take part in any coalition directed against the other party.

Article 5
The two contracting parties state that after the termination of the present war they will act in a spirit of friendship and cooperation for the purpose of further developing and consolidating the economic and cultural ties between the peoples of the two countries.

Article 6

The present treaty comes into force immediately it is signed and is subject to ratification in the shortest possible time. The exchange of ratification documents will be effected in Belgrade as early as possible.

The present treaty will remain in force for a period of twenty years. If one of the contracting parties at the end of this twenty years period does not, one year before the expiration of this term, announce its desire to renounce the treaty, it will remain in force for the following five years, and so on each time until one of the contracting parties gives written notice of its desire to terminate the efficacy of the treaty one year before the termination of the current five-year period.

In faith whereof the authorized persons signed the present treaty and thereto affixed their seals.

107 Izvestiya pays tribute to the significance of the Treaty of Friendship and the Partisans' role in World War II, 12 April 1945: excerpts (*p. 35*)

Both countries fought shoulder to shoulder against Hitlerite Germany. We all remember how, when the Germans were besieging Stalingrad, Partisan units in Yugoslavia waged a heroic struggle against the common enemy and held down part of the German armed forces. The Yugoslav Partisans kept the German forces of occupation under constant tension and prevented them using Yugoslavia's resources in the war against the USSR. They fought behind the German lines and kept them in constant dread of being taken in the rear. The Yugoslav patriots, heroically fighting under Marshal Tito's leadership, had unshakeable faith in the Soviet Union. They steadfastly believed that the Soviet Union would overthrow the enemy, drive it back from their native soil and help the fraternal peoples of Yugoslavia to free themselves from the yoke of the German fascists. They awaited the day when the Red Army should drive the hated enemy headlong from the land, enter the territory of Yugoslavia, liberate Belgrade together with the troops of Marshal Tito, and cast the Germans from Yugoslav soil.

The victory they have achieved together is now crowned by the Treaty of Friendship, Mutual Aid and Postwar Collaboration between the USSR and Yugoslavia, the aim of which is not only to lead to the end of the war but to make a contribution to the postwar organization of peace and security. This treaty serves the vital interests of both peoples. These vital interests require in the first place the construction of a firm barrier against German aggression . . . and not only against Germany, but against any other state which might unite with Germany, either directly or in any other form, in such a war. . . .

The treaty of 11 April 1945 will go down in the history of the USSR and Yugoslavia as an act of great international significance, destined to play its part in the further development and strengthening of friendly relations between the peoples of the USSR and Yugoslavia, between the Balkan peoples and the peoples of all democratic countries.

108 A Yugoslav profession of faith in the Soviet Union, 16 April 1945: excerpt (*p. 42*)

The Government of old Yugoslavia was openly hostile towards the Soviet

Union. Before the second World War Yugoslavia was a hot-bed of anti-Soviet intrigue and one of the bases for the formation of various terrorist groups which were sent to the Soviet Union. It is not accidental that Yugoslavia established diplomatic relations with the USSR only in 1940. Reactionary governments which were agents of various imperialist cliques, and especially of German fascism, acted contrary to the will of their own peoples.

The new Yugoslavia, resuscitated on the basis of fraternity, unity, and equality of all peoples belonging to our federation, pursues, and will consistently pursue, the most friendly policy towards the Soviet Union. The admiration, respect, and true love of our peoples for the peoples of the great Soviet Union which have been so brilliantly manifested during this war will grow and develop.

New Yugoslavia was born in the fire of the war of liberation in the days when our peoples were locked in a life and death struggle with the common enemy of the United Nations. We shall never forget that at the most difficult moment of our history, when the country was bleeding profusely and languishing in hunger under the yoke of brutal occupation, the great Red Army, led by the great Marshal Stalin, came to our assistance and fought shoulder to shoulder with us for the liberation of our Motherland.

There is no force on earth which could break the fraternal alliance of the peoples of Yugoslavia with the peoples of the Soviet Union born of this war. The guarantee of this is the fact that the leaders of new Yugoslavia have risen from the very midst of their peoples. They express the peoples' thoughts and aspirations, and it must be remembered that indissoluble friendship with Great Russia has been the age-old dream of all southern Slavs.

109 Soviet protest at alleged slanders against the Red Army, late 1944 or early 1945: excerpt (*p. 42*)

I understand the difficulty of your situation after the liberation of Belgrade. However, you must know that the Soviet Government, in spite of colossal sacrifices and losses, is doing all in its power and beyond its power to help you. However, I am surprised at the fact that a few incidents and offences committed by individual officers and soldiers of the Red Army in Yugoslavia are generalized and extended to the whole Red Army. You should not so offend an army which is helping you to get rid of the Germans and which is shedding its blood in the battle against the German invader. It is not difficult to understand that there are black sheep in every family, but it would be strange to condemn the whole family because of one black sheep.

If the soldiers of the Red Army find out that Comrade Djilas, and those who did not challenge him, consider the English officers, from a moral standpoint, superior to the Soviet officers, they would cry out in pain at such undeserved insults.

110 Tito at Ljubljana declares that Yugoslav interests must not be an object for 'barter and bargaining' in the Trieste dispute, 27 May 1945: excerpts (*pp. 45, 54*)

We believe that by virtue of our struggle, our sacrifices and our exertions for the allied cause, we have given proof enough that we are loyal to the general cause of the allies, that we want nothing more than to live in peace and that our brothers who were in slavery should be freed. . . . If, after the last war, injustices were committed—for when that war ended there was no Yugoslavia, but it was created round the conference table at Versailles and some politicians who represented that Yugoslavia had no qualms about giving away slices of our country and leaving thousands of our brothers and sisters under a foreign yoke—today the situation is different. There is a new Yugoslavia today. . . . We demand nothing more than that they should regard it as such. This Yugoslavia is not an object for barter and bargaining.

111 Instructions to the Soviet ambassador in Belgrade to protest against Tito's remarks as 'an unfriendly attack on the Soviet Union', June 1945: excerpt (*p. 45*)

We regard Comrade Tito's speech as an unfriendly attack on the Soviet Union and the explanation by Comrade Kardelj [that Tito's criticism was directed against the Western allies, not the Soviet Union] as unsatisfactory. Our readers understood Comrade Tito's speech in this way, and it cannot be understood in any other. Tell Comrade Tito that if he should once again permit such an attack on the Soviet Union we shall be forced to reply with open criticism in the press and disavow him.

112 Soviet ambassador's report of his interview with Kardelj following Tito's 'anti-Soviet' remarks, 5 June 1945: excerpt (*p. 45*)

Today, 5 June, I spoke to Kardelj as you suggested (Tito has not yet returned). The communication made a serious impression on him. After some thought, he said he regarded our opinion of Tito's speech as correct. He also agreed that the Soviet Union could no longer tolerate similar statements. Naturally, in such difficult times for Yugoslavia, Kardelj said, open criticism of Tito's statement would have serious consequences for them, and for this reason they would try to avoid similar statements. However, the Soviet Union would have the right to make open criticism should similar statements be made. Such criticism would benefit them. Kardelj asked me to convey to you his gratitude for this well-timed criticism. He said it would help to improve their work. The criticism of the political mistakes made in the Government declaration in March has been of great benefit. Kardelj was sure that this criticism would also help improve the political leadership.

   In an attempt to analyse (very carefully) the causes of the mistakes, Kardelj said that Tito had done great work in liquidating fractionalism in the CPY and in organizing the people's liberation struggle, but he was inclined to regard Yugoslavia as a self-sufficient unit outside the general development of the proletarian revolution and socialism. Secondly, such a situation had arisen in the Party that the Central Committee does not exist as an organizational and political centre. We meet by chance, and we make decisions by chance. In practice every one of us is left to himself. The style of work is bad, and there is not enough coordination in our work. Kardelj said he would like the Soviet Union to regard them, not as representatives of another country, capable of solving questions independently, but as representatives of one of the future

Soviet Republics, and the CPY as a part of the CPSU, that is, that our relations should be based on the prospect of Yugoslavia becoming in the future a constituent part of the USSR. For this reason they would like us to criticize them frankly and openly and to give them advice which would direct the internal and foreign policy of Yugoslavia along the right path.

I told Kardelj it was necessary to recognize the facts as they are at present, namely to treat Yugoslavia as an independent State and the CPY as an independent Party. You can and must, I said, present and solve your problems independently, while we would never refuse advice should you ask for it.

As regards Yugoslavia, we have obligations, undertaken by our treaties, and still more, we have moral obligations. As far as possible we have never refused advice and assistance, when these were needed. Whenever I pass Marshal Tito's communications on to Moscow, I receive replies immediately. However, such advice is possible and beneficial only if we are approached in time, prior to any decision being reached or any statement made.

113 Soviet–Yugoslav trade agreement, 25 July 1947: excerpt (*p. 43*)

. . . The Soviet Union will deliver to Yugoslavia equipment for the ferrous and non-ferrous metal industries, oil, chemical and timber industries, necessary for Yugoslavia in connection with the five-year plan for the development of the Yugoslav economy. The Soviet Union will also render Yugoslavia the necessary technical assistance in the designing and assembly of equipment, and in the mastering of the above undertakings. . . .

In addition, an agreement was signed on trade turn-over and payments between the USSR and Yugoslavia. The agreement has been concluded for the term of two years and may be prolonged for a further term. It determines the way in which trade turn-over and clearings between the USSR and Yugoslavia are to be realized.

At the same time the contracting parties have agreed on a list of mutual deliveries of goods from 1 June 1947 to 31 May 1948. According to this agreement the Soviet Union will deliver to Yugoslavia cotton, paper, cellulose, oil products, coal and coke, ferrous and non-ferrous metals, automobiles, tractors and other equipment, agricultural fertilizers and various other goods.

Yugoslavia will deliver to the Soviet Union lead, zinc and pyrite concentrates, copper, tobacco, hemp, plywood and agricultural goods. . . .

114 Founding of the Cominform, September 1947 (*p. 49*)

The Conference states that the absence of contacts among the Communist Parties participating in this Conference is a serious shortcoming in the present situation. Experience has shown that such a lack of contacts among the Communist Parties is wrong and harmful. The need for interchange of experience and the voluntary coordination of action of the various Parties is particularly keenly felt at the present time in view of the growing complication of the postwar international situation, a situation in which the lack of connections amongst the Communist Parties may prove detrimental to the working class.

In view of this, the participants in this Conference have agreed on the following:

1. To set up an Information Bureau consisting of the representatives of the CPY, the Bulgarian Workers' Party (Communists), the Communist Party of Romania, the Hungarian Communist Party, the Polish Workers' Party, the CPSU (Bolsheviks), the Communist Party of France, the Communist Party of Czechoslovakia and the Communist Party of Italy.

2. To charge the Information Bureau with the organization of the interchange of experience and, if need be, coordination of the activities of the Communist Parties on the basis of mutual agreement.

3. The Information Bureau is to consist of two representatives from each Central Committee, the delegations of the Central Committees to be appointed and replaced by the Central Committees.

4. The Information Bureau is to have a printed organ—a fortnightly, and subsequently a weekly. The organ is to be published in Russian and French, and when possible, in other languages as well.

5. The Information Bureau is to be located in the city of Belgrade.

115 Kardelj asks Vyshinsky for Soviet support of proposed minor modifications of Yugoslav–Austrian frontier, 20 April 1947 (*pp. 46, 60*)

Since there is the possibility that the Yugoslav territorial claims on Austria, in their present form, will be rejected in toto, and in the event of you wanting to advance a new proposal, I wish to call your attention to questions which are so important to the FPRY as to render necessary the finding of a solution for them. The positive solution of these questions would constitute the very minimum satisfaction of the demands contained in Yugoslavia's territorial claims.

The first question concerns the Zvabek [Schwabeck] and Labud [Lavamünd] electro-power plants. In my report to the Council of Foreign Ministers I emphasized the special importance which these power plants have for Yugoslavia's electric power industry. The Zvabek and Labud plants were erected after the Anschluss, for the most part during the war, by the German firm Alpen-Elektrowerke A. G., Vienna, and, moreover, in violation of the 1926 convention under which Austria undertook not to erect any installations on the Drava without first obtaining the consent of Yugoslavia. Consequently, these power plants are German property in the Western zone of Austria from which the FPRY, apart from the other countries that signed the decision of the Paris Reparations Conference, should receive part of her reparations. Further, these power plants were built without any account being taken of the needs of Yugoslavia's electric power industry, and under present conditions of exploitation they are causing enormous loss—in some months approximately 1,000,000 kw.-hrs.

The question may be solved by a slight alteration of the boundary line, drafts of two variants of which are enclosed; or, as a last resort, it may be solved by granting the FPRY special rights in the administration of these power plants. I am enclosing the plan for one such arrangement.

The second question concerns special provisions for safeguarding the national rights of the Carinthian Slovenes. After all the experience which the Slovene people has had with Austria, it can be taken for certain that following the signing of the Treaty, attempts will be made to intensify Germanization.

Even the demagogic measures (for example, the revival of bi-lingual schools) which Austria introduced in Carinthia after the collapse of Germany, at least on paper, with the aim of demonstrating its tolerance of nationalities, have already been abandoned de facto. For this reason it would be of great importance if the treaty provided that measures which have already acquired the force of law were augmented, and, as part of the Treaty, placed under Four-Power control. I enclose an outline of the main principles of one such arrangement.

116 Yugoslav objections to Soviet account of the British military mission's role during an incident in World War II, 26 November 1947: excerpt (*p. 53*)

Referring to . . . Mdivani's article 'The British Mission in the Drvar Cave', the Ministry of Foreign Affairs considers that Comrade Mijović [Yugoslav Press Attaché] should, in an appropriate way, draw the attention of the editors of the *Literaturnaya Gazeta* that it would be desirable if the editors, before publishing such articles, would inform the Embassy, especially if they refer to Yugoslav sources.

As Maclean [former head of the British military mission] visited Yugoslavia on several occasions after the war, and was during his last visit, not long ago, received by the Marshal, and as he is working on the implementation of an agreement concerning Displaced Persons which was signed between Yugoslavia and Great Britain, the Ministry considers that the publishing of this article would not serve our country's interests, although among others, this was one of its aims.

The Marshal, who is acquainted with the facts mentioned in the article, considers that they do not correspond to the truth.

THE CALL TO ORDER: THE INTER-PARTY POLEMIC

117 Tito protests to Molotov against the withdrawal of Russian advisers and enquires the reasons for Soviet displeasure, 20 March 1948 (*p. 52*)

On 18 March General Barskov [Head of the Soviet military mission] told us that he had received a telegram from Marshal Bulganin, Minister of People's Defence of the USSR, in which we are informed that the Government of the USSR has decided to withdraw immediately all military advisers and instructors because they are 'surrounded by hostility', that is, they are not treated in a friendly fashion in Yugoslavia.

Of course, the Government of the USSR can, when it wishes, recall its military experts, but we have been dismayed by the reason which the Government of the USSR advances for its decision. Investigating, on the basis of this accusation, the relations of the lower-ranking leaders of our country towards the Soviet military advisers and instructors, we are deeply convinced that there is no basis for this reason for their withdrawal, that during their entire stay in Yugoslavia relations with them were not only good, but actually brotherly and most hospitable, which is the custom towards all Soviet people in the new Yugoslavia. Therefore, we are amazed, we cannot understand, and we are deeply hurt by not being informed of the true reason for this decision by the Government of the USSR.

7

Secondly, on 19 March 1948, I was visited by the Chargé d'Affaires Arm-janinov and informed of the contents of a telegram in which the Government of the USSR orders the withdrawal of all civilian experts in Yugoslavia also. We cannot understand the reason for this decision and it amazes us. It is true that Srzentić, the Assistant to Minister Kidrič, stated to your commercial representative Lebedev that, according to a decision of the Government of the FPRY, he has not the right to give important economic information to anyone, but that for such information the Soviet people should go higher, that is, to the CC of the CPY and the Government. At the same time Srzentić told Lebedev to approach Minister Kidrič for the information which interested him. Your people were told long ago that the official representatives of the Soviet Government could obtain all important and necessary information direct from the leaders of our country.

This decision was issued on our part because all the civil servants in our Ministries gave information to anyone, whether it was necessary or not. This meant that they gave various people State economic secrets which could, and in some cases did, fall into the hands of our common enemies.

We have no special agreement, as mentioned in the telegram, regarding the fact that our people have the right to give economic information, without the approval of our Government or Central Committee, to Soviet workers in economy, except such information as is necessary to them in their line of duty. Whenever the Soviet Ambassador, Comrade Lavrentiev, asked me personally for necessary information, I gave it to him without any reservation, and this was also done by our other responsible leaders. We would be very much sur-prised if the Soviet Government were not in agreement with this attitude of ours from a State standpoint.

At the same time, in regard to this case, we are forced to reject the reason about some sort of 'lack of hospitality and lack of confidence' towards Soviet experts and Soviet representatives in Yugoslavia. Until now not one of them has complained to us of anything like this, although they have all had the opportunity to do so personally with me, because I have never refused to see any of the Soviet people. This is also true of all our responsible leaders.

From all this it can be seen that the above reasons are not the cause of the measures taken by the Government of the USSR, and it is our desire that the USSR openly inform us what the trouble is, that it point out everything which it feels is inconsistent with good relations between our two countries. We feel that this course of events is harmful to both countries and that sooner or later everything that is prejudicial to friendly relations between our countries must be eliminated.

In so far as the Government of the USSR is obtaining its information from various other people, we feel that it should use it cautiously, because such in-formation is not always objective, accurate, or given with good intentions.

118 Stalin complains to Tito of the anti-Soviet atmosphere in Yugoslavia
and shortcomings of the CPY, 27 March 1948 (*p. 53*)

Your answers of 18 and 20 March have been received.

We regard your answer as incorrect and therefore completely unsatisfactory.

1. The question of Gagarinov [Soviet official deemed to have shown disrespect

to Tito] can be considered closed, since you have withdrawn your accusations against him, although we still consider that they were slanderous.

The statement attributed to Comrade Krutikov [Soviet Deputy Minister for Foreign Trade] that the Soviet Government has allegedly refused to enter into trade negotiations this year, does not, as can be seen, correspond to the facts, as Krutikov has categorically denied it.

2. In regard to the withdrawal of military advisers, the sources of our information are the statements of the representatives of the Ministry of Armed Forces and of the advisers themselves. As is known, our military advisers were sent to Yugoslavia upon the insistent request of the Yugoslav Government, and far fewer advisers were sent than had been requested. It is therefore obvious that the Soviet Government had no desire to force its advisers on Yugoslavia.

Later, however, the Yugoslav military leaders, among them Koča Popović [Yugoslav Chief of Staff], thought it possible to announce that it was essential to reduce the number of advisers by 60 per cent. They gave various reasons for this; some maintained that the Soviet advisers were too great an expense for Yugoslavia; others held that the Yugoslav army was in no need of the experience of the Soviet army; some said that the rules of the Soviet army were hidebound, stereotyped and without value to the Yugoslav army, and that there was no point in paying the Soviet advisers since there was no benefit to be derived from them.

In the light of these facts we can understand the well-known and insulting statement made by Djilas about the Soviet army, at a session of the CC of the CPY, namely that the Soviet officers were, from a moral standpoint, inferior to the officers of the British army. As is known, this anti-Soviet statement by Djilas met with no opposition from the other members of the CC of the CPY.

So, instead of seeking a friendly agreement with the Soviet Government on the question of Soviet military advisers, the Yugoslav military leaders began to abuse the Soviet military advisers and to discredit the Soviet army.

It is clear that this situation was bound to create an atmosphere of hostility around the Soviet military advisers. It would be ridiculous to think that the Soviet Government would consent to leave its advisers in Yugoslavia under such conditions. Since the Yugoslav Government took no measures to counteract these attempts to discredit the Soviet army, it bears the responsibility for the situation created.

3. The sources of our information leading to the withdrawal of Soviet civilian specialists are, for the most part, the statements of the Soviet Ambassador in Belgrade, Lavrentiev, as also the statements of the specialists themselves. Your statement, that Srzentić allegedly told the trade representative, Lebedev, that the Soviet specialists seeking economic information should direct their requests to higher authorities, namely to the CC of the CPY and the Yugoslav Government, does not correspond in the slightest to the truth. Here is the report made by Lavrentiev on 9 March:

> Srzentić, Kidrič's [Head of Yugoslav State Planning Commission] assistant in the Economic Council, informed Lebedev, the trade representative, of a Government decree forbidding the state organs to give economic information to any one at all. Therefore, regardless of earlier promises, he could not give Lebedev the particulars required. It was one of the duties

of the state security organs to exercise control in this matter. Srzentić also said that Kidrič himself intended to speak about this with Lebedev.

From Lavrentiev's report it can be seen, firstly, that Srzentić did not even mention the possibility of obtaining economic information from the CC of the CPY or the Yugoslav Government. In any case, it would be ridiculous to think that it would be necessary to approach the CC of the CPY for all economic information while there still existed the appropriate ministries from which Soviet specialists had previously obtained the necessary economic information direct.

Secondly, it is clear from Lavrentiev's report that the reverse of what you write is true, namely that the Yugoslav security organs controlled and supervised the Soviet representatives in Yugoslavia.

One might well mention that we have come across a similar practice of secret supervision over Soviet representatives in bourgeois States, although not in all of them. It should also be emphasized that the Yugoslav Security agents not only follow representatives of the Soviet Government, but also the representative of the CPSU in the Cominform, Comrade Yudin. It would be ridiculous to think that the Soviet Government would agree to keep its civilian specialists in Yugoslavia in such circumstances. As can be seen in this case, too, the responsibility for the conditions created rests with the Yugoslav Government.

4. In your letter you express the desire to be informed of the other facts which led to Soviet dissatisfaction and to the straining of relations between the USSR and Yugoslavia. Such facts actually exist, although they are not connected with the withdrawal of the civilian and military advisers. We consider it necessary to inform you of them.

(a) We know that there are anti-Soviet rumours circulating among the leading comrades in Yugoslavia, for instance that 'the CPSU is degenerate', 'great power chauvinism is rampant in the USSR', 'the USSR is trying to dominate Yugoslavia economically' and 'the Cominform is a means of controlling the other Parties by the CPSU', etc. These anti-Soviet allegations are usually camouflaged by left phrases, such as 'socialism in the Soviet Union has ceased to be revolutionary' and that Yugoslavia alone is the exponent of 'revolutionary socialism'. It was naturally laughable to hear such statements about the CPSU from such questionable Marxists as Djilas, Vukmanović, Kidrič, Ranković and others. However, the fact remains that such rumours have been circulating for a long time among many high-ranking Yugoslav officials, that they are still circulating, and that they are naturally creating an anti-Soviet atmosphere which is endangering relations between the CPSU and the CPY.

We readily admit that every Communist Party, among them the Yugoslav, has the right to criticize the CPSU, even as the CPSU has the right to criticize any other Communist Party. But Marxism demands that criticism be aboveboard and not underhand and slanderous, thus depriving those criticized of the opportunity to reply to the criticism. However, the criticism by the Yugoslav officials is neither open nor honest; it is both underhand and dishonest and of a hypocritical nature, because, while discrediting the CPSU behind its back, publicly they pharisaically praise it to the skies. Thus criticism is transformed into slander, into an attempt to discredit the CPSU and to blacken the Soviet system.

We do not doubt that the Yugoslav Party masses would disown this anti-Soviet criticism as alien and hostile if they knew about it. We think this is the reason why the Yugoslav officials make these criticisms in secret, behind the backs of the masses.

Again, one might mention that, when he decided to declare war on the CPSU, Trotsky also started with accusations of the CPSU as degenerate, as suffering from the limitations inherent in the narrow nationalism of great powers. Naturally he camouflaged all this with left slogans about world revolution. However, it is well known that Trotsky himself became degenerate, and when he was exposed, crossed over into the camp of the sworn enemies of the CPSU and the Soviet Union. We think that the political career of Trotsky is quite instructive.

(b) We are disturbed by the present condition of the CPY. We are amazed by the fact that the CPY, which is the leading party, is still not completely legalized and still has a semi-legal status. Decisions of the Party organs are never published in the press, neither are the reports of Party assemblies.

Democracy is not evident within the CPY itself. The Central Committee, in its majority, was not elected but co-opted. Criticism and self-criticism within the Party does not exist or barely exists. It is characteristic that the Personnel Secretary of the Party is also the Minister of State Security. In other words, the Party cadres are under the supervision of the Minister of State Security. According to the theory of Marxism, the Party should control all the State organs in the country, including the Ministry of State Security, while in Yugoslavia we have just the opposite: the Ministry of State Security actually controlling the Party. This probably explains the fact that the initiative of the Party masses in Yugoslavia is not on the required level.

It is understandable that we cannot consider such an organization of a Communist Party as Marxist–Leninist, Bolshevik.

The spirit of the policy of class struggle is not felt in the CPY. The increase in the capitalist elements in the villages and cities is in full swing, and the leadership of the Party is taking no measures to check these capitalist elements. The CPY is being hoodwinked by the degenerate and opportunist theory of the peaceful absorption of capitalist elements by a socialist system, borrowed from Bernstein, Vollmar [former leaders of the German Social Democrat Party] and Bukharin [former prominent Bolshevik leader, executed in 1936].

According to the theory of Marxism–Leninism the Party is considered as the leading force in the country, which has its specific programme and which cannot merge with the non-party masses. In Yugoslavia, on the contrary, the People's Front is considered the chief leading force and there was an attempt to get the Party submerged within the Front. In his speech at the Second Congress of the People's Front, Comrade Tito said: 'Does the CPY have any other programme but that of the People's Front? No, the CPY has no other programme. The programme of the People's Front is its programme.'

It thus appears that in Yugoslavia this amazing theory of Party organization is considered a new theory. Actually, it is far from new. In Russia forty years ago a part of the Mensheviks proposed that the Marxist Party be dissolved into a non-party workers' mass organization and that the second should supplant the first; the other part of the Mensheviks proposed that the Marxist Party be dissolved into a non-party mass organization of workers and peasants, with the latter again supplanting the former. As is known, Lenin described these Mensheviks as malicious opportunists and liquidators of the Party.

(c) We cannot understand why the English spy, Velebit, still remains in the Ministry of Foreign Affairs of Yugoslavia as the first Assistant Minister. The Yugoslav comrades know that Velebit is an English spy. They also know that the representatives of the Soviet Government consider Velebit a spy. Nevertheless, Velebit remains in the position of first Assistant Foreign Minister of Yugoslavia. It is possible that the Yugoslav Government intends to use Velebit precisely as an English spy. As is known, bourgeois governments think it permissible to have spies of great imperialist States on their staffs with a view to ensuring their goodwill, and would even agree to placing themselves under the tutelage of these States for this purpose. We consider this practice as entirely impermissible for Marxists. With the best will in the world, the Soviet Government cannot place its correspondence with the Yugoslav Government under the censorship of an English spy. It is understandable, that as long as Velebit remains in the Yugoslav Foreign Ministry, the Soviet Government considers itself placed in a difficult situation and deprived of the possibility of carrying on open correspondence with the Yugoslav Government through the Yugoslav Ministry of Foreign Affairs.

These are the facts which are causing the dissatisfaction of the Soviet Government and the CC of the CPSU and which are endangering relations between the USSR and Yugoslavia.

These facts, as has already been mentioned, are not related to the question of the withdrawal of the military and civilian specialists. However, they are an important factor in the worsening of relations between our countries.

V. Molotov
J. Stalin
By order of the CC of the CPSU

119 Tito rejects the charges and defends his policies, 13 April 1948 (*p. 54*)
To Comrades J. V. Stalin and V. M. Molotov—

In answering your letter of 27 March 1948, we must first of all emphasize that we were terribly surprised by its tone and contents. We felt that the reason for its contents, that is, for the accusations and attitudes towards individual questions, is insufficient knowledge of the situation here. We cannot explain your conclusions otherwise than by the fact that the Government of the USSR is obtaining inaccurate and tendentious information from its representatives, who because of lack of knowledge, must obtain such information from various people, either from known anti-Party elements or from various dissatisfied persons. At the Plenum of the CC of the CPY, it became abundantly clear and was confirmed that S. Žujović and A. Hebrang were the main culprits in providing inaccurate and slanderous information to the Soviet representatives in Yugoslavia, both about alleged statements of certain leading people and about our Party in general. By this inaccurate, slanderous information, they desired to hide their anti-Party work and their tendencies and attempts, exposed earlier, to break up the unity of the leadership and the Party in general. Besides this, information from such people cannot be objective, or full of good intentions, or accurate, and usually has a definite purpose. In this concrete case, that information had as its aim to cause difficulties for the leadership of our Party, that is, for the new Yugoslavia; to make more difficult the already difficult task of the development of our country; to make the Five Year Plan impossible, and so to make impossible the realization of socialism in our country. We cannot understand why the representatives of the USSR, up to to-day, have not insisted on verifying such information with responsible people in our country, that is, on seeking such information from the CC of the CPY or from the Government. We regard the issuing of such information as anti-Party work and anti-State because it spoils the relations between our two countries.

No matter how much each of us loves the land of socialism, the USSR, he can, in no case, love his country less, which also is developing socialism—in this concrete case the FPRY, for which so many thousands of its most progressive people fell. We know very well that this is also similarly understood in the Soviet Union.

It particularly surprises us that none of this was mentioned when Kardelj, Djilas, and Bakarić were in Moscow as delegates of our Party and Government. As can be seen from your letter, your Government had the information in question, and similar information, prior to the arrival of our delegation in Moscow. It appears to us that at that time the question of relations with military and civilian experts, as well as other questions, could have been presented to our delegation.

We maintain that it was necessary to inform our Government through this delegation, and even before, that the Soviet Government was not satisfied with the behaviour of our people towards the Soviet experts, and that the situation should be cleared up in one manner or another. What happened was that the Government of the USSR, by its decision to withdraw military experts without any official notification, confronted us with a *fait accompli*, and in this way created unnecessary difficulties for us.

As for the withdrawal of Soviet military experts, we see no other reason for it than that we decided to reduce their number to the necessary minimum because of financial difficulties. In 1946 Premier of the Federal Government Tito officially informed the Soviet Ambassador, Comrade Lavrentiev, that, for many reasons, it was almost impossible for us to pay such high wages to the Soviet military experts and begged him to inform the USSR of this and of our desire that it moderate the conditions for paying the experts. Ambassador Lavrentiev received an answer from the USSR that the salaries could not be decreased and we could do as we pleased. Tito immediately told Lavrentiev that because of this we would have to reduce the number of experts as soon as it was possible to do so without creating great difficulties in the building up of our army. The wages of the Soviet experts were four times as high as the wages of the commanders of our armies and three times as high as the wages of our Federal Ministers. The commander of one of our armies, a lieutenant-general or a colonel-general, then had 9,000 to 11,000 dinars a month, and a Soviet military expert, lieutenant-colonel, colonel and general, had from 30,000 to 40,000 dinars. At the same time our Federal Ministers had a salary of 12,000 dinars a month. It is understandable that we felt that this was not only a financial burden but also politically incorrect because it led to misunderstanding among our men. Therefore, our decision to decrease the number of Soviet military experts was made for the reasons mentioned and for no other. On the other hand, we do not exclude the possibility that some of our men made untimely remarks. In these cases it is necessary to present us with the relevant information, duly substantiated, and without a doubt we would see that it did not happen again. Here we must mention that some of the Soviet experts did not always behave as they should and this caused dissatisfaction as a result of which, and against our will, various remarks came to be made which were later twisted and in this twisted version passed on to the command of the Soviet army. However, we consider these matters too insignificant to be allowed to play any part in straining relations between our states.

We were especially surprised by the part of the letter containing old matters about Djilas. There it states: 'In the light of these facts we can understand the insulting statement made by Djilas about the Soviet army, at a session of the CC of the CPY, namely that the Soviet officers were from a moral standpoint inferior to the officers of the British army.' Djilas never made such a statement in such a form. Tito explained this orally and in writing in 1945. Comrade Stalin and the other members of the Politbureau of the CC of the CPSU were satisfied then with this explanation. We cannot understand why you again repeat, as an argument, a charge which was proved to be distorted and inaccurate. We again emphasize that neither Djilas nor any one of our leading people has such an opinion of Soviet officers. Only a person who is not only an enemy of the USSR but also an enemy of Yugoslavia can have such an opinion.

There are matters which should be eliminated from our trade relations so that they can develop properly. We do not deny, in connection with this, that on our part there were oversights in commercial affairs, but we cannot believe that they could be reason enough to weaken our commercial co-operation. We cannot believe that the incident between Krutikov and our Foreign Trade representatives was a mere misunderstanding. Krutikov clearly told our representatives that our trade delegation, which was already waiting in Belgrade to leave for Moscow, did not have to go because the Government of the USSR would not be able to sign a protocol for further exchanges of goods in 1948 and that it would not be possible to discuss this question again until the end of 1948. Krutikov told this to our Deputy Minister of Foreign Trade, Comrade Crnobrnja, and to our Commercial Attaché in Moscow. When our commercial representatives asked if that was the attitude of the Soviet Government, Krutikov said that it was.

We think that if there were some irregularities on the part of our trade organs—and we believe that there might have been such cases in regard to the deliveries of materials and trade relations in general—then some means could have been found to agree on and eliminate all that interferes with the proper development of trade relations between our two countries.

We think that we should jointly investigate and eliminate everything which interferes with the proper functioning of economic co-operation between our two countries.

The allegations in your letter that UDBA [the Yugoslav State Security Service] follows Soviet specialists and other Soviet people are not true. No one has ever issued a decision of this sort, and it is not true that Soviet citizens are followed. This is someone's fabricated information. It is even less accurate that the representatives of the Soviet Government and Comrade Yudin of the Cominform were followed.

We cannot understand for whom such a slander, which led the Government of the USSR into error, was necessary. And in this case we would again like to be given concrete facts.

Your letter of 27 March states that we are making anti-Soviet criticisms and criticisms of the CPSU. It states that this criticism is being made among the leaders of the CPY. It further states that this criticism is being carried on behind the backs of the mass of the Party members; that this criticism is dishonourable, underhanded, hypocritical, etc. The names of Djilas, Vukmanović, Kidrič, and Ranković are mentioned, and, it is said, some others. That is, the letter mentions the names of some of the best known and most popular leaders of new Yugoslavia, who have proved themselves in many situations difficult for our Party.

It is very difficult for us to understand how such serious accusations can be advanced without mentioning their source. Further, it is more amazing to compare statements by our leaders with the one-time statements of Trotsky. The letter quotes parts of alleged statements, for example, 'the CPSU is degenerate', 'the USSR is trying to dominate Yugoslavia economically', 'great-power chauvinism is rampant in the USSR', 'the Cominform is a means of controlling the other Parties by the CPSU'. Further 'these anti-Soviet allegations are usually camouflaged by left phrases, such as "socialism in the USSR has ceased to be revolutionary", that only Yugoslavia is the true exponent of "revolutionary socialism" '.

On the basis of this and similar information gathered through a long period from various suspicious sources, which was tendentiously attributed to the leading men of the new Yugoslavia as if it were theirs and thus presented to the leaders of the USSR, it is without doubt possible to draw wrong conclusions and describe them as anti-Soviet statements. However, we feel that on the basis of unidentified persons and suspicious information, it is incorrect to draw conclusions and make accusations like those brought in the letter, against men who have performed invaluable services in popularizing the USSR in Yugoslavia and won priceless renown in the war of liberation. Is it possible to believe that people who spent six, eight, ten and more years in prison—among other things because of their work in popularizing the USSR —can be such as shown in your letter of 27 March? No. But these are the majority of the present high-ranking leaders of the new Yugoslavia, who on 27 March 1941, led the masses through the streets against the anti-popular regime of Cvetković–Maček, which signed the anti-Comintern pact and desired to harness Yugoslavia to the fascist axis wagon. They are the same people who, at the head of the insurgent Yugoslav people, with gun in hand, fought under the most difficult conditions on the side of the Soviet Union as the only true allies, believing in the victory of the USSR in the darkest days, just because they believed and believe today in the Soviet system, in Socialism.

Such people cannot work 'to blacken the Soviet system' because that would mean betraying their convictions, their past. We feel that these people should not be assessed on the basis of dubious information but on the basis of their long revolutionary activity.

To call such people two-faced because, in front of the masses they praise the CPSU 'to the skies'—as stated in the letter—is really terrible and insulting. In the letter it further states: 'We do not doubt that the Yugoslav Party masses would disown this anti-Soviet criticism, as alien and hostile, if they knew about it.' Yes, and we believe it too, if it were as shown in the letter. 'We think this is the reason why the Yugoslav officials make these criticisms in secret, behind the backs of the masses.' However, there could be no concealment from the masses for the simple reason that there was not and could not be any such criticism of the Soviet Union or the CPSU.

To oppose the leadership to the masses is incorrect. It is incorrect because the present leaders of Yugoslavia and the masses are one; because they are inseparably tied by their struggle against the anti-popular regime before the war, their struggle during the great war of liberation, and today by the great working efforts for the development of the country and the realization of socialism.

Among many Soviet people there exists the mistaken idea that the sympathy of the broad masses in Yugoslavia towards the USSR came of itself, on the basis of some traditions which go back to the time of Tsarist Russia. This is not so. Love for the USSR did not come of itself. It was stubbornly inculcated into the masses of the Party and the people in general by the present leaders of the new Yugoslavia, including, in the first rank, those so seriously accused in the letter. The present leaders of new Yugoslavia are the same who, long before the war, sparing neither efforts nor sacrifices, persistently revealed to the masses the truth about the Soviet Union and planted among the masses of Yugoslavia love for the land of socialism.

Comrade Molotov, for example, said that Djilas gave orders that the *History of the CPSU* should not be studied in Party schools and courses. This is completely inaccurate. Such an order does not exist nor did anyone give it. Even now the *History of the CPSU* is being studied in all our Party schools and in many courses. Of all this, the only thing true is that Djilas more than once said at Party meetings that the immature members in the basic Party organizations understood particular problems in the *History of the CPSU* erroneously, and mechanically compared them with the development of Yugoslavia. For example, the question of two periods of revolution, the question of war communism, the question of NEP, etc. He said it was better at the beginning to give these members the *Problems of Leninism* by Stalin, to study.

In connection with this it is necessary to emphasize that the *History of the CPSU* was issued four times illegally before and during the war and that it was printed in all national languages in 250,000 copies after the war. It is the same with the other works of Stalin and Lenin. The *Problems of Leninism*, for example, was issued in 125,000 copies.

As regards the question of the internal life of the CPY which is mentioned in your letter, it can be seen that you have received completely inaccurate information and have formed an erroneous picture. Accordingly we cannot agree with your evaluation of our Party.

The majority of the members of the CC of the CPY are not co-opted as is alleged in your letter. The matter stands thus. At the Fifth Party Conference, held in December (*sic*) 1940, when the CPY was completely illegal, attended by 110 delegates from all Yugoslavia, and which, by a decision of the Comintern, had all the powers of a congress, a CC of the CPY of thirty-one members and ten candidates was elected. Of this number, ten members and six candidates died during the war. Of the seven members of the Politbureau elected in 1940, five are still alive and working today. The Politbureau invites those members of the CC of the CPY who are in Belgrade to its sessions. In the CC of the CPY, in all only seven new members have been co-opted, and these were from the candidates and best leaders of the Party. Finally, during the war, two members were expelled from the CC of the CPY, so that there remain at work today nineteen members of the CC of the CPY elected at the Conference and seven co-opted members. Accordingly, the CC of the CPY is composed of twenty-six members; this is how the matter stands.

As regards the remark of not holding a Party congress, it is necessary to mention here that the Politbureau of the CC of the CPY has been making preparations for a congress of the CPY for a year. We feel that this congress should be prepared so that it has not only a demonstrational character, but that it be a congress in which a Statute and a Party programme will be brought forth. This programme will later be adopted in its essentials by the People's Front at its congress.

What is the basis of the allegation in the letter that there is no democracy in our Party? Perhaps information from Lavrentiev? Where did he get this information? We consider that he, as an ambassador, has no right to ask anyone for information about the work of our Party. That is not his business. This information can be obtained by the CC of the CPSU from the CC of the CPY.

The fact that the Organization Secretary in the CPY is also Minister of State Security in no case interferes with the self-initiative of Party organizations. The Party is not placed under the control of UDBA; this control is exercised through the CC of the CPY, of which the Minister of State Security is a member. Besides this, we must add that the chief of the Administration of Cadres under the CC of the CPY is Zeković and not Ranković.

It is not true that there is no freedom of criticism in our Party. Freedom of criticism and self-criticism exists in our Party and is carried out at regular Party meetings and conferences of the *aktiv*. Therefore, someone thought up this falsehood and passed it on as information to the CC of the CPSU.

The allegation that the policy of the class struggle is not realized in the CPY, and that capitalist elements in the villages and cities are being strengthened etc., is completely inaccurate. Where did this information come from, when the entire world knows that since the October revolution, nowhere in the world have there been such firm, consistent social changes as in Yugoslavia? These are facts which no one can dispute with us. Therefore, it is not understandable how any one can speak of Bernstein, Vollmar, Bukharin and rotten opportunism in connection with our Party. We cannot do other than defend ourselves against such inaccuracies and insults to our Party.

The letter further mentions the report of Tito to the Second Congress of the People's Front in Yugoslavia. A small extract is made from this report and a comparison is drawn with the attempt of the Mensheviks to break up the Social Democratic Party forty years ago.

First, that was forty years ago under Tsarism, and today we in Yugoslavia have power in our hands. That is, the CPY has the leading role in the Government. In watching social development in process, it is inevitable that organizational forms must be changed somewhat, methods of work changed, as well as forms of the leadership of the masses in order to achieve specific ends more easily.

Second, the People's Front of Yugoslavia, by its quality, is not only equal to some other Communist Parties, which accept anyone into their ranks, but is even better in its organization and activity. Not everyone can be a member of the People's Front of Yugoslavia, even though today it has approximately 7,000,000 members.

Third, the CPY has a completely assured leadership in the People's Front because the CPY is the nucleus of the People's Front. Therefore, there is no danger of its dissolving into the People's Front—as it said in the letter. Through the People's Front the CPY gradually realizes its programme, which the People's Front voluntarily adopts, considering it as its own programme. This is the basis of Tito's statement that the CPY has no other programme.

We are sorry that such things are written about us and we would like to draw attention to the fact that in some countries some CPs are changing, not only the forms of work but also the name of the Party, as is the case in Bulgaria and Poland, and this not without the approval of the CPSU. Of course, in these countries it is necessary for the Parties to take this course. However, here the combination of the People's Front, headed by the CPY, which is firmly organized from within, and which strongly binds about itself the million-strong masses of the People's Front, has shown itself most correct. And yet no one tells these other Parties that they will dissolve into the masses even though they have forms of work and forms of organization in harmony with the new given conditions in their country.

Why then does any one dispute facts which are undeniable and have been known for a long time? We are deeply convinced that the results achieved by our Party during the war and after the war speak for themselves: that the CPY is strong, monolithic, capable of leading the country to socialism, capable of leading the people of Yugoslavia in every situation however difficult it be.

Our Party is not semi-legal, as is mentioned in the letter. It is completely legal and known to every man in Yugoslavia as the leading force.

The fact of the matter is that unfortunately you are not acquainted with the nature of the Front in Yugoslavia and criticize us for not publishing reports of Party meetings and conferences. All the important decisions, from those of the Federal Government down, regarding all questions of social and state life, are either decisions of the Party or made on the initiative of the Party, and the people understand and accept them as such. Therefore, we do not feel it necessary to emphasize that this or that decision was made at this or that Party conference.

The great reputation of our Party, won not only in our country but in the whole world, on the basis of the results it has obtained, speaks for itself. On the other hand, we emphasize that our Party achieved all this thanks to the fact that it followed the doctrine of Marx, Engels, Lenin, Stalin; that it benefited by the experiences of the CPSU, applying these experiences to the given conditions. Therefore, we do not understand the allegation made in your letter that our leaders hypocritically and 'pharisaically praise the CPSU to the skies' and at the same time work against it.

We cannot believe that the CC of the CPSU can dispute the services and results achieved by our Party up to today because we remember that such acknowledgement was given us many times by many Soviet leaders and by Comrade Stalin himself. We are also of the opinion that there are many specific aspects in the social transformation of Yugoslavia which can be of benefit to the revolutionary development in other countries, and are already being used. This does not mean that we place the role of the CPSU and the social system of the USSR in the background. On the contrary, we study and take as an example the Soviet system, but we are developing socialism in our country in somewhat different forms. In the given period under the specific conditions which exist in our country, in consideration of the international conditions which were created after the war of liberation, we are attempting to apply the best forms of work in the realization of socialism. We do not do this, in order to prove that our road is better than that taken by the Soviet Union, that we are inventing something new, but because this is forced upon us by our daily life.

As to Velebit and why he still remains in the Ministry of Foreign Affairs, the matter stands thus. Kardelj and Djilas once told Molotov that all was not clear to us about Velebit. We never had any proof then and we have none today; the matter is still under investigation and we would not care to remove and destroy a man on the basis of suspicion.

What induces us not to be too hasty with Velebit, is, first, that he has been a Party member since 1939 and before that he did great services for the Party. In 1940 Tito gave him the confidential task of renting a villa in Zagreb in his name in which to place the radio station of the Comintern, and in which Valdés lived with his wife as wireless operator [see above, note 15]. Velebit was at the same time a courier. All this continued some time under the occupation and of course meant that his life was at risk. Then, in 1942, on the Party's instructions, Velebit joined the Partisans and conducted himself well. Later he received a task abroad and performed it well. We are now investigating his entire past. If the Soviet Government has something concrete about him we beg it to give us the facts. However, regardless of this, we shall immediately remove him from his position in the Ministry.

Therefore, the accusations in your letter in this connection are really surprising and insulting to the CC of the CPY and to the entire Government. You compare us with some bourgeois States which tolerate spies so that they may curry favour with certain great Powers. This is what is stated in your letter and what we consider impossible about a Government which is more than friendly and allied: 'it is possible that the Yugoslav Government intends to use Velebit precisely as an English spy. As is known, bourgeois governments think it permissible to have spies of great Imperialist States on their staffs, with a view to ensuring their goodwill, and would even agree to placing themselves under the tutelage of these States for this purpose.' That is how it is written in the letter. A man cannot read it without being deeply embittered and shocked by its manner, in a letter to a Government which represents a nation of 16 million people, which in the war of liberation on the side of the USSR sacrificed the most, and which in the future, if need be, will be a most faithful ally in the struggle.

If you were to ask us if there were anything with which we were not satisfied on your part, then we should openly say there are many reasons why we are dissatisfied. What are these reasons? It is impossible to mention all the reasons in this letter but we will mention a few. First, we regard it as improper for the agents of the Soviet Intelligence Service to recruit in our country, which is moving towards socialism, our citizens for their intelligence service. We cannot consider this as anything else but detrimental to the interests of our country. This is done in spite of the fact that our leaders and UDBA have protested against this and made it known that it cannot be tolerated. Those being recruited include officers, various leaders, and those who are negatively disposed towards the new Yugoslavia.

We have proof that certain agents of the Soviet Intelligence Service in recruting our Party members cast doubts on our leaders, seek to ruin their reputation, show them as inefficient and unreliable. For example, Colonel Stepanov did not hesitate in 1945, in recruiting one of our good comrades who was working in the central division of coding and decoding in UDBA, to blacken and cast doubts on all our leaders, stating 'for the present Marshal Tito works as he should'. Such cases are still occurring today. This also means that such recruiting is not done for the purpose of a struggle against some capitalist country, and we must inevitably come to the conclusion that this recruiting is destroying our internal unity, that it kills confidence in the leadership, demoralizes people, leads to the compromising of leading people and becomes a channel for collecting false information day by day. This work by the agents of the Soviet Intelligence Service cannot be called loyal and friendly towards our country, which is moving toward socialism and which is the most faithful ally of the USSR.

We cannot allow the Soviet Intelligence Service to spread its net in our country. We have our state security and our intelligence service for the struggle against various foreign capitalist elements and class enemies within the country, and if the Soviet intelligence agents need information or assistance in this direction they can obtain it whenever they want to; on our part, this has been done until now.

Such are the grounds—and there are many more like them—for our dissatisfaction. But can this be a reason for our mutual relations to deteriorate? No. These are questions which can be eliminated and explained.

It is clearly to the vital interest of the USSR and Yugoslavia to be firmly linked together. However, absolute mutual confidence is necessary for this; without it enduring and firm relations between our two countries cannot exist. The Soviet people, and in the first place the leaders, should believe the fact that the new Yugoslavia, under its present leadership, is moving unwaveringly towards socialism.

Further, they must believe that the USSR has in the present Yugoslavia under its present leadership, a most faithful friend and ally prepared to share good and evil with the people of the USSR in case of severe trial.

Finally, even though we know that the USSR has tremendous difficulties with the reconstruction of the devastated lands we rightfully expect the assistance of the USSR in the development of our country and the realization of the Five Year Plan without material deprivation to the people of the USSR, because we feel it is in the interest of the USSR for the new Yugoslavia to be as strong as possible, since it is face to face with the capitalist world which is endangering not only its peaceful development but the development of other countries of people's democracy and even the development of the USSR.

On the basis of everything set out above, the plenary session of the CC of the CPY cannot accept as justified the criticism in your letter about the work of our Party and its leaders. We are deeply convinced that this is the result of a grave misunderstanding, which should not have happened and which must rapidly be liquidated in the interest of the cause our parties serve.

Our only desire is to eliminate every doubt and disbelief in the purity of the comradely and brotherly feeling of loyalty of our CC of the CPY to the CPSU, to whom we will always remain thankful for the Marxist–Leninist doctrine which has led us until now and will lead us in the future—loyalty to the Soviet Union which has served us and will continue to serve us as a great example and whose assistance to our people we value so highly.

We are convinced that this disagreement can be liquidated only by full mutual explanation between our two Central Committees on the spot, that is, here.

Therefore, we propose that the CC of the CPSU send one or more of its members, who will have every opportunity here of studying every question thoroughly.

In the hope that you will accept our proposal we send you our comradely greetings.

By order of the CC of the CPY
Tito
Kardelj

120 Stalin rehearses his complaints and accuses the Yugoslav leaders of 'unbounded arrogance', 4 May 1940 (*p. 54*)

To Comrades Tito and Kardelj, the CC of the CPY—
Your answer and the announcement of the decision of the Plenum of the CC of the CPY of 13 April 1948, signed by Comrades Tito and Kardelj, have been received.

Unfortunately, these documents, and especially the document signed by Tito and Kardelj, do not improve on the earlier Yugoslav documents; on the contrary, they further complicate matters and sharpen the conflict.

Our attention is drawn to the tone of the documents, which can only be described as exaggeratedly ambitious. In the documents one does not see any desire to establish the truth, honestly to admit errors and to recognize the necessity of eliminating those errors. Yugoslav comrades do not accept criticism in a Marxist manner, but in a petit bourgeois manner, i.e. they regard it as an insult to the prestige of the CC of the CPY and as undermining the ambitions of the Yugoslav leaders.

So, in order to extricate themselves from the difficult situation for which they are themselves to blame, the Yugoslav leaders are using a 'new' method, a method of complete denial of their errors regardless of their obvious existence. The facts and the documents mentioned in the letter of the CC of the CPSU of 27 March 1948 are denied. Comrades Tito and Kardelj, it seems, do not understand this childish method of groundless denial of facts and documents can never be convincing, but merely laughable.

1 Concerning the withdrawal of Soviet military advisers from Yugoslavia
In its letter of 27 March the CC of the CPSU stated the reasons for the withdrawal of the Soviet military advisers, and said that the information of the CC of the CPSU was based on the complaints of these advisers of the unfriendly

attitude of the responsible Yugoslav officials towards the Soviet army and its representatives in Yugoslavia. Comrades Tito and Kardelj deny these complaints as unsubstantiated. Why should the CC of the CPSU believe the unfounded statements of Tito and Kardelj rather than the numerous complaints of the Soviet military advisers? On what grounds? The USSR has its military advisers in almost all the countries of people's democracy. We must emphasize that until now we have had no complaints from our advisers in these countries. This explains the fact that we have had no misunderstandings in these countries arising from the work of the Soviet military advisers. Complaints and misunderstandings, in this field, exist only in Yugoslavia. Is it not clear that this can be explained only by the special unfriendly atmosphere which has been created in Yugoslavia around these military advisers?

Comrades Tito and Kardelj refer to the great expenses in connection with the salaries of the Soviet military advisers, emphasizing that the Soviet generals receive three to four times as much, in dinars, as Yugoslav generals, and that such conditions may give rise to discontent on the part of Yugoslav military personnel. But the Yugoslav generals, apart from drawing salaries, are provided with apartments, servants, food, etc. Secondly, the pay of the Soviet generals in Yugoslavia corresponds to the pay of Soviet generals in the USSR. It is understandable that the Soviet Government could not consider reducing the salaries of Soviet generals who are in Yugoslavia on official duty.

Perhaps the expense of the Soviet generals was too great a burden for the Yugoslav budget. In that case the Yugoslav Government should have approached the Soviet Government and proposed that it take over part of the expenses. There is no doubt that the Soviet Government would have agreed to this. However, the Yugoslavs took another course; instead of solving this question in an amicable manner, they began to abuse our military advisers, to call them loafers, and to discredit the Soviet army. Only after a hostile atmosphere had been created around the Soviet military advisers did the Yugoslav Government approach the Soviet Government. It is understandable that the Soviet Government could not accept this situation.

2 Concerning the Soviet civilian specialists in Yugoslavia
In its letter of 27 March the CC of the CPSU stated the reasons for the withdrawal of the Soviet civilian specialists from Yugoslavia. In the given case the CC of the CPSU relied on the complaints of the civilian specialists and on the statements of the Soviet Ambassador in Yugoslavia. From these statements it can be seen that the Soviet civilian specialists, as well as the representative of the CPSU in the Cominform, Comrade Yudin, were placed under the supervision of the UDBA.

Comrades Tito and Kardelj in their letter deny the truth of these complaints and reports, stating that the UDBA does not supervise Soviet citizens in Yugoslavia. But why should the CC of the CPSU believe the unfounded assertions of Comrades Tito and Kardelj and not the complaints of Soviet men, among them Comrade Yudin?

The Soviet Government has many of its civilian specialists in all the countries of people's democracy but it does not receive any complaints from them and there are no disagreements with the Governments of these countries. Why have these disagreements and conflicts arisen only in Yugoslavia? Is it not because the Yugoslav Government has created a special unfriendly atmosphere around the Soviet officials in Yugoslavia, among them Comrade Yudin himself?

It is understandable that the Soviet Government could not accept this situation and was obliged to recall its civilian specialists from Yugoslavia.

3 Regarding Velebit and other spies in the Ministry of Foreign Affairs in Yugoslavia

It is not true, as Tito and Kardelj say, that Comrades Kardelj and Djilas, on the occasion of a meeting with Molotov, confined their doubts regarding Velebit to the remark 'that all was not clear about Velebit' to them. Actually, in their meeting with Molotov there was talk that Velebit was suspected of spying for England. It was very strange that Tito and Kardelj identified the removal of Velebit from the Ministry of Foreign Affairs with his ruin. Why could not Velebit be removed from the Ministry of Foreign Affairs without being ruined?

Also strange was the statement by Tito and Kardelj regarding the reasons for leaving Velebit in his position of First Assistant Minister of Foreign Affairs; it appears that Velebit was not removed from his position because he was under supervision. Would it not be better to remove Velebit just because he was under supervision? Why so much consideration for an English spy, who at the same time is so uncompromisingly hostile towards the Soviet Union?

Nor is Velebit the only spy in the Ministry of Foreign Affairs. The Soviet representatives have many times told the Yugoslav leaders that the Yugoslav Ambassador in London, Leontić, is an English spy. Is it not clear why this old and trusted English spy remains in the Ministry of Foreign Affairs?

The Soviet Government is aware that besides Leontić three other members of the Yugoslav Embassy in London, whose names are not yet established, are in the English Intelligence Service. The Soviet Government makes this statement with full responsibility.

It is also hard to understand why the United States Ambassador in Belgrade behaves as if he owned the place and why his 'intelligence agents', whose number is increasing, move about freely, or why the friends and relations of the executioner of the Yugoslav people, Nedić, so easily obtain positions in the State and Party apparatus in Yugoslavia.

It is clear that since the Yugoslav Government persistently refuses to purge its Ministry of Foreign Affairs of spies, the Soviet Government is forced to refrain from open correspondence with the Yugoslav Government through the Yugoslav Ministry of Foreign Affairs.

4 Concerning the Soviet Ambassador in Yugoslavia and the Soviet State

In their letter of 13 April 1948 Tito and Kardelj wrote: 'We consider that he (the Soviet Ambassador), as an ambassador, has no right to ask any one for information about the work of our Party. That is not his business.'

We feel that this statement by Tito and Kardelj is essentially incorrect and anti-Soviet. They evidently identify the Soviet Ambassador, a responsible communist who represents the Communist Government of the USSR, with an ordinary bourgeois ambassador, an ordinary official of a bourgeois State,

whose job it is to undermine the foundations of the Yugoslav State. It is difficult to understand how Tito and Kardelj could sink so low. Do these comrades
understand that such an attitude towards the Soviet Ambassador means the
negation of all friendly relations between the USSR and Yugoslavia? Do these
comrades understand that the Soviet Ambassador, a responsible communist,
who represents a friendly power which liberated Yugoslavia from the German
occupation, has not only the right but the duty, from time to time, to discuss
with the communists of Yugoslavia all questions which may interest them?
How can they be suspicious of these simple elementary matters if they intend
to remain in friendly relation with the Soviet Union?

For the information of Comrades Tito and Kardelj, it is necessary to mention that, unlike the Yugoslavs, we do not consider the Yugoslav Ambassador
in Moscow as a simple official; we do not treat him as a mere bourgeois ambassador and we do not deny his 'right to seek information about the work of
our Party from any one he chooses'. Because he became an ambassador, he
did not stop being a Communist. We treat him as a comrade and a communist
worker. He has friends and acquaintances among the Soviet people. Is he
'acquiring' information about the work of our Party? Most likely he is. Let
him 'acquire' it. We have no reason to hide from comrades the shortcomings
in our Party. We expose them ourselves in order to eliminate them.

We consider that this attitude of the Yugoslav comrades towards the Soviet
Ambassador cannot be regarded as accidental. It arises from the general atti-
tude of the Yugoslav Government, which is also the cause of the inability of
the Yugoslav leaders to see the difference between the foreign policy of the
USSR and the foreign policy of the Anglo–Americans; they, therefore, put the
foreign policy of the USSR on a par with the foreign policy of the English and
Americans and feel that they should follow the same policy towards the Soviet
Union as towards the imperialist States, Great Britain and the United States.

In this respect, the speech by Comrade Tito in Ljubljana in May 1945 is very
characteristic. He said:

> 'It is said that this war is a just war and we have considered it as such.
> However, we seek also a just end; we demand that every one shall be
> master in his own house; we do not want to pay for others; we do not
> want to be used as a bribe in international bargaining; we do not want to
> get involved in any policy of spheres of interest.' [See **110** for a different
> version of the relevant passage.]

This was said in connection with the question of Trieste. As is well known,
after a series of territorial concessions for the benefit of Yugoslavia, which the
Soviet Union extracted from the Anglo–Americans, the latter, together with
the French, rejected the Soviet proposal to hand Trieste over to Yugoslavia
and occupied Trieste with their own forces, which were then in Italy. Since all
other means were exhausted, the Soviet Union had only one other method left
for gaining Trieste for Yugoslavia—to start war with the Anglo–Americans
over Trieste and take it by force. The Yugoslav comrades could not fail to
realize that after such a hard war the USSR could not enter another. However,
this affair caused dissatisfaction among the Yugoslav comrades which was
expressed in Comrade Tito's speech. The statement by Tito in Ljubljana that
'Yugoslavia would not pay for others', 'would not be used as a bribe', 'would

not be involved in any policy of spheres of interest', was directed not only against the imperialist States, but also against the USSR, and in the given circumstances the relations of Tito towards the USSR are no different from his relations towards the imperialist States, as he does not recognize any difference between the USSR and the imperialist States.

In this anti-Soviet attitude of Comrade Tito, which met no resistance in the Politbureau of the CC of the CPY, we see the basis for the slanderous propaganda of the leaders of the CPY, pursued in the narrow circles of the Yugoslav Party cadres, regarding the 'degeneration' of the USSR into an imperialist State which desires to 'dominate Yugoslavia economically', the basis for the slanderous propaganda of the leaders of the CPY regarding the 'degeneration' of the CPSU which desires 'through the Cominform, to control the other parties' and the allegation that 'socialism in the USSR has ceased to be revolutionary'.

The Soviet Government was obliged to draw the attention of the Yugoslav Government to the fact that this statement could not be tolerated, and since the explanations subsequently given by Tito and Kardelj were unsatisfactory, the Soviet Ambassador in Belgrade, Comrade Sadchikov, was instructed by the Soviet Government to make the following statement to the Yugoslav Government, which he did on 5 June 1945 . . . [text given in **111**].

From this anti-Soviet attitude of Comrade Tito to the USSR arises the attitude of the Yugoslav leaders towards the Soviet Ambassador, by which the Soviet Ambassador in Belgrade is put on a level with bourgeois ambassadors.

It seems that the Yugoslav leaders intend to retain this anti-Soviet attitude in future. The Yugoslav leaders should take note that retaining this attitude means renouncing all friendly relations with the Soviet Union, and betraying the united socialist front of the Soviet Union and the people's democratic republics. They should also take note that retaining this attitude means depriving themselves of the right to demand material and any other assistance from the Soviet Union, because the Soviet Union can only offer aid to friends.

For the information of Comrades Tito and Kardelj, we emphasize that this anti-Soviet attitude towards the Soviet Ambassador and the Soviet State is only found in Yugoslavia; in other countries of people's democracy the relations were and remain friendly and perfectly correct.

It is interesting to note that Comrade Kardelj, who is now in complete agreement with Comrade Tito, three years ago had a completely different opinion of Tito's speech in Ljubljana. Here is what the Soviet Ambassador in Yugoslavia, Sadchikov, reported about his conversation with Kardelj on 5 June 1945 . . . [text given in **112**].

We leave aside the primitive and fallacious reasoning of Comrade Kardelj about Yugoslavia as a future constituent part of the USSR and the CPY as a part of the CPSU. However, we would like to draw attention to Kardelj's criticisms of Tito's anti-Soviet declaration on Ljubljana and the bad conditions in the CC of the CPY.

5 Regarding the anti-Soviet statement by Comrade Djilas about the Intelligence Service and trade negotiations

In our letter of 27 March, we mentioned the anti-Soviet statement by Comrade Djilas made at a session of the CC of the CPY, in which he said that the

Soviet officers, from a moral standpoint, were inferior to the officers in the English army. This statement by Djilas was made in connection with the fact that a few officers of the Soviet army in Yugoslavia indulged in actions of an immoral nature. We described this statement by Djilas as anti-Soviet because in referring to the behaviour of Soviet officers this pitiful Marxist, Comrade Djilas, did not recall the main difference between the Socialist Soviet army, which liberated the peoples of Europe, and the bourgeois English army, whose function is to oppress and not to liberate the peoples of the world.

In their letter of 13 April 1948, Tito and Kardelj state 'that Djilas never made such a statement in such a form', and that 'Tito explained this in writing and orally in 1945' and that 'Comrade Stalin and other members of the Polit-bureau of the CC of the CPSU' accepted this explanation.

We feel it necessary to emphasize that this statement by Tito and Kardelj does not correspond with the facts. This is how Stalin reacted to the statement by Djilas in a telegram to Tito . . . [text given in **109**].

In this anti-Soviet attitude of Djilas, which passed unchallenged among the other members of the Politbureau of the CC of the CPY, we see the basis for the slanderous campaign conducted by the leaders of the CPY against the representatives of the Red Army in Yugoslavia, which was the reason for the withdrawal of our military advisers.

How did the matter with Djilas end? It ended with Comrade Djilas arriving in Moscow, together with the Yugoslav delegation, where he apologized to Stalin and begged that this unpleasant error, which he committed at the session of the CC of the CPY, be forgotten. As can be seen, the affair is entirely different from the account given in the letter of Tito and Kardelj. Unfortunately, Djilas's error was not an accident.

*   *   *

Comrades Tito and Kardelj accuse the Soviet representatives of recruiting Yugoslavs for their intelligence service. They write . . . [text given in **119**].

We declare that this statement by Tito and Kardelj, which is full of hostile attacks against the Soviet officials in Yugoslavia, does not at all correspond to the facts.

It would be monstrous to demand that the Soviet people who are working in Yugoslavia should fill their mouths with water and talk and chat with no one. Soviet workers are politically mature people and not simple hired labourers, without the right to be interested in what is happening in Yugoslavia. It is only natural for them to talk with Yugoslav citizens, to ask them questions and to gain information, etc. One would have to be an incorrigible anti-Soviet to consider these talks as attempts to recruit people for the intelligence service, especially such people, who are 'negatively disposed towards the new Yugoslavia'. Only anti-Soviet people can think that the leaders of the Soviet Union care less for the welfare of new Yugoslavia than do the members of the Politbureau of the CC of the CPY.

It is significant that these strange accusations against the Soviet representatives are met only in Yugoslavia. To us it appears that this accusation against the Soviet workers is made solely for the purpose of justifying the actions of UDBA in placing the Soviet workers in Yugoslavia under surveillance.

It must be emphasized that Yugoslav comrades visiting Moscow frequently visit other cities in the USSR, meet our people and freely talk with them. In no case did the Soviet Government place any restrictions on them. During his last visit to Moscow, Djilas went to Leningrad for a few days to talk with Soviet comrades.

According to the Yugoslav scheme, information about the Party and State work can only be obtained from the leading organs of the CC of the CPY or from the Government. Comrade Djilas did not obtain information from these organs of the USSR but from the local organs of the Leningrad organizations. We did not consider it necessary to inquire into what he did there, and what facts he picked up. We think he did not collect material for the Anglo–American or French intelligence service but for the leading organs of Yugoslavia. Since this was correct we did not see any harm in it because this information might have contained instructive material for the Yugoslav comrades. Comrade Djilas cannot say that he met with any restrictions.

It may be asked now: Why should Soviet Communists in Yugoslavia have fewer rights than Yugoslavs in the USSR?

In their letter of 13 April, Tito and Kardelj again refer to the question of trade relations between the USSR and Yugoslavia, namely the alleged refusal of Comrade Krutikov to continue trade negotiations with the Yugoslav representatives. We have already explained to the Yugoslav comrades that Krutikov has denied the statements attributed to him. We have already explained that the Soviet Government never raised the question of suspending trade agreements and trade operations with Yugoslavia. Consequently we consider this question closed and have no intention of returning to it.

6 On the incorrect political line of the Politbureau of the CC of the CPY in regard to the class struggle in Yugoslavia

In our letter we wrote that the spirit of the policy of class struggle is not felt in the CPY, that the capitalist elements are increasing in the cities and the villages and that the leaders of the Party are not undertaking any measures to check the capitalist elements.

Comrades Tito and Kardelj deny all this point blank and consider our statements, which are a matter of principle, as insults to the CPY and evade answering the essential question. Their arguments amount only to statements that fundamental and consistent social reforms are being carried out in Yugoslavia. But this is totally insufficient. The denial on the part of these comrades of the strengthening of the capitalist elements, and in connection with this, the sharpening of the class struggle in the village under the conditions of contemporary Yugoslavia, arises from the opportunist contention that, in the transition period between capitalism and socialism, the class struggle does not become sharper, as taught by Marxism–Leninism, but dies out, as averred by opportunists of the type of Bukharin, who postulated a decadent theory of the peaceful absorption of the capitalist elements into the socialist structure.

No one will deny the depth and fundamental nature of the social transformation which occurred in the USSR after the October Revolution. However, this did not cause the CPSU to conclude that the class struggle in our country was weakening, nor that there was no danger of the strengthening of the capitalist elements. In 1920–21 Lenin stated that 'while we live in a country of small-holders there is a stronger economic basis for capitalism in Russia, than there is for communism', since 'small-scale individual farming gives birth to capitalism and the bourgeoisie continually, daily, hourly, spontaneously and on a mass scale'. It is known that for fifteen years after the October revolution, the question of measures for checking capitalist elements and later the liquidation of the kulaks as the last capitalist class, was never taken off the daily agenda of our Party. To underestimate the experiences of the CPSU in matters relating to the development of socialism in Yugoslavia is a great political danger, and cannot be allowed for Marxists, because socialism cannot be developed only in the cities and in industry, but must also be developed in the villages and in agriculture.

It is no accident that the leaders of the CPY are avoiding the question of the class struggle and the checking of the capitalist elements in the village. What is more, in the speeches of the Yugoslav leaders there is no mention of the question of class differentiation in the village; the peasantry are considered as an organic whole, and the Party does not mobilize its forces in an effort to overcome the difficulties arising from the increase of the exploiting elements in the village.

However, the political situation in the village gives no cause for complacency or benevolence. Where, as in Yugoslavia, there is no nationalization of the land, where private ownership of the land exists and land is bought and sold, where hired labour is used, etc. the Party cannot be educated in the spirit of camouflaging the class struggle and smoothing over class controversies without disarming itself for the struggle with the main difficulties in the development of socialism. This means that the CPY is being lulled to sleep by the decadent opportunist theory of the peaceful infiltration of capitalist elements into socialism, borrowed from Bernstein, Vollmar and Bukharin.

Nor is it by accident that some of the most prominent leaders of the CPY are deviating from the Marxist–Leninist road on the question of the leading role of the working class. While Marxism–Leninism starts by recognizing the leading role of the working class in the process of liquidating capitalism and developing a socialist society, the leaders of the CPY have an entirely different opinion. It is enough to quote the following speech by Comrade Tito in Zagreb on 2 November 1946 (*Borba*, 2 November 1946): 'We do not tell the peasants that they are the strongest pillar of our State in order that, eventually, we may get their votes, but because we know that that is what they are'.

This attitude is in complete contradiction to Marxism–Leninism. Marxism–Leninism considers that in Europe and in the countries of people's democracy, the working class and not the peasantry is the most progressive, the most revolutionary class. As regards the peasantry, or rather its majority—the poor and middle peasants—they can be or are in a union with the working class, the leading role in that alliance belonging to the working class. However, the passage quoted not only denies the leading role to the working class, but proclaims that the entire peasantry, including that is the kulaks, is the strongest pillar in the new Yugoslavia. This attitude consequently expresses opinions which are natural to petty-bourgeois politicians, but not to Marxist–Leninists.

7 On the incorrect policy of the Politbureau of the CC of the CPY on the question of mutual relations between the Party and the People's Front
In our previous letter we wrote that in Yugoslavia the CPY is not considered

as the main leading force, but rather the People's Front; that Yugoslav leaders diminish the role of the Party and are in fact dissolving the Party into a non-party People's Front, committing in this way the same cardinal error committed by the Mensheviks in Russia forty years ago.

Comrades Tito and Kardelj deny this, stating that all decisions of the People's Front are decisions of the Party, but that they do not consider it necessary to state at what Party conference these decisions were approved.

In this lies the greatest error of the Yugoslav comrades. They are afraid openly to acclaim the Party and its decisions before the entire people so that the people may know that the leading force is the Party, that the Party leads the Front and not the reverse. According to the theory of Marxism–Leninism the CP is the highest form of organization of workers, which stands above all other organizations of workers, among others over the Soviet in the USSR, over the People's Front in Yugoslavia. The Party stands above all these organizations of working men not only because it has drawn in all the best elements of the workers, but because it has its own special programme, its special policy, on the basis of which it leads all the organizations of the workers. But the Politbureau of the CC of the CPY is afraid to admit this openly and proclaim it at the top of its voice to the working class and all the people of Yugoslavia. The Politbureau of the CC of the CPY feels that if it does not emphasize this factor, the other parties will not have occasion to develop their strength and their militancy. It also appears that Tito and Kardelj think that by this cheap cunning they can abolish the laws of historical development, fool the classes, fool history. But this is an illusion and self-deception. As long as there are antagonistic classes there will be a struggle between them, and as long as there is a struggle it will be expressed in the work of the different groups and parties, legally or illegally.

Lenin said that the Party is the most important weapon in the hands of the working class. The task of the leaders is to keep this weapon in readiness. However, since the Yugoslav leaders are hiding the banner of their Party and will not emphasize the role of the Party before the masses, they are blunting this weapon, diminishing the role of the Party and disarming the working class. It is ridiculous to think that because of the cheap cunning of the Yugoslav leaders the enemy will relinquish the fight. Because of this the party should be kept fighting fit and ever ready for the struggle against the enemy. Its banner should not be hidden and it should not be lulled to sleep by the thought that, provided he is not provoked, the enemy will give up the struggle and cease to stop organizing his forces, legally or illegally.

We consider that this limiting of the role of the CPY has gone very far. We refer here to the relations between the CPY and the People's Front, which we consider incorrect in principle. It must be borne in mind that in the People's Front a great variety of classes are admitted: kulaks, merchants, small manufacturers, bourgeois intelligentsia, various political groups, including some bourgeois parties. The fact that, in Yugoslavia, only the People's Front enters the political arena and that the Party and its organizations do not take part in political life openly under their own name, not only diminishes the role of the Party in the political life of the country but also undermines the Party as an independent political force, called upon to gain the confidence of the people and to spread its influence over ever broader masses of workers through open political work, through open propaganda of its opinions and its programme. Comrades Tito and Kardelj forget that the Party develops and that it can develop only in an open struggle with the enemy; that cheap cunning and machinations of the Politbureau of the CC of the CPY cannot replace this struggle as a school for educating Party cadres. Their obstinate refusal to admit the error of their statements—namely that the CPY has no other programme than the programme of the People's Front—shows how far the Yugoslav leaders have deviated from Marxist–Leninist views on the Party. This might start liquidation tendencies regarding the CPY which would be a danger to the CPY itself and lead eventually to the degeneration of the Yugoslav People's Republic.

Comrades Tito and Kardelj state that the errors of the Mensheviks regarding the merging of the Marxist Party into a non-party mass organization were committed forty years ago and therefore can have no connection with the present mistakes of the Politbureau of the CC of the CPY. Comrades Tito and Kardelj are profoundly mistaken. There can be no doubt of the theoretical and political connections between these two events, because, like the Mensheviks in 1907, so, today, Tito and Kardelj forty years later, are equally debasing the Marxist Party, equally denying the role of the Party as the supreme form of organization which stands over all other mass workers' organizations, equally dissolving the Marxist Party into a non-party mass organization. The difference lies in the fact that the Mensheviks committed their errors in 1906–07, and after being condemned by the Marxist Party in Russia at the London Conference, did not return to these errors, whereas the Politbureau of the CC of the CPY, in spite of this instructive lesson, are bringing the same error back to life after forty years, and are passing it off as their own Party theory. This circumstance does not lessen but, on the contrary, aggravates the error of the Yugoslav comrades.

8 Regarding the alarming situation in the CPY

In our previous letter we wrote that the CPY retains a semi-legal status, in spite of the fact that it came into power more than three and a half years ago; that there is no democracy in the Party; there is no system of elections; there is no criticism or self-criticism, that the majority of the CPY Central Committee is not composed of elected persons but of co-opted persons.

Comrades Tito and Kardelj deny all these charges point blank.

They write that 'the majority of the members of the CC of the CPY are not co-opted', that 'in December 1940, when the CPY was completely illegal . . . at the Fifth Conference, which by the decision of the Comintern, had all the powers of a congress, a CC of the CPY was elected consisting of thirty-one members and ten candidates . . .' that 'of this number ten members and six candidates died during the war' that besides this 'two members were expelled from the CC', that the CC of the CPY now has 'nineteen members elected at the Conference and seven co-opted members', that now 'the CC of the CPY is composed of twenty-six members'.

This statement does not quite correspond to the facts. As can be seen from the archives of the Comintern, at the Fifth Conference, which was held in October and not in December 1940, thirty-one members of the CC of the CPY and ten candidates were not elected, but twenty-two members of the CC and sixteen candidates. Here is what Comrade Valter (Tito) reported from Belgrade at the end of October 1940 . . . [text given in 7].

If, out of twenty-two elected members of the CC, ten died, this would leave twelve elected members. If two were expelled this would leave ten. Tito and Kardelj say that now there are twenty-six members of the CC of the CPY—therefore, if from this number we subtract ten, this leaves sixteen co-opted members of the present CC of the CPY. It thus appears that the majority of the members of the CC of the CPY were co-opted. This applies not only to the members of the CC of the CPY but also to the local leaders, who are not elected but appointed.

We consider that such a system of creating leading organs of the Party, when the Party is in power and when it can use complete legality, cannot be called anything but semi-legal, and the nature of the organization sectarian-bureaucratic. This sort of situation is quite inadmissible, where meetings are either not held or held in secret, which must undermine the party's influence over the masses, and when party membership is fixed up behind the backs of the workers, whereas acceptance into the party should play an important educational role in linking the party to the working class and to all the workers.

If the Politbureau of the CC of the CPY had real regard for the Party it would not tolerate such a condition in the Party and would, immediately on gaining power, that is, three and a half years ago, have asked the Party to call a Congress in order to reorganize on the lines of democratic centralism and start work as a completely legal Party.

It is entirely understandable that under such conditions in the Party, when there is no election of the leading organs, but only their appointment from above, there can be no talk of internal Party democracy, and much less of criticism and self-criticism. We know that members are afraid to state their opinions, are afraid to criticize the system in the Party and prefer to keep their mouths shut, in order to avoid reprisals. It is no accident that the Minister of State Security is at the same time the Secretary of the CC for Party cadres, or, as Tito and Kardelj say, the organization secretary of the CC of the CPY. It is evident that the members and cadres of the Party are placed under the supervision of the Minister of State Security, which is completely impermissible and cannot be tolerated. It was sufficient, for example, for Comrade Žujović, at a session of the CC of the CPY, not to agree with a draft of the answer of the Politbureau of the CC of the CPY to the letter from the CC of the CPSU, to be immediately expelled from the Central Committee.

As can be seen, the Politbureau of the CC of the CPY does not consider the Party as an independent entity, with the right to its own opinion, but as a partisan detachment, whose members have no right to discuss any questions but are obliged to carry out all the demands of the 'chief' without comment. We call this cultivating militarism in the Party, which is incompatible with the principles of democracy within a Marxist Party.

As is known, Trotsky also attempted to force a leadership based on militarist principles on the CPSU, but the Party, headed by Lenin, triumphed over him and condemned him; militarist measures were rejected and internal Party democracy was confirmed as the most important principle of Party development.

We feel that this abnormal condition inside the CPY represents a serious danger to the life and development of the Party. The sooner this sectarian-bureaucratic regime within the Party is put an end to the better it will be both for the CPY and for the Yugoslav People's Democratic Republic.

9 On the arrogance of the leaders of the CC of the CPY and their incorrect attitude towards their mistakes

As can be seen from the letter by Tito and Kardelj, they completely deny the existence of any mistake in the work of the Politbureau of the CC of the CPY, as well as the slander and propaganda being conducted among the inner circles of Party cadres in Yugoslavia about the 'degeneration' of the USSR into an imperialist State and so forth. They consider that this arises entirely from the inaccurate information received by the CPSU regarding the situation in Yugoslavia. They consider that the CC of the CPSU has been a 'victim' of the slanderous and inaccurate information spread by Comrades Žujović and Hebrang, and maintain that if there had been no such false information regarding conditions in Yugoslavia there would have been no disagreements between the USSR and Yugoslavia. Because of this they came to the conclusion that it is not a matter of mistakes of the CC of the CPY and the criticism of these mistakes by the CC of the CPSU, but of the inaccurate information of Comrades Žujović and Hebrang who 'fooled' the CPSU with their information. They feel that everything would be put right if they punished Comrades Hebrang and Žujović. In this way a scapegoat has been found for their sins.

We doubt whether Comrades Tito and Kardelj themselves believe the truth of this version, even though they seize on it as if it were true. They do this because they feel it is the easiest way out of the difficult situation, in which the Politbureau of the CC of the CPY finds itself. In emphasizing this false and apparently naïve version they desire not only to clear themselves of the responsibility for strained Yugoslav–Soviet relations by throwing the blame on the USSR, but also to blacken the CC of the CPSU by representing it as being greedy for all 'tendentious' and 'anti-Party' information.

We consider that this attitude of Tito and Kardelj towards the CC of the CPSU and their critical remarks regarding the errors of the Yugoslav comrades is not only frivolous and false, but also deeply anti-Party.

If Comrades Tito and Kardelj were interested in discovering the truth and if the truth were not painful to them, they should think seriously about the following:

(a) Why should the CPSU's information about the affairs in Poland, Czechoslovakia, Hungary, Romania, Bulgaria and Albania appear correct, and not cause any misunderstanding with the Communist Parties of those countries, while the information about Yugoslavia appears, according to the Yugoslav comrades, 'tendentious' and 'anti-Party' and causes from their side anti-Soviet attacks and an unfriendly attitude towards the CPSU?

(b) Why do friendly relations between the USSR and the countries of people's democracies develop and strengthen while Soviet–Yugoslav relations deteriorate?

(c) Why did the CPs of the people's democracies support the CPSU's letter of 27 March and condemn the mistakes of the CPY, while the Politbureau of the CPY, which would not admit its errors, remained isolated? Was all this accidental?

In order to reveal the errors of the Politbureau of the CPY it is not necessary to obtain information from individual comrades such as, for example, Comrades Hebrang and Žujović. More than enough can be found in the official statements of the leaders of the CPY, such as Tito, Djilas, Kardelj and others, which appeared in the press.

We declare that Soviet citizens did not obtain any information from Comrade Hebrang. We declare that the talk between Žujović and the Soviet Ambassador in Yugoslavia, Lavrentiev, did not reveal a tenth of what was contained in the erroneous and anti-Soviet speeches of Yugoslav leaders. The reprisals taken against these comrades are not only an impermissible settling of private accounts incompatible with the principles of internal Party democracy, but also bear witness to the anti-Soviet attitude of the Yugoslav leaders, who consider talk between a Yugoslav communist and the Soviet Ambassador a crime.

We feel that behind the attempts of the Yugoslav leaders to clear themselves of the responsibility for straining Soviet–Yugoslav relations, lies the lack of desire by these comrades to admit their mistakes and their intention to continue an unfriendly policy towards the USSR.

Lenin says:
> The attitude of a political party towards its mistakes is one of the most important and most significant criteria of the seriousness of the party and the fulfilment of its obligations towards its class and towards the working masses. To admit errors frankly, to discover their cause, to analyse the situation which has been created by these errors, to discuss measures for correcting them—that is the sign of a serious party, that is the fulfilment of its obligations, that is the education of the class and the masses.

Unfortunately, we must state that the leaders of the CPY, who will not admit and correct their errors, are crudely destroying the principle formulated by Lenin in this directive.

We must also emphasize that, in contrast to the Yugoslav leaders, the leaders of the French and Italian Communist Parties honourably admitted their errors at the Conference of Nine Parties, conscientiously corrected them and thus enabled their Parties to strengthen their ranks and to educate their cadres.

We feel that underlying the unwillingness of the Politbureau of the CC of the CPY honourably to admit their errors and to correct them is the unbounded arrogance of the Yugoslav leaders. Their heads were turned by the successes achieved. They became arrogant and now feel that the depth of the sea reaches only up to their knees. Not only have they become arrogant, but they even preach arrogance, not understanding that arrogance can be their own ruin.

Lenin says:
> 'All revolutionary parties, which have existed in the past, perished because they were arrogant and because they did not see where their strength lay and were afraid to speak of their weaknesses. We will not perish because we are not afraid to speak of our weaknesses and we will learn to overcome them.'

Unfortunately we must state that the Yugoslav leaders, who do not suffer from undue modesty and who are still intoxicated with their successes (which are not so very great) have forgotten Lenin's teaching.

Comrades Tito and Kardelj, in their letter, speak of the merits and successes of the CPY, saying that the CC of the CPSU earlier acknowledged these services and successes, but is now supposedly silent about them. This, naturally, is not true. No one can deny the services and successes of the CPY. There is no doubt about this. However, we must also say that the services of the Communist Parties of Poland, Czechoslovakia, Hungary, Rumania, Bulgaria and Albania are not less than those of the CPY. However, the leaders of these Parties behave modesty and do not boast about their successes, as do the Yugoslav leaders, who have pierced everyone's ears by their unlimited self-praises. It is also necessary to emphasize that the services of the French and Italian CPs to the revolution were not less but greater than those of Yugoslavia. Even though the French and Italian CPs have so far achieved less success than the CPY, this is not due to any special qualities of the CPY, but mainly because after the destruction of the Yugoslav Partisan Headquarters by German paratroopers, at a moment when the people's liberation movement in Yugoslavia was passing through a serious crisis, the Soviet army came to the aid of the Yugoslav people, crushed the German invader, liberated Belgrade and in this way created the conditions which were necessary for the CPY to achieve power. Unfortunately the Soviet army did not and could not render such assistance to the French and Italian CPs. If Comrade Tito and Comrade Kardelj bore this indisputable fact in mind they would be less boastful about their merits and successes and would behave with greater propriety and modesty.

The conceit of the Yugoslav leaders goes so far that they even attribute to themselves such merits as can in no way be justified. Take, for example, the question of military science. The Yugoslav leaders claim that they have improved on the Marxist science of war with a new theory according to which war is regarded as a combined operation by regular troops, partisan units and popular insurrections. However, this so-called theory is as old as the world and is not new to Marxism. As is known, the Bolsheviks applied combined action of regular troops, partisan units and popular insurrections for the entire period of the civil war in Russia (1917–21), and applied it on a much wider scale than was done in Yugoslavia. However, the Bolsheviks did not say that by applying this method of military activity, they produced anything new in the science of war, because the same method was successfully applied long before the Bolsheviks by Field-Marshal Kutuzov in the war against Napoleon's troops in Russia in 1812.

However, even Field-Marshal Kutuzov did not claim to be the innovator in applying this method because the Spaniards in 1808 applied it in the war against Napoleon's troops. It thus appears that this science of war is actually 140 years old and this which they claim as their own service is actually the service of the Spaniards.

Besides this, we should bear in mind that the services of any leader in the past do not exclude the possibility of his committing serious errors later. We must not close our eyes to present errors because of past services. In his time Trotsky also rendered revolutionary services, but this does not mean that the

CPSU could close its eyes to his crude opportunist mistakes which followed later, making him an enemy of the Soviet Union.

* * *

Comrades Tito and Kardelj in their letter proposed that the CPSU should send representatives to Yugoslavia to study Soviet–Yugoslav disagreements. We feel this course would be incorrect, since it is not a matter of verifying individual facts but of differences of principle.

As is known, the question of Soviet–Yugoslav disagreements has already been communicated to the CC of the Nine Communist Parties who have their Cominform. It would be incorrect to exclude them from this matter. Therefore, we propose that this question be discussed at the forthcoming session of the Cominform.

V. Molotov
J. Stalin
By order of the CC of the CPSU

121 Tito remains unrepentant but declares the CPY will show by its deeds that the accusations are unfounded, 17 May 1948 (*p. 54*)

To Comrades J. V. Stalin and V. M. Molotov—

We received your letter of 4 May 1948. It would be superfluous to write of the discouraging impression created on us by this letter. It has convinced us of the fact that all our explanations, though supported by facts showing that all the accusations against us were the result of wrong information, are in vain.

We do not flee from criticism about questions of principle, but in this matter we feel so unequal that it is impossible for us to agree to have this matter decided now by the Cominform. Even before we were informed, the nine Parties received your first letter and took their stand in resolutions. The contents of your letter did not remain an internal matter for individual Parties but were carried outside the permissible circle, and the results are that to-day, in some countries such as Czechoslovakia and Hungary, not only our Party but our country as a whole is being insulted, as was the case with our parliamentary delegation in Prague.

The results of all this have been very serious for our country.

We desire that the matter be liquidated in such a way that we can show by our deeds that the accusations against us are unjust, namely that we are resolutely building socialism and that we remain loyal to the Soviet Union, loyal to the doctrine of Marx, Engels, Lenin, and Stalin. The future will show, as did the past, that we will realize all that we promise you.

J. B. Tito
E. Kardelj
By order of the CC of the CPY

122 CPY/CC disclaims any intention to execute Hebrang and Žujović and refuses Soviet demands for participation in the investigation, May 1948: excerpt (*p. 55*)

The Central Committee has never made preparations to kill anyone, and that includes Hebrang and Žujović. They are being investigated by regular authorities.

The Central Committee considers it improper for the Central Committee of the CPSU to pose the question in this manner and emphatically rejects the very thought of our party leaders being described as 'criminal murderers'.

Consequently the Central Committee feels that the participation of the Central Committee of the CPSU in the investigation of Hebrang and Žujović cannot even be considered. . . .

123 Renewed denunciation of Tito's 'anti-Soviet' policies, 22 May 1948
  (*p. 55*)

To Comrade Tito and other members of the CC of the CPY—
Your letters of 17 May 1948, and 20 May 1948, signed by Comrades Tito and Kardelj, have been received. The CPSU considers that in these letters the leaders of the CPY have gone a step further in aggravating their crude mistakes in matters of principle, the harmfulness and danger of which the CPSU indicated in its letter of 4 May 1948.

1. Comrades Tito and Kardelj write that they feel 'so unequal that it is impossible for us to agree to have this matter decided now by the Informbureau', and further they allowed themselves the allusion that the Yugoslav leaders had allegedly been placed in that position by the CPSU.

The CC of the CPSU considers that there is not a scrap of truth in this assertion. There is no inequality for the Yugoslav Communist Party nor can there be in the Informbureau of nine Parties. All know that during the organization of the Informbureau of nine Communist Parties, all Communist Parties started from the indisputable position that every Party should submit a report to the Informbureau, just as every Party has the right to criticize other Parties. From this point the Conference of nine Parties started when, at its meetings in September 1947, it listened to the reports of the Central Committees of all Parties without exception. The Conference of nine Communist Parties established that each party has an equal right to criticize any other party when the work of the Italian and French Communist Parties was subjected to stern Bolshevik criticism.

It is a known fact that the Italian and French comrades did not oppose the right of other Parties to criticize their mistakes. They have, on the contrary, borne the brunt of Bolshevik criticism and benefited from its conclusions. Moreover, the Yugoslav comrades, like all the others, took advantage of the opportunity to criticize the mistakes of the Italian and French comrades and did not consider, any more than did the others, that by so doing they were infringing the equality of those parties.

Why then are the Yugoslav comrades making this radical change, and demanding the liquidation of already established precedents in the Informbureau? Because they believe that the Yugoslav Party and its leadership ought to be placed in a privileged position, and that the statute of the Informbureau does not apply to them; that, having the privilege of criticizing other Parties, they should not themselves submit to the criticism of other parties. But such moral standards, if such we may call them, have nothing in common with equality. They amount to nothing less than a demand on the part of the Yugoslav leaders for a privileged position on behalf of the CPY which no party has or can have. We have taken and continue to take this stand, for without it the work of the Informbureau could not continue. Each Communist Party is obliged to submit reports to the Informbureau, each Communist Party has the right to criticize any other Communist Party. The refusal of the Yugoslavs to submit reports on their actions to the Cominform, and to hear criticisms from other Communist Parties, means a violation of the equality of Communist Parties.

2. In their letter of 17 May, Comrades Tito and Kardelj repeat the claim made in their previous letter, alleging that the CPSU criticism of Yugoslav Communist Party leadership is based on incorrect information.

But the Yugoslav comrades do not produce any evidence to prove this statement. The statement remains without substantiation and the CPSU's criticism remains unanswered, even though Comrades Tito and Kardelj state in their letter that they do not seek to avoid criticism on questions of principle. Maybe the Yugoslav leaders simply have nothing to say to justify themselves?

It is one of two things: either the Politbureau of the CPY, deep in its soul, is aware of the seriousness of the mistakes committed, but wishing to conceal this from the CPY and to deceive it, declares that the mistakes do not exist, in the meantime laying the blame on innocent men, who were supposed to have misinformed the CPSU; or it really does not understand that by its mistakes it is deviating from Marxism–Leninism. However, in that case it must be admitted that the Politbureau's ignorance of the principles of Marxism is extremely great.

3. Although they refuse to answer the direct questions of the CPSU and aggravate their mistakes by their stubborn unwillingness to admit and correct them, Comrades Tito and Kardelj assure us with words that they will show with deeds that they will remain true to the Soviet Union and the teachings of Marx, Engels, Lenin and Stalin. After what has happened we have no reason to believe in these verbal assurances. Comrades Tito and Kardelj have on many occasions given promises to the CPSU which have not been fulfilled. From their letters and especially from their last letter we are becoming ever more certain of this. The Politbureau of the CPY, and especially Comrade Tito, should understand that the anti-Soviet and anti-Russian policy which they have recently pursued in their everyday work has done all that was needed to undermine faith in them on the part of the CPSU and the Government of the USSR.

4. Comrades Tito and Kardelj complain that they have got into a difficult position and that the consequences of all this is very serious for Yugoslavia. This of course is true, but the blame for this lies exclusively with Comrades Tito and Kardelj and with other members of the Politbureau of the CPY, who have put their own prestige and ambition above the interests of the Yugoslav people, and, instead of admitting and correcting their mistakes in the interests of the people, have stubbornly denied their mistakes, which endanger the Yugoslav people.

5. Comrades Tito and Kardelj claim that the CC of the CPY refuses to attend the meeting of the Informbureau to discuss the question of the Yugoslav Communist Party. If this is their final decision, then it means that they have nothing to tell the Informbureau in their defence, and that they are tacitly admitting

their guilt and are afraid to appear before their fraternal Communist Parties. Moreover, refusal to report to the Informbureau means that the CPY has taken the path of cutting itself off from the united socialist people's front of people's democracies headed by the Soviet Union, and that it is now preparing the Yugoslav Party and people for a betrayal of the united front of people's democracies and the USSR. Since the Informbureau is a Party foundation of the united front, such a policy leads to the betrayal of the work done for international solidarity of the workers and to the adoption of an attitude of nationalism which is hostile to the cause of the working class.

Irrespective of whether the representatives of the CC of the CPY attend the meeting of the Informbureau, the CPSU insists upon the discussion of the situation in the CPY at the next meeting of the Informbureau.

In view of the request of the Czechoslovak and Hungarian comrades that the meeting of the Informbureau take place in the second half of June, the CPSU expresses its agreement with this proposal.

V. Molotov

J. Stalin

By order of the CC of the CPSU

THE FRONTAL ASSAULT

Yugoslavia's expulsion from the Cominform

124 CPY summoned to attend a meeting of the Cominform, 19 June 1948
  (p. 55)

The Communist Information Bureau, convened to discuss the situation in the Communist Party of Yugoslavia, invites representatives of the Central Committee to participate in the work of the Cominform.

In case of your concurrence, the Cominform will expect your representatives not later than June 21 in Bucharest where they should report to Comrade Gheorghiu-Dej at the Central Committee of the Rumanian Workers' Party for instructions on how to reach the place where the Cominform will sit in session.

We expect an urgent reply through Filipov—Moscow.

125 CPY defies the summons to attend, 20 June 1948 *(p. 55)*

Having received an invitation to send its representatives to the meeting of the Informbureau, which has already met for 'Discussion on the Situation in the CPY', the CPY CC requests that the Informbureau session be informed of the following:

The CPY CC is always ready to participate in the work of the Informbureau. But it cannot send its representatives to this meeting of the Bureau because it does not accept the agenda of the meeting, considering that the solution of the question of disagreement between the CPSU CC and the CPY CC, which constitutes the agenda sent to us, has from the beginning up until this meeting of the Bureau been put on an incorrect basis, for the following reasons:

1. The first letter of the CPSU CC to our CC was not composed in a spirit of comradely criticism to which the CPY CC could answer in the same tone, but was rather in the form of a rude and unjust accusation which we, considering

its falsity, could accept only to the detriment of our Party and state, or not accept at all.

2. The CPY CC considers it thoroughly incorrect to base accusations of a brotherly CP on one-sided information of what someone said or on isolated quotations, and not on the basis of analysis of the entire activity of our Party, which passed through such great tests before, during, and after the war.

3. Some of the most serious accusations of the CPSU CC are obviously based on the information of anti-Party elements against which our Party waged a struggle before, during, and after the war. The CPY CC considers it impermissible for such well-known remnants of former fractionalism in the CPY to receive the support of the CPSU CC.

4. The leaders of the member Parties of the Informbureau, uncritically accepting the accusations of the CPSU CC against our Party and without seeking any information from us, condemned our Party in written statements and refused to take into consideration the arguments in our answer to the first letter of the CPSU CC. Some of them, both within broad circles in their Parties and publicly, acted in a way harmful to our country.

5. The CPSU CC did not accept even one argument from our answer to its first letter but in response to that letter and later, too, brought out ever greater and totally unfounded accusations against the CPY. It is clear that such a stand makes it impossible for us to discuss matters on an equal footing.

All these facts are reasons why the CPY CC did not assent to the bringing out of the disagreements before the Informbureau, considering that this would only result in a deepening rather than in a solution of the disagreements.

The CPY CC points out that it proposed to the CPSU CC that it send its representatives to Yugoslavia for a joint investigation of disputed questions on the spot. The CPSU CC did not accept this procedure, which in our opinion represents the only correct one, but, even before receiving our answer, laid the disagreements before the other Parties of the Informbureau, that is, it sent them the text of the letter at the same time it was sent to us, at which the leaders of all the Parties, except the French and Italian, sent us written statements informing us of their judgment of our Party.

Such behaviour is not in the spirit of understanding or according to the principle of voluntariness upon which the Informbureau is based.

The CPY CC continues to adhere to its conviction that joint discussion of disputed questions by direct contact between the CPSU CC and the CPY CC in Yugoslavia itself is the correct way to solve the existing disagreements. The CPY CC expresses its deep sorrow at the fact that the disagreements have taken such a form on the part of the CPSU CC, and again appeals, both to the CPSU CC and to the Informbureau, that they agree with our opinion regarding the necessity for direct contact between the CPSU CC and the CPY CC for the solution of disagreements, and to this end to remove from the agenda the discussion of the situation in our Party, comprehending the incorrectness of such discussion without our consent.

The CPY CC greets the brotherly CPs and declares that no disagreements will prevent the CPY from remaining true to its policy of solidarity and of the closest co-operation with the CPSU CC and other CPs.

126 Cominform repeats Soviet charges, announces the expulsion of Yugoslavia, and calls on the CPY to replace its leaders, 28 June 1948: excerpt (*p. 55*)

1. The Information Bureau notes that recently the leadership of the CPY has pursued an incorrect line on the main questions of home and foreign policy, a line which represents a departure from Marxism–Leninism. In this connection the Information Bureau approves the action of the Central Committee of the CPSU (b), which took the initiative in exposing this incorrect policy of the Central Committee of the CPY, particularly the incorrect policy of Comrades Tito, Kardelj, Djilas and Ranković.

2. The Information Bureau declares that the leadership of the CPY is pursuing an unfriendly policy towards the Soviet Union and the CPSU (b). An undignified policy of defaming Soviet military experts and discrediting the Soviet Union has been carried out in Yugoslavia. A special regime was instituted for Soviet civilian experts in Yugoslavia, whereby they were under surveillance of Yugoslav state security organs and were continually followed. The representative of the CPSU (b) in the Information Bureau, Comrade Yudin, and a number of official representatives of the Soviet Union in Yugoslavia, were followed and kept under observation by Yugoslav state security organs.

All these and similar facts show that the CPY leaders have taken a stand unworthy of Communists, and have begun to identify the foreign policy of the Soviet Union with the foreign policy of the imperialist powers, behaving towards the Soviet Union in the same way as they do towards bourgeois states. As a result of this anti-Soviet position of the CC of the CPY, slanderous propaganda has been spread about the 'degeneration' of the CPSU (b), about the 'degeneration' of the USSR, and so on, borrowed from the arsenal of counter-revolutionary Trotskyism.

The Information Bureau condemns this anti-Soviet attitude of the leaders of the CPY as incompatible with Marxism–Leninism and appropriate only to nationalists.

3. In their domestic policy, the CPY leaders are departing from the positions of the working class and are breaking with the Marxist theory of classes and class struggle. They deny that there is a growth of capitalist elements in their country, and consequently, a sharpening of the class struggle in the countryside. This denial is the direct result of the opportunist tenet that the class struggle does not become sharper during the period of transition from capitalism to socialism, as Marxism–Leninism teaches, but dies down, as was affirmed by opportunists of the Bukharin type, who propagated the theory of the peaceful growing over of capitalism into socialism.

The Yugoslav leaders are pursuing an incorrect policy in the countryside by ignoring the class differentiation in the countryside and by regarding the individual peasantry as a single entity, contrary to the Marxist–Leninist doctrine of classes and class struggle, contrary to the well-known Lenin thesis that small individual farming gives birth to capitalism and the bourgeoisie continually, daily, hourly, spontaneously and on a mass scale. Moreover, the political situation in the Yugoslav countryside gives no grounds for smugness and complacency. In the conditions obtaining in Yugoslavia, where individual peasant farming predominates, where the land is not nationalized, where there is private property in land, and where land can be bought and sold, where much of the land is concentrated in the hands of the kulaks, and where hired labour is employed—in such conditions there can be no question of educating the Party in the spirit of glossing over the class struggle and of reconciling class contradictions without by so doing disarming the Party itself in face of the difficulties connected with the construction of socialism.

Concerning the leading role of the working class, the leaders of the CPY, by affirming that the peasantry is the 'most stable foundation of the Yugoslav state' are departing from the Marxist–Leninist path and are taking the path of a populist, kulak party. Lenin taught that the proletariat as the

> 'only class in contemporary society which is revolutionary to the end . . . must be the leader in the struggle of the entire people for a thorough democratic transformation, in the struggle of all working people and the exploited against the oppressors and exploiters.'

The Yugoslav leaders are violating this thesis of Marxism–Leninism.

As far as the peasantry is concerned it may be that the majority, that is, the poor and medium peasants, are already in alliance with the working class, with the working class having the leading role in this alliance.

The attitude of the Yugoslav leaders disregards these theses of Marxism–Leninism.

As can be seen, this attitude also reflects views appropriate to petty-bourgeois nationalism, but not to Marxists–Leninists.

4. The Information Bureau considers that the leadership of the CPY is revising the Marxist–Leninist teachings about the Party. According to the theory of Marxism–Leninism, the Party is the main guiding and leading force in the country, which has its own, specific programme, and does not dissolve itself among the non-Party masses. The Party is the highest form of organization and the most important weapon of the working class.

In Yugoslavia, however, the People's Front, and not the Communist Party, is considered to be the main leading force in the country. The Yugoslav leaders belittle the role of the Communist Party and actually dissolve the Party in the non-party People's Front, which is composed of the most varied class elements (workers, peasants engaged in individual farming, kulaks, traders, small manufacturers, bourgeois intelligentsia, etc.) as well as mixed political groups which include certain bourgeois parties. The Yugoslav leaders stubbornly refuse to recognize the falseness of their tenet that the CPY allegedly cannot and should not have its own specific programme and that it should be satisfied with the programme of the People's Front.

The fact that in Yugoslavia it is only the People's Front which figures in the political arena, while the Party and its organizations do not appear openly before the people in its own name, not only belittles the role of the Party in the political life of the country, but also undermines the Party as an independent political force, which has the task of winning the growing confidence of the people and of influencing ever broader masses of the working people by open political activity and open propaganda of its views and programme. The leaders of the CPY are repeating the mistakes of the Russian Mensheviks regarding the dissolution of the Marxist party into a non-party, mass organization. All this reveals the existence of liquidation tendencies in the CPY.

The Information Bureau believes that this policy of the Central Committee of the CPY threatens the very existence of the Communist Party, and ultimately carries with it the danger of the degeneration of the People's Republic of Yugoslavia.

5. The Information Bureau considers that the bureaucratic regime created inside the Party by its leaders is disastrous for the life and development of the CPY. There is no inner Party democracy, no elections, and no criticism and self-criticism in the Party. Despite the unfounded assurances of Comrades Tito and Kardelj, the majority of the Central Committee of the CPY is composed of co-opted, and not of elected members. The Communist Party is actually in a position of semi-legality. Party meetings are either not held at all, or meet in secret—a fact which can only undermine the influence of the Party among the masses. This type of organization of the CPY cannot be described as anything but sectarian-bureaucratic. It leads to the liquidation of the Party as an active, self-acting organism, it cultivates military methods of leadership in the Party similar to the methods advocated in his day by Trotsky.

It is a completely intolerable state of affairs when the most elementary rights of members in the CPY are suppressed, when the slightest criticism of incorrect measures in the Party is brutally repressed.

The Information Bureau regards as disgraceful such actions as the expulsion from the Party and the arrest of the Central Committee members, Comrades Žujović and Hebrang, because they dared to criticize the anti-Soviet attitude of the leaders of the CPY and called for friendship between Yugoslavia and the Soviet Union.

The Information Bureau considers that such a disgraceful, purely Turkish, terrorist regime cannot be tolerated in the Communist Party. The interests of the very existence and development of the CPY demand that an end be put to this regime.

6. The Information Bureau considers that the criticism made by the Central Committee of the CPSU (b) and Central Committees of the other Communist Parties of the mistakes of the Central Committee of the CPY rendered the latter fraternal assistance and provides its leaders with all the conditions necessary to speedily correct the mistakes committed.

However, instead of honestly accepting this criticism and taking the Bolshevik path of correcting these mistakes, the leaders of the CPY, suffering from boundless ambition, arrogance and conceit, met this criticism with belligerence and hostility. They took the anti-Party path of indiscriminately denying all their mistakes, violated the doctrine of Marxism–Leninism regarding the attitude of a political party to its mistakes and thus aggravated their anti-Party mistakes.

Unable to face the criticism of the Central Committee of the CPSU (b) and the Central Committees of the other fraternal Parties, the Yugoslav leaders took the path of outrightly deceiving their Party and people by concealing from the CPY the criticism of the Central Committee's incorrect policy and also by concealing from the Party and the people the real reasons for the brutal measures against Comrades Žujović and Hebrang.

Recently, after the Central Committee of the CPSU (b) and fraternal parties had criticized the mistakes of the Yugoslav leaders, the latter tried to bring in a number of new leftist laws. They hastily decreed the nationalization of medium industry and trade, though the basis for this is completely unprepared. In view of such haste the new decision only hampers the supply of goods to the population. In a similar hurried manner they brought in a new grain tax for which the way is also not prepared and which can, therefore, only dislocate grain supplies to the urban population. Finally, only recently the Yugoslav leaders in loud declarations declared their love for, and devotion to, the Soviet Union, although it is known that in practice they are pursuing an unfriendly policy toward the Soviet Union.

Nor is this all. Of late the leaders of the CPY have, with perfect aplomb, been declaiming a policy of liquidating the capitalist elements in Yugoslavia. In a letter to the Central Committee of the CPSU (b), dated 13 April, Tito and Kardelj wrote that 'the plenum of the Central Committee approved the measures proposed by the Political Bureau of the Central Committee to liquidate the remnants of capitalism in the country'.

In accordance with this line Kardelj, speaking in the Skupština on 25 April, declared: 'In our country the days of the last remnants of the exploitation of man by man are numbered.'

In the conditions prevailing in Yugoslavia this position of the leaders of the CPY in regard to the liquidation of the capitalist elements, and hence, the kulaks as a class, cannot be qualified as other than adventurous and non-Marxist. For it is impossible to solve this task as long as individual peasant economy predominates in the country, which inevitably gives birth to capitalism; as long as conditions have not been created for the large-scale collectivization of agriculture; and as long as the majority of the working peasantry is not convinced of the advantages of collective methods of farming. The experience of the CPSU (b) shows that the elimination of the last and biggest exploiting class—the kulak class—is possible only on the basis of the mass collectivization of agriculture, that the elimination of the kulaks as a class, is an organic and integral part of the collectivization of agriculture.

In order to eliminate the kulaks as a class, and hence, to eliminate the capitalist elements in the countryside, it is necessary for the Party to engage in detailed preparatory work to restrict the capitalist elements in the countryside, to strengthen the alliance of the working class and the peasantry under the leadership of the working class, to make socialist industry capable of producing machinery for the collective administration of agriculture. Haste in this matter can only lead to irreparable harm.

Only on the basis of these measures, carefully prepared and consistently carried out, is it possible to go over from restriction of the capitalist elements in the countryside to their liquidation.

All attempts by the Yugoslav leaders to solve this problem hastily and by means of decrees, signify either that the venture is foredoomed to failure or that it is a boastful and empty demagogic declaration.

The Information Bureau considers that by means of these false and demagogic tactics, the Yugoslav leaders are endeavouring to demonstrate that they are not only for class struggle, but that they go even further, beyond those demands which—taking into account the real possibilities—could be advanced by the CPY in the matter of restricting the capitalist elements.

The Information Bureau considers that since these leftist decrees and declarations of the Yugoslav leadership are demagogic and impracticable in the present conditions, they can but compromise the banner of socialist construction in Yugoslavia.

That is why the Information Bureau considers such adventurist tactics as an undignified manœuvre and an impermissible political gamble.

As we see, these leftist demagogic measures and declarations on the part of the Yugoslav leaders are designed to cover up their refusal to recognize mistakes and honestly correct them.

7. Taking into account the situation in the CPY and seeking to show the leaders of the Party the way out of this situation, the Central Committee of the CPSU (b) and the Central Committees of other fraternal parties, suggested that the situation in the CPY should be discussed at a meeting of the Information Bureau, on the same, normal party footing as that on which the activities of other Communist Parties were discussed at the first meeting of the Information Bureau.

However, the Yugoslav leaders rejected the repeated suggestions of the fraternal Communist Parties to discuss the situation in the CPY at a meeting of the Information Bureau.

Attempting to avoid the just criticism of the fraternal parties in the Information Bureau, the Yugoslav leaders invented the fable of their allegedly 'unequal position'. There is not a grain of truth in this story. It is generally known that when the Information Bureau was set up, the Communist Parties based their work on the indisputable principle that each party should report to the Information Bureau just as each party had the right to criticize other parties.

At the first meeting of the Nine Communist Parties, the CPY took full advantage of this right.

The refusal of the Yugoslavs to report to the Information Bureau on their actions and to listen to criticism by other Communist Parties means, in practice, a violation of the equality of the Communist Parties and is, in fact, tantamount to a demand for a privileged position for the CPY in the Information Bureau.

8. In view of this, the Information Bureau expresses complete agreement with the assessment of the situation in the CPY, with the criticism of the mistakes of the Central Committee of the Party, and with the political analysis of these mistakes contained in letters from the Central Committee of the CPSU (b) to the Central Committee of the CPY between March and May 1948.

The Information Bureau unanimously concludes that by their anti-Party and anti-Soviet views, incompatible with Marxism–Leninism, by their whole attitude and their refusal to attend the meeting of the Information Bureau, the leaders of the CPY have placed themselves in opposition to the Communist Parties affiliated to the Information Bureau, have taken the path of seceding from the united socialist front against imperialism, have taken the path of betraying the cause of international solidarity of the working people, and have taken up a position of nationalism.

The Information Bureau condemns this anti-Party policy and attitude of the Central Committee of the CPY.

The Information Bureau considers that, in view of all this, the Central Committee of the CPY has placed itself and the Yugoslav Party outside the united Communist front and consequently outside the ranks of the Information Bureau.

*   *   *

The Information Bureau considers that the basis of these mistakes made by the leadership of the CPY lies in the undoubted fact that nationalist elements, which previously existed in a disguised form, managed in the course of the past five or six months to reach a dominant position in the CPY leadership, and that consequently the leadership of the CPY has broken with the international traditions of the CPY and has taken the road of nationalism.

Considerably overestimating the internal, national forces of Yugoslavia and their possibilities, the Yugoslav leaders think that they can maintain Yugoslavia's independence and build socialism without the support of the Communist Parties of other countries, without the support of the people's democracies, without the support of the Soviet Union. They think that the new Yugoslavia can do without the help of these revolutionary forces.

Showing their poor understanding of the international situation and their intimidation by the blackmailing threats of the imperialists, the Yugoslav leaders think that by making concessions they can curry favour with the Imperialist states. They think they will be able to bargain with them for Yugoslavia's independence and, gradually, get the people of Yugoslavia orientated on these states, that is, on capitalism. In this they proceed tacitly from the well-known bourgeois-nationalist thesis that 'capitalist states are a lesser danger to the independence of Yugoslavia than the Soviet Union'.

The Yugoslav leaders evidently do not understand or, probably, pretend they do not understand, that such a nationalist line can only lead to Yugoslavia's degeneration into an ordinary bourgeois republic, to the loss of its independence and to its transformation into a colony of the imperialist countries.

The Information Bureau does not doubt that inside the CPY there are sufficient healthy elements, loyal to Marxism–Leninism, to the international traditions of the CPY and to the united socialist front.

Their task is to compel their present leaders to recognize their mistakes openly and honestly and to rectify them; to break with nationalism, return to internationalism; and in every way to consolidate the united socialist front against imperialism.

Should the present leaders of the Yugoslav Communist Party prove incapable of doing this, their job is to replace them and to advance a new internationalist leadership of the Party.

The Information Bureau does not doubt that the CPY will be able to fulfil this honourable task.

127 CPY CC rejects the charges and declares its solidarity with Tito, 29 June 1948 (*p. 55*)

The resolution of the Information Bureau 'On the Situation in the Communist Party of Yugoslavia' has a previous history, as is obvious from its contents.

Its basis lies in a number of letters dispatched by the CPSU CC to the CPY

CC. The first of these letters, dated 27 March of this year, in which the CPSU CC sets forth its accusations against the CPY CC, was also simultaneously dispatched to all other members of the Information Bureau, a fact of which the CPY CC had not been informed. In addition, a letter from the CC of the CP of Hungary was received through the CPSU CC which supported the attitude of the CPSU CC in its entirety. The letter of the Hungarian CC was sent to the other Parties also. Similar letters were received by the CPY CC from the other member Parties of the Information Bureau except from the French and Italian. The CPY CC points out that the Parties mentioned accepted as their base the standpoint of the CPSU CC without hearing the views or listening to the counter-arguments of the CPY CC. After this letter from the CPSU CC and the letters from the other Central Committees, as well as after the reply of the CPY CC dispatched to the CPSU CC dated 13 April, other letters from the CPSU CC were received on 4 and 22 May, which adhered more or less to the line of the first letter. The resolution of the Information Bureau 'On the Situation in the Communist Party of Yugoslavia' is essentially a repetition of these letters from the CPSU CC.

In these letters, the CPSU CC accuses the CPY CC and demands that it admit its mistakes, as: first, that the leading people of the CPY are paying lip service to the USSR while secretly slandering it and the CPSU; second, that leading personalities in Yugoslavia are slandering the Soviet army and that specialists from the Soviet Union are surrounded by enmity while Soviet citizens and Comrade Yudin are followed by state security agents; third, that the Party cadres are under the surveillance of the Minister of Internal Affairs and that there is no democracy and criticism within the Party but that it is ruled by a system of military leadership; fourth, that the Yugoslav Government wishes to get into the good graces of the imperialist countries through spies and to put itself under their control; fifth, that the Party submerges itself within the People's Front and cannot therefore be regarded as a Marxist–Leninist organization, that it is pervaded by Bernsteinist, Bukharinist, and Vollmarist theories of the peaceful withering away of the capitalist elements into socialism; sixth, that the ambassador of a certain imperialist power behaves as master of the house in Yugoslavia and that friends and relatives of the hangman of the Yugoslav peoples, Nedić, have easily found themselves positions of comfort in the Yugoslav Government and Party apparatus; seventh, that the Yugoslav leaders identify the foreign policy of the USSR with the foreign policy of the imperialist governments; eighth, that the leading members of the CPY have deviated from the Marxist–Leninist course in the question of the leading role of the working class; ninth, that German parachutists destroyed the 'Partisan' headquarters in Yugoslavia, that as a result of this a serious crisis ensued in the National Liberation Movement, and that thereafter the Soviet army came to assist, liberated Yugoslavia and created the conditions which enabled the CP to come to power; tenth, that the CPY has boasted excessively of its successes during the war although its services do not exceed those of the CPs of Poland, Czechoslovakia, Romania, Hungary, Albania, Bulgaria, etc. To these accusations should be added those made in the resolution of the Information Bureau but not specifically enumerated here.

From the statement submitted by the Politburo of the CPY CC to the session of the Informbureau, which will be given as an appendix, it is obvious that the CPY CC could not agree to a discussion based on the accusations of the CPSU CC founded on slanders, fabrications, and ignorance of the situation in Yugoslavia, before the actual state of affairs had been verified, and before the falsities had been separated from the actual grievances of principle, whether of the CPSU CC, or of any other CC of the member Parties of the Information Bureau.

In connection with the publication of the resolution of the Information Bureau, CPY CC makes the following statement:

1. The criticism contained in the resolution is based on inaccurate and unfounded assertions and represents an attempt to destroy the prestige of the CPY both abroad and in the country, to arouse confusion amongst the masses in the country and in the international workers' movement, to weaken the unity within the CPY and its leading role. It is therefore surprising that the CPSU CC refused to check its assertions on the spot as proposed in the letter of the CPY CC dated 13 April.

2. The resolution maintains, without citing any proof, that the leadership of the CPY carried out a hostile policy towards the USSR. The statement that Soviet military specialists in Yugoslavia have been treated with scant respect, and that Soviet civilian citizens have been under the surveillance of state security agents does not in the least correspond to the truth. Up to their withdrawal not one of the representatives of the Soviet Union brought such matters to the attention of the Yugoslav representatives. That any of the Soviet citizens, and least of all Comrade Yudin, were under observation in Yugoslavia, is altogether false. This statement, and especially that in connection with Comrade Yudin, is designed solely to discredit the CPY and its leadership in the eyes of other Parties.

On the contrary, it is correct, as stated in the letter to the CPSU CC on 13 April, and based on numerous reports of members of the CPY to their Party organizations as well as on statements of other citizens of our country, that from the liberation up to date the Soviet intelligence service sought to enrol them. The CPY CC considered and considers that such an attitude towards a country where the communists are the ruling party and which is advancing toward socialism is impermissible—and that it leads towards the demoralization of the citizens of the FPRY and towards the weakening and undermining of the governmental and Party leadership. The CPY CC considered and considers that the relationship of Yugoslavia toward the USSR must be based exclusively on confidence and sincerity and, in keeping with this principle, Yugoslav State organs never even dreamed of following or exercising any control over Soviet citizens in Yugoslavia.

3. The resolution criticized the policy of the CPY in regard to the conduct of the class struggle and particularly the policy of the CPY in the villages. In connection with this, well-known passages from Lenin are quoted. The CPY CC points out that in its policy of restricting the capitalist elements in the village, it is guided by the mentioned and similar passages from Lenin, which the authors of the resolution—had they taken the trouble—might have read in the published Party documents and articles, and might have convinced themselves concerning the practical execution of this policy. For this reason, the charges made in the resolution and by the CPSU CC in fact only knock on an open door; objectively, they inevitably tend to encourage and support

reactionary and capitalist elements in town and village, and to provoke confusion among the population, as if the CPY CC and its policy were to blame for objective difficulties especially in regard to supply, in the period of transition from capitalism to socialism. The CPY CC considers that as a method it is impermissible to evaluate its activities on the basis of individual quotations taken from the most varied periods of the struggle, or on the basis of individual, isolated, and distorted facts. The CPY CC considers that in assessing the policy of the CPY, as of other Parties, it is the practice of the Party that must be given primary consideration—whether the Party scores or does not score successes in the struggle for the socialist transformation of the country, whether as a whole the capitalist elements are growing weaker or stronger, whether the socialist sector of the national economy is growing weaker or stronger.

4. The CPY CC cannot but reject with deep indignation the assertions that the leading ranks in the CPY are deviating to the course of a kulak party, to the path of the liquidation of the CPY, that there is no democracy in the Party, that methods of military leadership are fostered within the Party, that the most basic rights of Party members are trampled upon in the Party and that the mildest criticism of irregularities in the Party is answered by sharp reprisals, etc. Could the members of the Party, who dauntlessly faced death in thousands of battles, tolerate in the Party a state of affairs unworthy of both men and communists? The assertion that criticism is not allowed in the Party and similar statements are a terrible insult to every member of our Party, a degradation of the heroic and glorious past of the Party and its present heroic struggle for the reconstruction and development of the country. The CPY CC emphasizes that because certain Party organizations have not yet held elections it cannot be maintained that there is no democracy within the Party. These are the remnants of the war period and the tempestuous postwar development through which the CPY passed and in their time they were to be found in other Parties and in the CPSU as well.

As regards the assertion that the Party is losing itself in the Front, that the leading ranks are taking the path of a kulak party, it leads objectively to the shattering of the union of the working masses realized under the leadership of the working class in the united organization, the People's Front, to isolating the Party from the working masses. The root of this assertion, apart from what was said, is to be found in the misunderstanding of the relationship between the Party and Front in Yugoslavia, in the lack of understanding of the essence of the Front in Yugoslavia and the manner of the realization of the leading role of the working class in it. In this question also the point of departure is not facts but fabricated assertions followed by polemics using well-known passages from Lenin which no responsible person in the CPY has ever disputed. The facts, as well as numerous declarations made throughout the war and after it—not only by communists but by non-communists in the Front—show, first, that the CP is the leading force in the Front; second, that the CP does not lose itself in the Front but that on the contrary the Party ideologically and politically is raising the masses of Front members, educating them in the spirit of its policy of Marxism–Leninism; third, that the People's Front of Yugoslavia is in practice fighting for socialism, which surely could not be the case if motley political groups played any important role in it—the bourgeois parties, kulaks, merchants, small industrialists and the like, as is said in the Resolution, or if it were a coalition between the CP and other parties or a form of agreement of the proletariat with the bourgeoisie; fourth, that the Party does not take over the Front programme but that rather the Front gets its basic direction and its programme from the CP, which is natural in view of its leading role in the Front.

The CPY CC emphasizes in this connection that the further ideological and political closing of the ranks of the Front masses, the linking of the political activity of the Party with the activity of the Front and the all-round activity of the Front, is one of the most important tasks of the Party.

Finally, the CPY CC points out that the majority of its members are not co-opted but elected. In its calculation, the CPSU CC did not take into account members of the Political Bureau who were separately elected at the 5th National Conference. For this reason, the seven members of the Political Bureau are to be added to the number of twenty-two members of the plenum of the CPY CC which is mentioned by the CPSU CC in one of its letters. It is odd to reproach the CPY CC, which lost ten of its members in the war, for having co-opted seven comrades in their place, chiefly from the ranks of candidates of the CPY CC.

The CPY CC rejects as ridiculous and untrue the assertion of the illegality of the CPY and considers that this also is a confirmation of the lack of understanding of the form of work of the CPY in the given conditions and at the given time. The forms of work of the CPY grew out of the concrete conditions of the long revolutionary practice of our Party; they were shown in practice to be correct and were an important factor in the Party's winning the confidence of the masses.

5. The CPY CC rejects as unworthy the accusation that a Turkish regime reigns in the CP and that the Yugoslav leaders concealed from the Party the 'criticism of the Central Committee's incorrect policy, concealed from the Party and the people the real reasons for the brutal measures against comrades Hebrang and Žujović'. The CPY CC could not publish the letters of the CPSU CC until this was done by the CPSU itself. The entire, broad, active body of the CPY, however, knows the contents of the letters of the CPSU CC and all party members are informed of the case of Hebrang and Žujović.

The CPY CC must express its amazement that representatives of the member Parties of the Information Bureau could take Hebrang and Žujović under their protection without asking for any details from the CPY CC. The CPY CC wonders why such men as Žujović are defended, for example, who in 1937 by decision of the Comintern, was expelled from the CPY CC together with Gorkić, or Hebrang who behaved treacherously before the Ustasha police, on the subject of which he deceived the Party—men who carried on fractionalist activity in the CPY and worked for its destruction and to sabotage the tempo of the development and industrialization of Yugoslavia. Is this not an encouragement to fractionalist activity, to traitors and to disruptive activity against the CPY? The CC in this connection publishes as a supplement its material concerning Hebrang and Žujović.

6. The CPY CC rejects as absurd the assertion that recently the Yugoslav leaders took measures for the nationalization of small-scale industry and small shops in a great hurry and for demagogical reasons. These measures as a

matter of fact were prepared six months before the charges made by the CPSU CC against the CPY CC and are the result of the strengthening and development of the socialist sector.

The quotation torn from the speech of Comrade Kardelj has only a general significance, while the whole of his speech in point of fact sets forth the line of the Party towards the gradual squeezing out of capitalist elements in the present phase.

In connection with all this it is comprehensible why the journal of the Informbureau, the Soviet press, and the press of certain other Parties have not been publishing any news of late about the successes in the economic development of Yugoslavia, as, for instance, the measures for the further weakening of capitalist elements, the successes in the realization of the plan, the mass pre-congress competitions of the working class and working people rallied in the People's Front, etc. But facts remain facts. By keeping silent concerning them one cannot conceal the arbitrary and completely unfounded criticism of the economic policy of the government of the FPRY and the line of the CPY CC in economic matters.

7. The CPY CC asserts that none of its leaders considers that Yugoslavia, in the struggle for the building of socialism and the preservation of independence, does not need the help of the countries of people's democracy and the USSR. Only people who have lost all contact with reality could assert anything of the kind. The CPY CC must emphasize in this connection that the extending of this aid and co-operation does not depend on it alone but also on the countries of people's democracy and the USSR. The CPY CC considers that this aid must be linked up with the internal and foreign policy of Yugoslavia and in no way with the fact that it could not accept the unfounded charges based on untruths.

The assertion that the Yugoslav leaders are preparing to make concessions to imperialists and to bargain with them concerning the independence of Yugoslavia is completely invented and is among the most grievous slanders against the new Yugoslavia.

The CPY CC must, however, emphasize that in certain countries of people's democracy a whole series of unprovoked acts have been committed by Party and state organs which are insulting to the peoples of Yugoslavia, their state, and state representatives and which lead toward the weakinging of the mentioned co-operation, toward the deterioration of relations with Yugoslavia. The CPY CC does not consider itself bound to remain silent in the future concerning similar acts.

8. The CPY CC does not consider that by refusing to discuss the mistakes of which it is not guilty it has in any way injured the unity of the communist front. The unity of this front is not based on the admission of invented or fabricated errors and slanders, but on the fact of whether or not the policy of a Party is actually internationalist. One cannot, however, ignore the fact that the Information Bureau has committed a breach of the principles on which it was based and which provide for the voluntary adoption of conclusions by every Party. The Informbureau, however, not only forces the leaders of the CPY to admit errors which they did not commit but also calls members of the CPY to rebellion within the Party, to shatter the unity of the Party. The CPY CC can never agree to a discussion about its policy on the basis of inventions and un-

comradely behaviour without mutual confidence. Such a basis is not one of principle and in this and only in this sense the CPY CC considered that it was not on an equal footing in the discussion and that it could not accept discussion on that basis. Further, in connection with the above, the CPY CC resolutely rejects the accusation that the CPY has passed on to positions of nationalism. By its entire internal and foreign policy, and especially by its struggle during the national liberation war and the proper solution of the national question in Yugoslavia, the CPY has given proof of the exact opposite.

By the above-mentioned unjust charges, the greatest historical injustice has been done to our Party, our working class and working masses, the peoples of Yugoslavia in general and their unselfish and heroic struggle.

It is clear to the CPY CC that the charges of the CPSU CC against the CPY CC will be used by enemy propaganda for the purpose of slandering the Soviet Union, Yugoslavia, and other democratic countries. The CPY CC, however, declares that it bears no responsibility for all these phenomena as it did not provoke them by any act of its own.

The CPY CC calls upon the Party membership to close their ranks in the struggle for the realization of the Party line and for even greater strengthening of Party unity, while it calls upon the working class and other working masses, gathered in the People's Front, to continue to work even more persistently on the building of our socialist homeland. This is the only way, the only method to prove in full and by deeds the unjustness of the above-mentioned charges.

128 Tito at 5th CPY Congress attacks Cominform, but affirms solidarity with the USSR and desire to resolve differences with the CPSU, July 1948: excerpts (*p. 56*)

This [Cominform Resolution], Comrades, is not only an attack on the leadership of our Party. This is an attack on the unity of our Party, an attack on the painfully achieved unity of our peoples, this is a call to all destructive elements to demolish what we have been building for the benefit of our peoples up to now; this is a call to civil war, a call to destroy our country.

We consider the most painful thing in the Resolution to be the accusation that we have turned our backs on the Soviet Union and the countries of People's Democracy, that we are nationalists and not internationalists, that we have renounced the science of Marxism–Leninism. . . .

In our foreign policy we have shown full accord with the foreign policy of the Soviet Union, for its policy corresponded, and corresponds, to the interests of our country, the interests of peace. Our attitude is known to all the world because it is written down or expressed in many speeches at international conferences and in our country. And this attitude of ours, that is, our faithfulness and solidarity with the Soviet Union and other countries of the People's Democracy in questions of foreign policy, consisted not only of words but of deeds—and this is very well known not only to every one of our citizens but to friends and enemies the world over.

The first foreign policy measure of the Central Committee of the CPY and our government after the liberation of our country was to link Yugoslavia as closely as possible with the Soviet Union and the countries of the new democracy, both economically, politically, and culturally. . . .

Everyone is now attempting to teach us the ABC of Marxism–Leninism, in which regard they are knocking on an open door and pulling quotations from the works of Marx, Engels, Lenin and Stalin, with no consideration of the fact that we have been using and are using these quotations in practice. They are now disputing the fact that we are Marxist–Leninists. On the basis of what science would we—that is, our Party—achieve such great results? Did we enter the life and death struggle of the Soviet Union in 1941 on the basis of Trotskyist conceptions, or because of loyalty to Marxism–Leninism, a theory that was being realised, and is being realised, in the USSR under the leadership of Comrade Stalin?

. . . Finally, comrades, I should like to emphasize that we shall work with all our might to mend the relations between our party and the CPSU. We hope that the comrades, leaders of the CPSU, will give us an opportunity to show them here, on the spot, everything that is inaccurate in the Resolution. We consider that it is possible to arrive at the truth only in such a case and in such a way.

Attempts to subvert the Party and state

129 Yugoslav Government informs Soviet authorities that it wishes to recall its citizens studying in the USSR, 6 July 1948: excerpt (*p. 57*)

. . . The Government of the FPRY learned that in the Soviet Union, and especially in civilian and military schools, in which the citizens of the FPRY are studying, as well as in other Soviet institutions where citizens of the FPRY are at work, Soviet organs were acting unfairly and slandering the political leaders and statesmen of the FPRY, particularly the Premier of the FPRY and Marshal of Yugoslavia, J. B. Tito.

The Government of the FPRY also learned of cases of certain persons and groups of Yugoslav citizens whom Soviet organs compelled to change their attitude towards the leaders of the FPRY or misled them into doing so, without allowing them to defend their viewpoint . . . [Specific cases cited . . . .

The above-mentioned cases, as well as a whole series of similar cases, clearly show that a situation is being created deliberately and systematically for the citizens of the FPRY that makes their further stay in the USSR impossible. The Government of the FPRY, therefore, decided to recall to Yugoslavia all its citizens in the USSR. The Government of the FPRY has in mind students, undergraduates, all those attending courses at military academies and schools, including students of the Suvorov Academy, the wounded and invalids, and citizens of the FPRY at work in the Radio Committee in Moscow, as well as in other Soviet institutions.

The Government of the FPRY expresses its readiness to settle in the shortest possible time all financial questions left outstanding in connection with the agreement on the training of Yugoslav citizens in the USSR.

The Government of the FPRY expresses its deep brotherly gratitude to the Government of the USSR for the help extended in the training and medical treatment of the citizens of the FPRY. . . .

130 Soviet rejection of Yugoslav note, 6 July 1948 (*p. 57*)

The Ministry of Foreign Affairs of the USSR returns to the Yugoslav Embassy its Note of July 6, this year because of its improper, slanderous nature.

131 Yugoslav note protests against the retention of Yugoslav children in the USSR, 11 June 1949: excerpt (*p. 57*)

. . . The parents and guardians of the Yugoslav children in the USSR, who have not yet been repatriated, justly expect the speedy return of their children and wards. They are applying more and more often, persistently requesting the Government of the FPRY to enable them to realize their fundamental rights as parents and have their children returned to them. The Ministry of Foreign Affairs encloses herewith some of the many letters sent to the Government of the FPRY by parents thus separated from their children. In these letters, as in all the others, the desire and the resolute demand of the parents for the return of their children is clearly expressed.

The Ministry of Foreign Affairs of the FPRY expresses its surprise and anxiety at the fact that, in spite of repeated requests on the part of the FPRY, the Government of the USSR has still not allowed, or arranged for, the return of Yugoslav children to their homeland, and that these children are still being detained in the USSR against the explicit will of their parents and guardians.

The Government of the FPRY requests the Government of the USSR to take steps for the return of the Yugoslav children to their parents in Yugoslavia. . . .

132 Yugoslav note protests against the encouragement of anti-Tito Yugoslavs in the USSR, 23 May 1949: excerpt (*p. 57*)

. . . In Moscow, on April 11, 1945, the Government of the FPRY and the Government of the USSR signed a Treaty of Friendship, Mutual Assistance and Post-War Cooperation for a period of twenty years. On not one single occasion has the Government of the FPRY violated its provisions, and it has remained faithful to this Treaty, as the Government of the USSR knows well, despite various hostile and discriminatory acts by the Government of the USSR against the FPRY.

The incomprehensible actions of the Government of the USSR, however, and its attitude towards the FPRY, are in fact transforming the above-mentioned Treaty into a dead letter.

New proof that a contrary policy is being pursued by the Government of the USSR towards the FPRY is the activity of certain Yugoslav traitors who have gathered in Moscow. In spite of the fact that their personal qualities are well known to the USSR Government, they are conducting hostile activity against the FPRY in Moscow with the full support of the USSR Government. At the beginning of April, 1949, a committee was created in Moscow which launched an anti-Yugoslav paper towards the end of April. The Soviet press and radio give a great deal of publicity to this anti-Yugoslav activity.

The support offered by the Soviet Government to these few traitors to their socialist homeland is in contradiction with the principle of non-interference in the internal affairs of other sovereign countries, a principle which should especially be observed in the relations between socialist States. This support is also in complete contradiction with the proclaimed principle of Soviet foreign policy repeated in the statement of the Head of the Soviet delegation during the second part of the Third Session of the UN General Assembly, namely that 'no State has the right to interfere in the internal affairs of another State, utilizing for this purpose various mercenary groups in order to undermine the foundations of another State'.

By enabling the traitors of a friendly, allied socialist country to gather and organize in Moscow, and by offering them help in their work aimed at combatting the FPRY and at the forcible destruction of the socialist order in Yugoslavia—the Government of the USSR is proving in practice that it is the one that is not pursuing a friendly policy towards the FPRY.

The Ministry of Foreign Affairs of the FPRY protests most energetically against the help being offered by the Soviet authorities to the few persons who have a hostile attitude towards the building of socialism in Yugoslavia. This is an inadmissible and flagrant interference in the internal affairs of the FPRY. The Government of the USSR is requested to prohibit such hostile activities and the further publication of the paper, because the support of such anti-Yugoslav work is in complete contradiction with the spirit and letter of the existing Treaty of Friendship, Mutual Assistance and Post-War Cooperation between the FPRY and the USSR.

133 Soviet reply claims the right to assist Yugoslav 'patriot-exiles', 31 May 1949: excerpts (*p. 57*)

The attitude of the Soviet Government towards the present Yugoslav Government should not be confused with its attitude towards Yugoslavia, its attitude towards the peoples of Yugoslavia. The Yugoslav Government deprived itself of the right to expect a friendly attitude on the part of the Soviet Government inasmuch as the Yugoslav Government pursued a hostile policy towards the Soviet Union, inasmuch as it established an anti-communist and undemocratic regime of terror in Yugoslavia, inasmuch as, waging a struggle against the Soviet Union, and owing to the logic of events, it fell so low as to join the camp of the enemies of the Soviet Union, inasmuch as it transformed the Yugoslav press into a loudspeaker for the furious anti-Soviet propaganda being disseminated by the fascist agents of imperialism. . . .

The Soviet Government decided to receive and give shelter to the Yugoslav patriot-exiles, persecuted by the Yugoslav anti-democratic regime for their democratic and socialist convictions, and gave them asylum. The Soviet Government declares that it will, in the future, extend its hospitality to the Yugoslav revolutionary exiles. This, however, does not mean—as incorrectly maintained in the Yugoslav note—that the Soviet Government or its state organs are allegedly offering 'full support to the revolutionary exiles'. Such dissimilar matters, as the right of revolutionary exiles to be offered shelter, cannot be confused with the 'full support' of their activity without the risk of creating a legal absurdity. . . .

The Yugoslav revolutionary exiles in the USSR are described in the Yugoslav note as 'traitors to their homeland'. The Soviet Government holds a different opinion. It considers that the Yugoslav revolutionary exiles are true socialists and democrats, faithful sons of Yugoslavia, resolute fighters for the independence of Yugoslavia, builders of friendship between Yugoslavia and the Soviet Union. If one is looking for traitors to Yugoslavia, one should not look for them amongst the revolutionary Yugoslav exiles, but amongst those gentlemen who are trying to undermine the friendship between the Soviet Union and Yugoslavia, weaken Yugoslavia and thus lead her to the same fate that befell those countries which became the slaves of imperialism and lost their independence.

134 Soviet note protests against the alleged maltreatment of Soviet citizens in Yugoslavia, 25 July 1949: excerpt (*p. 57*)

According to information at the disposal of the Embassy, the numerous repressive measures to which the Yugoslav authorities subject Soviet citizens permanently residing in Yugoslavia continue. There are numerous cases of arrests of Soviet citizens, and the arrested are kept in Yugoslav prisons without being presented with any indictment and in general without any grounds, without trial or investigation for many months.

This proves that the actual cause of the repressive measures to which the Yugoslav authorities subject Soviet citizens does not lie in the perpetration of any crimes by them, but merely in the fact that the Yugoslav authorities see in them advocates of friendly relations between the peoples of Yugoslavia and the Soviet Union.

It is necessary to point out that the Yugoslav authorities have instituted an absolutely intolerable, outrageous regime of imprisonment for the arrested, subjecting them whilst imprisoned to brutal violence, beating and all kinds of ill-treatment, dooming them to hunger and sickness. The management of the prisons has illegally deprived the imprisoned Soviet citizens of food parcels, not excluding even the sick, thus endangering their health and life. As a result of the ill-treatment and illegalities on the part of the Yugoslav authorities many of the arrested are brought to a state of exhaustion and their health is in a very poor state.

No protests of the imprisoned lodged with the prison administration against this inhuman regime have yielded any results and the position of the imprisoned Soviet citizens is deteriorating with every day. This particularly refers to those Soviet citizens imprisoned in Yugoslav jails, of whom a list which includes thirty-one names is enclosed herewith.

Drawing the attention of the Yugoslav Government to the impermissibility of such treatment of Soviet citizens, the Embassy insists on immediate cessation of these arbitrary practices towards Soviet citizens and on the immediate release from detention of all the Soviet citizens unlawfully kept in Yugoslav prisons. . . .

135 Yugoslav Government vindicates its treatment of Soviet citizens, 30 July: excerpts (*p. 57*)

. . . Although the Government of the USSR gave such White Guard elements Soviet citizenship after the war, it never proposed their repatriation to the Government of the FPRY, nor did it attempt to effect such repatriation. On the contrary, particularly after the Cominform Resolution, such and similar elements were given new impetus in their anti-Yugoslav activity. They acted with the conviction that they would, in every one of their actions against socialist Yugoslavia, enjoy the protection of the Embassy of the USSR in Beograd since they were Soviet citizens.

On the other hand, the Government of the USSR, as it transpires from the Embassy's Note, quite unfoundedly considers that the Yugoslav authorities should tolerate such counter-revolutionary and espionage activities simply because the Government of the USSR had given these people Soviet citizenship after the war.

As regards the Yugoslav citizens of whom the Embassy of the USSR groundlessly asserts that they are Soviet citizens and whose names also appear in the above-mentioned list, the Ministry of Foreign Affairs has, on several occasions, in its earlier Notes, given a competent answer confirming the fact that these persons were citizens of the FPRY for they either never requested or never obtained release from citizenship. Accordingly, persistent intervention in their favour on the part of the Embassy of the USSR represents inadmissible interference in the internal affairs of the FPRY.

Intentionally accusing the Yugoslav authorities of 'intolerable' and 'inhuman' treatment of the arrested persons, the Soviet Government in this case, too, attempts to conceal from the Soviet and the world democratic public the truth about the situation in Yugoslavia and maliciously to misrepresent the truly democratic socialist nature of the People's Government in our country.

The Government of the FPRY rejects these tendentious fabrications with the greatest indignation and notes that the methods imputed by the Soviet Government to the FPRY are entirely alien and unknown to the democratic socialist order established in Yugoslavia in the course of the revolutionary struggle of the peoples of this country.

The Government of the FPRY is certain that the facts stated in the previous Notes of the Ministry of Foreign Affairs will convince the Embassy of the USSR of the justifiability of the action taken by the Yugoslav authorities, and that the Embassy of the USSR will, in the interest of its own prestige and the prestige of the Soviet Union, cease intervening in favour of these counter-revolutionary elements. For this reason, the Government of the FPRY did not publish any of its Notes although their publication would have indicated certain activities by the Embassy of the USSR in Beograd which have nothing in common with the activities of the diplomatic mission of one socialist country in another.

The Soviet Government published the Note of the Embassy of the USSR in Beograd with the intention of giving new stimulus to the hostile, anti-Yugoslav campaign and offering support to the remnants of reaction in Yugoslavia and to all the counter-revolutionary elements in their endeavours to undermine the socialist order in the FPRY.

The Government of the FPRY resolutely rejects all the allegations contained in the Note of the Embassy of the USSR in Beograd as a deliberate insult and hostile act against the FPRY and again declares that it will not allow anyone, regardless of whose support he may enjoy, to undermine the building of the new socialist order in Yugoslavia. The Government of the FPRY will also in the future undertake legal action against all those who attempt to destroy the socialist order which was created with great sacrifices during their revolutionary struggle by the peoples of Yugoslavia who are now exerting tremendous efforts to develop and consolidate the socialist order further.

The Government of the FPRY finally emphasizes that the White Guard elements, who obtained Soviet citizenship after the Second World War, will not be allowed to stay in the FPRY unless they observe the Laws in force in this country.

136 Soviet charges repeated, 18 August 1949: excerpts (*pp. 57, 58*)

... The real reason for the persecution of the Soviet citizens is the fact that, together with all patriots of Yugoslavia, they disapprove of the generally-known, inadmissible attitude of the Yugoslav Government. The latter deserted from the camp of democracy and socialism to the camp of international capital and is trying to do as much mischief as possible to the Soviet Union, in order to win the praise of the representatives of international capital and thereby make a career for itself. ...

The Yugoslav Government itself was compelled to recognize this in its Note. Aware of the unfounded nature of the accusations based on the émigré past of these people, the Yugoslav Government in its Note alleges that there is another charge against them to the effect that certain imprisoned Soviet citizens have a negative attitude towards the existing regime in Yugoslavia, that they sympathize with the well-known Resolution of the Information Bureau of Communist Parties (Cominform), and that they help in its dissemination. But what kind of a charge is this? This is not so much a charge against the arrested Soviet citizens as against the existing political regime in Yugoslavia. The fact that the Yugoslav Government makes such accusations shows what kind of a political regime is now in force in Yugoslavia. In no other country excepting those with a fascist regime, is the free expression of democratic views considered a crime. Accordingly, in the present-day Yugoslavia, this serves as a pretext for unlawful arrests and merciless revenge upon people who criticize the fascist order in Yugoslavia.

Aware of the fact that such an argument is unconvincing and false, and in order to make it appear convincing, the Yugoslav Government falsely attributes propaganda for the forcible overthrow of the order in Yugoslavia to certain prisoners, linking this with the Resolution of the Cominform. Such fabrications, however, are outspoken provocations and slanders. In the Resolution of the Cominform there is no mention of 'propaganda for the overthrow of the order in Yugoslavia', nor of 'forcible' measures for the changing of this order. ...

There are only two Governments in Europe, the Greek and the Spanish, the Government of Tsaldaris and that of Franco, which consider the Resolution of the Cominform as a 'criminal leaflet'. These Governments are both fascist. Apparently, the Yugoslav Government is the third Government of this sort, which also thinks the Resolution of the Cominform is a 'criminal leaflet', considering its circulation and even its reading sufficient reason to imprison thousands of people. Is it not clear that this coincidence is not accidental? ...

If we only glance at what is happening now in Yugoslavia we can immediately see that there can be no question of any kind of people's government or democratic and socialist order in Yugoslavia. Can there be any question of a socialist order in Yugoslavia when the country has been placed under the control of foreign capital and the leadership of the CPY is at war with the Communist Parties of the whole world? Can there be any question of the democratic character of the Government when all of Yugoslavia is ruled by Gestapo methods of administration, when every free expression of ideas is persecuted, when all human rights are violated, when the Yugoslav prisons are crowded with supporters of the socialist camp, when the CPY has been transformed into a Department of the Political Police, subordinate to the chief of police Ranković? It is clear that the statements of the Yugoslav Government about the building of socialism, which is allegedly being carried out in Yugoslavia, are no more true than similar statements made in their time by Hitler and Mussolini. . . .

The Yugoslav Government apparently intends to continue its inhuman treatment of Soviet citizens, unlawfully arresting, beating and ridiculing them. The Yugoslav Government obviously does not intend to punish the offenders who are responsible for the fascist procedure. If this is so, the Soviet Government considers it necessary to state that it will not reconcile itself to such a state of affairs and that it will be compelled to resort to other, more effective means, indispensable for the protection of the rights and interests of Soviet citizens in Yugoslavia, and to take to task the fascist tyrants who have gone beyond all limits.

137 Yugoslav note rejects allegations, 23 August 1949: excerpts (*p. 57*)

The Government of the FPRY wonders how the arrest of several White Guard Soviet citizens, persons with an obscure past, who violated the laws and hospitality of the FPRY, could give rise to such an insulting, crude and unfounded Note from the Government of the USSR. The Government of the FPRY wonders even more why the Government of the USSR at the same time ignores the question of repatriation of the Yugoslav children from the USSR, repeatedly claimed both by the Government of the FPRY and by their parents and guardians, as well as the repatriation of citizens of Yugoslav nationality residing in the USSR to whom the Government of the USSR has still not issued exit visas although they have not violated its laws and are free.

The Government of the FPRY notes that the assertions about the acts of Yugoslav organs towards certain Soviet citizens, mostly White Guard émigrés, are completely invented, untrue and insulting. The above-mentioned persons, as stated in a number of Notes of the Government of the FPRY, are being detained for having seriously violated the laws of the FPRY by their espionage and hostile activities against the FPRY which, as a sovereign country, has the right to defend itself from such activities. However, although irrefutable proofs on the guilt of these persons are available, the Government of the FPRY, expressing its goodwill to settle the disputed question between the two Governments, is ready to hand over all these arrested persons to the Government of the USSR in the shortest possible time. At the same time, the Government of the FPRY expresses its readiness to enable all Soviet citizens permanently residing in the FPRY to leave Yugoslav territory immediately, if they express a desire to do so, and to put all the necessary facilities at their disposal.

The Government of the FPRY and its most responsible representatives have always expressed their readiness to settle with the Government of the USSR all the disputed issues between the two countries by way of agreement. The Government of the FPRY reiterates on this occasion its readiness to approach the settlement of all disputed questions with the Government of the USSR in accordance with, and in the spirit of, the international obligations assumed by both Governments.

Other forms of political pressure

138 USSR denounces the Treaty of Friendship, 28 September 1949 (*p. 57*)

At the trial concluded in Budapest on 24 September 1949 of the state criminal Rajk, and of his accomplices, who were also agents of the Yugoslav Government, it was revealed that the Yugoslav Government has for a rather long period of time been conducting an extremely hostile policy, and carrying on subversive activities against the Soviet Union, hypocritically disguised by false declarations of 'friendship' for the Soviet Union.

The trial at Budapest also revealed that the leaders of the Yugoslav Government have been and still are carrying on their hostile and subversive activities against the USSR not only on their own initiative but also under instructions from foreign imperialist circles.

The facts revealed at this trial further showed that the present Yugoslav Government is completely dependent on the foreign imperialist circles and that it has been transformed into an instrument of their aggressive policy which was bound to lead, and did so, to the liquidation of the independence of the Yugoslav Republic.

All these facts prove that the present Yugoslav Government has flagrantly violated and torn to shreds the Treaty of Friendship, Mutual Assistance, and Postwar Cooperation between the USSR and Yugoslavia, concluded on 11 April 1945 [106].

On the basis of the above-stated, the Soviet Government declares that the Soviet Union from now on considers itself free of the obligations deriving from the above treaty.

139 Yugoslav reaction to the Soviet denunciation, 1 October 1949: excerpts (*p. 57*)

The peace-loving and freedom-loving peoples of Yugoslavia and the entire democratic public of the world are witnesses to the unilateral and arbitrary breach of this Treaty of Friendship between the FPRY and the USSR. They are witnesses to the attempts of the Soviet Government to utilize this breach as a means of blackmail, and put pressure on the peoples of Yugoslavia and their free independent socialist homeland.

The Government of the USSR, aware of the gravity of this latest hostile act towards the peoples of the FPRY, and of the effect this unprecedented act will produce on the international democratic public, in its customary manner attempts to shift the responsibility upon the Government of the FPRY. In doing so, it resorts to slanders about the alleged hostile policy of the

Government of the FPRY towards the USSR, slanders based exclusively on the fabrications brought out at the recently staged trial in Budapest.

Facts regarding the development of relations between the FPRY and the USSR, however, show what is, in practice, the actual policy of the Government of the USSR towards Yugoslavia. It is well known that the representatives of the USSR tried to organize their own network of agents within the Government of the FPRY and the Yugoslav Army, in order to overthrow the legal Yugoslav Government by force. This outright interference in the internal affairs of a small, sovereign, independent, socialist country was to have imposed unequal relations upon the FPRY and put it into a politically and economically subordinate position. Having failed to achieve these intentions, certain leaders of the USSR, trying to disguise the actual ideological and material substance of their policy, used the Cominform as a front to carry out these non-socialist aims. Certain leaders of the USSR, as well as the press and radio, with the knowledge of the Government of the USSR, then started propagating openly for the overthrow of the existing socialist order in Yugoslavia, calling upon the Yugoslav peoples to rebel against their legal Government. They went even further than that, initiating and organizing the hostile activity of a group of States against the FPRY. Thus the Government of the USSR arbitrarily cast off the obligations assumed under the Treaty of Friendship long before it was formally broken.

Certain leaders of the USSR have been working for over a year on the organization of a furious and savage campaign of lies and calumnies against the FPRY, a campaign which is being carried out both by the press and the radio. The Government of the USSR organized economic pressure against Yugoslavia, pressure which went so far as to become an almost complete economic blockade by the USSR and the countries upon which the Soviet Government succeeded in imposing unequal relations. The Soviet Government gave full material and moral assistance to traitors and deserters from socialist Yugoslavia, using them as tools for the realization of its anti-Yugoslav plans. By diplomatic Notes full of brutal insults and threats, accompanied by conspicuous movements of Soviet troops in the neighbouring countries along the Yugoslav frontiers, and by other similar measures, the Government of the USSR tried to intimidate the peoples of Yugoslavia and put pressure on them in order to implement its anti-democratic and anti-socialist intentions with regard to the FPRY. . . .

The statements of the Soviet leaders regarding non-interference in the internal affairs of other States, the free will of peoples to organize their affairs in their own countries, and the peace-loving policy of the Soviet Government are words devoid of any meaning when compared with the present anti-democratic behaviour of the Government of the USSR towards the Government of an independent country like Yugoslavia, which has always pursued a policy of the sincerest friendship and cooperation with regard to the USSR and its Government.

This friendly policy of the Government of the FPRY towards the USSR was a natural expression of the liberation and revolutionary struggle, and of the socialist transformation carried out by the peoples of Yugoslavia in their country. They considered the support of the Soviet Union a guarantee of their independence and their unhindered national and State development. For this purpose a treaty of alliance was concluded with the USSR even before the end of the war. This alliance was the first treaty concluded by the Government of the FPRY with another country. The Government of the FPRY, pursuing with the utmost sincerity a policy of friendship towards the Soviet Union, concluded a number of economic and other agreements with the Soviet Government aimed at developing the closest friendly relations between Yugoslavia and the Soviet Union. The Government of the FPRY invited Soviet military and other specialists to come to Yugoslavia; it sent its best military and other personnel to schools in the Soviet Union; it entrusted the Soviet Government with the education of Yugoslav children, sent to schools in the Soviet Union. In conformity with the Treaty of Friendship, the Government of the FPRY, in all international forums and in all international relations, sincerely cooperated with, and actively supported the positions of the Government of the USSR in foreign policy—which is a generally known fact. In this way, the Government of the FPRY consistently implemented the Treaty of Friendship concluded with the USSR. Despite all the violations on the part of the Government of the USSR, the Yugoslav Government always invoked this Treaty and persistently endeavoured to solve all questions arising between our two countries in the spirit of the afore-mentioned Treaty. . . .

140 Soviet note accuses Yugoslav ambassador of espionage, 25 October 1949: excerpt (*p. 57*)

It was established in the course of the Budapest trial of the state criminal and spy Rajk, and his collaborators, that the present Yugoslav ambassador in the USSR, Mrazović, has for some time been engaged in spying and subversive activities in the Soviet Union, and that, as ambassador of Yugoslavia in the USSR, he published fabrications against the Soviet Union in the Yugoslav press.

For this reason the Soviet Government considers it impossible to allow Mrazović to remain in the capacity of diplomatic representative of Yugoslavia in the USSR.

141 Yugoslav reply, 29 October 1949: excerpt (*p. 57*)

The Ministry of Foreign Affairs of the FPRY considers entirely groundless the Note of the Ministry of Foreign Affairs of the USSR No 4 of October 25, 1949, by which the Soviet Government refuses to allow the former Ambassador of the FPRY in Moscow, Karlo Mrazović, to remain in the country. It is a well-known fact that, on October 15, 1949, at the Sixth Regular Session of the Sabor of the PR of Croatia at Zagreb, Karlo Mrazović was unanimously elected by the People's Deputies to the post of President of the Presidium of the Sabor of the PR of Croatia.

In connection with the insults and slanders against Karlo Mrazović contained in the note of the Soviet Government, however, the Government of the FPRY considers it necessary to underline that the Soviet Government is lending further support to the infamous conspiracy against Yugoslavia staged at Budapest and that it is attempting to sully the honour and prestige of the President of the Presidium of the Croatian Sabor.

It is well known that Karlo Mrazović joined the progressive revolutionary movement in his early youth, and took part in the revolutionary struggle of the Hungarian people after the First World War. He went from Moscow, where he spent seven years as a member of the CPSU (b), to Republican Spain, where he was seriously wounded in 1937 while fighting as a member of the International Brigade. Disabled, he left Spain and continued his self-sacrificing revolutionary struggle in the former Yugoslavia, upholding the honour and prestige of a true people's fighter. In 1941, Karlo Mrazović was one of the organizers and leaders of the people's uprising in Croatia, and was a high military and political leader in the National Liberation Struggle until the end of the war. After the war he was elected People's Deputy, and was a Minister in the Government of the PR of Croatia. He was then sent as Minister Plenipotentiary of the FPRY to Hungary and later to the USSR as Ambassador of the FPRY.

All these facts are well known to the Soviet Government. It therefore clearly follows from the above that the afore-mentioned Note of the Soviet Government is meant to give new impetus to the anti-Yugoslav campaign and, after the unilateral breach of the Treaty of Friendship, Mutual Assistance and Post-War Cooperation, to make relations between the FPRY and the USSR even more strained, on the one hand, and to calumniate the State leadership of the FPRY before the world public to the greatest possible extent, on the other hand. . . .

142 Soviet attempt to block the election of Yugoslavia to the UN Security Council, 20 October 1949: excerpt (*p. 57*)

Mr Vyshinsky: The results of the elections to the Security Council, as announced at the meeting of the General Assembly, have displayed the fact that these elections have taken place in violation of the Charter of the United Nations, and in particular in violation of Article 23, which recognises that in the election of non-permanent members of the Security Council due regard should be paid to the principle of equitable geographical distribution. The elections have entailed a violation of a firm tradition according to which expiring memberships in the Security Council are replaced by countries belonging to the same geographical region. . . .

It is well known that the delegation of the five countries of East Europe have unanimously advanced the candidacy of Czechoslovakia. The candidacy of Yugoslavia was not advanced by any one of these countries. However, despite the practice of previous elections to Security Council membership, in the present case a substantial number of countries failed to support the candidacy of Czechoslovakia, and instead gave their support to the candidacy of Yugoslavia. . . .

Yugoslavia is being dragged into the Security Council not as a result of free elections in accordance with the principles of the Charter and in accordance with established tradition, but as a result of a behind-the-scenes plot between Yugoslavia, the United States of America, and a number of other delegations that apparently decided to utilize for their own ends the political situation that has arisen between Yugoslavia, on the one hand, and the Soviet Union and the countries of the Peoples' Democracy, on the other.

The Soviet Union declares with full determination that Yugoslavia shall not, cannot, and will not be considered as a representative of the East European countries, and that the introduction of Yugoslavia to the Security Council shall be considered by the Soviet Union delegation as a new violation of the Charter undermining the very foundations of cooperation in the United Nations.

143 Cominform resolution on 'the CPY in the power of murderers and spies', November 1949: excerpts (*p. 58*)

The Information Bureau . . . having considered the question 'The Yugoslav Communist Party in the power of murderers and spies', unanimously reached the following conclusions:

Whereas, in June 1948 the meeting of the Information Bureau of the Communist Parties noted the change-over of the Tito–Ranković clique from democracy and socialism to bourgeois nationalism, during the period that has elapsed since the meeting of the Information Bureau this clique has travelled all the way from bourgeois nationalism to fascism and outright betrayal of the national interests of Yugoslavia.

Recent events show that the Yugoslav Government is completely dependent on foreign imperialist circles and has become an instrument of their aggressive policy, which has resulted in the liquidation of the independence of the Yugoslav Republic.

The Central Committee of the Party and the Government of Yugoslavia have merged completely with the imperialist circles against the entire camp of socialism and democracy; against the Communist Parties of the world; against the New Democracies and the USSR.

The Belgrade clique of hired spies and murderers made a flagrant deal with imperialist reaction and entered its service, as the Budapest trial of Rajk–Brankov made perfectly clear.

This trial showed that the present Yugoslav rulers, having fled from the camp of democracy and socialism to the camp of capitalism and reaction, have become direct accomplices of the instigators of a new war, and, by their treacherous deeds, are ingratiating themselves with the imperialists and kowtowing to them.

The change-over of the Tito clique to fascism was not fortuitous. It was effected on the order of their masters, the Anglo–American imperialists, whose mercenaries, it is now clear, this clique has been for long.

The Yugoslav traitors, obeying the will of the imperialists, undertook to form in the People's Democracies political gangs consisting of reactionaries, nationalists, clerical and fascist elements and, relying on these gangs, to bring about counter-revolutionary coups in these countries, wrest them from the Soviet Union and the entire socialist camp and subordinate them to the forces of imperialism.

The Tito clique transformed Belgrade into an American centre for espionage and anti-Communist propaganda.

When all genuine friends of peace, democracy and socialism see in the USSR a powerful fortress of Socialism, a faithful and steadfast defender of the freedom and independence of nations and the principal bulwark of peace, the Tito–Ranković clique, having attained power under the mask of friendship with the USSR, began on the orders of the Anglo–American imperialists a campaign of slander and provocation against the Soviet Union, utilizing the most vile calumnies borrowed from the arsenal of Hitler.

The transformation of the Tito–Ranković clique into a direct agency of imperialism, and accomplices of the warmongers, culminated in the lining up of the Yugoslav Government with the imperialist bloc at UNO, where the Kardeljs, Djilases and Beblers joined in a united front with American reactionaries on vital matters of international policy.

In the sphere of home policy, the chief outcome of the activity of the traitorous Tito–Ranković clique is the actual liquidation of the People's Democratic system in Yugoslavia.

Due to the counter-revolutionary policy of the Tito–Ranković clique which usurped power in the Party and in the State, an anti-Communist, police State—fascist type regime—has been installed in Yugoslavia.

The social basis of this regime consists of kulaks in the countryside and capitalist elements in the towns.

In fact, power in Yugoslavia is in the hands of anti-popular reactionary elements. Active members of the old bourgeois parties, kulaks and other enemies of People's Democracy, are active in central and local government bodies.

The top fascist rulers rely on an enormously swollen military-police apparatus, with the aid of which they oppress the peoples of Yugoslavia.

They have turned the country into a military camp, wiped out all democratic rights of the working people, and trample on any free expression of opinion.

The Yugoslav rulers demagogically and insolently deceive the people, alleging they are building socialism in Yugoslavia.

But it is clear to every Marxist that there can be no talk of building socialism in Yugoslavia when the Tito clique has broken with the Soviet Union, with the entire camp of socialism and democracy, thereby depriving Yugoslavia of the main bulwark for building socialism and when it has subordinated the country economically and politically to Anglo–American imperialists.

The State sector in the economy of Yugoslavia has ceased to be people's property, since State power is in the hands of enemies of the people.

The Tito–Ranković clique has created wide possibilities for the penetration of foreign capital into the economy of the country, and has placed the economy under the control of capitalist monopolies.

Anglo–American industrial-financial circles, investing their capital in Yugoslav economy, are transforming Yugoslavia into an agrarian–raw materials adjunct of foreign capital.

The ever-growing slavish dependence of Yugoslavia on imperialism leads to intensified exploitation of the working class and to a severe worsening of its conditions.

The policy of the Yugoslav rulers in the countryside bears a kulak–capitalistic character.

The compulsory pseudo-cooperatives in the countryside are in the hands of kulaks and their agencies and represent an instrument for the exploitation of wide masses of working peasants.

The Yugoslav hirelings of imperialism, having seized leadership of the CPY, unleashed a campaign of terror against genuine Communists loyal to the principles of Marxism and Leninism and who fight for Yugoslavia's independence from the imperialists.

Thousands of Yugoslav patriots, devoted to Communism, have been expelled from the Party and incarcerated in jails and concentration camps. Many have been tortured and killed in prison or, as was the case with the well-known Communist, Arso Jovanović, were dastardly assassinated.

The brutality with which staunch fighters for Communism are being annihilated in Yugoslavia, can be compared only with the atrocities of the Hitler fascists or the butcher Tsaldaris in Greece or Franco in Spain.

Expelling from the ranks of the Party those Communists loyal to proletarian internationalism, annihilating them, the Yugoslav fascists opened wide the doors of the Party to bourgeois and kulak elements.

As a result of the fascist terror of the Tito gangs against the healthy forces in the CPY, leadership of the party is wholly in the hands of spies and murderers, mercenaries of imperialism.

The CPY has been seized by counter-revolutionary forces, acting arbitrarily in the name of the Party. Recruiting spies and provocateurs in the ranks of the working class parties is, as is well-known, an old method of the bourgeoisie.

In this way the imperialists seek to undermine the Parties from within and subordinate them to themselves. They have succeeded in realising this aim in Yugoslavia.

The fascist ideology, and fascist domestic policy, as well as the perfidious foreign policy of the Tito clique, completely subordinated to the foreign imperialist circles, have created a gulf between the espionage fascist Tito–Ranković clique and the vital interests of the freedom-loving peoples of Yugoslavia.

Consequently, the anti-popular and treacherous activity of the Tito clique is encountering ever-growing resistance from those Communists who have remained loyal to Marxism–Leninism, and among the working class and working peasantry of Yugoslavia.

On the basis of irrefutable facts testifying to the complete change-over of the Tito clique to fascism and its desertion to the camp of world imperialism, the Information Bureau of the Communist and Workers' Parties considers, that:

1. The espionage group of Tito, Ranković, Kardelj, Djilas, Pijade, Gošnjak, Maslarić, Bebler, Mrazović, Vukmanović, Koča Popović, Kidrič, Nešković, Zlatić, Velebit, Koliševski and others, are enemies of the working class and peasantry and enemies of the peoples of Yugoslavia.

2. This espionage group expresses not the will of the people of Yugoslavia, but the will of the Anglo–American imperialists, and has therefore betrayed the interests of the country and abolished the political sovereignty and economic independence of Yugoslavia.

3. The 'CPY', as at present constituted, being in the hands of enemies of the people, murderers and spies, has forfeited the right to be called a Communist Party and is merely an apparatus for carrying out the espionage assignments of the clique of Tito–Kardelj–Ranković–Djilas.

The Information Bureau of Communist and Workers' Parties considers therefore, that the struggle against the Tito clique—hired spies and murderers —is the international duty of all Communist and Workers' Parties.

It is the duty of Communist and Workers' Parties to give all possible aid to the Yugoslav working class and working peasantry who are fighting for the return of Yugoslavia to the camp of democracy and socialism.

A necessary condition for the return of Yugoslavia to the socialist camp is active struggle on the part of revolutionary elements both inside the CPY and outside its ranks, for the regeneration of the revolutionary, genuine CPY, loyal to Marxism–Leninism, to the principles of proletarian internationalism, and fighting for the independence of Yugoslavia from imperialism.

The loyal Communist forces in Yugoslavia who, in the present brutal conditions of fascist terror, are deprived of the possibility of engaging in open action against the Tito–Ranković clique, were compelled in the struggle for the cause of Communism to follow the path taken by the Communists of those countries where legal work is forbidden.

The Information Bureau expresses the firm conviction that, among the workers and peasants of Yugoslavia, forces will be found capable of ensuring victory over the bourgeois-restoration espionage Tito–Ranković clique; that the toiling people of Yugoslavia led by the working class will succeed in restoring the historical gains of People's Democracy, won at the price of heavy sacrifice and heroic struggle by the peoples of Yugoslavia, and that they will take the road of building socialism.

The Information Bureau considers one of the most important tasks of the Communist and Workers' Parties to be an all-round heightening of revolutionary vigilance in Party ranks; exposing and rooting out bourgeois-nationalist elements and agents of imperialism no matter under what flag they conceal themselves.

The Information Bureau recognizes the need for more ideological work in the Communist and Workers' Parties; more work to train Communists in the spirit of loyalty to proletarian internationalism, irreconcilability to any departure from the principles of Marxism–Leninism, and in the spirit of loyalty to Democracy and Socialism.

Economic pressure

144 USSR applies trade sanctions, December 1948: excerpt (*p. 58*)

A protocol on the mutual delivery of goods for 1949 was signed, on 27 December, after the negotiations had ended between the Ministry of Foreign Trade of the USSR and the Yugoslav trade delegation, which had come to Moscow.

Owing to the hostile policy of the Yugoslav Government towards the Soviet Union, in consequence of which it is impossible to maintain large-scale economic exchange between the USSR and Yugoslavia, the protocol provides for reduced exchange of goods between the USSR and Yugoslavia for 1949. This exchange of goods will be reduced by 8 times as compared with 1948.

145 Yugoslavia protests to the USSR at her exclusion from Comecon, February 1949: excerpt (*p. 58*)

... 1. The Government of the FPRY notes with surprise that Yugoslavia was neither informed of, nor invited to participate in, the conference held in Moscow in January this year at which it was decided to establish a Council for Mutual Economic Assistance, although all the countries without exception which participated in that conference have treaties on political, cultural and economic cooperation, and mutual assistance with the FPRY. The surprise of the Government of the FPRY is the greater as it is a known fact that the Yugoslav leaders had several times posed the question of closer cooperation in the interests of the speedier recovery and economic rehabilitation of countries bound by treaties of close mutual assistance and cooperation. The Government of the FPRY proved its attitude by deeds for it was always guided by the principle of close economic cooperation with all the above-mentioned countries.

2. For the above-stated reasons, the Government of the FPRY considers that the Member-States of CMEA have discriminated against Yugoslavia, and that this act of discrimination is in complete contradiction with the existing treaties, economic and other, concluded and ratified between the FPRY and the above-mentioned countries.

3. The Government of the FPRY considers that such action cannot be justified by the existing abnormal relations between Yugoslavia and the Member-States of the Council, for if Yugoslavia had been invited to the consultation, and if her representatives had participated in them [*sic*], this would have created the possibility for an easier settlement of the misunderstandings existing between the FPRY and the Member-States of CMEA.

4. The Government of the FPRY notes that the conclusions of the consultation particularly with regard to the point dealing with the equality of rights of all countries which became parties to the mentioned council are identical with the standpoint of the Government of the FPRY. It therefore considers that, on this basis, it could participate in CMEA, created at these deliberations.

But on the other hand, the Government of the FPRY cannot help underlining at the same time that, if Yugoslavia were to participate in such economic cooperation as is provided for in the conclusions of the Moscow Consultation, it would be necessary;

Firstly, to proceed immediately to the fulfilment of all obligations assumed under, and confirmed by, the existing treaties between the USSR and the countries of People's Democracy, on the one, and the FPRY, on the other hand;

Secondly, to discontinue the campaign and actions directed against the FPRY as detrimental not only to the successful building of socialism in Yugoslavia but also to mutual economic cooperation between the FPRY and the above-mentioned countries. . . .

146 Soviet reply to Yugoslav protest, 11 February 1949: excerpt (*p. 58*)

. . . The Soviet Government considers the participation of Yugoslavia in Comecon as desirable. Participation in Comecon, however, will be possible only if the Yugoslav Government renounces its hostile policy towards the USSR and the countries of People's Democracy and if it returns to the former policy of friendship. The Soviet Government has no doubt that only a resolute break with the policy of hostility and a return to the policy of friendship can correspond to the essential interests of the Yugoslav peoples, the interests of their economic prosperity and the independence of the Yugoslav State.

147 Yugoslav complaint to the UN of Soviet exploitation through the medium of joint companies, 7 October 1949: excerpt (*pp. 43, 53, 58*)

In 1946, the Yugoslav Government and the Government of the Soviet Union had signed agreements by which two companies had been formed, a shipping company and an air transport company. A much larger number of such companies had been formed in other people's democracies. But Yugoslavia had realized that the activities of such companies would be prejudicial to Yugoslav economy and had not wished to increase their number, in spite of the insistence of the USSR Government.

Half the shares of those two companies had belonged to the Yugoslav Government and the other half to the Government of the Soviet Union. The active management had been in the hands of a director appointed by the USSR Government, while the assistant-director had been a Yugoslav. The Government of the Soviet Union had not invested the capital which it had undertaken to invest. Thus, in 1948, it had invested in one of the companies only 9·83 per cent of its share, while the Yugoslav Government had invested 76·25 per cent of its share; nevertheless, the director appointed by the USSR Government had directed the activities of the company in a manner which had served primarily the interests of the economy of the Soviet Union. Only 40 per cent of the transactions had been made for the benefit of Yugoslavia, and 60 per cent for the benefit of other countries. Yugoslavia had paid 0·4 dinar per ton-kilometre of transportation expenses, the USSR 0·19 dinar, and the other countries 0·28 dinar.

Under these conditions, Yugoslavia had preferred to wind up those two companies, which it had had to do by assuming responsibility for the deficits and by allowing the USSR to withdraw its capital, at any rate to the extent to which it had invested it.

The threat of invasion

148 Tito discounts rumours of armed invasion, but makes it clear that Yugoslavia would resist attack, 3 August 1949: excerpts (*p. 58*)

We cannot be sure today that someone will not make certain claims against us. You have heard, and still hear, rumours to this effect. At first, the rumours were spread by the West in the hope that we should believe their tales about the Red Army being about to attack us and so fall the more readily into their lap for protection. We did not believe this, since we knew that it was impossible for the Red Army to attack a socialist country, as that would be the end of socialism in the world. We knew what the capitalists were thinking and wanting when they scared us with this. But today those from the East are trying to scare us in the same way, spreading various rumours through underground channels of so many Soviet divisions over here and so much Soviet artillery over there. But I tell you, comrades, we are not the sort of people to be scared by such things. . . .

We know that these are mere rumours. All the same, we shall not be caught napping. As the comrade general remarked just now, we are ready to thwart any provocation, to defend our country against anyone, for whoever might attempt to hinder us from peacefully building socialism and to threaten our territorial integrity would be to us an enemy, whoever he might be. . . .

CONSEQUENCES OF THE RIFT

The reshaping of foreign policy

149 Note blaming the USSR for failing to support Yugoslavia's territorial claims against Austria and rejecting charges of secret negotiations with the Western powers, 3 August 1949: excerpts (*pp. 30, 60*)

The Government of the USSR is very well aware that there have never been any secret talks, conducted behind the back of the USSR, between the Yugoslav Government and the Government of Great Britain or of the Western powers, regarding the peace treaty with Austria. The Government of the USSR is similarly aware that the representatives of the USSR—Molotov, Vyshinsky, Gusev, Novikov and Zarubin—insisted from the beginning of 1946 that there should be a reduction of the legitimate territorial demands, reparations, and other Yugoslav claims regarding Austria. The Government of the FPRY, for its part, gave proof of its will to reach a conciliatory solution in the interests of safeguarding peace. . . .

The Soviet representatives advised the Government of the FPRY to try to reach an agreement on its own with the powers on this question, as the Government of the USSR is equally well aware. The Government of the USSR was thus kept informed, both from the start and subsequently, of all the proposals made on the Yugoslav side and also about the talks. From 20 April 1947, the Government of the USSR was informed in a letter addressed to M Vyshinsky of the proposal put by the Government of the FPRY, on 14 June 1947, to the British minister Noel-Baker, as also about the conversations taking place at that time in Moscow by the Yugoslav delegations and the responsible representatives of the USSR. It is thus untrue and absurd to allege, as is stated in the Soviet ambassador's note, that the Government of the USSR only learned by chance of the compromise proposal put forward by the Government of the FNRJ, seeing that it had been officially informed by the latter a good two months beforehand. . . .

. . . The Government of the USSR has not tried to explain by what logic the Soviet representatives continued to support all the Yugoslav claims with regard to Austria until the Paris decision, namely for two whole years after the alleged secret talks between the Yugoslav Government and the western states, nor why the Government of the USSR continued to concert with the Yugoslav Government regarding the interventions of the Yugoslav representatives and the scope of the Yugoslav demands. . . .

The Government of the FPRY notes with deep dissatisfaction that the guarantee of protection of minority rights given by the Paris decision, to which the representative of the USSR gave his consent, is precisely the same as that which, for three years, the Western powers wanted Yugoslavia to accept, in place of the real freedom and real national rights of Austria's Carinthian Slovenes and Croats, and which was modelled on the 'minority protection' given by the imperialist treaty of Saint-Germain after the first World War. This so-called guarantee of minority rights is nothing more than the continuation of the forced germanisation of Slovene and Croat national minorities in Austria. . . .

The Paris decisions, which give satisfaction to the demands of the USSR and assure its interests, whereas the interests of Yugoslavia are entirely neglected, demonstrate that the Soviet representatives did not support, before the adoption of the Paris decision, the legitimate interests of Yugoslavia for reasons of political principle or through conviction that the Yugoslav demands were well-founded, but on the contrary, so as to be able to make use of them at the right moment as bargaining counters in its transactions with the western states, with a view to achieving its own demands, without regard to the interests of Yugoslavia and to the detriment of Yugoslavia. . . .

150 USSR disclaims responsibility and puts the blame on the Yugoslavs, 11 August 1949: excerpts (*pp. 30, 46, 60*)

1. Following the conclusion of the second world war, the Yugoslav Government formulated its economic and territorial claims on Austria, including the demand that Slovene Carinthia and the Slovene frontier areas of Styria, covering a total territory of 2,600 sq. km. with a population of nearly 190,000, be transferred to Yugoslavia. The Soviet Government undertook to support these claims and did support them at the sessions of the Council of Foreign Ministers against the USA, Britain and France.

In April 1947, Mr Kardelj, the Vice-Premier of Yugoslavia, addressed a special letter to A. Y. Vyshinsky in which, on behalf of the Yugoslav Government, he set forth the new position of that Government in respect to Yugoslavia's claims on Austria. . . . [115]. Consequently, the Yugoslav Government, as early as April 1947, considered it necessary to abandon its demand not only for Slovene Carinthia, and not only for a small strip of territory in Slovene Carinthia, but all and every territorial claim on Austria.

This was at a time when at conferences with representatives of the Western Powers the Soviet Government was upholding the demand that Slovene Carinthia be transferred to Yugoslavia. That is the irrefutable fact.

In its note of 3 August, the Yugoslav Government qualifies the renouncement of the demand for Slovene Carinthia as treachery, as a betrayal of the interests of the Slovene population of Carinthia, as a violation of the right to national self-determination, as an expression of imperialist policy, as the conversion of Slovene Carinthia into a bargaining counter and so on. If there really has been treachery and betrayal of Yugoslavia's interests in this matter, then, as is evident from Kardelj's letter, it is the Yugoslav Government, and the Yugoslav Government alone, that must be regarded as the traitor and betrayer.

2. One would have thought that the Yugoslav Government, having decided to make such concessions and having abandoned its territorial claims, would have assumed responsibility for such a stand. But the Yugoslav Government calculated differently. It took the view that the Soviet Government must, on its own behalf, announce these concessions . . . while the Yugoslav Government was to remain in the background in order to create in the eyes of the peoples of Yugoslavia the false impression that the Yugoslav Government still adhered to its old demand for the transfer of Slovene Carinthia to Yugoslavia,

and that, accordingly, the refusal to press the demand for Slovene Carinthia originated not with the Yugoslav Government but with the Soviet Government. In other words, it was suggested that the Soviet Government become an instrument for the deception of the peoples of Yugoslavia, a deception engineered by the Yugoslav Government. The Yugoslav Government naïvely imagined that the Soviet Government would be a party to this political swindle. It stands to reason that the Soviet Government could not be a party to this sordid machination. . . .

3. At the same time, as was subsequently established, the Yugoslav Government was engaged, behind the back of the Soviet Government, in secret negotiations with British representatives in Belgrade and London . . . to renounce the claim to Slovene Carinthia. Despite the fact that the Soviet Union has a treaty of alliance with Yugoslavia, the Soviet Government does not to this day know what arrangement was reached by these gentlemen. . . . One thing is certain—that during these backstage negotiations a deal was struck at the expense of the interests of the Slovenes in Carinthia, to the detriment of Yugoslavia's national rights.

4. The Yugoslav Note falsely and slanderously asserts that the Soviet Government refuses to deny Austrian press reports alleging that 'Stalin promised President [Chancellor] Renner of Austria to guarantee Austria's 1938 frontiers.' The Yugoslav Government knows that such Austrian press reports are sheer inventions. . . .

5. All of these circumstances have led the Soviet Government to the conclusion that the Yugoslav Government is violating its obligations of ally with regard to the USSR; that it is behaving not as an ally, but as an enemy of the Soviet Union; that certain strong ties bind the Yugoslav Government, or the chief personages in that government, with the camp of the foreign capitalists; that the Yugoslav Government is to an ever greater degree merging with imperialist circles against the USSR and forming a bloc with them; that the Soviet Government can no longer regard the Yugoslav Government as an ally of the Soviet Union; that the Soviet Government can no longer support the claims of the Yugoslav Government, particularly the claims which the Yugoslav Government has itself abandoned, though it conceals this abandonment from the peoples of Yugoslavia; that if the Yugoslav Government prefers a united front with imperialist circles to a united front with the Soviet Union, then let these circles support its claims. . . .

6. . . . Let the peoples of Yugoslavia know that the Soviet Government regards the present government of Yugoslavia not as a friend and ally, but as a foe and enemy of the Soviet Union.

151 Further Yugoslav note on the question of the frontier with Austria, 29 August 1949: excerpts (*pp. 30, 60*)

The real facts are as follows:

1. In April 1947 a delegation from the FPRY arrived in Moscow to put its case before the Council of Foreign Ministers, but met with a completely negative attitude from the representatives of the USA, France, and Britain, and also with an ambivalent attitude on the part of the USSR in respect of its readiness to support the Yugoslav demands. The Soviet Government knows

9

very well that, in the course of several talks on that occasion between the head of the Yugoslav delegation E. Kardelj and the Yugoslav ambassador in Moscow, V. Popović, with the Soviet representatives Molotov and Vyshinsky, the latter assured the Yugoslav representatives that there was absolutely no prospect of the Yugoslav demands being accepted by the Council of Foreign Ministers and that they would probably be rejected in full. Foreign Minister Molotov told Kardelj that, despite this hopeless prospect, the Soviet delegation would continue to keep the Carinthian question open as a means of facilitating a positive solution on the question of German property in Austria in a sense favourable to the USSR. . . .

The Soviet stand on this question was moreover made clear at the meeting of the Council of Foreign Ministers at which Foreign Minister Molotov re-peatedly stated that, for the Soviet delegation, the main issue was that of the German property claimed by the USSR. This Soviet standpoint was naturally taken by the representatives of the Western powers as indicating a readiness to give ground over the question of Austria's frontiers provided that that of German property in Austria was settled to its advantage. . . .

The Soviet Government in fact gave up supporting the Yugoslav claims as soon as it reached agreement on the question of German property in Austria.
2. The Government of the FPRY cannot but link this official Soviet line with the letter sent by J. V. Stalin in May 1945 to Chancellor Renner:

> I thank you, most esteemed Comrade, for your message of 15 April.
> You may rest assured that your concern for the independence, integrity, and well-being of Austria is also my own.
> I am ready to send you all the friendly help needed for Austria which lies within my power and possibility.
> With apologies for the delay in replying to you,
>   J. Stalin.

The Soviet Government did not consider it necessary to inform the govern-ment of the FPRY of the contents of this letter, as might be expected from an allied government . . . that is to say, the promise that every help would be offered to preserve the immutability of the Austrian–Yugoslav frontier. . . .
3. In these circumstances, the FPRY delegation in Moscow endeavoured in conversations with the Soviet representatives Vyshinsky and Molotov to get the Soviet delegation to advocate at least a compromise settlement. The Soviet representatives thereupon asked the Yugoslav delegates to prepare a number of alternative minimal demands in writing, which was done in Kardelj's letter of 20 April 1947 to Vyshinsky [115].

It is thus not true, as is alleged in the Soviet note, that the Yugoslav Govern-ment gave up all its claims to Slovene Carinthia 'at the time when the Govern-ment of the USSR was supporting Yugoslavia's demands', but the fact is that the Government of the FPRY was compelled to request the Soviet Govern-ment to give support at least to a compromise settlement of the Carinthian question, once the Soviet Government had announced it was ceasing to support the Yugoslav demands.

The Yugoslav Government has never renounced and never stopped fighting for the incorporation of Slovene Carinthia in Yugoslavia, and was only forced to give in when required by the Soviet Government and because it had no other way out. It is widely known that the Soviet Government not only failed to support the Yugoslav claims for the incorporation of Slovene Carinthia but even the demand for minor frontier rectifications. The allegation that the Soviet Government had been willing to fight for the incorporation of Slovene Carinthia, but that the Yugoslav Government had not wanted it to do so is almost tantamount to making a mockery of a country which is fighting for its national liberation and unification. . . .

In the question of Slovene Carinthia, as well as on other issues affecting Yugoslav interests arising out of the Austrian Treaty, the Soviet Government has made common cause with the Western powers against a socialist state.

152 Soviet note repeats its case on the Yugoslav–Austrian frontier issue, 29 August 1949: excerpts (*pp. 30, 46, 60*)

The Yugoslav Government asserts that, in his letter to the Austrian Chancellor Renner [**151**], Stalin 'guaranteed the 1938 Austrian frontiers'. . . .
. . . in this letter of Stalin's, there is not one word about 'Austria's frontiers', or 'guaranteeing Austria's 1938 frontiers', or of the 'immutability of Austria's frontiers'. That is all an invention and concoction by the Yugoslav Government. . . . Does this mean that declaring himself against the partition of Austria and in favour of her independence is the same as recognizing Austria's frontiers as immutable and ruling out any rectification of them in favour of Yugoslavia? Of course not. The question of the integrity of this or that state and the question of 'the immutability of its frontiers' are two entirely different problems. Only people who have shed the last remnants of Marxism can confuse and equate the two issues. . . .

There can be no doubt that Yugoslavia could have got Slovene Carinthia had it not taken fright and betrayed by its cowardice Yugoslavia's national rights. . . .

The facts show, first of all, that as far back as 1947, the Yugoslav Government informed the British Government that it had dropped its territorial claims regarding Slovene Carinthia, and had concealed this from the Soviet Government. Secondly, that the Yugoslav Government was engaged in double-dealing both in 1947 and later, by passing itself off as fighting for Slovene Carinthia, whereas in reality the Yugoslav Government surrendered Slovene Carinthia in a secret understanding with representatives of the British Government two years ago. Thirdly, that the Western powers, after they had been informed about Yugoslavia's surrender of Slovene Carinthia, were perforce more resolute in opposing Yugoslavia's territorial claims, which made it impossible for the Soviet Government to succeed in supporting them. . . .

The Yugoslav Government has acted in this affair as an enemy and opponent of the Soviet Union, and as an agent of foreign imperialist circles.

When it became clear that the Yugoslav Government was playing this murky game, the Soviet Government naturally wished to have no hand in the Yugoslav Government's filthy policy of deceiving the peoples of Yugoslavia. It is also natural that the Soviet Government could no longer support Yugoslavia's territorial claims since the Yugoslav Government, as has now been made clear, had itself ceased to put forward those claims from the time of the secret understanding with the British Government in 1947, and so made further support for these claims on the part of the Soviet Government impossible.

Conscious that it had adopted a hopelessly defeatist attitude over Slovene Carinthia, and seeing that it could not conceal from public opinion Kardelj's letter giving up Slovene Carinthia, the Yugoslav Government took refuge in a third version of its slanderous invention. It alleged that the Soviet Government forced the Yugoslav Government into an agreement with the Western powers in respect to Yugoslavia's territorial claims against Austria, and that the Yugoslav Government 'had only been prepared to make concessions on this issue because the Soviet Government had demanded it.' . . .

The truth is that the Soviet representatives unmasked these false allegations of the Yugoslav Government by recalling in its note of 11 August that, in November 1947, the Soviet ambassador in Yugoslavia, in reply to an enquiry from the Yugoslav Ministry of Foreign Affairs, stated as follows: 'The USSR sees no reason for the Yugoslav Government to modify its territorial claims against Austria'. . . .

In 1948, the Soviet ambassador in Yugoslavia confirmed that the Soviet Government considered it inopportune to modify Yugoslavia's territorial claims. . . .

If the Soviet Government forced the Yugoslav Government to make territorial concessions, why did it not agree with Kardelj's letter? . . . Why did it not accept his proposals? Firstly, because the concessions proposed by Kardelj did not appear unavoidable, i.e., it was still possible to secure Yugoslavia's maximum territorial demands. Secondly, because the Yugoslav Government refused to assume responsibility for the territorial concessions put forward in Kardelj's letter. The Yugoslav Government wanted the Soviet Government, and not itself, to be answerable for the concessions. . . .

Everyone knows that the Yugoslav Government has deserted the camp of socialism and democracy for that of imperialism and fascism. . . . We hope that the Yugoslav Government will understand that it cannot count on the courtesy, still less on the respect, of the Soviet Government.

153 Kardelj announces that Yugoslavia has closed her frontier with Greece, 23 July 1949: excerpts (*p. 60*)

The great sympathy with which everyone in the new Yugoslavia has regarded the Greek liberation movement is generally known. It is also known that our official representatives at the UN have given moral and political support to the democratic struggle of the Greek people. It is known, furthermore, that the new Yugoslavia has received and given—and is still giving today—free medical care to thousands of refugees and children from the war zones in Greece. Finally, it is known that on account of her democratic stance regarding the war in Greece, Yugoslavia has been constantly exposed to attacks and accusations on the part of international reaction. All this the new Yugoslavia has done not to serve any political interests of her own, but on account of the deep sympathy felt for the democratic aspirations of the Greek people and for their struggle for freedom and independence.

However, shortly after the publication of the notorious Cominform resolution by some CPs [126] the leaders of the Greek CP began to pursue an openly unfriendly and devious policy towards Yugoslavia. . . . In return for everything we did for them the leaders of the Greek CP recently launched the vile and shameless invention that our representatives met on the Greek frontier with officers of the Anglo–American and Greek Governments with a view to permitting some Greek Government units to pass through our territory so as to attack formations of the Greek Democratic Army in the rear. . . .

The Government of the FPRY has replied to these slanders and also to the constant monarcho-fascist provocations by closing the Yugoslav–Greek frontier. . . .

If anyone bears the moral and political responsibility for the difficulties in which the Greek democratic movement finds itself, it is not Yugoslavia but the organizers of the anti-Yugoslav campaign who have striven to exploit the movement in their filthy agitation against Yugoslavia and have thereby gravely damaged that movement.

154 Soviet accusation that the Yugoslavs have 'stabbed the National Liberation Army of Greece in the back', 6 December 1949: excerpt (*p. 60*)

The shameless and hypocritical attempts by the despicable clique of Tito to conceal its true nature, a spying and murderous nature, under the false slogan of 'building socialism', have failed completely. The whole world today knows that the Tito–Ranković clique is in the service of Anglo–American imperialists and that it is fighting with them against the international camp of peace, democracy and socialism. . . .

The Belgrade gang of spies and murderers committed an act of perfidy against the Greek people, an act without precedent in history. They stabbed the national liberation army of Greece in the back at the most difficult moment in its struggle against the monarcho-fascist army and its Anglo–American patrons.

Emergence of the Yugoslav path to socialism

155 Tito places the Soviet–Yugoslav dispute in a global ideological context, 20 January 1951: excerpt (*p. 62*)

The path which we followed was at first that of complete reliance on the Soviet Union, and the clash between us and the Soviet leaders stemmed from the real relationship existing between the Soviet Union and other socialist states—in this particular case, Yugoslavia. The method of relationship between socialist states as practised by the Soviet Union was unacceptable to us not simply because it involved ourselves—Yugoslavia, a geographically small socialist state —but on general grounds, since we saw from the very outset that this was something very deep-rooted involving the whole future development of socialism throughout the world which was not in keeping with the teaching of Marx, Engels, and Lenin. We could not naturally know at first where all this would lead to, but we saw that it was wrong, and we thought that, by resisting such a standpoint in the specific case of Yugoslavia, we might promote a discussion on a basis of equality, that is, that the leaders of the Soviet Union would see that it was the wrong path. We thought that their mistakes regarding Yugoslavia stemmed from a lack of knowledge about conditions in our country which was the product of wrong or misleading information about Yugoslavia, and so on. But no; it later became clear over a period of three years—for the clash did not start with the resolution but long before, we might even say, from the war years—that things went much deeper than that, and that the leaders of the Soviet Union were applying in their international policy methods which are quite wrong and anti-socialist, in other words, that they had strayed from the path of socialism in the form conceived in broad outline by our great teachers Marx, Engels, and Lenin.

Our party has helped all progressive people in the world—not only socialists and communists but others—to look at the matter differently today. In many countries of Western Europe there are more and more people who breathe more freely today and see that it is possible to achieve socialism not in the way wanted by the rulers of the Soviet Union, but in the way which working folk in every country want it. I think this is a great service rendered by our Party which, through the example it has set, has given the impulse to make others think and feel that there are revolutionary forces latent in their countries able to build socialism without some armed power bringing it to them at bayonet point. For never in history has real freedom been brought at bayonet point, and still less can socialism be built in this way.

156 Kardelj in Skupština accuses the USSR of continuing its aggressive policy towards Yugoslavia, 27 February 1951: excerpts (*p. 62*)

There exist in the world today a number of danger-spots making for war. I want to refer particularly to the one which most directly concerns us and which threatens the independence, peace, and socialist construction of Yugoslavia, namely the USSR's hegemonistic policy towards Yugoslavia, and also the hostile policy pursued against Yugoslavia by some neighbouring governments in the service of Soviet foreign policy. . . .

The whole responsibility for this state of affairs rests with the USSR and the governments under its influence. The Yugoslav Government has done everything in its power to normalize relations between our country and the countries of the Soviet bloc. I should like to remind you that Comrade Tito and other official representatives of the Yugoslav government have taken every opportunity from 1948 down to the present to stress Yugoslavia's readiness for a normalization of relations and Yugoslavia's peaceful co-operation with the countries of the Soviet bloc, on one condition—that such co-operation should be based on respect for the independence of the peoples of Yugoslavia and non-intervention in our internal affairs. . . .

We do not ask of the Soviet Government that it should have a liking for the way we are building socialism. We have no liking for their unsocialistic methods which, furthermore, compromise the idea of socialism. We do not reproach them for failing to criticize that system. But what we demand from the Soviet Government is this; that they should behave with due respect for the independence of the peoples of Yugoslavia and their desire to work in peace, and without threatening anyone, for the great task of building socialism and increasing the prosperity of our working people.

157 Molotov at Polish CP rally predicts 'the liquidation of the Tito–Fascist clique', 21 July 1951: excerpt (*p. 62*)

Obvious to all is the fate of Yugoslavia, which fell by means of deceit into the hands of spies and provocateurs who betrayed their people and sold them out to the Anglo–American imperialists. Now all see that the Tito, Kardelj and Ranković gang have already re-established the capitalist system in Yugoslavia, deprived the people of its revolutionary victory, and transformed the nation into a weapon of the aggressive imperialist powers.

Realizing that the Yugoslav people hate this hired gang of criminals who stole its way to power, it holds itself in power by bloody terror and Fascist methods of ruling. This cannot continue long. The people of Yugoslavia will find a way to freedom and liquidation of the Titoist–Fascist regime.

158 Tito replies to Molotov's charges by accusing the Soviet leaders of genocide, 27 July 1951: excerpts (*p. 62*)

A few days ago the well-known Soviet leader Molotov found it necessary to go to Poland and there deliver a slanderous, warmongering speech aimed primarily against our country and its leaders. I shall tell you the reason why he attacked us, but first I should like to explain why it was Poland he went to. He went to Poland, Comrades, because it is not exactly all a bed of roses for them there, because he wanted to threaten them and tell the Poles what they could expect if they dared to follow Yugoslavia's example. The threats he uttered there against us are really aimed primarily against the Poles, as I believe that he should know very well by now that we are not afraid of his threats. He knows that, Comrades.

In this speech of his he, of course, hurled all sorts of threats and violent insults against the leaders of our country. He dubbed us, in customary style, spies and criminals who were murdering their people. But in this charge of theirs that we are criminals I see nothing else than their wish to cover up their own crimes. They have been murdering in Albania, Bulgaria, Hungary, Romania, Poland, and Czechoslovakia—not to mention Russia itself. And since this is the case, then they need to accuse *us* of murdering, so as to cover up their own deeds in this way. But which Cominformists have we killed up to now, which of those handful of wretches whom we could have ground into dust have we destroyed? Not one! Why should we kill anyone? Let them do what they want, let them then build socialism and think about themselves. What moral right has Molotov to throw in our face that we are criminals, that we are murdering the people and extirpating it? What right has he to speak—he who is one of the chief leaders of a country where an unheard of crime of genocide has been committed, where whole nations have been annihilated in the face of the whole world? Where is the German Republic of the Volga, where one of the most gifted of peoples used to live? It is in the forests of Siberia! Where is the Tartar Crimean Republic? It does not exist any more; it is in Siberia, vanished amidst the forests and swamps! Where are the Chechens of the Caucasus? They no longer exist—they have been driven out of the hills where, as a free people, they had been fighting for centuries for their liberty; they have disappeared into Siberia, swallowed up in the gigantic forests where they must slowly die, for they cannot support the climate. Where are the thousands and tens of thousands of Estonian, Latvian, and Lithuanian citizens? They do not exist any more; every day they are being sent to Siberia, to labour there in the hardest conditions and to perish from the face of the earth. This fate awaits every country and people which lets itself fall into their clutches. Who, then, is the criminal, who commits genocide, and who destroys peoples and carries out mass murders? Yes, Comrades—the answer is not difficult. So they have no moral right to throw such an insult in our face. . . .

Molotov has threatened that we shall disappear, that all the leaders of our country whom he has dubbed criminals will be swept away, and that the people will see to that. He said that because he knows that our people do not like to keep quiet. But I should like to see him here, I should like him to come here amongst us and say what he wants to you, whilst I shall say what I want, and then we shall see whom you believe. He has uttered this threat against us not only indeed to frighten the peoples of this country, but also if need be to frighten those amongst us who are not properly informed. But our people, Comrades, do not let themselves be frightened by any threats.

159 Yugoslavia complains to the UN of hostile activities by the USSR, 9 November 1951 (*p. 61*)

The Government of the Union of Soviet Socialist Republics has been instigating, organizing and exercising for more than three years—both directly and through the governments of Hungary, Bulgaria, Romania and Albania, as well as the governments of Czechoslovakia and Poland—all-round aggressive pressure against Yugoslavia for the purpose of encroaching upon her sovereignty and threatening her territorial integrity and national independence. These hostile actions have manifested themselves in all spheres of international relations. They have also broken up the basic conventional links between States, so that the existing diplomatic relations are merely nominal. It is clear that such actions are creating a situation endangering the maintenance of international peace.

2. The Government of the FPRY has done everything in its power to avoid the worsening of relations and to avoid being provoked. In spite of very grave offences, the Government of the FPRY has limited itself to customary and direct, but unfortunately unsuccessful, diplomatic steps. Only when it had become crystal clear that these hostile actions actually amounted to a system of aggressive pressure, which was being intensified according to plan, the Government of the FPRY began to draw attention to this situation in the course of the debates of the General Assembly of the United Nations on problems regarding the maintenance of peace. When all this failed to produce the desired effect, the Government of the FPRY published its 'White Book'. None of the accused Governments has even attempted to deny or contradict the facts brought out in the 'White Book', but, on the contrary, all of them have continued to increase the aggressive pressure in all spheres.

3. Consequently, the Government of the FPRY deems it necessary to draw the attention of the General Assembly formally to the existing situation, fraught with danger for peace, which has been brought about, and which is being deliberately aggravated, by the Government of the USSR, and under its

instigation, by the Governments of Bulgaria, Hungary, Romania, and Albania, and also those of Czechoslovakia and Poland.

4. The facts are:

5. That the Government of the USSR has organized and thoroughly carried out, together with the six aforementioned Governments, an economic blockade against the FPRY. Some of the above-mentioned States have already severed even all postal and railway connexions with Yugoslavia, thus violating not only their treaties with Yugoslavia, but also international conventions;

6. That the Government of the USSR has been pursuing for more than three years, together with the six aforementioned Governments, a crude campaign of incitement against the FPRY, which, as regards its scope and forms, has no parallel in international relations. The direct purpose of this propaganda is the creation of a war psychosis. The aim of this propaganda is to incite the hatred of the peoples of the aforementioned countries against Yugoslavia, and to stir up, among the Yugoslavs, agitation, excitement, and insecurity. In order to augment the effect of this propaganda which is being waged on the radio and in the Press, the highest representatives of the Government and of the army of the USSR, and of the other six States, are, in their public and official addresses, not only insulting the State and Government of the FPRY, but are also launching direct exhortations to the Yugoslavs to revolt and overthrow their legal Government;

7. That, with the same aim in view, they are organizing spying, subversive and terroristic activities against Yugoslavia. Special centres for the training of terroristic groups have been set up. Such groups are being sent into Yugoslavia from Bulgaria, Hungary, and Albania, with the direct assistance of State organs, for the purpose of committing acts of diversion and sabotage, in order to weaken the defensive power of Yugoslavia;

8. That, with the same aim in view, members of the Yugoslav minorities are being removed on a large scale from areas where they have been living for centuries. This is not only an inhuman act, but is also a violation of the truce agreements and peace treaties, under which the governments of the respective countries have pledged themselves to respect human rights and to refrain from discrimination;

9. That the Governments of Bulgaria and Hungary are, in contradiction with the provisions of the peace treaties, imposing their citizenship upon Yugoslav citizens born in those parts of Yugoslavia that Bulgaria and Hungary, as allies of Hitler, occupied during the war;

10. That, by withdrawing ambassadors and ministers from Belgrade and indulging in discriminatory practices and acts contrary to the law of nations and established international practice against Yugoslav diplomats—groundless rejections of diplomatic notes and failure to answer them; misuse of diplomatic correspondence for slanderous and abusive attacks on the FPRY—the aforementioned Governments are not only rendering it impossible to solve even the most insignificant disputes through diplomatic channels, but are also jeopardizing the nominal maintenance of diplomatic relations;

11. That the Governments of the USSR and of the other six States have unilaterally abrogated forty-six political, economic, cultural, and other agreements and conventions concluded with Yugoslavia;

12. That the Governments of Bulgaria, Hungary, and Romania, supported

by the Government of the USSR, have arbitrarily violated the military clauses of the peace treaties, by increasing the numerical strength of their armies and strengthening the quantity and quality of their armaments. Demonstrative troop movements and manœuvres have been taking place in the frontier areas bordering on the FPRY. The number and location of the troops of the USSR in Hungary and Romania are lending a much more dangerous character to these ostentatious provocations and are obviously encouraging them, because the provocations are increasing in number and intensity, so that many Yugoslav frontier guards and citizens have been killed and wounded in the course of incidents which have taken place along all the borders of the aforementioned States. Not only the number of incidents, but also the manner in which these incidents are being carried out, are proof of the intention to intensify the prevailing tension.

13. All these and similar actions of the Governments of the USSR, Hungary, Romania, Bulgaria, and Albania, as well as the Governments of Czechoslovakia and Poland, violate the generally accepted principles regarding relations among nations, as set forth in the United Nations Charter.

14. All the attempts that the Government of the FPRY has made so far in order to settle peacefully the questions under dispute, as well as the proposal of the Government of the FPRY to conclude agreements for a lasting peace and non-aggression with each of the neighbouring States, submitted by Mr Edvard Kardelj, Minister for Foreign Affairs, at the meeting of the General Assembly of the United Nations on 25 September 1950, have remained unsuccessful. On the contrary, the Governments of the States responsible for this state of affairs are constantly aggravating these relations, so that in October 1951, on the eve of the session of the General Assembly of the United Nations, they have been refusing even to accept notes regarding grave incidents, in which Yugoslav citizens were murdered on Yugoslav territory by agents of the said States.

15. The Government of the FPRY, having exhausted all normal diplomatic means for the elimination of a situation fraught with danger for international peace, and, bearing in mind that this situation is worsening, has the honour to request the General Assembly of the United Nations, in accordance with Article 10 of the United Nations Charter, that the following item: 'Hostile activities of the Government of the USSR and the Governments of Bulgaria, Hungary, Romania, and Albania, as well as the Governments of Czechoslovakia and Poland, against Yugoslavia', should be placed on the agenda of the General Assembly, so that the Assembly may discuss it and make recommendations which it may find appropriate.

160 Reply of the Soviet delegate to the UN to the Yugoslav complaint, 28 November 1951 (*p. 61*)

Mr SOBOLEV (USSR) recalled that the USSR had opposed inclusion in the agenda of the item proposed by Yugoslavia concerning alleged hostile activities of the USSR governments and the governments of Bulgaria, Hungary, Romania, and Albania, as well as the governments of Czechoslovakia and Poland, against Yugoslavia. The American bloc, however, had obliged the General Assembly to consider the complaint. It was not the first time that the American bloc had provoked and encouraged consideration of complaints against the USSR and the people's democracies. On each occasion the complaints had proved baseless, and the same thing would happen in the case of the Yugoslav complaint. The Soviet Union delegation deprecated the placing of that libellous complaint upon the General Assembly's agenda.

The statement made by the Yugoslav representative in the *Ad Hoc* Political Committee (8th and 9th meeting) was nothing but a tissue of lies and calumnies, and was a complete confirmation of the provocative character of the Yugoslav complaint. It was clear that the Yugoslav Government was attempting to mislead public opinion and the Yugoslav people and to conceal the misdeeds of the rulers of Yugoslavia.

4. What were the facts of the case? The Yugoslav Government attached great importance and special significance to the frontier incidents, for which it made the governments of Albania, Bulgaria, Hungary, and Romania responsible. In reality, as was shown by the numerous protests from those governments to the Yugoslav Government, the incidents had all been provoked by the Yugoslav authorities. Thus, 124 incidents had occurred on the Albanian–Yugoslav frontier in 1949, 65 in 1950 and 56 in the first seven months of 1951. On several occasions Yugoslav commandos had carried out raids on that frontier and Yugoslav aircraft had flown over Albanian territory in the same area, dropping leaflets hostile to the Albanian Government. On the Bulgarian–Yugoslav frontier, 63 incidents had been provoked by the Yugoslav authorities in 1949, and 123 in 1950. On the Hungarian frontier, the Yugoslav authorities had provoked 795 incidents in the course of 1950 alone.

5. Mr Sobolev quoted some typical incidents provoked by the Yugoslav authorities which had occurred recently on those frontiers and formed the subject of notes of protest from the governments concerned. All those incidents were being openly made use of by the Yugoslav Government for lying propaganda.

6. It was not the USSR Government or the governments of the people's democracies which were engaging in hostile activities against Yugoslavia; it was the Yugoslav Government itself which was carrying on subversive activities against the USSR and the people's democracies. That fact had been clearly brought out at the trial of the traitor Rajk in Budapest, when it had been proved that the Yugoslav Government had attempted to overthrow the Hungarian democratic regime. The trial of the traitor Kostov in Sofia had likewise demonstrated that an agreement had been concluded during the war between Marshal Tito and the representatives of the United Kingdom and United States Governments, providing that the Balkan countries, which would be liberated by the Red Army, must not be allowed to deviate from the Western bloc, and that Bulgaria was to be annexed to Yugoslavia for that purpose.

7. It was thus proved that the Yugoslav Government, acting at the instance and with the approval of the United States and the United Kingdom, had engaged in subversive activities directed against the Soviet Union and the people's democracies.

8. It had also been established that the Yugoslav Government had long been completely subject to the foreign imperialist circles and was now but an instrument of their aggressive policy.

9. The Yugoslav Government had cynically violated the treaty of mutual

assistance and friendship concluded with the USSR Government on 11 April 1945, and that was the reason for the USSR's note of 28 September 1949 to the Yugoslav Government, stating that it considered itself released from the obligations of the 1945 treaty [**138**].

10. Furthermore, Yugoslav diplomatic representatives had taken advantage of their privileges to engage in espionage in the countries to which they had been accredited and to organize subversive activities there, as was attested by innumerable facts brought to light during the trials which had taken place in Hungary, Bulgaria, Albania and Romania. The Yugoslav diplomats in Moscow had spread propaganda hostile to the USSR. They had therefore committed gross breaches of the rules of international law, under cover of the protection conferred upon them by diplomatic privileges and immunities.

11. Soviet Union, Albanian, Hungarian, Romanian, and Bulgarian nationals residing in Yugoslavia had been subjected to all kinds of outrage, ill-treatment and persecution, despite the protests of their governments, and especially of the USSR note of 18 August 1949 to Yugoslavia [**136**]. Moreover, the Yugoslav Government had made no effort to disguise the fact that such persecutions were in no way due to any crimes or offences which the victims might have committed, but to their open advocacy of friendship between the Soviet Union and Yugoslavia.

12. The Yugoslav Government's attitude was explained by the fact that that country had lost its independence and had become an American colony where human rights and democratic liberties were violated without scruple. The Yugoslav authorities had provoked frontier incidents with a view to creating a war psychosis to enable them to justify their policy of making Yugoslavia a bastion of aggression against the USSR and the people's democracies. That such was the role allotted to Yugoslavia by the Anglo–American ruling circles was not open to doubt in the face of certain statements made by President Truman and various American Senators. Furthermore, the militarization of Yugoslavia had been intensively developed to the detriment of its economic life as a result of the visit to Washington of General Popović, Chief of Staff of the Yugoslav army, and the visit to Yugoslavia of General Collins, Chief of Staff of United States land forces. American military missions were in charge of that militarization, their part being identical to that played by similar missions to other countries, notably Greece and Turkey.

13. Thus, it was not the USSR, whose armies had liberated Yugoslavia from German occupation, which was threatening that country's independence, but the present rulers of the country, with their policy of subordinating their country's national interests to those of their British and American masters.

14. Referring to the allegation that the Soviet Union had imposed an economic blockade of Yugoslavia, Mr Sobolev recalled that between 1945 and 1947 the USSR had furnished substantial aid to Yugoslavia in the form of goods for a total value of 451 million roubles and had granted loans amounting to 795 million roubles. Loyal to the principle of respect for the sovereign rights of other States, the USSR had not made that economic aid subject to any condition detrimental to the national interests of Yugoslavia. If the Soviet Union had reduced the volume of aid in 1948 and had later completely discontinued it, that was because the Yugoslav Government had from the beginning failed to fulfil its obligations and had, in 1949, suspended payments due under the

trade and loan agreement. Contrary to the Yugoslav allegations, the trade agreements had been violated not by the USSR but by Yugoslavia; and the same remark applied to the trade agreements with Albania, the railway agreements with Romania and Bulgaria, the convention on the navigation of the Danube, and other agreements. By violating those agreements, Yugoslavia had done serious economic injury to the countries concerned, in particular to Albania and Hungary, whose economic development had been retarded. Further, when it had invited Albania to consider the question of the improvement of relations between the two countries, the Yugoslav Government had let it be understood that that improvement would have to take the form of the annexation of Albania to Yugoslavia and on 12 November 1949 had broken off its treaty of friendship with Albania.

15. Many more examples could be cited to prove that Yugoslavia was following a hostile policy towards the USSR and the people's democracies. Nevertheless, while reserving the right to speak at a later stage of the debate, if necessary, Mr Sobolev said that he would refrain from mentioning any further instances at the moment. The facts he had brought forward sufficed to prove that the Yugoslav Government's allegations were empty slanders made for the sole purpose of diverting the attention of the peoples of Yugoslavia from the policy of betrayal their leaders were following with a view to making Yugoslavia a docile instrument of the aggressive policy of the United States. The USSR delegation was convinced that all such manœuvres were doomed to failure.

161 Malenkov at 19th CPSU Congress denounces the Yugoslav communist leaders as American agents, October 1952: excerpt (*p. 63*)

As for such 'free' countries as Greece, Turkey, and Yugoslavia, they have already managed to become American colonies, and the rulers of Yugoslavia—all those Titos, Kardeljs, Rankovićes, Djilases, Pijades and others—long ago signed up as American agents carrying out espionage and sabotage assignments from their American 'chiefs' against the USSR and the People's Democracies.

162 Tito at CPY 6th Congress assails 'Soviet imperialists' for having betrayed socialism in the USSR and for attempting to subvert the CPY, 3 November 1952: excerpts (*p. 62*)

Furious that such a fat morsel as the natural wealth of Yugoslavia has escaped them, the Soviet imperialists accuse us of selling ourselves to the West. . . . In his report—the veritable brainchild of intoxicated conquerors—Malenkov has called us American agents who are working against the USSR. . . . But this wolf wears his sheep's clothing in vain, for no one will be taken in by it. We know his voice too well. He has been singing the old song about his love of peace simply to deceive people and disguise his true imperialistic aims and so lull the world to sleep. But the Soviet leaders have their souls too stained by many dishonest things for anyone to believe them. . . .

Until Teheran we had great faith in them, but they gradually destroyed it all, so that we know them now, know their real face, their aims, their hypocrisy and ruthlessness when it comes to achieving their dishonest goals. . . . To all who believed in the unselfishness of the Soviet Union, her fame as the protector of small nations, that was the first moral blow, the first strong feeling of doubt about the USSR and the correctness of the policy of the Soviet Union. From Teheran down to the present day, the Soviet Union has revealed herself to the world in all her imperialistic greatness. Today we can confidentally say that the whole Soviet international policy, leaving aside her cheap propaganda tricks such as her alleged struggle for peace and so on, has been such as to make her the foremost contributor to the current tensions of the international situation. . . .

Has she not made of the former independent Eastern countries such as Czechoslovakia, Poland, Hungary, Romania, Bulgaria and so on, mere colonies in the heart of Europe? Not to speak of the enslavement of the Baltic states before the war . . . .

Stalin there at Teheran divided Yugoslavia into interest spheres on a fifty-fifty basis with a capitalist country which he had always attacked, and still attacks, as such. . . . He did this because he has completely betrayed socialist principles and taken the path of Czarist Russia, the path of great Russian state interests, and of imperialist methods to further them, whilst seeking to cloak them with the revolutionary interests of the international proletariat. . . .

The clash which occurred between ourselves and the USSR in 1948 was not accidental. . . . It happened at the moment when we clearly saw that the USSR was abandoning socialist principles, not only in its domestic but in its foreign policy, and was openly following the path of imperialist expansionism. . . .

Wherein lie the causes of such an unsocialistic foreign policy on the part of the USSR? They are to be found in the Soviet reality, in the whole domestic structure of that country—economic, political, cultural. The USSR has long since diverged in her internal evolution from socialist development into state capitalism and an unprecedented bureaucratic system. . . .

The 5th Congress of our Party rightly assessed the USSR's attack on our country, although all the causes of this attack were not clear at the time. . . . Immediately after the Congress it was discovered that the leaders of the CPSU had some agents in the ranks of our party . . . who had been recruited by the NKVD, some of them being assigned the task of attacking the policy of the CPY CC at the Congress. But the unanimity of the delegates to the Congress in condemning the letters of Stalin and Molotov, and the Cominform resolution, poured cold water over these traitors and they did not dare to proceed with their fractional work at the Congress. That was a new and mighty defeat for the Soviet leaders, following the Hebrang and Žujović case, in their attempt to break the unity of the Party and of our country's peoples. The 5th Congress unanimously approved the CC's answers to the letters of Stalin and Molotov, as also our decision not to attend the Cominform meeting in Bucharest. But at the 5th Congress, in its resolution regarding this dispute, the hope and desire were expressed that everything be done to improve relations between our Party and the CPSU and settle the dispute in friendly fashion.

There were several reasons for the 5th Congress adopting this position. Firstly, the rank and file of our party—and still more so, the people at large— were ignorant of the whole background of the clash. Secondly, there was the position—political, economic, and ideological—then prevailing, that is to say, the degree of awareness not only of the broad masses of the workers of our country, but also of many Party members, for the Party had for years and years been fostering in its members faith and love towards the Soviet Union as the one true ally on whom our people could rely in difficult times. So when all this was shown up in practice as a terrible blunder, when it became quite clear to us in the leadership what the USSR wanted for our country and for its policy in general, many Party members and the people were still in the dark. We found it hard to believe that the USSR had such dishonourable designs on us as were later to be shown in practice.

The illusion regarding the USSR was slowly shattered, but the process was accelerated by the slanders and insults heaped by the USSR and the Cominform on everything which were our people's greatest pride. It was accelerated by the pressure exercised on our country by the USSR through its economic blockade, the border provocations and the killing of our frontier guards, the military threats, the withholding from their parents of the children who had been sent to be educated in the USSR before the dispute, and many other hostile acts towards our country. They opened the eyes of every honest person in Yugoslavia.

The provocations on the borders of our country grew rapidly from year to year. Whilst the Soviet agents carried out 936 provocations in 1949, the number rose to 1517 in 1951, whilst for only the first ten months of the current year they have reached 1530, causing up to the present the death of 40 frontier-guards and citizens. All of this, together with their launching whole tons of slanderous propaganda material, has served to unmask their hostile intentions towards our country, and not only towards the leadership of the Party, as they tried to make out at first.

Although this attack by the Soviet Union and the other Eastern countries against our Party and people has from the outset been exceptionally fierce and constantly stepped up in different forms, yet it has not shaken the ranks of the party, as Stalin and the other leaders of the USSR and the Cominform hoped.

163 CPY 6th Congress resolution brands the USSR as a 'new aggressive imperialist power', November 1952: excerpt (*p. 62*)

A characteristic of the present international situation is the role of the Soviet Union as a new aggressive imperialist power, which aims at world hegemony.

The aggressive and hegemonistic policy of the Soviet Government is applied particularly against socialist Yugoslavia.

The Government of the USSR has increased international tension by erecting its imperialistic hegemony over a number of independent European states; it is increasing it still further by exerting pressure on other independent states and by persistent striving for spheres of interest which are particularly against the interests of small underdeveloped states and seriously endanger their independence. This policy of the Soviet Union is a threat to world peace and peaceful co-operation between nations.

III POST-STALIN RAPPROCHEMENT, RECOIL AND NON-ALIGNMENT

RUSSIAN OVERTURES FOR RECONCILIATION

164 Tito's statement on normalization of relations with the USSR, 14 June 1953: excerpts (*p. 63*)

The Soviet Union has recently shown a desire for ambassadors to be exchanged again. . . . We shall accept the offer. . . . However, the exchange of ambassadors does not necessarily imply a normalization or improvement of the relations between two countries, in so far as the worst enemies exchange diplomats. . . .

The harm they did to Yugoslavia will not easily be repaired. . . . We need relations which are normal and, if need be, formalized. We are now waiting to see from them how relations will be normalized. I do not trust words alone, but await deeds. . . .

If they think that this normalization will bring about a change in our policy towards the West they are mistaken. . . . We consider that we do not need the Atlantic Pact, and that in our specific circumstances it would bring us more harm than good. But we are always ready to co-operate; and we have said that we are on the side of those who are against aggression, and for the defence of world peace. . . .

My advice to the West is not to give way to nerves. The Soviet Union is now making certain concessions, and I would not say that they are all just manœuvres but rather that they are necessary on account of her present difficult situation. She needs to modify the Stalinist foreign policy and the narrow line which denied small countries the right to exist and held that freedom could only be brought to them on the tip of Soviet bayonets!

I believe that the leaders of the Soviet Union have a real desire to make some changes in the methods of their foreign policy, to behave in a rather different way, in a word, to make certain concessions, and perhaps later, some greater concessions. Of course I do not believe that they will renounce their aims. As long as the Stalinist conception of force as the main factor in the world persists, I do not believe they will give up their aims. It is for us to do our utmost to establish as good relations as we can with all countries, including the Soviet Union, and so avoid the difficulties we have had, and still have, on our borders with our eastern neighbours. We do not hate those peoples. We are sorry that Stalin's policy destroyed everything we built up after 1945 for rapprochement and improved co-operation with them. We are sorry—and I think that those who have not lost their wits are more than sorry—that they have not followed our path of self-management on their own soil. Friendship with the Soviet Union would then indeed have been a reality.

165 Moscow reappoints an ambassador to Belgrade, 17 June 1953 (*p. 63*)

The Presidium of the Supreme Soviet of the USSR has appointed Comrade Vasily Alexeyevich Valkov Ambassador Extraordinary and Plenipotentiary of the USSR to the FPRY.

166 Tito welcomes the Soviet initiative in seeking a normalization of relations based on respect for equal rights and non-interference, 21 December 1954: excerpt (*p. 63*)

The initiative for normalization has come from the Soviet Union, with the admission by today's responsible Soviet leaders that Yugoslavia was wrongly dealt with and condemned in 1948. These statements—and others which will some day see the light of day—helped to make us accept normalization, all the more so since it is in keeping with our wish to co-operate with all countries who want this and who respect the principle of equality of rights. Normalization is greatly facilitated by the Soviet leaders' statement that they respect relations based on equality of rights and non-interference in the internal affairs of our country, and in addition the fact that they accept our viewpoint that this normalization should not be detrimental to our relations with the western countries.

167 Molotov in the Supreme Soviet claims progress in the normalization of relations, 8 February 1955: excerpt (*p. 63*)

It is well known that successes have been achieved recently in the relations between the Soviet Union and Yugoslavia.

We do not consider that everything has already been done in this direction, but we believe that this depends no less upon Yugoslavia also. In recent years Yugoslavia has, apparently, departed to some degree from the course she embarked upon during the first years after the Second World War. And this, of course, is entirely her own domestic concern. The Soviet Union strives to develop Soviet–Yugoslav relations in the economic, political and cultural spheres. At the same time we strive for a possible concerting of efforts in a matter of such decisive importance to all peoples as the safeguarding of peace and international security. We are convinced that the positive trend in the development of Soviet–Yugoslav relations is in the interests both of the peoples of the USSR and those of Yugoslavia.

168 Tito in the Federal Assembly takes issue with Molotov, 7 March 1955: excerpt (*p. 63*)

Towards the end of last year anti-Yugoslav propaganda was called off in the Eastern European countries and open hostile work of émigré organizations against our country was suspended. But it is characteristic that in almost all of these countries there are cases of efforts being made to describe us, in connection with that normalization, to party members and to the people at large at various meetings etc., as allegedly remaining what we have been accused of, but having nonetheless realized to a certain extent our delusions and making efforts to correct ourselves—and similar nonsense. This of course may give rise in our country to doubts as to the complete sincerity of statements made in direct contacts by the most responsible persons in those countries concerning the unjust accusations made against our country in 1948. Mr Molotov's wording when he referred to Yugoslavia in the statement submitted to the Supreme Soviet is, of course, not in keeping with the facts and in a way coincides with these utterings. We consider this as an attempt to hush up the actual facts before their peoples, and this again at our expense. It is high time matters were explained as they really are and as they developed, instead of stopping normalization half-way and continuing to create elements of doubt among our peoples; for such manifestations do not contribute to the improvement of our mutual relations but, on the contrary, they check this process which any-how is not easy after all that has been done to our country and after all the insults which we had to endure through no fault of our own.

169 A mild Soviet response to Tito's sharp words, 12 March 1955: excerpt (*p. 63*)

In his speech, President Tito considered it necessary to question the sincerity of the relations between the USSR and Yugoslavia. The sincerity of the policy of any particular state, however, must be judged from the facts, from the con-crete measures which, indeed, ensure normal relations between states. To what does President Tito's speech bear witness? Does it contain practical proposals directed at improving Yugoslav–Soviet relations further? The facts, unfor-tunately, indicate that this speech does not contain such proposals. Instead, President Tito turns to the past. He has decided to remind public opinion of the accusations against the government of Yugoslavia made in the past. But, in recalling the past, he did not by a single word recall those direct and varied manifestations of hostility towards the Soviet Union which took place in Yugoslavia. In taking up such a position it is truly possible, to use the words of President Tito, 'to halt normalization half-way, and create elements of doubt among the people'.

Thus, President Tito's stand, alleging that one of the parties is 'concealing facts from its people' does not correspond with reality.

This is the case with regard to the historical facts. But that is not the main point.

For anyone who looks forward and not backwards, for anyone desirous of ensuring truly firm and friendly relations between Yugoslavia and the Soviet Union, it is important to develop the successes already achieved in making relations normal, and to ensure the removal of former hostility. As has been repeatedly pointed out in recent years, the Soviet Union has decisively favoured the complete removal of hostility and the building of relations in the spirit of friendship and mutual respect. The making normal of relations between the USSR and Yugoslavia must rest on the basis of concerted efforts to strengthen peace and the observance of the principle of national independence. . . . The making normal of relations depends not only on the Soviet Union but equally upon Yugoslavia herself.

It is widely known that the Soviet Union adheres firmly to the position that every state has the right to pursue any line it wishes in domestic and foreign policy. No one in the Soviet Union would think of 'explaining' the successes achieved in the making normal of relations between the USSR and Yugoslavia by saying that the Yugoslav leaders have now 'realised their mistakes' or are trying to 'mend their ways'.

170 Joint communiqué announces high level Soviet delegation to confer with a view to healing the breach, 14 May 1955 (*p. 64*)

In their mutual wish to ensure the further improvement of relations between the two countries, and to contribute to the strengthening of peace, the Governments of the USSR and the FPRY have agreed to arrange for a meeting of their top level representatives. With this object in view the following delegations have been formed:

By the USSR—N. S. Khrushchev, member of the Presidium of the Supreme Soviet of the USSR and First Secretary of the Central Committee of the CPSU (head of delegation); N. A. Bulganin, President of the Council of Ministers of the USSR; A. I. Mikoyan, First Vice-President of the Council of Ministers of the USSR; D. T. Shepilov, President of the Foreign Affairs Committee of the Soviet of Nationalities of the Supreme Soviet of the USSR and editor-in-chief of the newspaper *Pravda*; A. A. Gromyko, First Deputy Foreign Minister; and P. N. Kumykin, Deputy Minister of Foreign Trade of the USSR.

For the FPRY—Josip Broz Tito, President of the Republic; Vice-Presidents of the Federal Executive Council, E. Kardelj, A. Ranković, and S. Vukmanović-Tempo; K. Popović, State Secretary for Foreign Affairs; Mijalko Todorović, member of the Federal Executive Council; and Veljko Mičunović, State Under-Secretary for Foreign Affairs.

The meeting will be held in Belgrade towards the end of May 1955.

171 Tito welcomes proposed talks but states terms on which they must be conducted, 15 May 1955: excerpt (*p. 64*)

The normalization of relations between Yugoslavia and the Soviet Union constitutes a huge success and a contribution to peace. . . . This has been the most acute problem during the last six years, when Yugoslavia had to withstand enormous pressure and to put up with every conceivable difficulty and injury. But we held out here and the leaders of the Soviet Union, who today are responsible before their people and before the whole world, have boldly approached that question and offered us normalization and improvement of relations between our two countries. . . .

Agreement has recently been reached for a Soviet delegation headed by the foremost Soviet state leaders to visit our country. This has greatly surprised a number of people, but I can only say that I—and all of us—welcome such a bold decision on the part of the responsible men of the Soviet Union and their resolve to come and conduct talks. In the course of the preparations for this meeting, we let them know what the world has known for many years, and to which our people continue to adhere, namely that we want to talk on an equal footing and as an independent country . . . and that we shall let no one, be it from the East or from the West, meddle in our domestic affairs.

The Soviet leaders have been directly informed of all this, and have decided to come on this basis to discuss problems which still exist between the two countries, so that the normalization of relations may acquire a realistic and firm foundation, without any illusions being harboured on either side. These talks will be carried on before the world; the East and the West and the rest of the world will know what we talked about and on what we reached agreement, for we have no intention of manœuvring behind the scenes or doing anything at the expense of someone else. It is not our fault if those in the West who had certain illusions about Yugoslavia becoming something other than what she is are disappointed. . . .

I think that relations should be the same between all countries. We shall not adhere to any bloc. . . .

We shall never be the tool of anyone else who might possibly harbour aggressive designs on someone else. We shall stay as we are, and we wish to maintain good relations with the West, just as we wish to see a great improvement in our relations with the Soviet Union and the other Eastern countries.

172 Soviet comment on proposed talks, 18 May 1955: excerpts (*p. 64*)

The prospects for the further improvement of Soviet–Yugoslav relations frighten only those who are interested not in easing, but in increasing, the strain in international relations. . . .

Yugoslavia is even being threatened with reprisals of a material and financial character in the event of the Soviet Government bringing about normal relations with Yugoslavia. . . .

Certain representatives of US reactionary circles, using their own yardstick in assessing relations between democratic countries, are coming out with deliberately false allegations to the effect that the Soviet side is intending to 'isolate' Yugoslavia from the so-called Western world, to break her relations with the West. The absurdity of these statements is obvious. The Soviet Union has repeatedly proved by its foreign policy that in the interests of strengthening peace it is necessary not to set up closed military groupings pitted against each other, but to follow the path of peaceful co-existence and business-like co-operation amongst all states, regardless of differences in their political systems.

The Soviet Union gives due consideration to Yugoslavia's desire to maintain normal relations with all states.

KHRUSHCHEV'S VISIT TO YUGOSLAVIA: THE BELGRADE
DECLARATION

173 Speech by Khrushchev on his arrival at Belgrade, 26 May 1955 (*p. 64*)

Dear Comrade Tito, dear comrades, members of the government and leaders of the LCY, dear comrades and citizens!

In the name of the Presidium of the Supreme Soviet of the USSR, of the government of the Soviet Union and of the CC of the CPSU, on behalf of the Soviet people, I extend cordial greetings to you and to the working people of the glorious capital of Yugoslavia, Belgrade, to all the fraternal peoples of Yugoslavia.

The Soviet delegation has arrived in your country in order to determine, together with the Yugoslav government delegation, the future course for the development and consolidation of the friendship and cooperation between our peoples, to discuss our common tasks in the struggle for the progress of our countries, for relieving international tension and strengthening general peace and the security of the nations.

The peoples of our countries are bound by ties of an age-old fraternal friendship and joint struggle against common enemies. This friendship and militant cooperation had been especially strengthened in the hard trials of the struggle against the Fascist invaders, in the years of the Second World War. In those hard years, all the Soviet people reacted with deep sympathy to the heroic struggle of their Yugoslav brothers, under the leadership of the Communists, and welcomed wholeheartedly the courageous military exploits of the People's Liberation Army of Yugoslavia under the leadership of Marshal Tito. Our peoples will remember for ever that it was here, in Belgrade, that the Yugoslav and Soviet soldiers together struck at the enemy and liberated this ancient Slav city from the Hitler invaders. The foundation of the FPRY was warmly acclaimed by the peoples of the Soviet Union.

It will be remembered that those years witnessed the development of the best relations between the peoples of the Soviet Union and Yugoslavia, between our states and our Parties. But those good relations were disturbed in the years that followed.

We sincerely regret that, and we resolutely sweep aside all the bitterness of that period.

On our part, we have no doubt about the part played in provoking that bitterness in the relations between Yugoslavia and the USSR by Beria, Abakumov [former Security Chiefs, executed after Stalin's death] and other exposed enemies of the people. We have thoroughly investigated the materials upon which the grave accusations against and insults to the leaders of Yugoslavia were based at that time. Facts indicate that those materials were fabricated by the enemies of the people, the contemptible agents of imperialism who had fraudulently wormed their way into the ranks of our Party.

We are deeply convinced that the cloudy period in our relations is past. We, on our part, are prepared to take all the necessary steps in order to remove all the obstacles to making the relations between our states completely normal, to the promotion of friendly relations between our peoples.

Now that definite headway has been made in making our relations normal, the Soviet delegation voices the conviction that the coming talks will lead to the development and strengthening of political, economic and cultural cooperation between our peoples. All the conditions for this cooperation exist; the age-old historic friendship of the peoples of our countries, the glorious traditions of the revolutionary movement, the necessary economic foundation and community of ideals in the struggle for the peaceful progress and happiness of the working people.

True to the teachings of the founder of the Soviet state, Vladimir Ilyich Lenin, the government of the Soviet Union bases its relations with other countries, big and small, on the principles of the peaceful co-existence of states, on the principles of equality, non-interference, respect for sovereignty and national independence, on the principles of non-aggression and recognition that any encroachments by states upon the territorial integrity of other states are impermissible.

We hope that the relations between our countries will in the future too develop on the basis of these principles, for the good of our peoples. And that will be another major contribution to the efforts to ease international tension, to sustain and strengthen general peace.

We fully appreciate Yugoslavia's desire to promote relations with all states, in the West and in the East. We believe that greater friendship and contact between our countries will help to improve relations between all countries, irrespective of social system, and to advance the cause of general peace.

The presidium of the Supreme Soviet of the USSR, the Soviet Government and the Central Committee of the CPSU have commissioned our delegation to hold a fraternal discussion of all pressing problems with you.

As representatives of the CPSU, the Party founded by great Lenin, we consider it desirable to establish mutual confidence between our Parties as well. The most enduring bonds develop between the peoples of those countries where leadership is given by the Parties which base all their work on the teachings of Marxism–Leninism. The Parties which rely for guidance upon Marxist–Leninist theory achieve complete mutual understanding because they have a common aim—the struggle for the interests of the working class and of the working peasantry, for the interests of the working people. It was for the triumph of socialism that the finest sons and daughters of the peoples gave their blood and, fighting against internal and foreign enemies, discarded the yoke of capitalism and won their freedom and independence. Steering the new, socialist course, the peoples of these countries are strengthening their forces through enduring, unshakeable friendship.

We would have failed in our duty to our own peoples, and to the working people of the whole world, if we had not done all that we could possibly do to promote mutual understanding between the Communist Party of the Soviet Union and the LCY, on the basis of the teachings of Marxism–Leninism.

In the interests of the workers and peasants, in the interests of the international labour movement and of the common aims of the struggle for the strengthening peace, for mankind's better future, the leaders of the Communist and Workers' Parties must develop mutual confidence between these Parties, on the basis of the principles of Marxism–Leninism.

Long live stable peace among nations!

Long live the fraternal friendship and close cooperation between the peoples of the Soviet Union and Yugoslavia!

Long live the peoples of Yugoslavia!

174 Yugoslav and Soviet leaders agree to bury the hatchet and pledge respect for the principles of sovereignty, equality, and non-interference; the Belgrade Declaration, 2 June 1955: excerpt (*p. 65*)

During the negotiations, which were held in a spirit of friendship and mutual understanding, views were exchanged on international problems affecting the interests of the USSR and the FPRY, and the political, economic and cultural relations between the two countries were also examined from every aspect.

1

The starting point for the negotiations was the mutual desire of the two governments that the method of negotiations be used for the peaceful settlement of international issues and the strengthening of cooperation between peoples and states.

The peoples of the two countries and their armed forces have, in particular, developed their friendship and fighting cooperation during the war which they waged jointly with other freedom-loving peoples against the Fascist invaders.

The two governments have agreed to undertake further measures for the normalization of their relations and the development of cooperation between the two countries, being confident that this is in line with the interests of the peoples of the two countries and is a contribution to easing tension and also to strengthening world peace. The sincere desire of the governments of the two countries for the further development of all-round cooperation between the USSR and the FPRY has been revealed in the course of the negotiations, which is fully in conformity with the interests of the two countries and also with the interests of peace and socialism, and for which objective conditions exist at the present time.

In examining the questions which were the object of the negotiations and for the purpose of strengthening confidence and cooperation between the peoples, the governments proceed from the following principles:

The indivisibility of peace, upon which collective security can alone be based.

Respect for sovereignty, independence, territorial integrity, and for equality between the states in their mutual relations and in relations with other states.

Recognition and development of peaceful co-existence between nations, irrespective of ideological differences and differences of social systems, which implies the cooperation of all states in international relations in general, and in economic and cultural relations in particular.

Mutual respect and non-interference in internal affairs for any reason— whether of an economic, political or ideological nature—since questions of the internal structure, differences of social systems and differences of concrete forms in developing socialism are exclusively a matter for the peoples of the different countries.

Development of bilateral and international economic cooperation and the elimination of all the factors in economic relations which hamper trade and retard the development of the productive forces both in the world and within the bounds of a national economy.

The rendering of assistance through the appropriate United Nations agencies, and also in other forms that are in conformity with the principles of the United Nations, both to the national economies and to economically under-developed areas, in the interests of the peoples of those areas and in the interests of developing the world economy.

Discontinuation of any form of propaganda and misinformation and other actions which spread mistrust and in one way or another hamper the creation of an atmosphere for constructive international cooperation and peaceful co-existence among the nations.

Condemnation of any aggression and any attempt to establish political and economic domination over other countries.

Recognition of the fact that the policy of military blocs increases international tension, undermines confidence amongst the nations and increases the danger of war.

2

Both governments proceed in their policy from the principles enunciated in the United Nations Charter and they are in agreement that further efforts should be made to enhance the role and prestige of the United Nations, which would, in particular, be confirmed by giving the People's Republic of China its legitimate seat in the United Nations. The admission to this organization of all other states meeting the requirements of the United Nations Charter could also be of importance.

Both governments agree that all nations should exert fresh efforts for achieving constructive results and agreements in negotiations on such essential problems of world peace as the reduction and limitation of armaments and the prohibition of atomic weapons, the establishment of general collective security, including a system of collective security in Europe based on a treaty, and the question of using atomic energy for peaceful purposes.

Such efforts would result in the creation of an atmosphere which would at the same time make it possible to settle peacefully such burning international issues of first importance as that of an agreed settlement of the German question on a democratic basis and in conformity with the wishes and interests of the German people and the requirements of general security, and that of the satisfaction of the legitimate rights of the People's Republic of China with regard to Taiwan.

Both governments acclaim the results of the Bandung Conference as a substantial contribution to the idea of international cooperation, as support for the efforts of the Asian and African peoples in strengthening their political and economic independence, and they consider that all this promotes world peace.

3

Full attention was given to an analysis of the relations between the two countries up to the present time and the prospects for their further development. Taking into account the fact that in recent years their relations have been considerably disturbed, which has done harm to both the interested parties and to international cooperation, the governments of the USSR and the FPRY, expressing their determination to develop their future relations in the spirit of friendly cooperation and proceeding from the principles outlined in the declaration, have agreed on the following:

1. That they will take all the necessary measures to introduce a normal treaty situation, on the basis of which they will regulate and ensure the normal development of relations with the aim of expanding cooperation between the two countries in all spheres in which the two governments are interested.

2. On the necessity for strengthening economic ties and expanding economic co-operation between the two countries.

To this end, the two governments have agreed to take the necessary measures that will eliminate the consequences which have arisen as a result of the disturbance of the normal treaty situation in the economic relations between the two countries.

They have also agreed to proceed with the conclusion of the necessary treaties which will regulate and facilitate the development of economic relations in the direction indicated above.

3. With the aim of developing cultural relations, both governments have expressed readiness to conclude a convention on cultural cooperation.

4. Attaching great importance to keeping the public informed in the interests of the development of friendly co-operation amongst the nations and desiring that the public be accurately and objectively informed, the two governments

have agreed on the need to conclude a convention on an information service in the spirit of the decisions of the United Nations and on the basis of reciprocity from the standpoint of the status and privileges of the agencies of this service on the territory of each of the contracting parties.

5. Supporting the recommendations of the United Nations on the development of cooperation among all countries in the peaceful uses of atomic energy, which is of essential interest to the strengthening of peace and to progress throughout the world, the two governments have agreed to establish mutual cooperation in this field.

6. The two governments have agreed to take measures for the conclusion of treaties with the aim of settling questions concerning the citizenship or the repatriation of citizens of one of the contracting parties who are on the territory of the other party. The two governments have agreed that the treaties should be based on respect for the principles of humanity and also on the generally recognised principles of the voluntary decision of the persons concerned.

The two governments have also agreed on ensuring the rights to protect the citizens of the other party on their respective territories, understanding that this also includes the right of citizens to retain the citizenship which they had prior to their arrival on the territory of the other contracting party.

7. In the spirit of the peace-loving principles outlined in the present declaration and also in order to make the peoples of their countries know and understand each other better, the two governments are agreed that they will support and facilitate co-operation of public organizations of the two countries through contact, exchange of socialist experience and free exchange of views.

8. The two governments have agreed that they will make every effort for the carrying out of the tasks and decisions of the present declaration in the interests of further developing relations between the two countries and of promoting international cooperation and strengthening peace.

175 Statement by Foreign Minister Koča Popović in the Federal Assembly on expansion of economic relations, 12 November 1955: excerpt (*p. 65*)

Our joint endeavours to apply the principles expressed in the Belgrade Declaration have had the most visible results in the field of economic relations.

In Moscow, in August 1955, the Vice President of the Federal Executive Council, Vukmanović, signed with the Vice-President of the Soviet Government, A. Mikoyan, a protocol on economic relations and cooperation. The protocol foresees the conclusion of agreements under which Yugoslavia receives considerable foreign currency and investment credits on favourable terms, as well as an agreement on technical cooperation and exchanges of experiences. The protocol further provides for the expansion of Yugoslav–Soviet trade, which will this year reach the value of almost 40 m. dollars while in 1957 to 1960 its yearly value will be almost 70 m. dollars.

TOWARDS THE RE-ESTABLISHMENT OF PARTY LINKS:
THE MOSCOW DECLARATION

176 Tito's message to the 20th CPSU Congress, 20 February 1956 (*p. 66*)

Permit me on behalf of the LCY and the Socialist Alliance of Working People of Yugoslavia to send to your 20th Congress of the CPSU comradely greetings and sincere wishes for successful and fruitful work for the benefit of your great socialist country and for the benefit of further peaceable development in international relations and cooperation.

I believe that this Congress will have great significance, not only for internal plans for aiding the development and adding to the strength of the USSR, but also in the foreign policy field, in the direction of strengthening peace and peaceful solutions to the various disputes whose acuteness and immediacy still cause anxiety in the world, and also because it is necessary to rally and strengthen all progressive forces in the world in order to prevent fresh armed conflicts and devastations with all their fearful consequences for the whole of mankind.

Our country is very well aware of the tremendous triumphs you have achieved in the industrialisation of your country, and we who in our time have seen the backwardness of your enormous country can best judge how tremendous were the efforts which the peoples of the USSR had to make, particularly the Communists with their Leninist consistency, firmness and tenacity, before they achieved these great triumphs. Our own experience, our efforts, our difficulties, and every kind of obstacle in the way of our building up socialism, have taught us how to make a correct appraisal of all the difficulties and labours which you had to overcome before reaching your present level of development.

The visit of your leaders, Comrades Khrushchev, Bulganin and Mikoyan, to our country last year, in 1955, and the announcement of the so-called Belgrade Declaration, not only ushered in a new period in the development of relations between our two countries and our relations with the other countries of people's democracy, but it also had a powerful, positive influence on the development of international relations, both in respect of giving strength to peaceable forces and also in respect of gradually establishing confidence and mutual understanding among nations and relaxing tensions and the fear of a new war.

I consider that we are far from having grounds for complacency about the present international situation, but it can be said with complete conviction that the voice of peace can be heard in increasing volume above the noise of certain appeals for war.

Finally, comrades, I think we can be satisfied with the gradual and continuous improvement in our relations and I think that the fact that it is gradual is a most healthy omen for the establishment of firm mutual trust and cooperation, and at the same time it makes it possible for all the elements which might hamper the strengthening of our mutual confidence to be eliminated from everyday practice.

177 Khrushchev's 'secret speech' to the 20th CPSU Congress criticizing Stalin's handling of the Soviet–Yugoslav dispute, 25 February 1956: excerpts (*p. 66*)

... The wilfulness of Stalin showed itself not only in decisions concerning the internal life of the country but also in the international relations of the Soviet Union.

The July Plenum of the Central Committee studied in detail the reasons for the development of the conflict with Yugoslavia. It was a shameful role which Stalin played here. The 'Yugoslav Affair' contained no problems which could not have been solved through Party discussions among comrades. There was no significant basis for the development of the 'affair'; it was completely possible to have prevented the rupture of relations with that country. This does not mean, however, that the Yugoslav leaders did not make mistakes or did not have shortcomings. But these mistakes and shortcomings were magnified in a monstrous manner by Stalin, which resulted in a break of relations with a friendly country.

I recall the first days when the conflict between the Soviet Union and Yugoslavia began artificially to be blown up. Once, when I came from Kiev to Moscow, I was invited to visit Stalin who, pointing to the copy of a letter lately sent to Tito, asked me, 'Have you read this?' Not waiting for my reply he answered, 'I will shake my little finger—and there will be no more Tito. He will fall.'

We have dearly paid for this 'shaking of the little finger'. This statement reflected Stalin's mania for greatness, but he acted just that way. . . . But this did not happen to Tito. No matter how much or how little Stalin shook, not only his little finger but everything else that he could shake, Tito did not fall. Why? The reason was that, in this case of disagreement with the Yugoslav comrades, Tito had behind him a state and a people who had gone through a severe school of fighting for liberty and independence, a people which gave support to its leaders.

You see to what Stalin's mania for greatness led. He had completely lost consciousness of reality; he demonstrated his suspicion and haughtiness not only in relation to individuals in the USSR but in relation to whole parties and nations.

We have carefully examined the case of Yugoslavia and have found a proper solution which is approved by the peoples of the Soviet Union and of Yugoslavia as well as by the working masses of all the People's Democracies and by all progressive humanity. The liquidation of the abnormal relationship with Yugoslavia was done in the interest of the whole camp of socialism, in the interest of strengthening peace in the whole world. . . .

178 Joint communiqué on Tito's state visit to Moscow, June 1956: excerpt (*p. 66*)

. . . The governments of both countries have reaffirmed their allegiance to the policy of peaceful and active co-existence, based on the principles of sovereignty, independence, territorial integrity, non-aggression, equality, mutual respect and non-interference in home affairs, which are a product of the requirements brought out by the international developments of the past years, and which are the most effective means for further consolidating and strengthening all-round cooperation between states, regardless of the difference in their social, economic or political systems.

Especial attention has been given during the talks to the consideration of the relations existing between the two countries, and it has been noted with great satisfaction that the principles put forward in the Declaration of the Soviet and Yugoslav governments of 2 June 1955 [**174**] which include their mutual relations, have provided a foundation for all-sided friendly cooperation and have rendered good service to the interests of peace and international cooperation.

Owing to the efforts of both sides, substantial results have been achieved in adjusting the treaty status provided for in the Declaration.

Both governments note with satisfaction the successful settlement of the question of mutual claims, which has facilitated the resumption of the economic relations which had been disrupted earlier and the development of economic cooperation on a mutually advantageous basis. In this sense a correct trade exchange has been established and long-term credit and investment agreements concluded, along with agreements on scientific and technical cooperation, cooperation in the field of using atomic energy for peaceful purposes, etc.

A cultural convention providing a broad basis for fruitful cultural cooperation and exchange has been concluded.

An agreement has also been reached on an information service.

The complete normalisation of political and other Soviet–Yugoslav relations and the results achieved have shown that the cooperation of the two countries, guided by the interests of peace and socialism, cooperation based on mutual respect for the principles of the Belgrade Declaration on independence, equality and non-interference in home affairs—principles which are finding ever wider application in the practice of a growing number of governments and countries of the world—open up the broadest possibilities for the all-round and fruitful development of their friendly relations. The talks have given both governments an exceptionally useful opportunity to consider the further possibilities of mutual cooperation. Both governments express their desire and intention to continue their personal contacts in the future, and that their representatives should regularly exchange views on political and other questions of mutual interest.

The parties to the talks have noted the possibility of, and have reached agreement on, the further extension of economic contracts and the level of trade, and have emphasised the usefulness of long-term economic agreements.

It has been decided to extend scientific cooperation and the exchange of scientists, specialists, students, and scientific literature. On the basis of the cultural convention concluded, the necessary working plans for cultural cooperation will be drawn up. Both governments attach great importance to the recently signed convention on dual citizenship, considering it an important contribution to the cause of normalising their relations. They will do everything in their power to facilitate its implementation.

Taking into consideration the fact that the contacts of political, public, and trade union organisations which have been maintained so far, and which had the purpose of exchanging socialist experience and opinions, have developed and yielded positive results, both governments have agreed that these kinds of contact on a working basis, which are in the interests of both countries, should be further facilitated and expedited.

The governments of the USSR and the FPRY hold that the fruitful exchange of views on all the questions considered during the negotiations shows that the visit to the Soviet Union of the FPRY delegation, led by President Josip Broz Tito, will be a new important stage in the development of cooperation and friendship between the peoples of the USSR and the FPRY, and will be of benefit to the peoples of both countries and to the strengthening of peace and socialism.

179 Statement on relations between the LCY and the CPSU: the Moscow Declaration, 20 June 1956: excerpt (*p. 66*)

In the course of the official visit of the government delegation of the FPRY to the Soviet Union, from 1 to 23 June 1956 . . . the two sides exchanged views, in a spirit of comradely sincerity and frankness, on the relations and cooperation between the LCY and the CPSU.

In the course of these meetings they agreed on the following:
1. The Belgrade Declaration of 2 June 1955 [174] placed the relations between the two socialist countries on a sound basis, and in their cooperation the principles proclaimed in it are being increasingly applied.
2. The cooperation and the general development of relations between the two countries following the Belgrade Declaration, as also the contacts between the political and other public organisations of their peoples, have created favourable political conditions also for cooperation between the CPSU and the LCY.

Proceeding from this, the delegations of the LCY and the CPSU, taking into consideration the specific conditions in which present-day socialist movements are developing and guiding themselves by the internationalist principles of Marxism–Leninism, have agreed that it is necessary and beneficial to continue to develop the existing contacts between the two parties with a view to cooperation in the interests of further consolidating the prosperity of our socialist countries, for cooperation in the international working-class movement on the numerous issues of the present-day development of socialism, and also for the development of peaceful coexistence and cooperation between all the peoples of the world, irrespective of differences in their social and political systems, and in the interests of peace, freedom and the independence of the peoples.

The representatives of the two parties proceed from the fact that the further development of relations and cooperation between the CPSU and the LCY— as the ruling parties in countries in which the working class holds power and which set themselves the common aim of building a completely socialist society in their countries, of ensuring the progress of mankind and lasting peace—will undoubtedly contribute to the further development of cooperation between the USSR and the FPRY, and to strengthening firm friendship between the peoples of Yugoslavia and the Soviet Union.
3. Believing that the ways of socialist development vary in different countries and conditions, that the wealth of the forms of socialist development contributes to its strength, and proceeding from the fact that any tendency to impose their views as regards the ways and forms of socialist development is alien to both sides, the two sides have agreed that the aforementioned cooperation should be based on complete voluntariness and equality, on friendly criticism, and on comradely exchange of views on contentious issues between our parties.
4. Basing themselves on these foundations, the LCY and the CPSU will develop their cooperation primarily through all-round mutual acquaintance

with the forms and the methods of socialist construction in the two countries, free and comradely exchange of experience and views on matters of common interest for the development of socialist practice and for the advancement of socialist thought, and also on questions concerning peace, rapprochement and community among the peoples, and the progress of mankind in general.
5. The present material and spiritual transformation of the world—which finds expression in the tremendous growth of the forces of socialism, in the upsurge of the national liberation movements and the growing part that the working class is playing in the solution of concrete issues of international development today—confronts the international working-class movement with a number of major problems.

This fact also indicates the need for a scientific analysis of the phenomena and the principal material and social factors and trends of development in the world today. For this reason they have agreed that, guided by the principles of Marxism–Leninism, they will give every encouragement—both in their mutual relations and in the international working-class movement in general—to mutual cooperation and exchange of views in the sphere of socialist scientific thought.
6. With regard to the specific forms of cooperation between the LCY and the CPSU, the delegations have agreed that it should be effected through personal contacts, written and oral expositions and exchanges of views, through the exchange of delegations, materials and literature, and, as the need arises, by holding meetings between party leaders to discuss pressing issues of mutual interest and, generally, through all forms of constructive, comradely discussion.
7. The representatives of the CPSU and the LCY consider such mutual cooperation to be an integral part of their contacts with other communist and workers parties and also with the socialist and other progressive movements of the world.
8. The CPSU and the LCY consider that the struggle for lasting peace and the security of the peoples and for social progress calls for the broad cooperation of all progressive and peaceable forces, which is increasingly being manifested in most diverse forms and on a world-wide scale. This cooperation is one of the prerequisites of modern social development. Such ties should be equal, frank, democratic, and open before world public opinion. They should aid mutual acquaintance and consultation on various problems of mutual interest and contribute to mutual understanding on the basis of patient explanation of the attitudes and views of the different sides. This means, at the same time, that each individual participant in this cooperation should be free to act in accordance with the conditions of its development and in conformity with the common progressive aims aspired to.

The representatives of the LCY and the CPSU are convinced that cooperation between the working class movement of the FPRY and the Soviet Union, on the basis of the aforementioned principles and forms, will serve the interests of their peoples and the interests of socialist construction in their countries. They are convinced that thereby they are making their contribution to the cause of the general rapprochement between the socialist and other progressive movements in the world, and that this will equally serve the interests of world peace and the interests of the general progress of mankind.

REPERCUSSIONS IN EASTERN EUROPE: THE HUNGARIAN RISING

180 Soviet alarm at the growing independence of the East European CPs; secret CPSU directive circulated before the Hungarian crisis, summer or autumn, 1956: excerpt (*p. 66*)

. . . The CPSU considers that it remains the 'directing party' amongst all the Communist organizations of the world. Each Communist Party is judged in the light of the more or less intimate relations which it has with the CPSU, for the interests of the CPSU are closely tied in with those of the other sister parties, and similarly, the evolution of the CPSU could not be considered as an individual and distinct phenomenon.

It is in accordance with the theories of Lenin to respect national differences in the building of Socialism and in the setting up of popular democracy, on the condition that the principle mentioned above is not forgotten. A permanent collaboration of the different Communist Parties will only be possible with those of them which keep strictly to the Marxist Leninist doctrines. Other proletarian parties must be led to collaborate with the Communist Parties on the fundamental problems of the working class. Better and more frequent contacts will have to be established.

However, it must be affirmed that Socialism can only be built under the banner of internationalism, and in close liaison with the socialist countries, and not under the banner of nationalism, without liaison with the socialist countries. The unalterable ideological basis of each Communist Party is limited to Marxism–Leninism, which must thus be the object of always more profound study in the light of historical developments.

In conclusion, the CPSU makes an appeal with a view towards preserving unity and firmly combating modern capitalism. The Communist Parties have the duty of strengthening their mutual relations and establishing ties with all the organizations which are fighting for the liberty of the peoples. The development of the USSR, and of the other popular democracies, is furthered by these struggles for liberation.

181 Tito's speech to the LCY activists at Pula on events in Poland and Hungary, 11 November 1956: excerpts (*pp. 67, 69*)

. . . You are aware, in the main, of the causes which have led to the events in Poland and Hungary. It is necessary that we go back to the year 1948, when Yugoslavia was the first to give an energetic answer to Stalin and when she said that she desired to be independent, that she desired to build up her life and socialism in accordance with the specific conditions in her country, and that she was permitting no one to interfere in her internal affairs. Of course, it did not then come to armed intervention because Yugoslavia was already united. Various reactionary elements were not able to carry out various provocations because we had liquidated their main force already during the People's Liberation War. Second, we had a very strong, united and monolothic Communist Party, steeled in both the prewar period and during the People's Liberation War. We also had a powerful and steeled Army, and most important, we had the unity of the people which personifies all these things.

Once the truth about our country had been victorious and the period of normalization of relations with the countries which had severed relations with us after the ill-famed Resolution had begun, the leaders of the Eastern countries expressed the desire that we no longer mention that which had been done to us, that we let bygones be bygones, and we accepted this only in order that relations with those countries might be improved as soon as possible. . . .

Because of her desire and on her initiative, we have normalized relations with the Soviet Union. When Stalin died, the new Soviet leaders saw that, thanks to Stalin's madness, the Soviet Union found itself in a very difficult situation, in a blind alley both in foreign and internal policy and in the other countries of people's democracy as well, thanks to his nagging and by forcing his methods on them. They understood where the main cause of all these difficulties lay and at the 20th Congress they condemned Stalin's acts and his policy up to then, but they mistakenly made the whole matter a question of the cult of personality and not a question of the system. But the cult of personality is in fact the product of a system. They did not start the fight against that system, or if they have, they have done so rather tacitly, saying that on the whole everything has been all right but that of late, because Stalin had grown old, he had become a little mad and started to commit various mistakes.

From the very beginning we have been saying that here it was not a question of the cult of personality alone, but of a system which had made possible the creation of that cult, that therein lay the roots, that this is what should be struck at incessantly and tenaciously, and this is the most difficult thing to do. Where are those roots? In the bureaucratic apparatus, in the method of leadership and the so-called one-man rule, and in ignoring the role and aspirations of the working masses. . . .

The Moscow Declaration intended for a Wider Circle of Countries than Yugoslavia and the Soviet Union
As far as we are concerned, we have gone a considerable way in our relations with the Soviet Union. We have improved these relations and have concluded a whole series of economic arrangements, very useful for us, on very favourable terms, and so forth. Two Declarations have also been adopted, one in Belgrade and the other in Moscow [**174, 179**]. Both Declarations should in fact be significant not only in our mutual relations but also in relations among all socialist countries. But, unfortunately, they have not been understood in this way. It was thought as follows; good, since the Yugoslavs are so stubborn, we will respect and implement these Declarations, but they do not concern the others because the situation there is, nevertheless, a little different than in Yugoslavia. Yugoslavia is an organized and disciplined state. The Yugoslavs have proved their worth because they have succeeded in maintaining themselves even in the most difficult times and in not allowing a restoration of the capitalist system, and so forth, to wit, they are something different from you in the Eastern countries where we brought you to power. And this was wrong, because those same elements which provoked such resistance on the part of Yugoslavia in 1948 also live in these Eastern countries, in Poland, Hungary, and in others, in some more and in some less. During the time that we were preparing the Declaration in Moscow on our party relations, mainly on the relations between the LCY and the CPSU, this was a little difficult to settle. Here we could not

completely agree, but, nevertheless, the Declaration was issued which, in our opinion, is intended for a wider circle than Yugoslavia and the Soviet Union. We warned that those tendencies which once provoked such strong resistance in Yugoslavia existed in all countries, and that one day they might find expression in other countries, too, when this would be far more difficult to correct.

You know that Khrushchev was here for a rest. On that occasion, we had talks here and many more in Belgrade. Since I and Comrades Rankovic and Pucar were invited to the Crimea, we went there and continued the talks. We saw that it would be rather difficult going for other countries, since the Soviet leaders had a different attitude toward other countries. They had certain wrong and defective views on relations with these countries, with Poland, Hungary, and others. However, we did not take this too tragically, because we saw that was was not the attitude of the entire Soviet leadership, but only of a part which to some degree had imposed this attitude on others. We saw that this attitude was imposed rather by those people who took and still take a Stalinist position, but that there were still possibilities that within the Soviet leadership those elements would win—through internal evolution—who stand for stronger and more rapid development in the direction of democratization, abandonment of all Stalinist methods, the creation of new relations among Socialist states, and the development of foreign policy in this same direction as well. From certain signs and also from the conversations, we saw that these elements were not weak, that they were strong, but that this internal process of development in a progressive direction, in the direction of abandoning Stalinist methods, was also hindered by certain Western countries, which by their propaganda and ceaseless repetition of the need for the liberation of these countries were interfering in their internal affairs and hindering a rapid development and improvement in relations among these countries. The Soviet Union believes that in view of the fact that this interference in internal affairs has assumed rather extensive proportions through propaganda on the radio, the dispatch of material by balloons, and so forth, unpleasant consequences could result if it left those countries completely and gave them, say, a status such as that enjoyed by Yugoslavia. They are afraid that reactionary elements might then be victorious in these countries. In other words, this means that they lack sufficient confidence in the internal revolutionary forces of these countries. In my opinion, this is wrong, and the root of all later mistakes lies in insufficient confidence in the socialist forces of these peoples.

Yugoslav influence blamed for events in Poland and Hungary
When the Poznan affair happened—you know about it—there occurred among the Soviet people a sudden change of attitude toward us. They started to grow colder. They thought that we, the Yugoslavs, were to blame. Yes, we are to blame because we live in this world, for being such as we are, for having created a Yugoslavia such as she is, because her acts reverberate even beyond our country. Even if we did not desire it, our country still acts, and she does so very positively and usefully. Thanks to the fact that there still remained in Poland, in spite of all persecutions and Stalinist methods of destruction of cadres, a hard core of leaders with Gomulka at their head who at the Eighth Plenum managed to take matters strongly into their own hands, boldly to put their stamp on the new course, that is, the course toward democratization,

10

toward their full independence, but also for good relations with the Soviet Union, resolutely to offer resistance to interference in their internal affairs— thanks to this, reactionary forces in Poland could not make themselves heard, although these forces certainly did exist and had hoped that they would be able to rise to the surface as a result of a clash between Communists. . . .

Soviet intervention in Hungary—to what extent was it justified?
When we were in Moscow there also was talk of Poland and Hungary and other countries. We said that Rákosi's regime and Rákosi himself had no qualifications whatever to lead the Hungarian state and to bring about inner unity, but that, on the contrary, their actions could only bring about grave consequences. Unfortunately, the Soviet comrades did not believe us. They said that Rákosi was an old revolutionary, honest, and so forth. That he is old, this is granted, but that is not enough. That he is honest—this I could not say, inasmuch as I knew him, especially after the Rajk trial and other things. To me, these are the most dishonest people in the world. The Soviet comrades said he was prudent, that he was going to succeed, and that they knew of no one else whom they could rely upon in that country. Just because our policy, both state and Party policy, is opposed to interference in the internal affairs of others, and in order not again to come into conflict with the Soviet comrades, we were not insistent enough with the Soviet leaders to have such a team as Rákosi and Gerö eliminated.

When I went to Moscow, there was great surprise that I did not travel via Hungary. It was precisely because of Rákosi that I did not want to do so. I said that I would not go through Hungary even if it would have meant making the journey three times shorter. When increasingly strong dissatisfaction began to rise to the surface in the ranks of the Hungarian Communists themselves, and when they demanded that Rákosi should go, the Soviet leaders realized that it was impossible to continue in this way and agreed that he should be removed. But they committed a mistake by not also allowing the removal of Gerö and other Rákosi followers, who had compromised themselves in the eyes of the people. They made it a condition that Rákosi would go only if Gerö remained. And this was a mistake, because Gerö differed in no way from Rákosi. He pursued the same kind of policy and was to blame just as much as Rákosi was. . . .

There is no point now in investigating who fired the first shot. The Army was called out by Gerö. It was a fatal mistake to call the Soviet Army at a time when the demonstrations were still in progress. It is a great mistake to call in the Army of another country to teach a lesson to the people of that country, even if there is some shooting. This angered the people even more, and thus a spontaneous revolt broke out in which the Communists found themselves, against their will, together with various reactionary elements. The reactionary elements got mixed up in this uprising and exploited it for their own ends. . . . The justified revolt and uprising against a clique turned into an uprising of the whole nation against Socialism and against the Soviet Union. And the Communists who were in the ranks of the rebels willy-nilly found themselves in a struggle not for socialism but for a return to the past, as soon as the reactionaries took matters into their own hands. Against their own will they found themselves in such a situation.

Was it now possible to prevent this? It seems that it was already late. Had Nagy's Government been more energetic, had it not wavered this way and that, had it stood firmly against anarchy and the killing of Communists by the reactionary elements, had it offered decisive resistance to the reactionaries, perhaps matters would have taken a correct turn and perhaps there would not have been any intervention by the Soviet Army. And what did Nagy do? He called the people to arms against the Soviet Army and appealed to the Western countries to intervene. . . . Renewed fighting broke out in Hungary. Soviet troops were reinforced. Nagy fled and a new Government was set up. I can say to you, comrades, that I know these people in the new Government and that they, in my opinion, represent that which is most honest in Hungary. They were persecuted under Rákosi, they were in prisons and stand sincerely for a new kind of development. And the very program announced by Kádar, which you have read, proves this. But Soviet intervention weakens that whole program and the Government itself is in a very serious position.

The question may now be asked whether Soviet intervention was necessary. The first intervention was not necessary. The first intervention, coming at the invitation of Gerö, was absolutely wrong. The second mistake consisted in the fact that the men responsible, instead of waiting for the second intervention, did not do at once what they did later on, when the second Soviet intervention took place, that is, form a new Government and issue a declaration. Had they first created a new Government and issued such a declaration, the worker and Communist elements would probably have separated themselves from the reactionary elements and it would have been easier to find a way out of this critical situation. . . .

Many people are now asking why the second Soviet intervention took place. It is clear, and we have said so and will continue to say it, that we are against interference and the use of foreign armed forces. Which was now the lesser evil? There could be either chaos, civil war, counter-revolution, and a new world war, or the intervention of Soviet troops, which were there. The former would be a catastrophe and the latter a mistake. And, of course, if it meant saving socialism in Hungary, then comrades, we can say, although we are against interference, Soviet intervention was necessary. But had they done everything that should have been done earlier, there would not have been any need for military intervention. This error was, unfortunately, a result of their idea that military power solves everything. And it does not solve everything. . . . The first thing was the worst that could have happened and the second, the intervention of Soviet troops, was also bad, but if it leads to the preservation of socialism in Hungary, that is, to the further building up of socialism in that country, and to peace in the world, then one day this will become a positive thing, provided that the Soviet troops withdraw the moment the situation in that country is settled and quiet.

We said this to the Soviet comrades. We concealed nothing. The Soviet comrades stated that their troops would then leave. It should be borne in mind that the Soviet Union, too, is now in a very difficult situation. Their eyes have now been opened and they realize that not only are the Horthyites [supporters of the prewar right-wing regime of Admiral Horthy] fighting but also workers in factories and mines, that the whole nation is fighting. Soviet soldiers go unwillingly, with heavy hearts. Therein lies the tragedy. . . .

You can rest assured that we have never advised them to go ahead and use the army. We never gave such advice and could not do so even in the present crisis. In this grave situation we can tell them nothing except that they should take care to correct their old mistakes. That is the crux of the matter. Therefore, we should combat those rumours in our country which see in the Soviet intervention a purely interventionist act. That is not correct. I, comrades, am deeply convinced of this. I am deeply convinced that the bloodshed in Hungary and those dreadful sacrifices made by the Hungarian people will have a positive effect and that a little light will reach the eyes of the comrades in the Soviet Union, even those Stalinist elements, and that they will see that it is no longer possible to do things in this way. It is our tragedy—the tragedy of all of us— that socialism has been dealt such a terrible blow. . . . I believe that the events in Hungary will probably be the last tragedy necessary to jolt the Soviet comrades and leaders who are still blind to this in other countries into doing everything in their power to prevent such a situation as now prevails in Hungary from arising in other countries as well.

182 Soviet reply to Tito's comments on the events in Hungary, 23 November 1956: excerpts (*p. 69*)

. . . Tito's speech contains, along with correct judgments on the Hungarian events, judgments which cannot but evoke legitimate objections. . . . Speaking of the Hungarian events, Comrade Tito also made a number of critical remarks about the CPSU. Particular note should be taken of these remarks. We are not, of course, opposed to criticism. The Moscow Declaration states as the consensus of the CPSU and the LCY that our cooperation will be based on friendly criticism and on comradely exchange of opinions on issues contended between our two Parties. We have no reason to retract this decision. Comrade Tito's critical remarks, however, arrest our attention because they were made in a tone that had nearly disappeared in the recent period.

Let us take the major proposition set forth by Tito with regard to the Soviet system. He persistently emphasized that the 'cult of the individual leader was essentially the product of a specific system'. He said that it is necessary to speak of the system 'that gave rise to the creation of the cult of the individual'. However, in reality, the cult of the individual was a blatant contradiction of our entire Soviet Socialist system. It was by proceeding from our political and economic system that we were able to conduct the struggle against the cult of the individual and to achieve in a short time great success in eliminating its results. . . .

How, then, can we interpret Tito's remarks about our system except as an attempt to cast a shadow on the Soviet people's system of social life? How can we fail to ask if this is not a repetition of earlier attacks on the Soviet Union, which were fashionable in the past when relations between the USSR and Yugoslavia were deteriorating? It is up to the Yugoslav people themselves and the LCY to decide what forms and methods they wish to use in building Socialism, but is it right to denigrate the Socialist system of other countries, and to praise one's own experience, publicizing it as universal and the best? One cannot help but see that more and more frequently in the Yugoslav press the idea is appearing that the 'Yugoslav road to Socialism' is the most correct or even the only possible road for nearly all the countries of the world. In addition, no mention is made of the good aspects and achievements of Socialist construction in other countries. . . .

. . . In Yugoslavia there are also unique forms of Socialist construction. New methods and techniques of administration and economic management are being put to the test of practice. The workers' councils in Yugoslavia appeared relatively recently. Every year of their existence brings corrections in their functions, but certain virtues of this institution are already apparent. This cannot be said of another innovation, which has had an adverse effect, namely certain measures in the field of planning which have weakened the planned basis of the Yugoslav economy and increased the influence of market relations, a fact about which the Yugoslav press has also written. . . .

It is well known that agriculture plays a large role in the Yugoslav economy, yet grain production has not yet reached the prewar level, and unfortunately there is still a long way to go to the victory of Socialist relations in the country-side. It is also well known that Yugoslavia has an annual wheat deficit of about 600,000 to 650,000 tons.

It is quite obvious what great importance for the Yugoslav economy aid from capitalist states, above all the USA, has. Because of the situation that arose, Yugoslavia had for many years an opportunity to exploit the aggravated contradictions between imperialism and the Socialist countries. But if aid from capitalist countries accounts for a substantial part of its economy, it cannot be considered that this road has any particular advantages. After all, all the countries in the Socialist camp cannot rely on such aid; they cannot base their policy on the assumption of aid from the imperialists. Therefore such a path is by no means universally applicable. It is well known that the imperialist circles have not given aid to Yugoslavia because they sympathize with Socialism and Socialist construction in Yugoslavia.

. . . In his speech Comrade Tito puts forth the slogan of 'independence' of Socialist countries and Communist Parties from the Soviet Union and the CPSU. Everyone knows, however, that the Soviet Union does not require the dependence or subordination of anyone. This is stated with the utmost force in the decisions of the 20th Party Congress. These principles are reaffirmed in the USSR government's declaration of October 30, 1956, on the Principles of Development and Further Strengthening of Friendship and Cooperation Between the Soviet Union and Other Socialist States. Our Party and our government are correcting past mistakes on this score with the greatest determination. This is borne out by the experience of our relations with Yugoslavia in recent years. We acted boldly to erase all past errors in our relations with Yugoslavia, disregarding all questions of prestige, and we were the first to offer our hand to the Yugoslav government and to the League of Communists. No one can deny that for its part the CPSU has done and is doing everything needed to improve relations on the ideological basis of Marxism–Leninism in the interests of strengthening friendship and cooperation with the fraternal people of Yugoslavia and in the interests of the struggle for peace and Socialism.

While making a generally favorable evaluation of the development of Soviet–Yugoslav relations and of the agreements made between the USSR and Yugoslavia, Tito rebukes the Soviet leaders for allegedly not wanting to extend the principles set forth in these agreements to other Socialist countries. Tito needed this strange and entirely far-fetched assertion to attribute to the Soviet Union 'insufficient trust' in the Socialist forces of the people's democracies. . . .

What does Comrade Tito call for in his speech? To go it alone? But it may be asked: What does this path promise? What advantage does it offer for Socialist countries? There are no such advantages. The appeal to break with the other Socialist states, with the whole fraternal family of Socialist countries, cannot have any benefit for the cause of building a Socialist society. . . .

. . . In the light of the requirements of Socialist internationalism, one cannot but be astonished at the tone in which Comrade Tito found it possible to speak of the Communist Parties and their leaders. Groundlessly, he lists as 'Stalinists' all the leading persons of the fraternal Parties of the West and East who disagree with his point of view, and he attributes the worst characteristics to them. He does not talk of them in any way other than as 'inveterate Stalinist elements', 'irresponsible elements in various Communist Parties', etc. The entire speech at Pula is rife with such attacks against Communist figures. Having chosen the question of mutual relations among Communist Parties as the subject of his speech, Tito did not, in fact, conduct a comradely discussion, did not debate, but tried to lecture or, rather, abused various leaders of the Communist and Workers' Parties. The speech was not delivered in a tone of conversation or debate on an equal basis, with proper respect for difference of opinion.

. . . After all that has been said, it is not surprising that Comrade Tito's speech met with jubilation in bourgeois circles abroad. . . . Our enemies are now jumping to the conclusion that this speech will cause serious differences between Soviet and Yugoslav Communists and will lead to a deterioration in Soviet–Yugoslav relations. . . .

The CPSU, for its part, will continue to conduct a policy of cooperation between our Parties on a principled Marxist–Leninist basis in the interests of the fraternal peoples of the USSR and Yugoslavia and in the interests of defending peace, democracy, and Socialism. We are convinced that disputed questions should be discussed and clarified in a calm friendly atmosphere by a comradely exchange of views.

183 Yugoslav Government note to Hungarian Government on how Soviet authorities seized Imre Nagy in defiance of the agreement between them, November 1956: excerpt (*p. 69*)

On the grounds of the agreement reached between the two Yugoslav and Hungarian governments and the guarantees given in regard to Imre Nagy and the other mentioned persons, these, of their free will, left the Yugoslav embassy on 22 November 1956, at 18.30 in a bus which was placed at their disposal to take them to their homes by the Hungarian vice-premier and minister of the armed forces and public security, Dr Ferenc Munnich. . . .

When the above-mentioned persons boarded the bus, Soviet military organs intervened with the request that they should take these persons away by bus. One Soviet military official entered the bus, despite the energetic protest of the Yugoslav minister in Budapest. In consequence, the Yugoslav minister sent diplomatic official Milan Djordjević and military attaché Milan Drobac with the Imre Nagy group so that they might personally see that the persons mentioned would be taken to their homes. However, the bus was driven to the

Soviet Kommandatura of the city where a lieutenant-colonel of the Soviet army forced the two Yugoslavs to leave the bus. In reply to the protest of the Yugoslav military attaché, the Soviet lieutenant-colonel declared that he was executing the orders of his command. After that, the bus with the above-mentioned persons, escorted by Soviet armoured cars, drove off to an unknown destination. . . .

THE SECOND SOVIET-YUGOSLAV DISPUTE

184 Pravda wishes Yugoslavia success in 'building socialism' in its own way, but declares that it should not claim to be a model for other countries, December 1956: excerpts (*p. 69*)

E. Kardelj, at a session of the Yugoslav Federal People's Skupština, tried in his speech, which was devoted mainly to the Hungarian events, to present some sort of 'third line', but in substance he only proved that there can be no such line. . . .

Hungary [he said] should have followed approximately the same road which has been worked out in theory and is being carried into practice in Yugoslavia. He leads all his listeners to this conclusion in making the following statement, for example: 'Instead of making fruitless attempts to restore Communism and other political parties, the progressive socialist forces in Hungary should actually have fought during the past revolutionary days for the victory of the principle of direct democracy by creating united workers councils and self-governing communes as the basic foundations for a new socialist regime.' . . .

E. Kardelj asserts that Yugoslav socialism was the first to embark on the road which, in his opinion, all socialist development should follow. In this connection he emphasises the importance of 'workers' councils', communes and other democratic forms of social administration. We do not wish to say anything unfavourable about these agencies. It seems obvious, however, that it is still too early to sum up the results of Yugoslavia's advance along its chosen road. . . .

We advocate that the most diverse forms of socialist economic activity develop in all countries. But practical experience is the criterion of truth. The real verification of any form of economic activity is primarily how it contributes to a rise in the national economy, without which it is impossible to solve the most important problem of socialist construction—improvement of the material well-being of the people. It is still too early to say that the new forms of economic administration in Yugoslavia are having a favourable effect on the economy and are the example which should be followed everywhere. . . .

Soviet people do not intend to interfere in the internal affairs of Yugoslavia. The peoples of Yugoslavia, like those of any other country, are entitled to arrange their life in their own way. The right is indisputable. The Soviet Union sincerely wishes the glorious Yugoslav people success in building Socialism, whatever concrete forms the Yugoslav comrades prefer to use in its construction. But why *contrast* the development of Yugoslavia with the development of other socialist countries? Such a course is obviously contrary to the principles of Marxism–Leninism, the principles of socialist internationalism.

185 Foreign Minister Shepilov informs the Supreme Soviet that relations with Yugoslavia have been normalized, but blames 'certain elements' for the continuation of ill will, February 1957: excerpt (*p. 70*)

As a result of efforts made by the Government of the Soviet Union, which were met half way by the Government of Yugoslavia, relations have been normalized between the USSR and the FPRY. We shall continue to take all the necessary steps to ensure the successful development of Soviet–Yugoslav relations on a basis of friendship and equality. At present, however, this depends chiefly on the leaders of the Yugoslav Republic, since within Yugoslavia there are still manifestations of ill will and even direct attacks against the USSR and a number of peoples democracies on the part of certain elements. We regret this because these facts undoubtedly hamper our common cause. . . .

186 Foreign Minister Popović reasserts Yugoslavia's wish to remain outside the Soviet bloc and declares that Stalinism has harmed the socialist cause more than any 'imperialist conspiracies', 26 February 1957: excerpts (*p. 70*)

The heart of our dispute with the Soviet Union and satellites lies, in our opinion, in the differing viewpoints regarding our relations and standpoints towards the Socialist 'camp'. We do not wish to enter the 'camp', as this would not be in accord with our established principles or the trend of our foreign policy, nor with the general interests of peace and socialism. But if the camp did not exist, or if we do not wish to join it, that would not mean that good and friendly relations between our countries should be ruled out or made more difficult. . . .

[*On Hungary:*] Far from all the difficulties in building socialism come from outside in the form of plots and subversion. It is all the more necessary to recognize this so as to avoid a regression into Stalinism which, I am deeply convinced, has been responsible in the postwar period for inflicting incomparably more harm on the cause of socialism than all the imperialist conspiracies taken together. . . .

The fact remains that differing views and ideas about the concept of the 'camp', and even about Stalin and Stalinism, should not be an obstacle to friendly relations and cooperation.

187 *Pravda* qualifies Popović's statement as 'monstrous and revolting sacrilege', 11 March 1957: excerpts (*p. 70*)

The Yugoslav press makes frequent use of the artificial term 'Stalinism' in order to slander the Soviet social and political system, the policy of the CPSU, to slander the Socialist camp. But how can one make such attacks and call oneself a Communist?

Even if Mr Popović had in mind Stalin's mistakes, which our Party has condemned, it would be monstrous and revolting sacrilege for any Communist even to compare those mistakes with the subversive activities of the imperialists. . . .

It is common knowledge that the Soviet Union has for its part done, and is continuing to do, everything to have the friendship and cooperation between the peoples of the Soviet Union and Yugoslavia develop and gain in strength on the basis of the principles of proletarian internationalism. It is necessary for Yugoslav statesmen to strive to work out the differences between us instead of aggravating them, to strengthen Yugoslavia's friendship and cooperation with the countries of the Socialist camp.

188 Tito blames the views of 'certain individual leaders' in the USSR for the renewed deterioration of relations and asks 'whom are we to trust?', 19 April 1957: excerpts (*p. 70*)

... I would not like to dramatize the existing dispute any more. On the contrary, we hoped it would not go beyond the domain of ideology, since at the beginning, the Soviet comrades themselves said that in the realm of ideology there might be some different views which, however, should not lead to any inter-governmental conflicts. ...

In our country the question is often being raised whether we may trust them at all, since it is already the second time that we are placed in an awkward situation. I think that in this regard the main role is played by the subjective element and by the views of individual leaders who are not able as yet to get rid of old concepts of relationships between socialist countries. ...

In our country, confidence in the Soviet Union made its way with very great difficulty. When comrades Khrushchev, Bulganin, and Mikoyan stayed in Belgrade we told them a rather long period would be necessary to restore such confidence towards the Soviet Union as prevailed up to 1948 and which had been built up in our people by our Party long before the war. At that time and later on when I was in Moscow with a delegation we appealed to them that they should be patient and understand that all these things cannot be brought about so smoothly, that they should not cling immediately to every word put down in some newspaper, which unfortunately keeps on recurring against our will, that they should not consider such elements as a kind of insincerity of our policy towards the Soviet Union, but that they should rather be patient. We said that, on the other hand, we shall undertake everything in order not only to normalize, but also to create more friendly relations with both the Soviet Union and other Eastern countries. Unfortunately, there was no patience there and their reactions were impatient and improper. ...

Whereas of late Khrushchev spoke in the Kremlin in a very conciliatory manner ... we are suddenly faced with Suslov's attack because of our alleged 'revisionism' and 'national communism'. ...

Now, whom are we to trust, comrades? Today, one talks like this, while tomorrow another turns this upside down. ... We shall have to tell them in a certain manner that things cannot go on like this.

189 Khrushchev purges the 'anti-Party group'; Molotov's 'erroneous stand on the Yugoslav question' in CPSU CC resolution cited as one reason for his disgrace, June 1957; excerpt (*p. 70*)

... As Minister of Foreign Affairs, Comrade Molotov for a long time not only failed to take any measures through the Ministry of Foreign Affairs to improve relations between the USSR and Yugoslavia but repeatedly came out against those measures which the Presidium of the Central Committee carried out to improve relations with Yugoslavia. Comrade Molotov's erroneous stand on the Yugoslav question was unanimously condemned by the July 1955 plenary session of the Party Central Committee as 'not corresponding to the interests of the Soviet state and the Socialist camp and not conforming to the principles of Leninist policy'. . . .

190 Tito and Khrushchev meet in Romania and agree to work for better relations, 2 August 1957: excerpt (*p. 71*)

. . . The representatives of the two parties and governments examined a number of issues bearing upon relations between the USSR and Yugoslavia and also questions concerning the activity of the two parties and common interests for socialism and world peace, particularly issues hindering the further successful development of mutual relations.

The delegations also discussed international affairs and a number of problems related to the international working class movement and the fight for peace and the security of the nations.

The agreement of both sides to work for the further all-round extension of mutual relations and for the removal of the obstacles hampering this development was confirmed in the course of the conversations.

Agreement on key issues relating to present-day international affairs was also confirmed.

It was emphasised that the all-round consolidation of the unity and fraternal cooperation among the Communist and Workers Parties and the peoples of all the Socialist countries and among peace-loving and progressive forces the world over, and the unity of the international working class movement acquires special significance.

The two delegations emphasised that relations between the Soviet Union and the FPRY would continue, as hitherto, to develop on the basis of equality, mutual assistance and cooperation, and respect for sovereignty and independence and non-interference. The delegations affirmed the momentous importance of the Belgrade and Moscow Declarations [**174, 179**] for the development of friendly relations between the two countries and cooperation between the CPSU and the LCY on the basis of the principles of Marxism–Leninism, and expressed their readiness to continue to implement the principles set forth in these Declarations.

The two delegations agreed on concrete forms of cooperation between the two parties and on the maintenance of constant links through the exchange of party delegations, reciprocal information and publications.

191 Tito, at 7th LCY Congress, reports progress in improving Soviet–Yugoslav relations, 22 April 1958: excerpt (*p. 71*)

After the visit of the Soviet delegation to Yugoslavia in 1955 and the visit of our delegation to Moscow in 1956, after the talks which then took place and after the announcement of the now familiar Declarations, fertile soil was prepared for very successful progress in establishing mutual confidence and cooperation.

However, clouds again began to gather in our common sky. Due to the events in Hungary, relations between us and the Soviet Union again became strained; but during our talks with the Soviet leaders in Romania, in August, 1957, the matter was cleared up. On that occasion we put an end to some of our disagreements; and very little remained that could disturb our thorough cooperation and friendly relations. The important thing is that all this is now behind us, the important thing is to get going along the new, right road of cooperation and to forget things in the past which might affect our present and future good and friendly relations. The essential thing is that there is more trust between us, that we understand each other, that we can in a comradely and sincere fashion talk about our experiences in building socialism and exchange views on the subject, that mutual respect exists, and that there is no interference by one in the internal development of others—as was stated in the Belgrade Declaration [174] which was a reflection of the efforts of both sides to eliminate completely all traces of the former, abnormal situation and to establish relations between us on new, healthy foundations.

Yugoslav–Soviet relations, founded on the Belgrade Declaration, are developing very successfully today. Extensive trade exchanges are also developing. A whole range of agreements have been concluded such as, for example: agreements on building industrial enterprises in Yugoslavia to the value of 110 million dollars, on a credit for goods to the total of 54 million dollars, on scientific and technical cooperation, on a loan, in gold or foreign exchange, to the value of 30 million dollars. and on cooperation in the field of atomic energy. In addition, a cultural convention has been signed on the basis of which wide cooperation has developed, and also a convention to regulate dual nationality; a separate agreement was concluded for the building of an aluminium combine and a fertilizer factory, and so on. All this shows that normalisation and the establishment of good and friendly relations have acquired their material basis in economic cooperation, which is very beneficial to both countries. . . .

192 LCY defines its position; the Draft Programme of the 7th Congress, April 1958: excerpts (*pp. 71, 72*)

The tides of the Great October Revolution have for forty years now been ceaselessly and powerfully impelling socialist chain reactions in the social relations of all peoples and of the whole world, stimulating and steering numerous revolutionary and evolutionary processes towards the achievement of socialist goals. Inter-linked with these processes and continuing through them, the Great October Socialist Revolution has truly developed into a world process of socialist development. . . .

During the period of Stalin's leadership, the CPSU and the Soviet working people succeeded in preserving the achievements of the October Revolution, in consolidating them by successful industrialisation and by raising the general cultural and technical levels of the country, and in maintaining and developing the Soviet Union as a support of all socialist and progressive movements, in face of the relentless pressure of the forces of capitalism and imperialism. However, for both objective and subjective reasons, Stalin did not fight the bureaucratic-statist tendencies stemming from the great concentration of power in the state machinery, from the merging of the party and state machinery, and from lopsided centralism. He himself, moreover, became their political and ideological champion. It was along these lines that a pragmatic revision of certain fundamental scientific postulates of Marxism–Leninism was carried out—first in the sphere of the theory of the state and party, and then also in the sphere of philosophy, political economy, and the social sciences generally. The Marxist–Leninist theory of the dictatorship of the proletariat, as a political system of power in the state which is withering away, and as an instrument of working-class struggle in the process of destroying the economic foundations of capitalism and the creation of political and material conditions for the free development of new socialist relations, was gradually replaced by Stalin's theory of the state which does not wither away and which must grow ever stronger in all fields of social life, the state whose machinery is assigned too great a role in the construction of socialism, in the solving of internal contradictions of a transition period, a role which sooner or later must begin to obstruct the development of social and economic factors.

Phenomena of this type began to make their appearance after the Second World War in the international sphere as well, i.e., in certain elements of Soviet foreign policy and in relations between socialist countries. This was particularly evident in Stalin's action against socialist Yugoslavia, which the 20th Congress of the CPSU unanimously condemned as clearly contrary to the real interests of socialism.

In resisting such pressure and fighting for the independence of their country, the Yugoslav Communists and the peoples of Yugoslavia were not only fighting for their right to pursue free socialist development, but were also offering their contribution to the indispensable struggle against statist-bureaucratic and other anti-socialist distortions in the development of socialism, and in the relations between the peoples who had chosen the socialist path. Their resistance was consistently socialist and progressive, and by virtue of this, it contributed to the strengthening and the progress of socialism throughout the world.

All these and other well-known negative phenomena and errors caused damage—in particular as some of them were transferred to and repeated in certain other socialist countries—both to international socialism and to socialist construction in the Soviet Union. They were unable however to distort seriously or hamper lastingly the development of socialism in the Soviet Union, because the socialist forces in that first country of Socialism had grown and become so strong that they were able to break through the barriers of bureaucracy and the 'cult of personality'. This was precisely the reason why certain distortions, which had manifested themselves under the influence of the above-mentioned negative tendencies, began to be eliminated gradually in the Soviet Union shortly after Stalin's death, and after the Twentieth Congress of the CPSU. . . .

The interest of further socialist development demands free socialist, democratic relations between the parties of the socialist countries. In the struggle for the victory of socialism, the working class of one or another country may, for a certain period of time, be the standard-bearer of that struggle, its vanguard, or possess greater material power; but that does not entitle it to a monopoly position in the workers' movement, least of all in the sphere of ideology. Past experience has shown—and it is even clearer today—that cooperation in the workers' movement is possible only between equals. . . .

During the October Revolution and after, when the Soviet Union was the only socialist country, defence of the Soviet Union as the main stronghold of international socialism was one of the principal criteria of proletarian internationalism. Today the criterion is broader. Proletarian internationalism requires correct relationships, support of and solidarity with every socialist country and every socialist movement which is genuinely fighting for socialism, for peace, and for active peaceful co-existence between peoples. . . . In all its relations with other Communist, socialist, progressive and anti-imperialist movements, as well as in all its international relations in general, the LCY is guided by the great idea of proletarian, socialist internationalism.

193 Soviet criticism of the Draft Programme and the 7th LCY Congress, 9 May 1958: excerpts (*p. 73*)

. . . To describe the content of the Soviet Union's policy in the first postwar years as a striving 'to gain domination over other peoples', as was done in the statements at the 7th Congress of the LCY, is to repeat the fabrication of imperialist propaganda about a 'Soviet empire' that surrounded itself with 'satellites'. . . .

The leaders of the LCY do not agree with the characterization, generally recognized by the Communists of all countries, that the world is divided today into two opposed camps, those of Socialism and Imperialism. They declare that Yugoslavia stands outside these camps. . . . Two economic systems exist and will continue to exist for a long time to come. The task is to organize peaceful economic co-existence of the two systems, to normalize economic relations between the Socialist world and the Capitalist world. . . .

The line pursued in the speeches at the Congress of the LCY is aimed at substantiating separation of the Socialist countries, and counterposing them to one another. . . . The very existence of each country as a Socialist country and its successful advance are possible only because the Socialist camp exists, because it is possible to rely on the economic might and political unity of this camp. . . .

Reading such speeches, accompanied by deep bows and genuflections to the ruling circles of the US, one involuntarily asks: Why are the American monopolists so well disposed towards Yugoslavia? . . . Is it not because the Yugoslav leaders seek to smear the Soviet Union, to weaken the unity of the international Communist and workers' movement? . . . Everybody knows that American aid to any country is by no means disinterested and it leads to one form or another of economic and political dependence. . . . Whilst the American 'aid' has the aim of making recipient countries dependent on the USA, the Soviet Union seeks actively to help other Socialist countries, as well as the economically under-developed countries, to strengthen and develop their economy and to carry out industrialization. . . .

Yet the authors of the Draft Programme of the LCY, grossly distorting the nature of the relations amongst the Socialist countries, ascribe to them, in unfriendly manner and even slanderously, a striving for hegemony, and claim that in the early phases of the development of Socialism individual peoples or states have an opportunity 'to utilize one form or another of economic exploitation of another country'.

Do some people in Yugoslavia consider that such a tendency to 'exploitation' is manifested in the economic relations between the Soviet Union and the FPRY? If so, Yugoslavia could be relieved of such 'exploitation'. . . .

The Yugoslav leaders say that ideological differences must not lead to a deterioration of state relations between Yugoslavia and the Socialist countries. But a mere repetition of this truth, as experience shows, is not enough. We cannot but see that ideological differences, if they are not eliminated but deepened, naturally entail differences on political questions as well.

The Soviet Union and its Communist Party have resolutely undertaken to eliminate the injustices and mistakes committed in the past with regard to Yugoslavia. It must be said straightforwardly, however, that the Yugoslav side in 1948 and subsequent years made mistakes of a nationalist character and deviated from the principles of Marxism–Leninism on some important questions. . . . The 7th Congress of the LCY and the Draft Programme graphically showed that the Yugoslav leaders continue to hold to their positions, contrary to the principles of Marxism–Leninism.

194 USSR proposes a revision of existing economic agreements, 27 May 1958: excerpt (*p. 73*)

. . . These agreements [of 12 January and 1 August 1956] envisage that the Soviet Union will grant Yugoslavia credits for the period from 1957 to 1964 to finance the construction of an aluminium plant and to pay for equipment for fertiliser and other enterprises and also for designing and other work enumerated in the agreements.

At the present time there is a need to revise the period of the credits granted to Yugoslavia in accordance with the above-mentioned agreements. This need has arisen in connection with the decision recently taken in the Soviet Union to speed up the development of the chemical industry, and particularly the production of synthetic materials and goods to satisfy the requirements of the population and the needs of the national economy, the implementation of which will require large new capital investments in the chemical industry of the USSR in the next few years. The Soviet government is therefore making changes in its financial plans with a view to ensuring that financial resources are used in the most effective way from the economic standpoint.

Owing to this circumstance, the government of the USSR is faced with the necessity of proposing some later periods for the use of the credits granted to Yugoslavia, namely:

> Under the agreement of 12 January, 1956, in the part relating to the further use of the credit, to establish that this credit will be used in the period from 1962 to 1969;
> Under the agreement of 1 August, 1956, to establish that the credit will be used in the period from 1963 to 1969.

The time for the delivery of equipment and the fulfilment of designing and other work provided for by the agreements should be made to accord with the changes in the period for the use of the credits.

However, Soviet foreign trading organisations, should the government of the FPRY so desire, could deliver equipment to Yugoslav organisations and carry out designing and other work in the period established by the protocols of 29 July 1957 and could deliver equipment of various kinds in accordance with the protocol of 2 August 1956, not, however, on credit, but to be paid for under current trade turnover.

As regards the time of the postponement of the putting in operation of the enterprises envisaged by the agreements, including enterprises for the production of fertilisers, the Soviet side, should the Yugoslav side so desire, could by way of mutual trade turnover deliver to Yugoslavia a definite quantity of mineral fertilisers and also industrial goods by agreement between the parties.

The proposals stated above are, in the opinion of the Soviet Government, in keeping with the principles of economic cooperation between states which is profitable for both sides. The government of the USSR expresses confidence that the government of the FPRY will correctly understand the proposals made in the present note and will adopt a positive attitude to them. . . .

195 Yugoslavia objects to the Soviet proposals, 3 June 1958: excerpts (*p. 73*)

The Government of the FPRY cannot accept the proposals of the USSR government put forward in the above note. . . . The proposals . . . would lead to changes in the current and long-term national economic plans of the FPRY in the sense that they would change the distribution of the national income already adopted, particularly at the expense of investments and, accordingly, the living standards of the population. Furthermore, in view of the fact that the construction of certain enterprises envisaged under the above agreements has been partly begun, and that the Yugoslav side has assigned an organisation which is to work in this direction, and that considerable manpower and resources are engaged in this, any postponement of the periods provided for under the agreements would do direct harm to Yugoslavia and to the Yugoslav economy. . . .

The Government of the FPRY cannot but note the fact that the Soviet side has already on one occasion raised the question of postponing the periods of fulfilment of these agreements and that then, with the aim of displaying maximum good will and in spite of considerable material losses, the Yugoslav side went as far as possible to meet the suggestions of the Soviet side half way and accepted the proposed postponement.

In its note of 27 May, this year, the Government of the Soviet Union again proposes, after nearly ten months, to postpone the period of fulfilment, and this would mean that, as regards the initial agreements, the period of fulfilment would accordingly be postponed from six to ten years for the first agreement and from seven to twelve years for the second agreement.

The Government of the FPRY is obliged to declare that such acts on the part of the USSR Government introduce a lack of confidence in the economic relations between the FPRY and the USSR, and this can only do harm to the general normal relations between our countries. The Government of the FPRY would also like to draw the attention of the Soviet Government, in so far as it adheres to its positions, to the responsibility which the USSR Government is taking upon itself as regards losses inflicted on the Yugoslav economy. In this case the FPRY reserves the right to demand just compensation. . . .

196 Soviet Government justifies its intention to suspend credits, 28 June 1958: excerpts (*p. 73*)

. . . The content and the tone of the note of 3 June of this year, like the entire approach of the Yugoslav side to this question, and in particular the groundless allegation that the USSR has torn up these agreements, indicate an attempt to present the Soviet Union's position on Soviet–Yugoslav economic relations in a wrong light and at the same time to cast doubt on the fulfilment by the Soviet Union of its commitments under international agreements.

There is no need to say that the Soviet Union, pursuing a policy designed to strengthen peace and develop cooperation amongst all states, strictly abides by its international commitments.

It is common knowledge that a change in certain terms of agreements as a result of negotiations between the parties does not go beyond the bounds of the normal, generally recognised practices of states in relation to international treaties, and that agreements as such do not deprive the parties of the right to raise the question of changing particular terms of the agreements.

The Soviet Government, in making the aforementioned proposal, also took into account the interests of the Yugoslav side. . . . Thus it is a question of bringing the terms of the economic agreements between the USSR and Yugoslavia closer to the principles upon which mutually advantageous agreements between states are concluded.

In submitting the proposal to defer the period for the use of credits, which to some extent would balance the advantageous character of the agreement for both sides, and not only for Yugoslavia, the Soviet Government does not propose to change the other terms of the agreements, although these terms, too, are exceptionally easy for the FPRY and are not applied in cases in which the parties proceed only from the purely commercial aspects of mutual benefit. This, too, cannot but be taken into account in discussing the Soviet proposal.

Proceeding from what has been stated above, the Soviet government would consider it correct for representatives of the two governments to meet in the immediate future, discuss in a business-like way the questions raised in the Soviet note of 27 May, and reach understanding on introducing changes in the agreements of 12 January and 1 August 1956, as proposed by the government of the USSR.

197 Khrushchev, at the 7th Bulgarian CP Congress, renews his denunciation of Yugoslav revisionism, but keeps the door open for détente, 3 June 1958: excerpts (*p. 73*)

. . . Why do the imperialist bosses, whilst striving to obliterate the Socialist states from the face of the earth and suppress the Communist movement, at the same time finance one of the Socialist countries, granting that country credits and free gifts? . . . If the imperialists agree to give assistance to a Socialist state, they do not take such a step in order to strengthen it. . . . Present-day revisionism is in its way a Trojan horse. The revisionists are striving to corrupt the revolutionary parties from within and to disrupt the unity of Marxist–Leninist theory. . . .

In 1948, a conference of the Informburo issued a Resolution on the state of affairs in the CPY which contained just criticism of the activity of the CPY on a number of questions of principle [126]. This Resolution was fundamentally correct and corresponded to the interests of the revolutionary movement. Later on, from 1949 to 1953, a conflict arose between the CPY and other fraternal parties. In the course of this struggle, mistakes and rigidities were permitted to arise which caused damage to our common cause. Fully conscious of its reponsibility to our countries and peoples and the international Communist movement, the CPSU took the initiative in liquidating this conflict and achieved a normalization of relations between our countries, and established contacts, cooperation and alliance according to Marxist–Leninist principles. . . .

It proved, however, that the burden of the past was too heavy for these Yugoslav leaders, and they proved to be incapable of giving up their wrong position and standing firmly on a Marxist–Leninist position. . . . During the counter-revolutionary rebellion in Budapest the Yugoslav Embassy became in substance a centre for those who started the war against the people's democratic regime in Hungary. . . . Remember the unprecedented speech of Comrade Tito [181] in which the rebels in Hungary were defended and the fraternal assistance of the USSR to the Hungarian people was called Soviet intervention. . . . As a result of this attitude of the Yugoslav leaders, we were forced to come out with open criticism of their views and actions. . . .

In August 1957, on the initiative of the Yugoslav leaders, a well-known meeting of delegations of the Soviet Union and Yugoslavia took place in Bucharest. . . . Agreement was reached to the effect that the delegation of the LCY would take part in the forthcoming conference of fraternal parties of Socialist countries and in the drawing up of a draft declaration at the conference. Subsequent events showed, however, that the Yugoslav leaders retreated from the positions agreed upon. While having refused to sign the declaration of the Communist and Workers Parties of the Socialist countries, the Yugoslav leaders decided to come out with their platform, a Draft Programme of the LCY [192] opposed to the coordinated views of the Marxist–Leninist Parties and pretending to be a programme of the international Communist and workers movement. . . . Having rejected fraternal criticism based on principles voiced by fraternal parties, the Yugoslav leaders once again found themselves isolated and continued persistently to maintain their mistaken anti-Marxist views. . . .

We have stood and continue to stand on this position: that it is necessary to strengthen cooperation between all states in every way in the struggle for peace and the security of nations. We want to maintain such relations with the FPRY. But we as Communists would like more. We would like to reach mutual understanding and cooperation on the party level. The Yugoslav Communists have considerable revolutionary experience and have achieved great merits in the struggle against our common class enemies. The working class and all the working people of Yugoslavia made a considerable contribution to the struggle against Fascism in the years of World War II. Of course, if cooperation on the party plane cannot succeed, then we shall support and develop normal relations with Yugoslavia on the state plane. . . .

**198 Tito rebuts Khrushchev's charges and defends Yugoslav policy,
15 June 1958: excerpts** (*p. 73*)

... The main reason for this campaign is that we refused to sign the Declaration of the 12 countries in Moscow last November and to join the so-called Socialist camp because, as is well known, we opposed the division of the world into camps. . . . It does not follow that because we did not sign the Declaration and join the Socialist camp we are against the best possible cooperation with all Socialist countries. On the contrary, we are for such cooperation in all fields, but in the present tense international situation we consider it better to conduct a constructive peaceful policy together with other peace-loving countries which also do not belong to any bloc rather than to join a camp and thus intensify the present tense world situation even further. . . .

This is a campaign led by state and party leaders of the Socialist countries against Socialist Yugoslavia, and because of this, state relations inevitably deteriorate. That this has already affected state relations is proved by several facts.

First, immediately after our Congress, the Soviet Government for the second time in the last two years violated an interstate agreement on extending credit for some projects of importance to us. Second, immediately after our Congress, the Soviet Union cancelled a return state visit. . . . In order to deceive the world Comrade Khrushchev made a speech at the 7th Congress of the Bulgarian CP recently held in Sofia in which, among other things, he attacked Yugoslavia and the leadership of the LCY without justification and with expressions which have no connection with comradely criticism. . . . He not only attacked the Yugoslav leaders, but also our people. Our people suffered a lot from Stalin's policy of economic and political pressure and we are deeply hurt to hear Comrade Khrushchev repeat and justify this now, even though he sharply condemned such Stalinist policies at the Twentieth Congress of the CPSU [177]. . . .

The United States started giving us aid in 1949, not so that Socialism would triumph in our country—they do not like Socialism and they do not conceal this; they state openly that they do not like it— but because we were threatened by famine and because Yugoslavia would in this way be able more easily to resist Stalin's pressure and strengthen its independence.

If certain US circles possibly entertained other hopes, that was no concern of ours. The Stalinist policy of economic blockade and threats inflicted enormous damage on Yugoslavia which amounted to about 600 billion dinars according to the estimates of experts. Thus the tripartite aid of the United States, Great Britain, and France helped Yugoslavia in her distress due to the blockade and Cominform pressure. And the United States, Great Britain, and France gained a lot in the world, in the moral respect, as a result of this aid.

Comrade Khrushchev often says that Socialism cannot be built on US wheat, but I think that those who know how can do it, whilst those who do not know how will not even be able to build on their own wheat. . . . After all, US wheat is no worse than the Soviet wheat which we are not getting, and we *are* getting wheat from the United States.

. . . Finally, what moral right have those who are attacking us to reproach us on account of US aid or credits, when Comrade Khrushchev himself recently offered extensive trade exchanges to the United States in order to get credits? There is no logic in this, and it is pure cynicism to attack and slander us as selling ourselves for US aid and credits. . . .

It appears that it is our fate to have to build Socialism in our country under constant blows from all sides, and the worst blows are coming from those who should be our most loyal and best friends. It appears to us that history bestowed on us this hard road to preserve the development of Socialism from degeneration and to enable Socialism to emerge from the chaos which today prevails in the world with such moral strength that it will hew a victorious road in its further development. . . . We did not want this struggle, because we already have enough to worry about. However, since this struggle has been imposed on us, we will defend ourselves and nothing will scare us out of fighting for what we believe to be correct and just.

199 Khrushchev, at the 5th Congress of the Socialist Unity Party, reviews the course of Soviet–Yugoslav relations and returns to the attack, 11 July 1958: excerpt (*p. 73*)

. . . The Yugoslav leadership is stubbornly trying to impose on the Yugoslav people and the LCY the idea that the current sharpening of relations between the LCY and the Communist and Workers' Parties is, so they say, nothing more than a continuation of the 1948 events, i.e., a continuation of the previous conflict.

But what took place in 1948? At that time our party criticized the opportunist and nationalistic errors committed by the CPY leadership. Our criticism, which we have never renounced, was not incorrect; it was the appeal for a change in the leadership of the CPY contained in the Cominform's resolution that was incorrect. That is all that bears on 1948. There were errors on both sides—let me emphasize that—on both sides, in the sense that the disputes and bad relations between the Parties were carried over into the relations between the states. The Yugoslavs blame the Cominform for all the errors of the past— an organ which they helped to found and in which they actively participated until June 1948.

We have subjected the errors made on our side to honest and open criticism. The Yugoslavs did nothing of the sort when relations were re-established, although they had good grounds for self-criticism, for subjecting their own errors to criticism. It is sufficient to recall, for instance, the slanderous resolution of the 1952 6th Congress of the LCY at which it was asserted that the USSR was not a socialist country but an imperialist power conducting an expansionist policy [163]. The Western imperialists at that time generously subsidized them with hundreds of millions of dollars in return for such ravings. But the Yugoslav leaders still did not engage in any self-criticism. Moreover, they even concealed from the members of the LCY the fact that at the very beginning of the Belgrade talks in 1955 we told them that we considered our criticism of their errors in 1948 and the Cominform's 1948 Resolution basically correct.

The Yugoslav leaders' assertions that the present sharpening of relations between the LCY and all the other Communist parties is a continuation of the conflict begun in 1948 does not stand up under criticism. It is known that this conflict was settled in 1955 with the signing of the Soviet–Yugoslav Declaration [**174**]. Our relations with Yugoslavia along state lines were restored to normal, and it can be said that they became good relations. At the same time, contacts were also established on the party level; these also began to develop considerably. Thus the conflict which had begun in 1948 could be regarded as superseded.

In 1955 we agreed with the Yugoslav representatives when they declared that they considered it expedient to draw the line and not revive the past, so that a gradual, step-by-step improvement in the relations between our parties could be achieved. The leaders of the LCY, as everyone knows, have now violated this agreement also.

During the time of the Hungarian events in the autumn of 1956, the Yugoslav leadership again strengthened its activity directed against the unity of the countries of the socialist camp. Our party energetically repulsed the development of these activities. But after the well-known Soviet–Yugoslav meetings in Bucharest, the situation was again restored to normal. Even the decision of the Yugoslavs not to take part in the Conference of Communist and Workers' Parties of the Socialist countries in Moscow in autumn of 1957, and not to sign the Declaration of these parties, did not call forth open conflict.

Our party refrained, at that time, from any kind of open criticism of the action of the Yugoslav comrades which might break relations that had been worsening up to then. Naturally each of the fraternal Communist parties drew its own conclusion from what happened. The position taken then by the Yugoslav leaders could not but call for vigilance; their activities were for all of us a serious signal. However, even beforehand it was well known that there was a whole series of questions on which the Yugoslavs held their own particular views that contradicted the spirit of Marxist–Leninist ideology; nevertheless, our party considered it possible to maintain links and contacts with the Yugoslav comrades on those questions on which there was a definite community of views.

But for the Yugoslav leaders this was too little. They apparently wanted more. In deliberately counterposing themselves to the other Communist and Workers' Parties and speculating on disagreements with them, they sought to raise their price on the international market. It can be assumed that when our parties showed no open reaction to the Yugoslav leadership's decision not to participate in the Conference of Communist and Workers' Parties, when we merely drew our own conclusions from this, that it was then that the Yugoslavs decided to move to overt attacks against the CPSU, the Chinese Communist Party and all the Communist and Workers' Parties. Such a situation made it necessary for our parties to refuse to send their delegations to the 7th Congress of the LCY. . . .

Once more, just as in the past, impertinent and filthy caricatures have appeared in *Borba, Komunist, Politika*, and other organs of the Yugoslav press. People who in the past made a career out of anti-Soviet and anti-Communist concoctions are once again at work in the Yugoslav press and on the radio. By granting them complete freedom of action, the LCY leadership has apparently approved their views, which are right in line with those of the most shameless propagandists of imperialism. . . . Since Comrade Tito's speech at Labin [**198**] it has become plain who is actually organizing and inspiring this campaign against the Communist parties and socialist countries. . . .

Now the Yugoslavs are attempting to defame our system and our methods of socialist construction. They assert that we are somehow distorting Marxist–Leninist doctrine and that they themselves are the authentic preservers of Marxism–Leninism. We have heard and read all this many times before. But how then has it happened that the Soviet Union has achieved, and continues to achieve every year, results renowned throughout the whole world? . . .

In Yugoslavia, only about two per cent of the peasant farms have been combined into producers' cooperatives, and no consistent work is being waged for the socialist transformation of agriculture. It appears that as far as the peasant question is concerned the Yugoslav comrades are patently out of step with Marxism–Leninism. They talk a great deal about Marxism–Leninism in Yugoslavia, but they do many things which contradict Marxist–Leninist doctrine.

Recently, Yugoslav propaganda has been misleading the public by asserting that the low living standard of the Yugoslav population is due to the fact that some sort of economic blockade against Yugoslavia has supposedly been established. If a blockade is the point at issue, it should be stated quite definitely that one has never existed before and certainly does not exist now. We Soviet citizens are quite familiar with blockades. Yugoslavia has not only not been under blockade but has even enjoyed special protection and received substantial funds when the United States, considering the situation, decided National Communism of the Yugoslav type deserved special support. In addition, it should be recalled that Yugoslavia received large amounts of aid from the Soviet Union during the first four years after the war, and afterwards from the USA, Britain, France, and West Germany. . . . There are reports that the United States is already making its new 'contribution' to the cause of the 'building of Yugoslav socialism'. But the Yugoslav leaders are ashamedly keeping quiet about this latest hand-out because the peoples will know the price of American generosity. The capitalists don't give away something for nothing; when they give you something they take your soul in return and their aid is later paid for dearly.

The Yugoslavs say that they stand outside power blocs, condemn the policy of forming blocs, etc. This declaration of theirs does not correspond to reality, since Yugoslavia herself has joined with Turkey and Greece in the Balkan Pact and through her allies in this bloc are to some extent tied up with both NATO and the Baghdad Pact. . . .

The Yugoslav leaders claim that the Soviet Union and the CPSU aspire to some sort of special role, to hegemony, that they want to give orders, but that they, the Yugoslavs, won't agree to this. Such declarations are utter lies. It would be understandable if it were the propagandists of the imperialist camp who were trumpeting about this, but when people who call themselves Marxists talk this way, one involuntarily asks how they could sink to such vile slander. . . . There can be no question whatever of any sort of orders, or of the subordination of certain parties or countries to others in the camp of the socialist countries and in the international Communist movement. Indeed, there is no need for this; there is not even an agency which could give orders. . . .

In their speeches and official documents, the Yugoslav leaders have openly espoused their revisionist views, views which contradict the revolutionary essence of Marxism–Leninism. They have adopted a clearly schismatic and revisionist line and are thus abetting the enemies of the working class in their struggle against Communism; they are abetting the imperialists in their struggle against the Communist Parties and against the unity of the international revolutionary workers' movement. . . .

In our struggle for the total Communist cause we should not devote greater attention to the Yugoslav revisionists than they actually deserve. The more attention we pay them, the more they will think they are some sort of force playing a great role in the world. . . . We of the leadership of the CPSU are of the opinion that we should not fall in with the plans of the Yugoslav leaders, who are trying to aggravate the current conflict between us. We shall not contribute to the inflaming of passions or to the sharpening of relations. Even at the present stage of our relations with the LCY it would be useful to preserve some spark of hope, to search for acceptable forms of contact along certain lines.

200 Khrushchev, at a Friendship Meeting of the Polish People's Republic and the USSR, continues to denounce revisionism, but advocates more interchange of delegations, 10 November 1958: excerpts (*p. 73*)

. . . Evidence of the solidarity of the world Communist movement is the unanimous stand taken by all Communist and Workers' Parties against present-day revisionism, which found its fullest expression in the programme of the LCY. There was not a single Marxist party in the world or any sizeable group within such a party which would share the anti-Marxist views set forth in the programme of the LCY or would defend the position of the Yugoslav leadership. All the revolutionary parties of the working class assessed the Yugoslav programme as revisionist and severely condemned the subversive, splitting actions of the leaders of the LCY.

We have reiterated how highly we value the past services of the CP and the people of Yugoslavia, who have made such great sacrifices in the struggle against German and Italian Fascism. In that struggle our peoples fought shoulder to shoulder against a common enemy.

Unfortunately, the leaders of Yugoslavia, the individuals who head the party, are backsliding from a working-class position to the position of its enemies. Therefore one can hardly expect mutual understanding now in our relations with the LCY on a Party level, although we should not like to give up hope in this respect.

On a state level we shall strive to promote friendly relations with Yugoslavia, to extend trade and cultural intercourse. In the future, too, we are ready to maintain trade with Yugoslavia on a mutually profitable basis. . . .

We stand for a broad interchange of various delegations with Yugoslavia—delegations of persons engaged in cultural activities, delegations of collective farmers, workers, and others. It would be extremely beneficial, for instance, for our collective farmers to visit Yugoslavia and for Yugoslav peasants to come to our country, or for workers of the Soviet Union to be able to visit Yugoslavia and for Yugoslav workers to visit our country more often. Let the working people of our countries familiarize themselves with each other's life.

Let them see that no one bears any enmity for Yugoslavia, that our peoples have only one desire—closer friendship.

After the normalization of relations with Yugoslavia, after the elimination of all extraneous elements which existed in the relations between our countries, after the clearing up of absurd accusations, quite a few positive results have been achieved both in the relations between our countries and with regard to problems of cooperation in the struggle for peace. We may note with satisfaction that on many major international issues our positions often coincide, and we hope that in the future too our countries will join their efforts in an active struggle for the preservation and consolidation of peace.

As for our differences on ideological problems, we shall continue to wage an irreconcilable struggle against all distortions of Marxism–Leninism. All fraternal Communist and Workers' Parties are united in this. They regard revisionism as the main danger at the present stage. The struggle against revisionism is the struggle for the purity of our ideas, for the monolithic unity and solidarity of the international communist movement. . . .

201 The 21st CPSU Congress confirms the denunciation of the LCY 'revisionist programme', January–February 1959: excerpt (*p. 73*)

. . . The revisionist programme of the LCY has been unanimously condemned by all Marxist–Leninist parties. The theory and practice of the Yugoslav leaders are a departure from the positions of the working class and the principles of international solidarity. The views and policy of the leaders of the LCY jeopardise the achievements of the people's revolution and socialism in Yuogslavia.

The Soviet Communists and the entire Soviet people entertain friendly feelings for the fraternal peoples of Yugoslavia and for the Yugoslav Communists. The USSR will continue to seek cooperation with Yugoslavia on all the questions on which our views coincide in the struggle against imperialism and for peace.

202 Yugoslavia accused at Moscow CP Conference of revisionism and betraying Marxism–Leninism, December 1960: excerpt (*p. 74*)

. . . The Communist Parties have unanimously condemned the Yugoslav variety of international opportunism, a variety of modern revisionist 'theories' in concentrated form. After betraying Marxism–Leninism, which they termed obsolete, the leaders of the LCY opposed their anti-Leninist revisionist programme to the Declaration of 1957; they set the LCY against the international Communist movement as a whole, severed their country from the socialist camp, made it dependent on so-called 'aid' from U.S. and other imperialists, and thereby exposed the Yugoslav people to the danger of losing the revolutionary gains achieved through a heroic struggle. The Yugoslav revisionists carry on subversive work against the socialist camp and the world Communist movement. Under the pretext of being outside blocs, they engage in activities which prejudice the unity of all the peace-loving forces and countries. Further exposure of the leaders of the Yugoslav revisionists and active struggle to safeguard the Communist movement and the working-class movement from the anti-Leninist ideas of the Yugoslav revisionists remain an essential task of the Marxist Leninist Parties. . . .

The Communist and Workers' Parties unanimously declare that the CPSU has been, and remains, the universally recognized vanguard of the world Communist movement.

203 Tito, in the Federal Assembly, replies to criticisms by Moscow CP Conference, 26 December 1960: excerpts (*p. 74*)

. . . Even now, after twelve years of repetition of that assertion that the Yugoslav Communists were 'revisionists', they were not able to produce any at all convincing evidence to show in what this revisionism consisted, they were unable to give any sort of reasoned statement of their charges, which had rather the character of interference in our internal affairs and a distorted presentation of the realities of our development and our foreign policy. For these reasons all this does not really greatly worry us. But when in the same Declaration it is said that the policy of the LCY is a menace to the achievements of our people's liberation struggle, we have more than a crude falsehood, we have a deliberate attempt to destroy the unity which exists between the Communists and the other citizens of our country. . . .

An equally crude falsehood is the assertion in that Declaration that the Yugoslav Government, in its policy of non-alignment, allegedly works to the detriment of the unity of all world peace-loving forces. . . .

We are charged with having cut ourselves off from the Socialist countries. But who was it that denounced economic agreements we had concluded with the Socialist countries? We did not! Who harmed us in that way, compelling us under most arduous conditions to seek substitutes on the other side, in the West? All that is common knowledge today, and the authors of this new Declaration about Yugoslavia cannot have forgotten it. Do they really then think anybody has a right to reproach Yugoslavia with turning for cooperation and aid to where it was possible to get it without strings, without in any way endangering the achievements of our revolution or the building up of socialism? Nobody has any right to reproach us. . . .

Not only shall we never betray the class struggle of the proletariat, we shall also never fail the struggle of the subject peoples for freedom and independence, but at the same time we shall not allow anybody to slander us without cause, but will give our answer to every such attempt. And in our policy, a policy of peace, we shall continue to stand consistently and stoutly for those principles which we have hitherto always made our own.

204 A move towards détente: communiqué on the Yugoslav Foreign Minister's visit to Moscow, July 1961: excerpt (*p. 75*)

The Yugoslav State Secretary for Foreign Affairs Koča Popović paid an official visit to the Soviet Union from 7–13 July 1961. During his stay, Koča Popović was received by the President of the Soviet Ministerial Council, N. S. Khrushchev, and the First Vice President of the Ministerial Council, A. I. Mikoyan. He also met the Soviet Foreign Minister A. Gromyko. . . .

Both sides expressed satisfaction that Soviet–Yugoslav relations were developing normally and that the two countries' attitudes on fundamental international questions were either similar or identical. . . .

205 Khrushchev repeats his criticisms at the 22nd CPSU Congress, October 1961: excerpt (*p. 75*)

. . . The leaders of the LCY, who plainly suffer from national narrowmindedness, have turned from the straight Marxist–Leninist road onto a winding path that has landed them in the bog of revisionism. The Yugoslav leaders responded to the 1957 Declaration of the fraternal parties, which resounded throughout the world as a charter of Communist unity and solidarity, with a revisionist, anti-Leninist programme that all the Marxist–Leninist parties criticized decisively and justly.

Revisionist ideas pervade not only the theory but also the practice of the leadership of the LCY. The line they have adopted—that of development in isolation, apart from the world socialist community—is harmful and dangerous. It plays into the hands of imperialist reaction, foments nationalist tendencies and may in the long run lead to the loss of socialist gains in the country, which has broken away from the friendly and united family of builders of a new world.

Our party has criticized and will continue to criticize the Yugoslav leaders' revisionist conceptions. As internationalists, we cannot but feel concern for the destiny of the fraternal peoples of Yugoslavia, who fought selflessly against Fascism and after victory chose the path of socialist construction.

THE SECOND RECONCILIATION

206 Détente resumed: communiqué on Brezhnev's visit to Yugoslavia, October 1962: excerpts (*p. 75*)

The talks proceeded in a friendly and cordial atmosphere and in a spirit of mutual understanding and respect. They touched on questions of Soviet–Yugoslav cooperation, and also pressing international problems. During the talks the President of the Presidium of the USSR Supreme Soviet and the President of the FPRY recorded with satisfaction that the declaration of the governments of the USSR and the FPRY of 2 June 1955 [174] was a good basis for fruitful cooperation and expressed their conviction that mutual friendly relations and cooperation would continue to develop and grow in the same spirit in all spheres.

An identity or proximity of the views of the two sides was recorded in the course of a broad exchange of views on pressing international problems and tendencies of world development. . . .

They stressed the common interest in achieving the further extension of economic cooperation and their determination to achieve this. . . .

It was noted that informing the public in the two countries more widely and on a mutual basis about the topical events and processes taking place in them is essential for broadening mutual acquaintance and better understanding as well as for achieving a more comprehensive development of friendly relations between the USSR and the FPRY.

207 Tito, in the Supreme Soviet, declares that despite certain differences Yugoslavia and the USSR pursue the same socialist aims, and praises Khrushchev's statesmanship, December 1962: excerpt (*p. 76*)

. . . I should not like to speak of the past, for it is a long and complicated story· Since there still exist some differences of views, we shall eliminate them jointly, in constructive cooperation. In this short time we have become convinced that not only the leaders but your whole people want friendship and cooperation with the peoples of Yugoslavia. . . .

In the past few years the relations between the Soviet Union and Yugoslavia have been developing gradually in the direction of friendly cooperation in both the sphere of our bilateral relations and the sphere of foreign policy as well. The barriers that were artificially erected in our relations in the past are gradually being removed, and realistic relations and confidence are being created, bringing great benefit not only to our two countries but to the strengthening of world peace and the further successful development of socialism and the strengthening of mankind's progressive forces. . . .

We pursue the same goals—the building of a new society; the construction of socialism, of communism; and ensuring the peace that is essential to achieve these goals, for they can be achieved only in conditions of peace, in view of the fact that with the existence of ruinous modern means of warfare, nuclear and other weapons, war would be a catastrophe for mankind as a whole. There our views on all major international questions coincide or are very close. On the question of war and peace, on peaceful coexistence, on disarmament, on the elimination of colonialism, on the German question and on other questions troubling the world today, our viewpoints are identical or close to one another. . . .

We too shared with you and with the peoples of the whole world the deepest anxiety over the very dangerous events of recent months. In particular, I have in mind the crisis in the Caribbean. We were placed face to face with a very dangerous alternative. Now, when the crisis is already behind us, thanks to the peace-loving and constructive decision of the Soviet government and the action of the United Nations, I wish to express my satisfaction and the satisfaction of the peoples of Yugoslavia with this ending of the Cuban affair, although we still cannot say that everything is settled. For my part, I should like to express gratitude to the Soviet government and to Comrade Nikita Sergayevich [Khrushchev] personally for acting so boldly at a most critical moment, for acting with regard for the interests of all mankind and showing the farsightedness of true statesmen.

208 Tito explains to the LCY CC the implications of rapprochement with Moscow, May 1963: excerpts (*p. 76*)

We Yugoslav Communists, and the Yugoslav people, welcomed the decisions of the 20 and 22nd CPSU Congresses. This is not only because Stalin's mistakes were condemned there, but also because they laid the basis for a new process in the development of economic and social relations in the Soviet Union through comprehensive, more rapid development in all areas of economic and social life. Practice has confirmed the importance of those decisions both in the Soviet Union and in the international workers' movement. Thanks to Comrade Khrushchev and his colleagues, we are slowly but surely improving our relations with the Soviet Union and other Socialist countries. . . .

Good relations and cooperation with the Soviet Union and other Socialist countries are not in conflict with our previous policy, a policy of cooperation with all countries desiring to maintain cooperation with us on the basis of equal rights. This does not mean that we want in any way to worsen our international relations with the capitalist countries, to refuse to cooperate with them on problems of mutual or international interest. No, if we were to act thus, it would be inconsistent with the principles of active peaceful coexistence; we would be furthering not the easing but the exacerbation of the tense international situation. This would have an unwelcome adverse effect on our relations and cooperation with the non-aligned countries and on the constructive role these countries play in present-day international politics. . . .

It seems to me that amongst the members of the LCY are people who do not understand the great positive importance of our establishing not only normal but good relations with the Soviet Union and the other Socialist countries. Our recent visit to the Soviet Union has great importance not only from the standpoint of state interests and the interests of the international workers and progressive movement in general, but it is also useful for world peace. This is closely linked with our duty to participate actively in really clearing up misunderstandings and deformations in the socialist and workers movement.

When I say that misunderstandings in the Communist movement must be cleared up on the basis of principle, I have in mind also the recent past—the resolutions of the 81 parties at the 1960 Moscow Conference in connection with Yugoslavia [202] which did not correspond to the truth, and therefore were not based on principle. That is now past, and we Communists must look to the present and to the future. We must not on account of that harbour, as it were, a sort of distrust towards the Soviet Union and the other Socialist states and parties. We must take into account how they behave towards us, and which standpoints these parties adopt in the most important international problems. The views of the LCY on those questions must be one and the same. There can be no differences of view when it comes to the unified policy of the LCY and attitudes towards events not only in internal developments but in the international scene in general. The international revolutionary workers movement must have a special interest for us. We must be conscious that we are a part of that movement, and not something outside it. . . .

209 Tito and Khrushchev discuss 'urgent problems' with 'complete mutual understanding and agreement', August 1963: excerpt (*p. 76*)

. . . In the course of the talks, the international situation; the activity of the two countries in the preservation and consolidation of peace the world over and the possibility of further steps in this direction; urgent questions of pursuing the policy of peaceful coexistence among states with different social systems; further efforts toward general and complete disarmament and toward Soviet–Yugoslav cooperation in the cause of rendering aid to the developing countries; the complete liquidation of colonialism; and other questions related to settling the international situation and strengthening constructive cooperation among peoples were comprehensively discussed.

Comrades N. S. Khrushchev and J. Broz Tito exchanged opinions on urgent problems of the international workers' movement and on strengthening the unity of the socialist and other progressive forces in the struggle for peace, democracy and socialism.

Special attention was paid to the comprehensive development of Soviet–Yugoslav relations.

In the course of these talks between the Chairman of the USSR Council of Ministers and the Yugoslav President, complete mutual understanding and agreement on basic questions of the international situation and mutual relations between the two countries was apparent.

210 Communiqué on Tito's Talks with Khrushchev in Leningrad, June 1964: excerpts (*p. 77*)

Both sides noted with satisfaction the successful development of Soviet–Yugoslav relations in political, economic, cultural and other domains, and discussed opportunities for the further strengthening of friendly relations and the broadening of general cooperation between the Soviet Union and the SFRY in the interests of the peoples of Yugoslavia. . . .

Both sides reaffirmed unanimity of views on major problems of the contemporary world, and their loyalty to the principles of peaceful coexistence between states with different social systems, as the general line of the foreign policy of the USSR and the SFRY. . . .

Attaching great importance to the unity of all progressive forces that are struggling for peace, democracy, and socialism, they emphasised the necessity for every Communist and Workers' Party to make its contribution to overcoming the difficulties arisen in the world communist movement, and to achieving unity and a monolithic structure of the fraternal Communist and Workers' Parties, based on principles of Marxism–Leninism, in the interests of the strengthening of peace through the world and in the vital interests of mankind.

RELATIONS FOLLOWING KHRUSHCHEV'S FALL

211 Tito, in report to the 8th LCY Congress, alludes to the divisions within the world communist movement in the post-Khrushchev period, 7 December 1964: excerpt (*p. 77*)

. . . The Chinese leaders, apparently overestimating their role in the world, expected that the intensive campaign they have been waging for many years, added to their atomic bomb tests, and their continued efforts to discredit the policy of active and peaceful co-existence, would influence the Soviet Government and party to change their whole domestic and foreign policy, and revert to those of the Stalin period. When these hopes were not realized, the Chinese leaders stepped up their press attacks against the present leadership of the Soviet government and the CPSU. These attacks indeed, have hitherto been indirect, but it has been quite clear against whom they were aimed. The main target is now, and always has been, the former Secretary of the CC of the CPSU and President of the Council of Ministers, N. S. Khruschchev, whose resignation has been accepted by the Presidium and Plenum of the CC of the CPSU.

The Chinese journal *Hung Chi* has published a notorious attack, couched in loathsome terms, not only against Khrushchev, who for more than ten years was at the head of the CPSU and the Government, but against the CC of the CPSU and the whole Soviet people. Even if Comrade Khrushchev has been to blame in recent years for a number of mistakes and failures, he still, whilst leader of the party and government, played an important part in de-Stalinization and greater freedom of expression for the citizens, and he did great service for the preservation of peace in the world and for the curbing of various imperialist ploys, such as the Suez crisis, the Cuban crisis, etc. And I must take this opportunity of emphasizing that he deserves great credit for the normalization and improvement of relations between Yugoslavia and the Soviet Union. Naturally, he was not alone in this; the CC of the CPSU, the Supreme Soviet, and the Soviet Government also played their part, but no one denies his services in these issues. . . .

Yugoslavia will continue most actively to promote close cooperation with the Soviet Union and other Soviet countries. . . .

212 Communiqué affirming co-operation between the CPSU and the LCY, 1 July 1965: excerpts (*p. 77*)

During the talks on relations between the USSR and the SFRY the sides noted with satisfaction that cooperation between the two countries, particularly in recent years, has been developing successfully in all fields. The mutual cooperation is based on the principles of socialist internationalism, complete equality, respect for sovereignty and non-interference in one another's internal affairs contained in the 2 June 1955 Belgrade Declaration [174]. . . .

Both sides agreed that a steady and significant rise is being observed in the field of economic cooperation, and that this cooperation is assuming increasingly broad and diverse forms. The level of trade achieved and the number of interstate economic agreements signed between the USSR and the SFRY are a major contribution to the cause of further expansion of economic relations. . . . An intergovernmental Soviet–Yugoslav Committee on Economic Cooperation has been established. . . .

The sides affirmed the identity or similarity of their views in the evaluation of the main problems of the present-day international situation. . . . [They] noted with satisfaction that contacts between the CPSU and the LCY have become broader and stronger in recent years.

213 Soviet and Yugoslav Foreign Ministers confer in Moscow, May 1966: excerpt (*p. 78*)

The two Ministers noted the successful development of Soviet–Yugoslav relations and the expansion of all-round economic, scientific-technical and cultural ties. . . . The review of international questions reaffirmed the closeness or identity of the two countries' views on the chief problems of the present international situation.

214 Communiqué on the 'friendly talks' between Brezhnev and Tito in Yugoslavia, 25 September 1966: excerpt (*p. 79*)

Friendly talks took place between Comrades L. I. Brezhnev and Josip Broz Tito. . . .

There was a discussion of questions of Soviet–Yugoslav relations. Satisfaction was expressed with the development of these relations, as was a common desire for their further expansion and strengthening in the interests of the peoples of both countries and the cause of peace and Socialism.

INVASION OF CZECHOSLOVAKIA AND THE DOCTRINE OF
LIMITED SOVEREIGNTY

215 LCY CC affirms support for Czechoslovakia and warns against outside interference, 18 July 1968: excerpt (*p. 80*)

The CC of the LCY is in agreement with the support extended to the CP of Czechoslovakia and its present leadership. It feels that the present significant changes in Czechoslovakia are, above all, a reflection of the objective need to consolidate socialist social relationships and develop them still further. The LCY takes the position that the working class and its CP and other socialist and progressive forces in Czechoslovakia are the only ones called upon to assess the situation in their country and to solve the problems that have been piling up over a number of years. They know best their own conditions, requirements and possibilities. The CC is profoundly convinced that the working class and progressive forces in Czechoslovakia are sufficiently strong to counter all attempts to jeopardise the achievements of socialism and further socialist development.

The LCY is of the opinion that the right of the working class and peoples of Czechoslovakia to independent development must be respected, and that the CP of Czechoslovakia, its present leadership and all socialist forces in Czechoslovakia deserve confidence and support.

The CC of the LCY feels that any outside action representing interference or an effort to limit the independence of the CP of Czechoslovakia or in any way whatsoever to jeopardise the sovereignty of Czechoslovakia would have grave consequences for the development of socialism in Czechoslovakia and in the world. Any such action would extend support to conservative and reactionary forces in Czechoslovakia and elsewhere. . . .

216 Tito expresses confidence that force will not be used against Czechoslovakia, which would be 'extremely wrong', 12 July 1968: excerpt (*p. 80*)

The events in Czechoslovakia have a different character from those that took place in relation to Yugoslavia in 1948 and I think that they should not be over-dramatised. I do not believe there are, in the Soviet Union, people so short-sighted that they would have recourse to a policy of force to solve internal problems in Czechoslovakia. There were some things that represented a certain amount of pressure, but now we can read in the press that the troops are withdrawing. Without question, it would be extremely wrong for one or more countries to interfere in the internal affairs of another country.

Secondly, the situation is such that Socialism in Czechoslovakia is not in jeopardy. If there should be any intervention or strong pressure from the West posing a direct threat to the social system, Czechoslovakia has its own army to defend it; it has its own CP, its own working class.

Similarly, we in Yugoslavia have our own army, CP and socially conscious working people and nobody needs to save socialism for us. We have the strength to do it ourselves. . . .

217 Tito's statement on the news that Czechoslovakia had been invaded, 21 August 1968: excerpt (*p. 81*)

The entry of foreign military units into Czechoslovakia, without invitation or consent by the legal government, has given us cause for deep concern. By this step the sovereignty of a Socialist country has been violated and trampled upon, and a serious blow inflicted on socialist and progressive forces all over the world.

During my stay in Prague and in my talks with the Czech leaders headed by Comrade Dubček, I became convinced that the leadership was determined to prevent any attempt by anti-socialist elements to hinder the normal development of democracy and normal socialist development in Czechoslovakia. This was confirmed by the joint document adopted on that occasion.

However, the latest events have unilaterally terminated the joint decisions taken by the Six in Bratislava, while at the same time measures have been taken which will have far-reaching and very negative consequences for the entire revolutionary movement everywhere in the world. . . .

218 Statement by the Federal Executive Council of the SFRY denouncing the Soviet invasion, 22 August 1968: excerpts (*p. 81*)

. . . The armed intervention by the Warsaw Pact countries committed without invitation and against the will of the Government and other constitutional organs of the CSR is the grossest form of violation of the sovereignty and territorial integrity of an independent country, and a direct negation of the generally accepted principles of international law of the United Nations Charter.

The Government of the SFRY considers that no State or group of States has the right to decide on the fate of any other country and on its internal development, nor to take measures which are in contradiction with the publicly expressed will of its people and its constitutional organs.

The military intervention against the CSR and the invasion of its territory cannot be justified in any way, the more so since this Socialist country did not threaten anybody, nor did it—as was recently unambiguously stated by its legal government and other constitutional institutions—itself feel endangered.

The Governments of the countries taking part in the military intervention against the CSR bear full responsibility for the far-reaching consequences of their action. The armed intervention against the CSR encourages policies of force and aggression and the dangerous practice of constant interference in the internal affairs and free development of other countries. The negative consequences do not only concern the CSR; they also affect the interests and relations of other countries, their international security and the stability of peace in Europe and throughout the world. . . .

The Government of the SRFY fully supports the demands of the legitimate representatives of the CSR, demands which call for the withdrawal of occupying troops, respect for the independence and territorial integrity of the CSR, respect for the sovereignly expressed will of the people of Czechoslovakia, and which urge that the constitutional bodies and political forums of the CSR be allowed to work under normal conditions.

The Government of the SFRY appeals to the Governments of the USSR, the People's Republic of Poland, the German Democratic Republic, the People's Republic of Hungary, and the People's Republic of Bulgaria, in the expectation that they will take urgent measures to put an immediate end to the occupation of the CSR.

219 LCY CC resolution condemns the invasion and reaffirms its resolve to resist all attempts at external pressure, 23 August 1968: excerpts (*p. 81*)

The Communists, the working people, the peoples and the various nationalities of this country have in recent days massively expressed their deep indignation and protest against the occupation of Czechoslovakia. . . .

In the situation we face, the CC of the LCY particularly stresses:

1. The LCY does not recognize the right of anyone wilfully to interfere in the internal development and affairs of an independent country by recourse to military intervention or any other form of pressure.

2. The LCY rejects as completely unacceptable all the arguments submitted by the governments of the five countries of the Warsaw Treaty designed to justify the invasion of Czechoslovakia. The LCY offers full support to the Communist Party, the working class and the peoples of Czechoslovakia in their struggle for the independence of their country and free socialist development.

3. The LCY demands the urgent termination of the occupation of Czechoslovakia and the release of the democratically elected representatives and leaders of the SCR and the Communist Party of Czechoslovakia, and creation of all the conditions necessary for the socialist development of Czechoslovakia unhampered by outside interference.

4. The League of Communists and Socialist Yugoslavia will continue striving for the broadest possible cooperation with the socialist and all other anti-imperialist and democratic forces and movements in the struggle for freedom, peace and social progress, and for equality amongst states and nations, for full respect for the right of independent development for each country and party and for non-interference in their policies and internal development.

In the development of relations with socialist countries and the Communist and Workers Parties, we consistently adhere to and strive for implementation of the principles expressed in the Belgrade and Moscow Declarations issued by the Governments and Parties of Yugoslavia and the USSR in 1955 and 1956 [**174, 179**].

5. The League of Communists and Socialist Yugoslavia do not recognize any agreements—open or tacit—regarding spheres of interest which transform the small nations into pawns of power politics. Just as we opposed the Yalta Agreement, which carved out spheres of interest for the great powers, so we today oppose any such arrangement at the expense of other peoples. Historical practice has shown that the policy of the division into spheres of interest and of hegemony by the big powers is not only a disaster for the peoples concerned but also a constant threat to world peace.

6. Today, as before, we are resolved to use all our forces and means to defend our independence, revolution and our own way of socialist develop-ment. We shall strive to strengthen the defensive power and security of our country. This is a matter that concerns all the citizens, all the peoples and all the nationalities of our Socialist community. Created and educated in the revolution, the Yugoslav national army is ready unwaveringly to do its duty in defending the country.

7. By the promoting of political vigilance and by energetic, uncompromising action we must oppose all attempts to undermine the foundations of our system, to hinder our independent democratic socialist development and to strike at the unity of our peoples and our working folk, and also oppose any provocative action geared towards weakening the strength of our resistance and interference from any quarter whatever.

220 *Pravda* **accuses Yugoslavia of joining NATO countries in supporting the 'anti-socialist forces' in Czechoslovakia, 25 August 1968: excerpt** (*p. 81*)

The imperialist circles, which are whipping up political hysteria in their countries and in the UN, have now rushed to their [the 'counter-revolution-aries'] assistance. It is noteworthy that the leaders of Yugoslavia and Romania, who are giving active assistance to the Czechoslovak anti-socialist forces, have joined this imperialist chorus, and it is precisely in Belgrade and Bucharest that the political adventurers from Prague who find themselves outside Czechoslovakia during this period are weaving their intrigues.

An example of how far the Yugoslav patrons of the anti-socialist forces have gone is provided by a provocational statement sent by the Yugoslav Govern-ment to the UN on the so-called Czechoslovak question; this statement fully coincides with the positions of the NATO countries. The Mao Tse-tung group in Peking, which has joined with the USA and Yugoslavia on this question, is also acting in the same spirit. . . .

221 Soviet protest at the Yugoslav attitude towards the invasion of Czechoslovakia, 30 August 1968: excerpt (*p. 82*)

In connection with the unfriendly position adopted by Yugoslavia regarding the aid operation undertaken by the five Socialist countries for the benefit of Czechoslovakia, Mr Benediktov [Soviet Ambassador to Yugoslavia], acting on instructions of the CC of the Party and of the Soviet Government, made a statement to the effect that 'The CC of the Party and the Soviet Government are astonished in the highest degree that the leadership of the LCY and the Yugoslav Government should have taken the same line as those countries which have adopted measures designed to give active support to . . . [the counter-revolutionaries]'

222 Tito calls for the withdrawal of the Warsaw Pact forces from Czechoslovakia, 5 September 1968: excerpt (*p. 82*)

Yugoslavia welcomed the agreement concluded in Bratislava by the six Socialist countries, which recognised the right to an independent road to Socialist development, and confirmed the principles of non-interference and cooperation on terms of equality, and so today we cannot approve of the present situation in the CSR and direct interference in internal affairs of a people. We consider that the brotherly peoples of Czechoslovakia alone have the right and ability to solve their problems. Because of this, it is indispensable, after the Moscow Agreement, to enable the peoples of the CSR and their legal representatives, the Communist Party and working class of Czechoslovakia, to solve their problems by themselves and to extend to them for the purpose all possible and sincere help, respecting their full independence. To this end the speedy withdrawal of the troops of the five Warsaw Pact countries should be achieved as this would create conditions for the establishment of confidence and for the development of cooperation, on terms of equality, amongst socialist countries and Communist Parties. . . .

223 Tito defends the Yugoslav concepts of self-management and socialist democracy and attacks the doctrine of limited sovereignty, 20 October 1968: excerpts (*p. 82*)

Our views on the case of Czechoslovakia we have openly presented before the whole world, and we shall abide by them for ever. I consider that the principles of non-interference, independence, territorial integrity and sovereignty must apply to all countries in the world, regardless of which bloc they belong to. . . .

This policy of ours caused revolt amongst some of our friends and neighbours in Eastern countries—Poland, the Soviet Union, Hungary, the Democratic Republic of Germany and especially in Bulgaria. And of course they have again begun, as they did in 1948, to attack our country in the press and published speeches. . . .

What is involved here is that they do not find our social system to their liking, our Socialist system based on self-management, our road to Socialism and Communism. They do not like our Socialist democracy. In short, it is our self-management which galls them most, and that is why they have launched their attacks on our internal system. . . . They attack our reform, at the same time they themselves are trying to discover some kind of reform. These are some of the basic elements that stand between us and them. And in the case of Czechoslovakia, the central issue was, in my opinion, the democratization of social development in the sense of changes which would have enabled the people to live a better life. . . .

Amongst justifications for the Czechoslovak case—that is, the invasion committed by the troops of the five Socialist countries—some kind of theory has made its appearance according to which sovereignty is not essential for small nations. It has not been explicitly stated that this refers to small nations but this is what was actually meant. This is in fact an attempt to legalise something that is altogether untenable, something that does not even exist in the Atlantic Charter, or anywhere else for that matter. . . .

224 *Pravda* **plays down Yugoslav alarm following the invasion of Czechoslovakia, 3 December 1968: excerpts (*p. 83*)**

The Yugoslav press has published the statements made by J. Broz Tito, President of the SFRY, at a press conference for Yugoslav and foreign journalists in the city of Jajce, where a celebration was held on the occasion of Yugoslavia's national holiday, Republic Day.

In reply to questions from correspondents, Tito spoke about Yugoslavia's relations with other countries. He noted that Yugoslavia, which is building socialism, desires to have the best possible relations not only with the socialist countries but with all other countries as well, regardless of their social systems.

Asked about his views on the international Communist movement after the events in Czechoslovakia, Tito said: 'It is not desirable to dramatize the situation at present. We must make a start on normalization, so that the best possible cooperation can be established in the international workers' movement'.

Tito gave a resolute rebuff to the provocative rumors being spread by NATO circles to the effect that the Soviet Union intends to attack Yugoslavia. Tito declared that he sees no reason for this. . . .

To a question about the prospects for Soviet–Yugoslav relations, Tito reported that he had received telegrams of congratulation from the leaders of the Soviet Union. These telegrams, he noted, 'express in very precise and strong terms a desire to develop durable good relations with Yugoslavia'. Tito added that he believes this is the desire of the entire Soviet people. 'Evidently', he continued, 'ideological differences will continue to exist, but both they and we have an interest in good relations, since we are socialist countries'.

225 Tito, at the 9th LCY Congress, renews his criticism of limited sovereignty, March 1969: excerpt (*p. 83*)

We have on several occasions, especially at the 10th meeting of the League's Central Committee, expressed our views on intervention in Czechoslovakia. This action, which constitutes a violation of the independence of a sovereign country and which is in direct contradiction with the generally accepted principles of international law and of the United Nations Charter, has dealt a heavy blow to the interests of progress, peace, and freedom, all the more so since it was committed by Socialist countries and in the name of the protection of Socialism. At the same time in some East European countries there also appeared an unacceptable doctrine about 'collective', 'integrated', and in essence restricted sovereignty. This doctrine negates, in the name of an alleged higher degree of relationship amongst Socialist countries, the sovereignty of these countries and strives to legalize the rights of one or more countries to impose their will upon other socialist countries, according to their own judgement and even by means of military intervention. We, of course, resolutely reject such a conception as contrary to the basic right of all peoples to independence and as contrary to the principles of international law. In addition, such a conception is at variance with the interests of the struggle for socialism.

'NORMALIZATION' AND THE TACTICS OF LIMITED RAPPROCHEMENT

226 Tito urges that economic relations should not be prejudiced by political or ideological differences or by hostile press criticism, 1 May 1969: excerpts (*p. 83*)

In the Soviet Union there is sometimes indignation about what some of our newspapers write. But what is the position in their country with regard to ours? They are always speaking against us. A great number of lectures are organized criticizing us in every way. They say we have gone over to capitalism and the like. . . .

What sort of relations should we have with the socialist states? . . . I consider we should have normal, and if possible, good and friendly relations. Economic relations should be broader and more all-embracing, as we have to some extent already achieved, and we should not let them be prejudiced by political or ideological differences. . . . They should certainly not be allowed to be affected by the publication of one or two articles in the newspapers.

227 Communiqué of the Moscow conference of CPs is conciliatory towards the LCY, July 1969: excerpt (*p. 84*)

The Soviet Union attaches great importance to the development of relations with Socialist Yugoslavia, although these relations do not always take a smooth form. We are convinced that the allegiance of the peoples of the USSR and Yugoslavia to the ideas of Socialism and their mutal interest in expanding ties and contacts creates the prerequisites for the further development of Soviet–Yugoslav relations and we are completely in favour of this. . . .

228 Yugoslav and Soviet Foreign Ministers confer in Belgrade, September 1969: excerpts (*p. 84*)

. . . Particular attention was devoted to an examination of bilateral relations between our countries, and hope was expressed for the further development of friendship and cooperation between the USSR and the SFRY. Both sides stressed the importance of the principles of the Belgrade Declaration [174]. . . . Much attention was also devoted to the status of Soviet–Yugoslav economic, scientific-technical and cultural cooperation. . . . There were discussions of the possibility of establishing long-term cooperation in the machine-building and pharmaceutical industries. . . .

The exchange of views between the two Ministers on major international problems demonstrated their agreement on many questions. . . . Particular mention should be made of the importance of political cooperation between our countries in the interests of peace in the Balkans. The Soviet Union steadily advocates the transformation of this area into a zone of tranquility and peace, free of nuclear weapons. On this question our countries' positions are identical.

229 Tito declares that Yugoslav–Soviet relations have been placed on the right path, 10 October 1969: excerpts (*p. 84*)

I wish particularly to stress the importance of the visit by the Soviet Foreign Minister A. Gromyko. . . . The common view was reached that the dissensions noted in the recent past should be overcome, that we should turn to the future and foster all that we have in common and that is profitable to both countries.

Whilst striving for the further promotion of relations with the Soviet Union and socialist countries a common course should be adopted, aimed primarily at those things that truly tend to promote cooperation, while differences of view, where they may appear, should be discussed and in a principled manner on the basis of equal rights and complete mutual respect. In view of the recent meetings and talks, I can say that we are on the right path. . . .

230 Visit of Prime Minister Ribičič to the USSR; communiqué affirming that 'differences of opinion' should not restrict the development of normal and friendly relations', July 1970: excerpts (*p. 84*)

During the discussion of questions of bilateral relations, a positive assessment was given to their development, and both sides expressed a desire to continue to make efforts towards expanding and strengthening cooperation, mutual understanding and friendly relations, based on the principles of the 1955 Belgrade Declaration [174] and other joint documents—principles of respect for sovereignty and territorial integrity, equal rights, non-interference in each other's internal affairs, and mutual respect. . . .

They expressed the opinion that the existence of some differences of opinion on certain questions should not restrict the development of normal and friendly relations between the two countries.

231 Communiqué on talks between Soviet and Yugoslav Foreign Ministers 'in a sincere and friendly atmosphere', February 1971: excerpt (*p. 86*)

The meeting and talks took place in a sincere and friendly atmosphere.

During the talks great attention was devoted to the status of Soviet–Yugoslav relations.

Both sides noted with satisfaction that relations and cooperation between the USSR and the SFRY, which are based on respect for sovereignty, equality of rights and non-intervention in domestic affairs, have been developing successfully. In this connection they emphasized the significance of the meetings that have been taking place in recent years between leading figures of the USSR and SFRY.

The sides expressed readiness to continue to assist in the strengthening of relations and of manifold cooperation between themselves, which accords with the fundamental interests of both countries and furthers the cause of peace, progress and international cooperation on a foundation of equality of rights.

Both sides reaffirmed that the development of political contacts and of the exchange of views at various levels, as well as the strengthening of ties and of cooperation between appropriate public, scientific, cultural and other organizations, and broader mutual familiarization with the life and achievements of the peoples of both countries will foster better mutual understanding and a strengthening of trust and friendship between them.

Having placed a positive appraisal on their cooperation in the sphere of culture, education, science and other fields, the sides stressed the need to seek new opportunities for further developing this cooperation.

Satisfaction was expressed with the successful development of economic relations between the two countries. The trade agreement for 1966–1970 has been implemented, and this has laid a firm foundation for a further growth of trade. This favorable trend in economic relations has found reflection too in the agreement on trade during the period 1971 to 1975.

The sides stressed the need to seek new opportunities for expanding economic cooperation, particularly in production specialization and cooperation. . . .

232 Brezhnev, at 24th CPSU Congress affirms the Soviet people desire 'socialism to gain strength' in Yugoslavia, March 1971: excerpt (*p. 86*)

Soviet–Yugoslav relations continued to develop. The Soviet people want Socialism to gain strength in Yugoslavia and its ties with the Socialist Commonwealth to become firmer. We are for Soviet–Yugoslav cooperation and for the development of contacts between our people. . . .

233 Communiqué on Brezhnev's state visit to Yugoslavia: rapprochement gathers momentum, September 1971: excerpts (*p. 88*)

The cooperation between the USSR and the SFRY is based on the closeness of their historical destiny, the common nature of the foundations of their social systems and the similarity in their approaches to many international problems, on their allegiance to the principles of socialist internationalism, the common struggle for peace, independence and equal international cooperation and the struggle against imperialism.

This creates favorable conditions for fruitful cooperation between our peoples, parties and states and for the constructive resolution of all questions arising in mutual relations, no matter how complicated they may be.

The CPSU and the LCY proceed from the premise that only the teachings of Marx, Engels, and Lenin, creatively applied and developed in accordance with the special features of each country, can be the invariable foundation today and in the future for the policy of the Communist and Workers' Parties that stand at the head of their peoples and the working class in the struggle for the construction of a socialist society. The methods of the construction of socialism, which reflects the experience and specific character of the development of individual countries, are the affair of the peoples and the working class of these countries and should not be counterposed to one another.

The development of comprehensive Soviet–Yugoslav relations is based on the principles set forth in the 1955 Belgrade Declaration, the 1956 Moscow Statement and Declaration and the 1965 Joint Soviet–Yugoslav Statement [174, 179, 212].

The two sides deem it necessary to continue to develop on this basis the friendly cooperation between the CPSU and the LCY, as parties guiding socialist and communist construction in their respective countries, and to strengthen the confidence that should characterize relations between the two parties and two sovereign states.

The two sides will stimulate more frequent meetings, exchanges of opinion and consultations at various levels between the CPSU and the LCY and between the USSR and the SFRY on questions of bilateral relations and foreign policy. . . .

Taking into account the practice of mutually useful inter-party ties, the CPSU and the LCY will expand exchanges of party delegations, encourage the cooperation of party and scientific institutions, and develop contacts and ties between local party organizations.

The CPSU and the LCY will promote the all-round development of cooperation between the USSR and the SFRY in the political and economic fields and also in the spheres of science, technology and culture.

The two sides are convinced that there are great possibilities for the expansion and deepening of economic, scientific and technical cooperation between the USSR and the SFRY on a bilateral and multilateral basis, including cooperation based on the treaty between the SFRY and the Council for Mutual Economic Aid. . . . In this connection, the two sides welcome the conclusion of the 1971–1975 agreement between the USSR and the SFRY. . . .

An intergovernment committee on economic, scientific and technical cooperation and the appropriate economic agencies and organizations of the two countries will study the possibilities and take the necessary steps for the more efficient and swifter development of economic relations.

The CPSU and the LCY emphasize the importance of the further development on the basis of reciprocity of ties in the field of the press, radio, television, culture and the arts. . . .

The two sides attach great importance to the expansion of direct contacts between the working people of the USSR and the SFRY and to the development of cooperation between trade union, young people's, women's, tourist, sports and other mass organizations with the aim of better mutual understanding and familiarization with the life of the peoples of the two countries.

The Soviet side supports the anti-imperialist trend in the policy of the non-aligned countries and, in this connection, takes a positive view of its role in the strengthening of peace and international cooperation in the struggle of the peoples against colonialism and neo-colonialism and for independence and social progress.

The USSR and the SFRY, as well as the CPSU and the LCY, are in favour of the development of broad and equal cooperation between countries and peoples with the aim of guaranteeing peace and international security. By their policy, they will continue actively to promote the affirmation of international relations of the principles of the peaceful coexistence of states regardless of their social systems. . . .

The Soviet Union and Yugoslavia support the strengthening of lasting peace and security on the Balkan Peninsula, an important element in which could be the proclamation of the Balkans as a zone free of nuclear weapons. . . .

234 Tito's visit to Moscow: 'relations have become still friendlier', June 1972: excerpts: (*p. 89*)

During the negotiations, which were held in a cordial, frank and friendly atmosphere and in a spirit of mutual respect and equality, there was a comprehensive exchange of opinions on the results of the strengthening cooperation between the USSR and the SFRY, and between the CPSU and the LCY, on further possibilities for development of that cooperation, and on topical international problems. . . .

Noting the vital nature of the principles of the Belgrade Declaration and the Moscow Statement [**174, 179**], the two sides emphasized the great importance of the Joint Soviet Yugoslav Statement adopted in Belgrade on 25 September 1971 during the visit to the SFRY of L. I. Brezhnev, Secretary General of the CPSU [**233**]. The two sides also stated with satisfaction that the implementation of the ideas and proposals in that statement have already yielded substantial positive results.

Relations between the USSR and the SFRY have become still friendlier. Emphasis was placed on the significance of the fruitful personal meetings between party, state and public figures of the two countries, the broadening of cooperation between the USSR Supreme Soviet and the SFRY Federal Executive Council, and the deepening of contacts and cooperation at various levels. Both sides pointed out the need for the further development and enrichment of all forms of cooperation on the basis of working plans elaborated jointly; this will no doubt facilitate better mutual acquaintance with the development and accomplishments of both socialist states and a deepening of the exchange of experience in socialist and communist construction. . . .

The two sides evaluated highly the results from the cooperation between the CPSU and the LCY. The CPSU and the LCY, guided by the teachings of Marx, Engels and Lenin and creatively applying them in accordance with the specific features of their respective countries, will continue—in a spirit of internationalist traditions and of friendship, mutual respect and equality—to favour the fruitful comprehensive exchange of opinions and experience, the improvement of mutual understanding, and the further expansion of cooperation.

235 Kosygin, on a visit to Yugoslavia, stresses the value of closer economic co-operation, 2 October 1973: excerpts (*p. 90*)

. . . The heads of government emphasized that fruitful Soviet–Yugoslav cooperation is being carried out in the two countries' mutual interests, with respect for the principles of sovereignty, equality and non-interference and in accordance with the Belgrade Declaration of 1955, the Joint Statement of 1971, and the Joint Communiqué of 1972 [**174, 233, 234**] which constitute a firm and unchanging foundation for the further comprehensive development of relations between the two socialist countries. They . . . noted with satisfaction that cooperation between the CPSU and the LCY is very fruitful and is constantly expanding, as is the cooperation between the USSR Supreme Soviet and the SFRY Federal Assembly, and between individual republics, people and political organisations and cities of the two countries.

The heads of government devoted a great deal of attention to economic cooperation and noted with satisfaction that it is developing steadily and dynamically.

The two sides agreed that the achieved level of economic cooperation creates a realistic and broad basis for its further comprehensive development. They took note of the need to make further efforts aimed at the development of productive cooperation in the motor vehicle, electronic and machine-building industries and other fields, and the intensification of cooperation in light industry, metallurgy, agriculture, transportation and tourism.

236 Brezhnev stresses that Yugoslavia and the USSR have a common 'social formation', November 1973: excerpts (*p. 91*)

The Belgrade and Moscow Declarations of 1955 and 1956, the Soviet–Yugoslav Statement of 1971, and the Joint Communiqué adopted in 1972 [**174, 179, 233, 234**]—these are the significant milestones that mark the progressive development of our relations. . . .

. . . the dominant tendency in relations between the Soviet Union and Yugoslavia—countries of the same social formation—is determined by what unites us; it is determined by the common objective laws governing the development of socialism, laws discovered by Marx and Lenin and confirmed by the experience of many Communist and Workers' Parties.

Our states' cooperation is being filled with ever richer content, and this applies not only to the sphere of bilateral relations but also to the field of foreign policy. In the struggle for lasting peace and the security of peoples, the Soviet Union cherishes the solidarity of Yugoslavia, whose peace-loving foreign policy is making a positive contribution to the improvement of the international atmosphere.

237 Tito acknowledges the 'common goal' but stresses 'different methods', November 1973: excerpts (*p. 91*)

. . . Practice has shown that mutual respect for jointly adopted principles—equality, independence, noninterference and consideration for the special features of our countries' internal development and international positions—is a firm foundation on which our long-term cooperation can develop successfully. However, I think there are still unused possibilities for the further development of cooperation, specially in the economic field. . . .

Our common goal—the building of socialism and communism, despite our different methods of and specific paths in the creative application of the teaching of Marx, Engels and Lenin, depending on the special features of each country—leads us along the path of the strengthening of mutual trust, the steady expansion of relations and strengthening of friendship between two socialist countries and parties. . . .

238 Tito and Brezhnev in joint communiqué salute the improvement in state and Party contacts, November 1973: excerpt (*p. 91*)

. . . Leonid Brezhnev and Josip Broz Tito informed each other about the progress in building Socialism and Communism, had an exchange of views on the development and cooperation between the CPSU and the LCY, and between the USSR and the SFRY, and the prospects of strengthening Soviet–Yugoslav relations, and also discussed topical international problems and questions concerning the international Communist and Working Class movement.

12

They noted with satisfaction the successful development of Soviet–Yugoslav cooperation in the political, economic, scientific, technical and cultural spheres and emphasized the important efforts made by both sides in implementing the provisions of the joint document adopted earlier. The General Secretary of the CPSU Central Committee and the Chairman of the LCY expressed great appreciation of the results achieved in the field of cooperation between the CPSU and the LCY. In the opinion of the two sides, the level achieved in Soviet–Yugoslav relations ensures the fullest development of all-round cooperation.

Both sides emphasized that improvement in party and state contacts and enrichment of Soviet Yugoslav cooperation accorded with the interests of building Socialism and Communism, and they advocated the expansion of long-term cooperation in the political and economic fields and in culture, education, science, information, tourism and other spheres. The two sides consider that the participation of the SFRY in the activities of the Council for Mutual Economic Assistance, on the basis of the existing treaty between the SFRY and the Council, are helping to strengthen economic cooperation between the Soviet Union and Yugoslavia.

SOURCE NOTES

ABBREVIATIONS

BFSP   *British & Foreign State Papers*
CDSP   *Current Digest Soviet Press**
DGFP   *Documents on German Foreign Policy*
FRUS   *Foreign Relations of the United States*
GAOR   *General Assembly Official Records*
RIA   *Review of International Affairs* (Belgrade)
YWB   *White book on aggressive activities by the governments of
                        the USSR, Poland, Czechoslovakia, Hungary, Rumania,
                        Bulgaria and Albania towards Yugoslavia* (Ministry of
                        Foreign Affairs, Belgrade 1951)
Dedijer, *Prilozi*   V. Dedijer, *Josip Broz Tito: Prilozi za biografiju* (Belgrade,
                        1953)
Knezevich, *Mihailović* Z. Knezevich, *Mihailović and the USSR* (Washington [?]
                        1945)
Pijade, *Legend*   M. Pijade, *About the legend that the Yugoslav uprising
                        owed its existence to Soviet assistance* (London, 1950)
Plenča, *Medjunarodni* D. Plenča, *Medjunarodni odnosi Jugoslavije u toku drugog
   odnosi   svetskogarata* (Inst. društvenih nauka, Belgrade, 1962)
Tito, *Govori*   Josip Broz Tito, *Govori i članci* (Zagreb, 1959–)
Zbornik dokumenata   *Zbornik dokumenata, podataka o narodno- oslobodilačkom
                        ratu jugoslovenskih naroda* (Belgrade, 1949–65)

* Published weekly by the American Association for the Advancement of Slavic Studies at
the Ohio State University. Copyright 1953, 1957, 1958, 1962, 1963, 1965, 1966, 1968, 1969,
1970, 1971, 1972, 1973 by permission.

*Document
No.*
  1 *Aprilski rat 1941* (Vojnoistorijski Inst., Belgrade, 1969), vol. i, pp. 374–5.
  2 Pero Damjanović, *Tito na čelu partije* (Belgrade, 1968), pp. 153–4.
  3 *Aprilski rat 1941* (1969), p. 504.
  4 *Pravda*, 20 Apr. 1940.
  5 Ibid., 12 May 1940.
  6 Ibid., 25 June 1940.
  7 Quoted in Letter of 4 May 1948 from the CC of the CPSU to the CC of the CPY (see
     Document **120**).
  8 *Komunist* (Belgrade), Oct. 1946, pp. 59–100.
  9 *Aprilski rat 1941* (1969), pp. 826–7.
 10 *Komunist* (Belgrade), Oct. 1946, pp. 101–22.
 11 *Pravda*, 1 Apr. 1941.
 12 DGFP, ser. D, vol. xii, pp. 451–2.
 13 *Pravda*, 6 Apr. 1941; BFSP, 1941, vol. 144, pp. 878–9.
 14 *Pravda*, 6 Apr. 1941.
 15 DGFP, ser. D., vol. xii, p. 480.
 16 Ibid., p. 485.
 17 Plenča, *Medjunarodni odnosi*, pp. 28–9.

18 Undated report by Tito, registered as received by the Comintern on 28 June 1941: ibid., p. 21; Tito, *Selected military works* (Belgrade, 1966), pp. 40–5.
19 *Zbornik dokumenata,* vol. i, pp. 11–17.
20 Dedijer, *Prilozi,* p. 295.
21 *The Times,* 14 July 1941.
22 Plenča, *Medjunarodni odnosi,* p. 33.
23 Dedijer, *Prilozi,* p. 296.
24 Ibid., pp. 318–19.
25 Ibid., pp. 319–20.
26 Ibid., p. 321.
27 Ibid.
28 Ibid., p. 320.
29 Ibid.
30 Ibid., pp. 332–3.
31 Ibid., pp. 344–5.
32 Knezevich, *Mihailović,* p. 11.
33 Ibid., p. 12.
34 Plenča, *Medjunarodni odnosi,* p. 116.
35 Knezevich, *Mihailović,* p. 16.
36 Ibid.
37 Ibid., p. 17.
38 Ibid.
39 Archives, Inst. for Military History, Belgrade, 12/2–64, 65, k.20.
40 Knezevich, *Mihailović,* pp. 7–9.
41 *The Times,* 3 Sept. 1942.
42 Dedijer, *Prilozi,* pp. 360–1.
43 Ibid.
44 Ibid., p. 362.
45 Pijade, *Legend,* pp. 18–19.
46 Dedijer, *Prilozi,* p. 362.
47 Ibid., p. 363.
48 Archives, Inst. for Military History, Belgrade, 23/1–5, k.269.
49 Dedijer, *Prilozi,* p. 345.
50 Ibid., p. 346.
51 Ibid.
52 Ibid., pp. 351–2.
53 Ibid., p. 354.
54 Ibid.
55 Ibid., p. 355.
56 Pijade, *Legend,* p. 20.
57 Dedijer, *Prilozi,* p. 368.
58 Ibid., p. 369.
59 Pijade, *Legend,* p. 22.
60 Dedijer, *Prilozi,* p. 320.
61 Ibid., p. 323.
62 Ibid., p. 349.
63 Pijade, *Legend,* p. 11.
64 Dedijer, *Prilozi,* p. 350.
65 Pijade, *Legend,* p. 12.
66 Dedijer, *Prilozi,* p. 353.
67 Ibid., p. 356
68 Ibid., pp. 356–7.
69 Ibid., p. 366.
70 Pijade, *Legend,* p. 17.
71 Ibid., p. 20.
72 Dedijer, *Prilozi,* p. 365.
73 Ibid.
74 Ibid., pp. 378–9.
75 Ibid., p. 380.
76 Ibid., pp. 382–3.

77   Ibid., p. 385.
78   Ibid., p. 297.
79   *Zbornik dokumenata,* vol. ii/6, pp. 143–5.
80   Ibid., vol. vii/1, p. 15.
81   Dedijer, *Prilozi,* pp. 321–2.
82   *Istorijski arhiv KPJ* (Belgrade), vol. vii, pp. 45–8.
83   *Zbornik dokumenata,* vol. ii/6, pp. 148–9.
84   *Istorijski arhiv KPJ* (Belgrade), vol. vii, p. 61.
85   Ibid., p. 62.
86   Ibid., p. 287.
87   Dedijer, *Prilozi,* p. 346.
88   Ibid., p. 347.
89   Ibid., p. 351.
90   Ibid.
91   Pijade, *Legend,* p. 12.
92   V. Dedijer, *Tito Speaks* (London, 1953), pp. 197–8.
93   Ibid.
94   W. S. Churchill, *Closing the ring* (London, 1952), p. 414.
95   *Pravda,* 10 Mar. 1944.
96   *Soviet foreign policy during the patriotic war* (U.S.S.R. Government, 1946), vol. ii, p. 184.
97   *Pravda,* 28 Jan. 1945.
98   FRUS, *The Conferences at Malta and Yalta, 1945,* p. 974.
99   407 HC Deb., pp. 398–9.
100 *Pravda,* 14 Dec. 1943; FRUS, *1943,* vol. ii, p. 1026.
101 Dedijer, *Prilozi,* p. 388.
102 Ibid., p. 413.
103 *Završne operacije za oslobodjenje Jugoslavije 1944–5* (Belgrade, 1957), p. 313.
104 *Pravda,* 21 Oct. 1944.
105 Villa Resta telegram of 8 Nov. 1944, FO 371/44282.
106 *Pravda,* 12 Apr. 1945; BFSP, 1943–5, vol. 145, pp. 1177–8.
107 *Izvestiya,* 12 Apr. 1945.
108 Article by Djilas, ibid., 16 Apr. 1945.
109 Quoted in Letter of 4 May 1948 from the CC of the CPSU to the CC of the CPY (see Document **120**).
110 Tito, *Govori,* vol. i, pp. 300–4.
111 Quoted in Letter of 4 May 1948 (see Document **120**).
112 Ibid.
113 Moscow Radio; *Soviet News,* 30 July 1947.
114 Cominform Journal, 10 Nov. 1947.
115 *New Times* (Moscow), suppl., 17 Aug. 1949.
116 Dedijer, *Tito Speaks* (London, 1953), p. 216.
117 Official English version (slightly amended) of the correspondence: Savez Komunista Jugoslavije, *The correspondence between the Central Committee of the Communist Party of Yugoslavia and the Central Committee of the All-Union Communist Party, Bolshevik* (Belgrade, 1948).
118 Ibid.
119 Ibid.
120 Ibid.
121 Ibid.
122 V. Dedijer, *The battle Stalin lost* (New York, 1971), p. 124.
123 Official English version, as for notes 117–21.
124 Dedijer, *The battle Stalin lost* (1971), p. 128.
125 *Jugoslovenska knjiga* (Belgrade, 1948).
126 Cominform Journal, 1 July 1948.
127 *Jugoslovenska knjiga* (Belgrade, 1948), slightly amended.
128 Official English version, as for notes 117–21.
129 YWB, p. 81.
130 Ibid.
131 Ibid., pp. 203–5.
132 Ibid., pp. 107–8.

133 *Izvestiya*, 2 June 1949.
134 *Soviet News,* 27 July 1949.
135 YWB, pp. 122–4.
136 Ibid., pp. 124–6.
137 Ibid., pp. 127–8.
138 *Izvestiya*, 30 Sept. 1949.
139 YWB, pp. 141–5.
140 *Izvestiya*, 26 Oct. 1949.
141 YWB, pp. 183–4.
142 Ibid., pp. 181–2.
143 Ibid., pp. 174–8.
144 *Pravda*, 31 Dec. 1948.
145 YWB, pp. 283–4.
146 *Izvestiya*, 12 Feb. 1949.
147 Statement by Dr Vilfan, Yugoslav Representative to the Economic Committee of the UN General Assembly: GAOR, 4th sess., 2nd cttee, pp. 40–3.
148 Tito, *Govori*, vol. iv., pp. 261–2.
149 *Borba*, 7 Aug. 1949; RIIA, *Documents on International Affairs 1949–50* (London), pp. 457–9 (slightly amended).
150 *New Times* (Moscow), suppl., 17 Aug. 1949.
151 *Borba*, 22 Aug. 1949.
152 *Vneshnaya Politika SSR 1949 god* (Moscow, 1953), pp. 144–59.
153 *Borba*, 24 July 1949.
154 *Pravda*, 6 Dec. 1949.
155 Tito, *Govori*, vol. v, pp. 377–8.
156 Kardelj, *Problemi naše socijalističke izgradnje* (Belgrade, 1954), pp. 181–8.
157 *New York Times*, 23 July 1951.
158 Tito, *Govori*, vol. vi, pp. 75–9.
159 Explanatory Memorandum sent to the UN Secretary-General for circulation to members of the General Assembly: GAOR, 6th sess., annexes, vi/a.i.68.
160 Statement by M. Sobolev at the 10th meeting of the Ad Hoc Political Committee of the General Assembly: GAOR, 6th sess., A/AC.53/SR.10.
161 *Pravda*, 23 Sept. 1952 (CDSP, vol. iv/38, 1 Nov. 1952).
162 Savez Komunista Jugoslavije, *Borba Komunista za socijalističku demokratiju VI Kongres KPJ* (Belgrade, 1952), pp. 11–78.
163 Ibid.
164 Tito, *Govori*, vol. viii, pp. 133–9.
165 *Pravda*, 17 June 1953 (CDSP, vol. v/24, 25 July 1953).
166 Tito, *Govori*, vol. x, p. 31.
167 *Soviet News*, 17 Feb. 1955.
168 RIA, 15 Mar. 1955.
169 *Pravda*, 12 Mar. 1955.
170 RIA, May 1955.
171 Tito, *Govori*, vol. x., pp. 172, 180.
172 *Pravda*, 18 May 1955.
173 *Soviet News*, 27 May 1955.
174 Ibid., 3 June 1955.
175 RIA, 16 Nov. 1955.
176 *Borba*, 20 Feb. 1956; Tito, *Selected speeches & articles 1941–61* (Zagreb, 1963), pp. 181–2.
177 Special release, US Dept of State, 4 June 1956; [Khrushchev], *Khrushchev remembers* (London, 1971), vol. 1, pp. 559–618.
178 *Soviet News*, 25 June 1956.
179 Ibid.
180 *Washington Post*, 17 Oct. 1956.
181 RIIA, *Documents on International Affairs, 1956* (London), pp. 497–508.
182 *Pravda*, 23 Nov. 1956.
183 R. H. Bass & E. Marbury, eds, *The Soviet-Yugoslav controversy 1948–58* (New York, 1959), p. 85.
184 *Pravda*, 18 Dec. 1956 (CDSP, vol. vii/51, 30 Jan. 1957).

185 Ibid., 13 Feb. 1957 (CDSP, vol. ix/11, 24 Apr. 1957).
186 *Borba*, 27 Feb. 1957.
187 *Pravda*, 11 Mar. 1957; *Soviet News*, 13 Mar. 1957.
188 RIA, 1 May 1957.
189 *Pravda*, 4 July 1957 (CDSP, vol. ix/23, 17 July 1957).
190 *Soviet News*, 6 Aug. 1957.
191 Tito, *Selected speeches & articles 1941–61* (Zagreb, 1963), pp. 236–7.
192 *Program SKJ* (Belgrade, 1958).
193 *Pravda*, 9 May 1958 (CDSP, vol. x/19, 18 June 1958).
194 *Soviet News*, 2 July 1958.
195 Ibid.
196 Ibid.
197 *Pravda*, 4 June 1958 (CDSP, vol. x/22, 9 July 1958).
198 Tito, *Govori*, vol. xiii, pp. 250–64.
199 *Pravda*, 12 July 1958 (CDSP, vol. x/28, 20 Aug. 1958, expanded).
200 Ibid., 11 Nov. 1958.
201 *Current Soviet policies* (New York, 1960), p. 214.
202 *World Marxist Review*, Dec. 1960.
203 *Yugoslav Survey*, Mar. 1961, pp. 576–7.
204 RIA, 5–20 Aug. 1961.
205 *Pravda*, 18 Oct. 1961.
206 *Soviet News*, 5 Oct. 1962.
207 *Pravda*, 14 Dec. 1962 (CDSP, vol. xiv/51, 16 Jan. 1962).
208 *Komunist* (Belgrade), May 1963.
209 Joint communiqué: *Pravda*, 28 Aug. 1963 (CDSP, vol. xv/35, 25 Sept. 1963).
210 *Yugoslav Survey*, Oct.–Dec. 1964.
211 Tito, *Govori*, vol. xix, pp. 378–9, 404.
212 *Pravda*, 2 July 1965 (CDSP, vol. xvii/26, 21 July 1965).
213 *Izvestiya*, 2 June 1966 (CDSP, vol. xviii/22, 22 June 1966).
214 *Pravda*, 25 Sept. 1966 (CDSP, vol. xviii/39, 19 Oct. 1966).
215 RIA, 5–20 Aug. 1968.
216 Ibid.
217 *Yugoslav Survey*, Nov. 1968.
218 Ibid.
219 RIA, 5 Sept. 1968.
220 *Pravda*, 25 Aug. 1968 (CDSP, vol. xx/34, 11 Sept. 1968).
221 *Le Monde*, 4 Sept. 1968.
222 *Yugoslav Survey*, Nov. 1968.
223 Ibid.
224 *Pravda*, 3 Dec. 1968 (CDSP, vol. xx/49, 25 Dec. 1968).
225 *Yugoslav Survey*, Aug. 1970.
226 *Borba*, 3 May 1969.
227 *Izvestiya*, 12 July 1968 (CDSP, vol. xxi/58, 6 Aug. 1969).
228 Ibid., 11 Sept. 1969 (CDSP, vol. xx/37, 8 Oct. 1969).
229 RIA, 20 Oct. 1969.
230 *Pravda*, 1 July 1970 (CDSP, vol. xxii/26, 28 July 1970).
231 Ibid., 28 Feb. 1971 (CDSP, vol. xxiii/9, 30 Mar. 1971).
232 Ibid., 31 Mar. 1971 (CDSP, vol. xxiii/12, 20 Apr. 1971).
233 Ibid., 26 Sept. 1971 (CDSP, vol. xxiii/39, 26 Oct. 1971).
234 Ibid., 11 June 1972 (CDSP, vol. xxiv/23, 5 July 1972).
235 Ibid., 2 Oct. 1973 (CDSP, vol. xxv/39, 24 Oct. 1973).
236 Ibid., 13 Nov. 1973 (CDSP, vol. xxv/46, 12 Dec. 1973).
237 Ibid.
238 *Soviet News*, 20 Nov. 1973.

INDEX

Abakumov, G. T., 64, 108, 253
Agriculture in Yugoslavia: Soviet criticism of, 173, 179, 190, 202–3, 269, 285; collectivization, 42, 61, 205
Albania: Yugoslav influence in, 30, 44, 46, 60, 86, 153; proposed annexation of, 46, 50–1; tension with Yugoslavia, 74, 240–5; tension with Soviet Union, 73–5
Alexander, Harold, 38, 44
Alexander, King, 3, 5
Amery, Julian, 98
Andropov, Yuri, 112
Anti-Fascist Council (AVNOJ), 25–7, 32, 151–2, 156, 158, 160
Arab-Israeli war, 79, 91, 110–11
Armjaninov, D. M., 170
Atanasov-Viktor, Sterija, 100
Atherton, Terence, 24, 99–100
Austria: Partisan activity in, 30; frontier dispute with Yugoslavia, 30, 44–6, 60, 168–9, 231–6

Bakarić, Vladimir, 50, 106, 111, 175
Balkan Pact, 60, 74, 285
Balkans: proposed confederation of, 4, 18, 47, 50; proposed nuclear-free zone, 88, 300, 303
Barskov, A. N., 52
Belgrade: Soviet Legation in, 6, 11, 94; liberation of, 39–41, 104; non-aligned conference at, 75
Belgrade, Declaration of, 64–5, 254–8
Benediktov, I. A., 297
Beria, L. P., 64, 107–8, 253
Bihać, 25–6
Blažević, Jakov, 89
Bled, 47–8
Bogomolov, A. E., 18, 20, 128, 135–7
Bosnia, 13, 21–2, 27, 130, 133, 136, 141–2, 148
Boznitch, Sava D., 104
Brezhnev, Leonid: visits Yugoslavia (1962), 75, 79, 87, 189, 294, 302–3; and Czechoslovakia, 80; and limited sovereignty doctrine, 82–3, 87, 298–300; friendly references to Yugoslavia, 86, 91, 112, 302–5
Brioni, 68, 78, 85
Bukharin, N., 173, 179, 189–90, 202
Bulganin, N., 64, 66, 85–6, 169, 251, 258, 273
Bulgaranov, Boyan, 101
Bulgaria, 30–2, 44, 46–7, 50–2, 152–6, 240–5

Carinthia, 30, 45–6, 60, 168–9, 231–6
Ceauçescu, Nicolae, 81

Chetniks: clashes with Partisans, 13–21, 23–4, 97, 131–41; reported collaboration with enemy, 14, 18–21, 24–5; Soviet attitudes towards, 15–21, 39–40, 104, 132–41, 147, 162; see also Mihailović
China: interest in E. Europe, 68, 72; tension with Yugoslavia, 72, 76, 292; rapprochement with Yugoslavia, 83, 86; rift with USSR, 74–7, 83
Churchill, Winston: and Yugoslav Government in Exile, 20, 34–5, 159–60; and Tito, 32–5, 37–8, 103–4; proposes '50–50 agreement' with Stalin, 34, 45, 102
Cincar-Marković, Aleksandar, 116
Comecon (CMEA), 58, 76, 228–30, 303, 306
Cominform: establishment of, 49, 167–8; Soviet-Yugoslav dispute referred to, 54, 197–214; Yugoslavia expelled from, 55, 202–7; attacks on Yugoslavia by, 55, 58, 202–7, 219, 225–8; Yugoslav counter-charges, 55, 200–2, 207–14; dissolution of, 65
Cominformists, 57, 86, 93, 112
Comintern: pre-war relations with CPY, 4–8, 11, 93, 115, 118, 120–1; clandestine radio links, 6–7, 11, 16, 21, 96–7, 181; directives for armed action, 10, 13, 23, 25, 128–9; operates Radio Free Yugoslavia, 14, 18, 25–7; military assistance requested from, 21–3, 141–5; political directives from, 23–32, 99, 145–52, 156–7; directives for Italy, 29–30, 152–3; directives for Austria, 30; directives for Albania, 30, 153; directives for Macedonia and Bulgaria, 30–2, 47, 153–6; dissolution of, 27, 157–8
Communist Party of the Soviet Union: relations with CPY, 43–4, 52–6, 63–6, 71, 77, 84, 89, 91, 166–7, 169–200, 263, 275–6, 292–3; polemics with CPY, 169–213; rapprochement with CPY, 91–2, 214, 246, 261–2, 264, 274, 293, 303–4, 306; and anti-party group, 70, 273–4; and Chinese, 73–5; 19th Congress, 245; 20th Congress, 66, 77, 257–9, 290; 21st Congress, 73, 77, 287; 22nd Congress, 75, 77; 24th Congress, 86, 302
Communist Party of Yugoslavia: inter-war period, 4–8, 93, 115–16, 120–1, 126; membership and organization, 126, 178–9; attitude to World War II, 7, 94, 115, 117–21; role during invasion, 7–8, 125–6; and

DATE DUE